(Canadian Forces Photo PL29567)

To my brother, F/L Frank Joel Clark, who died in the fiery explosion of his Spitfire over the beaches of Normandy one week after D-Day.

SEE P. 78

iii

Angels Eight

Normandy Air War Diary

By

David Clark

ISBN: 1-4107-2236-8 (e-book)
ISBN: 1-4107-2241-4 (Paperback)
ISBN: 1-4107-2242-2 (Dust Jacket)

Library of Congress Control Number: 2003091445

This book is printed on acid free paper.

Printed in the United States of America
Bloomington, IN

Cover photograph: Mike Red sector of JUNO beach at Graye-sur-Mer midday 6 June 1944, oblique taken from 8,000 feet altitude – 'angels eight' (Imperial War Museum CL27)

1stBooks - rev. 06/13/03

ACKNOWLEDGMENTS

Editing and correcting manuscripts is gruelling work and I want to thank my friends Ron Pickler of Burlington, Allan Hillman of Cornwall and my daughter Lynn Clark for the fine job they did. Larry Milberry of Toronto provided much expert advice. Many performed research or contributed material for the book -- I must thank Bill McRae of Ottawa, Bill Mason of Victoria, Philippe Chéron of Rouen, Ken Arnold of Philadelphia, Ernie Burton of Worcester, Hugh Halliday of Ottawa, Mike Bechthold of Wilfrid Laurier University, Sharon McElroy of Toronto, Elizabeth Lang of Toronto, Franek Grabowski of Krakow, Steve Cooke of Clinton and Bill Cook of Goderich, Laura Bamford of Stoney Creek, Pierre Le Coq of Tampa and many more who answered questions on bulletin boards or dropped off notes. In addition, thanks must go to those airmen who produced the daily history of 127 Wing, 403 Squadron, 416 Squadron and 421 Squadron. And no acknowledgment would be complete without mentioning the names of those who provided the foundation of research upon which this work is based -- Jean-Bernard Frappé who provided the detailed Luftwaffe data, Frank Olynyk who provided the massive listing of USAAF claims, Paul Andrews and William Adams who compiled the US Eighth Air Force loss data, Norman Franks who compiled the Fighter Command loss data, Ken Rust who chronicled the history of the US Ninth Air Force and the dedicated staffs of the National Archives of Canada, Imperial War Museum, Public Records Office and Canadian Forces Photo Section who assisted in assembling material. Without the eager assistance of these many people this book could not have been completed.

David Clark

Table of Contents

List of Tables

List of Figures

PART ONE –
The Normandy Campaign

This photograph of Pegasus Bridge, greatly enlarged, was taken by a photo-reconnaissance aircraft from 27,000 feet shortly after D-Day. Several gliders landed close enough to the bridge to permit the attacking British 6th Airborne troops to take the bridge by complete surprise.

(Photo courtesy of Wilfrid Laurier University LCMSDS 309/3163)

David Clark

Chapter One – Prelude

Preparation for OVERLORD -- invasion of Europe

The British Army together with remnants of French and Belgian forces evacuated the beaches of Dunkirk in the summer of 1940. They left all their equipment behind and they slunk home as a defeated army, but the soldiers together with every British and Commonwealth citizen around the world knew that one day they would have to return -- to invade France and defeat Hitler.

The United States joined the war against Germany and Japan in December 1941 and within months argued for an invasion of Europe, however it was clearly out of the question at that time. The Battle of the Atlantic was running in Germany's favour, threatening the flow of essential war materials to Britain -- this battle had to be won first. Only after establishing safe seaways could the US and Britain amass the necessary military supplies in England. A not so obvious second requirement before an invasion of Europe could be accomplished, was the taking and assembling of massive amounts of photographic intelligence of enemy defences and of the topography. And there was an even more obvious requirement -- the numbers of available assault landing craft to accomplish the crossing were not nearly enough to handle five divisions. As late as the fall of 1943 this was still the case.

Germany invaded the Soviet Union in the summer of 1941, halted in winter and resumed in spring 1942. After a year of ferocious fighting the initiative passed to the Russians after Stalingrad in February 1943. The British and Americans sent massive military aid to the Soviet Union to fuel this reversal, but the Soviet effort was achieved at an enormous cost in lives and Stalin insisted the Allies invade Europe as soon as possible to further relieve the pressure on his forces. At a summit conference in Teheran on 28 November 1943, President Franklin Roosevelt of the USA and Prime Minister Winston Churchill of the UK met Marshal Joseph Stalin of the Soviet Union for the first time. The Western Allies told Stalin they would invade Europe in May 1944. An official communiqué released after the meeting referred to, "complete agreement as to the scope and timing of operations which will be undertaken from the east, west and south."[1] Stalin was also told that General Dwight Eisenhower would be appointed Supreme Commander of the invasion forces.

The Allied leaders knew that smashing through Hitler's Atlantic Wall defences, landing in Europe, resisting counter-attack and breaking out of the beachhead would be an 'all-or-nothing' affair. If the assault was beaten at the beaches – as both Adolph Hitler and his generals insisted it must – the Allies would have to wait a year or more to try it again for the invasion would directly involve some two million people – a million landed as military forces and another million dealt with people, materials and logistics in the United Kingdom. Apart from the horrendous loss of lives and materiel should the invading forces be thrown back into the sea, the blow to morale would cripple efforts to re-group.

Preparation for the invasion of Normandy required not only the usual assemblage of men and materials to give it any chance of success, but it required many other ingredients in order to guarantee that success. Surprise – a most unlikely element to achieve – would have to be striven for; every effort had to be made to mislead the Germans as to time and place. Air supremacy over the landings and over the lodgement was an absolute necessity; enemy aircraft must not be allowed to attack the crowded beaches or hamper ground operations. Intelligence from the interception of communications, French Underground and saturation photography of the target areas were another essential. Naval control of the Channel crossing lanes was another essential; enemy surface vessels or U-boats could cause a disaster if they broke through the ring of defenders.

ULTRA and Photographic Reconnaissance

In all the accounts written by the key players immediately after the war – Churchill, Eisenhower, Montgomery, and others -- no reference was made to breaking the German military communication code. Thirty years passed before the first leak occurred regarding one of the most astounding accomplishments of the entire war. The world learned that as early as 1939 the Polish and the British had secretly seized a German encoding machine called ENIGMA. With the machine in hand they broke the German code and when hostilities were hot in 1940, British code-breakers were able to regularly interpret German military messages. The German Army used its ENIGMA machines to direct troop movements and for all forms of military communiqués and the navy used it to communicate with U-boats. The Germans were convinced that the code could not be broken.

A message was broken into four-letter segments and entered into the ENIGMA machine. The machine had a series of wheels whose coordinated positioning provided various combinations to scramble the letters. Without prior knowledge of the combination of wheels, there were thousands of billions of solutions – impossible to de-code. However, it is now known that the German operators took short cuts, including in the message a master setting necessary for de-coding, rather than having the master setting transmitted in some other way. In so doing, the number of possible solutions to the unscrambling of a message was reduced to a point where the British electro-mechanical computers could decode it.

The decoding endeavour was called Operation ULTRA, and the activity was centred at Bletchley Park in Buckinghamshire. By war's end 10,000 people were employed there. They picked up radio signals from all over the world, de-coded them, translated them and passed them to the highest Allied leadership. In Churchill's memoirs he refers to information he received daily from a 'secret source'. Only in recent years has it become known what that source was, for only in 1994 were decodes of Churchill's ULTRA messages de-classified and made public.

This marvellous scoop by the intelligence community provided the planners of the invasion of Europe with the disposition of German forces literally as they occurred. At the end of May 1944 for instance, the Allies received a fairly precise location for most of the 28 German divisions between Amsterdam and Brest, and a very accurate account of where the armour was located. This last came in an intercepted message announcing that the Inspector-General of Armour would inspect all units in Western Europe, and the message went on to give his itinerary, with the number of days to be spent at each location.

Admiral Karl Dönitz, commander of Germany's U-boat fleet, used the ENIGMA machine to communicate with his U-boats, and the British regularly intercepted and acted upon those communications. Throughout the Normandy Campaign intercepts proved of great value – the difficulty was that the Allies had to act with extreme caution not to reveal their secret. Between the volume of intelligence gathered by ULTRA and corroboration of much information from the French Underground, the Allies had an enormous advantage over the Germans whose intelligence sources became more scarce and less reliable as the war progressed.

Another essential body of information required for the successful invasion of Europe was knowledge of the countryside. Starting in 1942, every foot of shoreline from Holland to the Spanish border was systematically photographed in a variety of forms. Obliques were shot at wave-top level from three miles out to sea. Photos were then crudely montaged into long concertina pages for the Navy to use as landfall identifiers -- 15 such foldouts of this type covered the Normandy coast. Additional obliques were flown at 1,500 yards from the shore at wave-top level to furnish recognition material for landing craft commanders. Still more obliques were flown at 1,500 yards from the shore and two thousand feet altitude to provide views of the hinterland beyond the beaches for use by the assaulting troops. Mustang and Mosquito aircraft of the Royal Air Force (RAF) and Royal Canadian Air Force (RCAF), and then P-38 aircraft of the United States Army Air Force (USAAF) carried out this low-level photography. High altitude photography of the whole 600-mile coast, as well as all bridges, towns and thousands of special targets was also needed. This activity accelerated as D-Day -- the actual invasion day -- approached so that in the two months before the actual assault, 4,700 photo-reconnaissance sorties were flown and thousands of photographs taken.

The Importance of Air Supremacy

The Allied forces that invaded Europe in June 1944 were pitted against a German army that had better weapons, more experienced soldiers and the benefit of chosen defensive positions. Even given the important advantages of intelligence, deception, the Royal Navy and the huge numerical advantage in weapons, it is certain that the Normandy Campaign would not have succeeded without Allied air supremacy. Not a single historian of the war has failed to note this. It was the most important feature of the Normandy Campaign, and to a large extent, the remainder of the war in the west. How had air superiority come about?

Throughout 1942 and 1943, RAF Bomber Command under Air Marshal Sir Arthur Harris, and the US 8thAF under Major General Carl Spaatz, conducted a strategic bombing campaign aimed at bringing Germany to its knees. The RAF was forced to halt daylight operations in the early years of the war because the losses incurred were too great to bear. Instead they began night bombing, but the Americans, with their heavily armed four-engine B-17s, were convinced they could withstand enemy fighter attack and get through to heartland Germany. Besides, the Americans insisted their superior bombsight could achieve pin-point accuracy only in daylight. The US 8thAF bombed Germany by day while RAF Bomber Command bombed it by night.

In 1943 the number of available US 8thAF heavy bombers increased to a point where they could mount a 1,000-plane raid, just as RAF Bomber Command had done the year before. As this became a possibility, the German Luftwaffe reduced the strength of its fighter units in the Mediterranean and on the Eastern and Western fronts and stationed over 1,000 fighter aircraft in Germany to battle the bombers.

In June 1943 a remarkable fighter – the P-51D – made its sudden appearance. This aircraft had the performance to fully compete with any German fighter, but more importantly its increased internal and external fuel capacity permitted it to fly on 1,000-mile missions – an unheard of feature for any fighter aircraft at the time. On 14 October

1944 American losses reached a zenith when 291 bombers were despatched for a raid on Schweinfurt. 60 bombers were shot down and 17 were damaged so badly that they were written off when they returned. The combination of the two – 77 aircraft destroyed out of 291 -- is 26 percent. In no time at all, this loss rate could lead to the complete destruction of the US 8thAF. The Americans suspended their attacks on Germany; the Luftwaffe had won air superiority over the Fatherland. But the victory was to be a very short-lived one.

By January 1944, large numbers of P-51D aircraft became operational in the US 8thAF and the bombing of Germany resumed, now accompanied by the P-51Ds. In a period in February that became known as Big Week, the balance of air superiority was tilted and turned the other way. Between 20 February and 25 February, 13 major bomber strikes involving as many as 1,000 bombers and 900 fighters (mostly P-51Ds) were launched and although the losses were high – 210 heavy bombers and 38 fighters according to Spaatz – the losses to the Luftwaffe were far greater. The immediate claim was 600 German fighters destroyed, and although this figure is undoubtedly too high, the Germans themselves later confirmed losing 1,000 fighters in the first four months of 1944. It was not the loss of the machines that hurt the Luftwaffe so much as the loss of many of their best pilots and commanders. The Americans had won a major victory. After Big Week and the early months of 1944, the ability of the Luftwaffe to respond to Allied aerial initiatives deteriorated continuously. Allied air superiority had been achieved; Allied air supremacy was about to become a reality.

Comparison of Fighters

The leading fighter aircraft of the British and Commonwealth was the Supermarine Spitfire Mark IX. Earlier versions of the Spitfire had been flying since 1936, but it was the Mark IX that came into service in mid-1942 that was the favourite, powered by the 1700-horsepower Rolls-Royce Merlin inline engine. The mainstay fighter of the US 8thAF in 1943, and later the leading fighter of the US 9thAF (the tactical air force that supported US Army operations in Normandy) was the Republic P-47 powered by the huge 2300-horsepower Pratt &

Whitney R-2800 radial engine. Popular with both forces was the North American P-51D powered by a Rolls-Royce Merlin inline engine built under licence by Packard in the United States. The leading fighter aircraft of the Luftwaffe was the FW 190A, driven by a powerful Junkers Jumo radial engine. It was supported by the Bf 109G powered by the BD 601 inline engine.

The aircraft known by every Allied airman and soldier as the Me 109, was called by the Germans, the Bf 109 because it was built in the Bayerische Flugzeugwerke factory. However, since Allied combat reports refer to the Me 109, that is the term retained in the quoted combat reports, while Bf 109 is used elsewhere.

A comparison of the characteristics and performance of the Spitfire, P-47, P-51, Bf 109 and FW 190 aircraft is as follows:

		Super-marine Spitfire MkIXb	Republic Thunder-bolt P-47D	North American Mustang P-51D	Messer-schmitt Bf 109G	Focke Wulf FW 190A
wingspan	ft	36.8	40.8	37.0	32.5	34.4
length	ft	30.5	36.1	32.3	29.0	33.4
height	ft	12.5	14.2	12.6	11.2	11.0
wing area	sq ft	242	300	233	173	197
Engine	hp	1710	2300	1700	1800	2240
loaded wt.	lb	7500	14,600	10,100	6945	9480
wing loading	lb/sq ft	31	49	43	40	48
power loading	hp/lb	0.228	0.158	0.168	0.259	0.236
max speed	mph	408	429	437	387	426
service ceiling	ft	44,000	40,000	40,000	38,500	39,400
rate of climb	ft/min	4150	2780	3470	4100	4200

Table 1 – Aircraft comparison. A key to performance of the five most powerful fighter aircraft in 1944 is the power of their engines compared to their wing surface and overall weight. These combine to provided 'wing loading' and 'power loading'. Wing loading is a key factor in turning capability; power loading in speed and acceleration. Power varied greatly with altitude. In terms of power per pound of weight, the Spitfire, Bf 109 and FW 190 were half again higher than the P-47 and P-51, however aerodynamics and engine performance at high altitude evened things out, providing the US aircraft an advantage in speed attained at higher altitude.

The Spitfire was considered by its pilots to be extremely agile and almost flew itself. The P-47 was heavy and ponderous but at high altitudes it came into its own and those who flew it loved it for its ruggedness and it is said that a P-47 got back to base with a whole engine cylinder shot away. The P-51's praises are sung not just for its unbelievable range for a fighter, but as a very versatile and manoeuvrable airplane, faster than the others. The Bf 109 was difficult to fly and difficult to land, but was revered by many German veterans for its agile performance and heavy armament. The FW 190 was formidable – quick to roll, very manoeuvrable, hard hitting. When first introduced in the summer of 1941, it so dominated the airspace over western Europe that it was called 'the butcher bird'. Since those early days several versions had improved its performance even more. The air-cooled engines of the FW 190 and the P-47 were not as vulnerable to damage as the Spitfire, Bf 109 or P-51 liquid-cooled engines where a chance rupture of an engine-coolant line was often the downfall for any of these types.

The P-47 was twice the size of a Spitfire or Bf 109, while the P-51 and FW 190 were slightly larger than the Spitfire. The pilots who flew it affectionately dubbed the P-47 'the Jug'. Wing loading (lower the better) is a determinant of turning ability, although acceleration into the roll allowing the turn to be established quickly, is just as important. Thus the Spitfire, Bf 109 and the FW 190 are known for their ability to turn tightly. The greater weight and speed in the American planes was advantageous when chasing an opponent in a dive.

The Transportation Plan

The invasion planners devised the Transportation Plan – a program to systematically destroy the French railway and communication systems. Every major marshalling yard, every main railway trunk line and every bridge was identified and made a target for heavy bombing. Radar stations and command centres were added to the list. In addition to heavy bombing by the Lancasters of RAF Bomber Command and the B-17s of the US 8thAF, medium bombers, fighter-bombers and fighters flew regular train busting and bridge bombing missions. The bombing began early in April even though many like Harris and Spaatz and a lukewarm Churchill were opposed. In spite of its political unpopularity[2], it proved very successful -- in some ways essential. The bombing activity reduced the effectiveness of the French railroad system to less than 20% by June 1944, and resulted in the destruction of all but two of the twenty bridges across the Seine and Loire Rivers that together isolate Normandy. The result of this activity was that by 6 June, Normandy was almost completely cut off from the rest of Europe.

Operation The Naval Plan – NEPTUNE

Lt Gen Frederick Morgan was officially appointed as Chief-of-Staff to the Commander of the invasion forces in January 1943 (although eleven months would go by before the commander he was to report to was named!). His primary function was to start the planning of the assault of the French mainland called Operation OVERLORD, and the naval operation called Operation NEPTUNE.

From the earliest planning stages, selecting the precise invasion date was difficult. Full moonlight was necessary to aid the crossing and landfall of the ships, and to make possible airborne troop landings in the middle of the night. Dawn was thought the best hour to land the beach assault troops, however to ensure that the submerged coastal defences were visible, the landing must be made when the tides were low enough to reveal the obstacles, but rising so as to facilitate the landing after the mined obstacles were disarmed. Thus the landing required a dawn attack after a night of bright moonlight and a morning when the tides would be highest about three hours after the dawn. Several windows occurred in April and May, the time favoured by the planners, but the insufficiency of landing craft required that the date be extended until at least the end of May. The 5th, 6th and 7th of June provided these conditions, but failure to hit that window of time would mean a delay of two weeks until 19 June. D-Day was initially set for Monday, 5 June 1944.

As that date approached however the weather worsened to severe storm conditions. Sunday night the 4th of June a vicious storm raged, but the meteorologists predicted that the storm would let up somewhat in another few hours. The decision was made to delay D-Day by one day. When the delay was announced, troops travelling the longest distances from Wales and south-western England were already at sea and the loading at the south coast ports was just about completed. Ships were called back, but no troops could be disembarked because there was not sufficient time. Although the effect upon the troops was most undesirable, it turned out that the decision to delay was an excellent one. Actual conditions on the morning of 5 June were impossible. All night long 10/10ths cloud covered Normandy with a solid base at one thousand feet ceiling. Winds blew at 30 to 40 knots, and high waves pounded all along the Normandy coast. Under these conditions, an aerial drop, heavy bombing and an assault of the beaches would have been disastrous.

The go ahead set in motion the most massive operation ever undertaken by man, performed with a degree of coordination and international and inter-service cooperation that had never been seen before – nor since. The closest modern equivalent -- the massive build-up of forces to oppose Saddam Hussein in 1990 – was only a third of the magnitude of OVERLORD.

Operation NEPTUNE -- was under the command of Admiral Sir Bertram Ramsay. Six thousand ships of the invasion fleet were loaded with scrupulous care to carry nothing but essentials and with cargoes located within the vessels for proper sequential unloading on the assault beaches. Monday night they moved out of almost every port on the south coast from Plymouth to Eastbourne, slipped anchor and formed up in convoys in an orchestrated stream. The first wave of the armada started a flow that lasted for nearly a year, and grew in magnitude as ships from further afield joined the endless stream of people and materials necessary to supply the Allied army in Europe.

Leading the armada of ships were minesweepers. OVERLORD planners predicted that 30% to 50% of the minesweepers would be lost because these gallant little ships had to hold their course straight and true to ensure there were no holes in the swept channels into the beaches. The planners assumed that the invasion armada would be detected many miles out to sea, and that it would be met with a steady stream of fire from the 27 large coastal batteries along the Calvados coast and the minesweepers would be out in front of everyone, like sitting ducks. The crews knew their chances of survival were slim, but went about the job anyway. In the largest operation of its type ever undertaken, 247 minesweepers swept ten channels to the assault area, cleared bombardment and transport marshalling areas parallel to the coast and finally swept paths into each of the five assault beaches. The job was only completed an hour before the actual landings, and as the minesweepers turned to go home they passed the duplex drive (DD) floating tanks going the other way and the small landing craft filled with troops. Many of these vessels greeted the minesweepers with the cry, "which way to Red Beach?" The minesweepers did their job thoroughly and notwithstanding the dire predictions of the planners, only one minesweeper was lost to enemy shore batteries.

Two naval task forces – an eastern and a western – had been patrolling the extremities of the Channel for weeks before the assault took place. They did so in naval hunting groups in conjunction with squadrons of Coastal Command maritime patrol aircraft. In the Channel, Germany's Kriegmarine consisted of a mere seven destroyers, three flotillas of E-boats and the fleet of U-boats. U-boats were Germany's most dangerous weapon and were the gravest threat to the landings in Normandy, but the Allies had a distinct advantage, for through ULTRA the Royal Navy knew where all of Admiral Dönitz's U-boats were at any one time. The Germans had 22 U-boats in Norwegian ports, 36 in the Brittany ports and 17 on patrol in the Atlantic – although, unknown to Dönitz, three of these had been sunk.

On the night of the 6th and 7th of June, a Coastal Command aircraft destroyed two U-boats while six more were damaged. The following night two more were destroyed and two damaged. The protection offered was so effective that in thousands and thousands of crossings in the first two weeks of the Normandy Campaign, only four ships and two escort vessels were sunk by U-boats. During that period Germany lost 20 U-boats in the Channel or on passage to the Channel by the Allied naval forces. Three German destroyers from Brest were neutralized (one sunk, one purposely beached and the third damaged) by Royal Navy and Royal Canadian Navy units in the Bay of Biscay. Meanwhile at Le Havre, three of the four destroyers and two of the three flotillas of E-boats were destroyed in RAF heavy bombing raids. The invasion armada was never seriously threatened. More important is the fact that it was not even detected until it was just off the Normandy coast.

The armada was awesome in size consisting of large and small landing ships for infantry, landing ships and smaller landing craft for tanks, flak landing craft, rocket launching landing craft, landing craft unloaded from ships, landing craft for ship-to-shore liaison, and landing craft with machine gun support. In addition to all of these there were the Allied capital ships, Erebus, Black Prince, Nevada, Enterprise, Glasgow, Ajax, Argonaut, Belfast, Warspite, etc. -- a total of 27 huge battleships and cruisers committed to specific targets of large shore batteries. Five headquarter ships, one for each beach, and two command ships, USS Augusta for the commander of the American forces and HMS Scylla for the command of the British and Canadian forces and hundreds of destroyers were part of the assemblage. Tugs towed 147 floating concrete blocks for the building of two 'Mulberries' and there were the 247 minesweepers.

The Mulberry was an ingenious invention. Hitler's views regarding where the Allies would land in Europe started with the premise that a huge army would need a large port to provide men, ammunition and supplies. The Allied planners answer was "we will bring our own port." Several varieties of massive concrete caisson consisting of hundreds of modules, were built in East Sussex, towed across the Channel with the invasion fleet and installed within days of the initial assault. A row of sunken ships and break-water caissons formed a ring at OMAHA beach and another at Arromanches at GOLD beach. Within the ring were several lines of caisson unloading wharves reaching out into the harbour. And at the end of each wharf were several caissons designed to rise and fall with the tides. Ships docked at the wharves in high or low tide and disgorged vehicles full of supplies that drove straight onto the beach and thence to the front. Within days of the invasion the Mulberries were each the size and capacity of the port of Dover. In addition to these dock facilities, the Allies had laid a fuel pipeline across the Channel called PLUTO (Pipe Line Under The Ocean)

The planning that went into NEPTUNE and OVERLORD was truly unbelievable. Consider the planning required to ensure that every one of the ships of the invasion armada was in the place at the time it was supposed to be. Taking GOLD beach as an example: two separate landings were planned, each about a mile across with about a mile between them. The sequence of landings for just one of these two was as follows[3]:

TIME	RED BEACH	GREEN BEACH
H-Hour minus 5 min	4 – LCTs with 12 DD tanks	4 – LCTs with 12 DD tanks
H-Hour	5 – LCTs with 20 AVRE s	9 – LCTs with 36 AVREs
H-Hour plus 5 min	14 – LCAs with assault troops	10 – LCAs with assault troops
H-Hour plus 20 min	12 – LCAs with reserve troops	12 – LCAs with reserve troops
H-Hour plus 45 min		12 – LCAs with reserve troops
H-Hour plus 47 min		12 – LCAs with reserve troops
H-Hour plus 47 min	3 – LCTs with 12 Crocodiles	
H-Hour plus 60 min	5 – LCTs with 20 trucks	5 – LCTs with 20 trucks
H-Hour plus 90 min	5 – LCTs with 20 trucks	5 – LCTs with 20 trucks
H-Hour plus 105 min		3 – LCTs with artillery
H-Hour plus 120 min	4 – LCTs with 16 trucks	
H-Hour plus 90 min		1 -- LST launching 21 DUKWs

*Table 2 -- **Landing schedule**. DD tank's are Duplex Drive floating tanks, LCTs are Landing Craft Tank, LCAs are Landing Craft Assault infantry, AVREs are Armoured Vehicle Royal Engineers, Crocodiles are flame-throwing tanks, LSTs are Landing Ship Tank and DUKWs are amphibious trucks.*

The 72 LCAs each carrying about 30 troops were off-loaded from larger ships while the 53 LCTs carrying tanks and other vehicles had been loaded in the UK and sailed across with the armada under their own steam. However every one of the 125 vessels had to be formed up and kept in proper position to permit an orderly build-up on the beaches. Double these figures for GOLD beach, and multiply the total by five for all beaches, and that gives some indication of the coordination required. Getting them out of the south coast ports, across the English Channel and in place before the beaches was a monumental challenge.

David Clark

The assembly and orchestrated movement of the armada began on 4 June 1944 and continued through to May 1945, for although the 6,000-ship initial armada was essential to transport everything needed to establish the beachhead on D-Day, the daily volume of food, supplies, parts, fuel and ammunition required to fuel the invasion would increase as more and more troops poured into France, so the number of ships required to provide personnel and material would increase with time. A measure of the magnitude of this seaborne supply system can be summarized with the following[4]:

	Personnel Landed	Vehicles Landed	Tons of Stores
By 11 June	367,142	50,228	59,961
by 18 June	621,986	95,750	217,624
Great Storm – 19 June to 21 June			
by 30 June	861,838	157,633	501,834

Table 3 -- Landings 152,000 troops landed in France 6 June. The number of personnel landed doubled by the eleventh, and nearly doubled again one week later.

Surprise – Operation FORTITUDE

Through ULTRA, planners gleaned a steady stream of information, developed complex deceptions designed to mislead the Germans, and then listened to confirm whether the deceptions worked or not. The British Intelligence Service MI5 had turned 40 German agents in Britain and some in Spain into double agents. They fed false information through these spy networks and then waited for ULTRA to provide feedback on how much had been believed. Two elaborate deceptions were developed.

Operation FORTITUDE NORTH was designed to convince the Germans the invasion would be through Norway, and Operation FORTITUDE SOUTH that it would be straight across the Channel at the Pas de Calais. A Commando raid in February blew up a heavy water plant in Norway and soon after, purposely-staged radio traffic led the Germans to believe there were six divisions in Scotland – poised for an invasion of Norway in conjunction with the Soviets.

16

Operation FORTITUDE SOUTH planted the information that a huge US army was stationed in Kent. Fictitious divisions were assigned, fields were filled with dummy tanks and trucks, and a steady stream of false radio messages simulated the daily chatter of a massive army awaiting orders. Throughout April and May, while the Allied air offensive was preparing the Normandy area, twice as many bombs were dropped on Pas de Calais as upon Normandy. Furthermore the commander of the fictitious army in East Anglia was Lt Gen George Patton – the Allied general Hitler most admired. Patton made public speeches and was seen in many places in Kent. The fiction was reported through the double-agent network that the Norway attack would be a feint and that as soon as the Germans moved troops to defend Norway, the main thrust of some 20 divisions would cross at Pas de Calais. Early in May, a note from von Runstedt to one of his colleagues virtually repeated this fiction -- FORTITUDE SOUTH was working. Later, as the Normandy landings were taking place, turned German operatives in England reported that Normandy was a feint and that the real invasion was coming shortly to the Pas de Calais.

The German Plan of Defence

The Germans knew that an invasion was coming. In November 1943 Hitler's Directive 51 stated that the Western theatre would be the decisive defence area, and that called for intensification of defence forces in terms of men and equipment along the Atlantic Wall and for specific defence plans aimed at concentrating the armoured Panzer divisions to counter-attack and throw the enemy back into the sea. In the preamble, Hitler noted,

> "Everything indicates that the enemy will launch an offensive against the western front of Europe, at the latest in the spring, perhaps even earlier." [6]

Hitler appointed Generalfeldmarschall Erwin Rommel to oversee construction of the defences under the command of

Generalfeldmarschall Gerd von Runstedt. Time was short, but Rommel threw himself into the job and inspired or cajoled a vast army of forced-labour workers to build massive defences all along the coast. One of the innovations introduced was called 'Rommel's Asparagus' – above ground and underwater obstacles with mines attached to smash through the sides of assaulting vessels.

Hitler was convinced that the most likely stretch of coast for an Allied landing was the Channel Sector – the coast between the Seine and the Scheldte -- because the Allies would need a major port like Le Havre or Antwerp. However, the Germans reasoned it could be anywhere from Norway to Spain – about 600 miles of coast. From the first days of 1944, all coastal defenders were put on high alert whenever the weather and tides might favour a landing. But on 5 June, with high winds and seas high enough to turn back some heavily-laden German mine-laying ships, it seemed certain there would be no invasion in the next few days. The commander of the German Seventh Army in Normandy, Generaloberst Friedrich Dollmann relaxed the alert and summoned his senior officers to Rennes for a map exercise while Rommel took the weather forecast as an opportunity to drive back to Germany to celebrate his wife's birthday. Thus none of the commanders who could have responded to the invasion were there when they were needed.

Chapter Two – D-Day, 6 June 1944

Beginning about midnight and throughout the night of 5/6 June, the skies of southern England were filled with lines of small red and white navigation lights and the steady drone of heavy bombers and transports. As predicted, the sky was clear and the moon bright. Three streams of large aircraft created a continuous roaring sound like thunder. To the east flying south over Beachy Head, an armada of 606 four-engine transports and 327 towed gliders carried the 6th British Airborne Division headed for a landing on the eastern flank of the lodgement at the River Orne. In the west flying south over Exeter, 378 C-47s and 229 gliders carried the 82nd US Airborne Division and 443 C-47s and 84 gliders carried the 101st US Airborne Division headed for the base of the Cotentin Peninsula on the western flank of the assault area. Hours after midnight the third stream, 1,365 heavy bombers of RAF Bomber Command and the US 8thAF flew south over Portsmouth and Southampton on a course to bomb the beach defences for two hours before the start of the beach assault troop landings.

Below them, all night long the massive fleet of invasion vessels moved. Out in the Channel, 10 motor launches guided the streams of the assault armada into the 10 swept lanes left by the minesweepers. This traffic control worked well, and the ungainly mass of ships navigated easily into position throughout the night. With the moon shining on glistening wave tops but not a single light showing from any craft, the armada sailed in an air of unreality. Everyone had been alerted to the assumption that the armada would be detected by the Germans in mid-Channel and each lookout thought that any minute a ship might blow up – hit by a torpedo or from a shore battery. However, apart from the persistent wind and the choppy seas there was no sound or sign that indicated that the vast carpet of invasion ships had been detected.

The Airborne Landings

Shortly after midnight in the eastern end of the assault area, the pathfinder and 'coup de main' forces in nine gliders, together with three hundred paratroopers of the 6th British Airborne Division touched down north of Caen east of the canal and Orne River. Their accuracy in coming in to the planned Drop Zones (DZ) was truly remarkable. Three gliders of the coup de main force were intended to land as close as possible to Pegasus Bridge and rush the pillbox. One of these landed 200 feet from the pillbox and the unbelieving sentry was overpowered before he recovered from the shock. ACM Sir Trafford Leigh-Mallory, commander of all the invasion air force units, said of this landing, it was the finest piece of aerial navigation in the entire war.

Maj Gen Richard Gale commanded the 6th British Airborne Division. Its first objective was to secure two bridges at Benouville (later to be called Pegasus bridge and Horsa bridge) and the one at Ranville to stop reinforcements coming from Le Havre and Paris. This they did handily with a small group of soldiers. The German defenders woke up but were quickly overcome when a force of just 150 men captured the Merville battery a couple of miles north of the bridges and destroyed the guns. By 0400 hours the last of their objectives was achieved as the airborne troops secured the high ridge to the east of the Orne River. German opposition stiffened and the 6th Airborne dug in to await a major counter-attack. The Airborne experienced about 500 casualties.

In the west, the airborne assault was a very different story. The 82nd US Airborne Division under the command of Maj Gen Matthew Ridgway, was originally intended to drop in the centre of the peninsula near the town of St. Sauveur le Vicomte to stop reinforcements being brought in from Cherbourg. In the weeks before D-Day, aerial photography indicated a growing number of defensive obstacles in the planned DZ and a fresh German infantry division – the 91st -- was reported to have moved into the area. It was decided to move the DZ 10 miles to the east, closer to the intended DZ of the 101st US Airborne Division. The C-47s that carried the airborne troops flew west of the Cotentin Peninsula, almost over the Channel Islands and turned east to approach Normandy. They met heavy anti-aircraft fire the moment they crossed the coast of the Cotentin Peninsula for the clear night made them easy targets and 21 troop carrying C-47s and two C-47s towing gliders were shot down. Taking evasive action to avoid the flak and driven by a strong tailwind, the C-47s drifted away from their intended routes and dropped sticks of paratroopers miles away from the intended DZ and after leaving the aircraft, the paratroopers drifted in the high winds. On average the sticks landed between 3 and 5 miles east of the DZ though some sticks landed 25 miles away -- glider landings were as widely dispersed as the paratroopers. Many paratroopers drowned under their heavy equipment in the vast flooded areas and many others landed in the midst of German positions and were captured. At first only a few hundred members of the 82nd could be gathered together, however even though they were so widely dispersed, isolated groups teamed together and moved to secure bridges and strategic positions while moving in the direction of the UTAH landing. The process was slow, and even by D-Day-plus-two only about 2,000 of the 6,000 troops dropped on D-Day could be mustered.

The dispersion of the 101st US Airborne Division, led by Maj Gen Maxwell Taylor, was even greater than that of the 82nd Division, but they recovered faster, for out of 6,600 men dropped or landed, about 1,100 were mustered on D-Day. They had two objectives, to secure the causeways that crossed flooded sections of the coast behind UTAH beach and to take the town of Ste. Mère Église. Both the airborne divisions achieved every one of their objectives with far fewer men than planned, partly because the extreme dispersion of the landings caused the Germans to be completely confused as to what was happening. Casualties were very high for the two units, estimated at over 2500 for the first three days.

Landings on the Assault Beaches

The bombarding ships of the Allied armada moved virtually unopposed into positions just before dawn broke. With the help of their spotting aircraft, the battleships laid down a withering fire on the

27 shore batteries from HMS Warspite firing its 15-inch guns on Villerville just south of Le Havre to HMS Erebus firing 15-inch guns on Barfleur just east of Cherbourg. Closer to shore than the 27 huge battlewagons, 54 cruisers and destroyers pounded the coast as well.

After a clear and relatively calm night, just before dawn, a blustering wind blew up over the assault beaches growing in strength until it attained 15 knots, punctuated with stronger gusts. Waves breaking on the beaches were much reduced from the previous day, but were still about 3 feet high -- heaviest at OMAHA. The sky was fair over the Channel, but beginning to cloud up over the coast.

The Normandy assault beachhead area was divided in two. To the west – the Western Assault Area – was the 25-mile stretch of coastline from UTAH beach at the base of the Cotentin Peninsula, past the mouth of the Vire River, along the cliffs past Pointe du Hoc and OMAHA beach to Port-en-Bessin. To the east – the Eastern

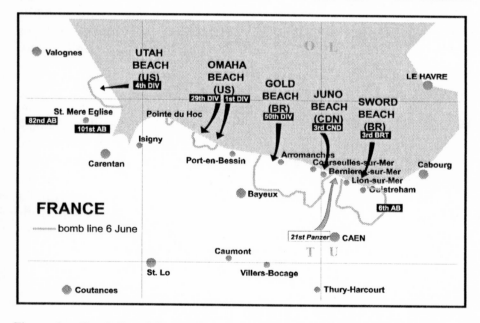

Figure 1 -- Bomb line 6 June. Three Allied airborne divisions landed during the night, while six seaborne divisions landed at the five beaches on D-Day. The extent of beachheads secured by midnight 6 June was less than planned but the landing was very successful.

Assault Area – was the 25-mile coast from Port-en-Bessin, past the British beach at GOLD, the Canadian beach at JUNO and the British beach at SWORD at the mouth of the Orne River. Commander of all the First US Army troops in the Western Assault Area was Lt Gen Omar Bradley. Stationed on his headquarters vessel the USS Augusta, Bradley commanded the landings at UTAH, OMAHA, Pointe du Hoc and the airborne troops of the 82nd and 101st Airborne Divisions. Commander of all the British Second Army troops in the Eastern Assault Area was Lt Gen Sir Miles Dempsey. Stationed on his headquarters vessel HMS Scylla, Dempsey commanded the landings at GOLD, JUNO, SWORD and the British 6th Airborne Division.

Assaulting troops landed at OMAHA beach at 0636 hours on D-Day. The beach was at the base of a 100-foot high 45-degree slope, the summit of which commanded a view of every part of the beach area. Four gullies afforded more gradual access to the higher ground, but the Germans had built concrete strong points to guard each of these access places. The strong points were supposed to have been destroyed by the heavy bombardment before the troops landed, however heavy bombing and naval gunfire failed to knock out any of them. An eight-foot seawall provided the only protection for the assaulting troops. Seas were heaviest in front of OMAHA beach and 27 of the 32 Dual Drive tanks, intended to swim in and clear the concrete machine-gun nests before the troops landed, were flooded and lost with their crews before they could get to the beach. Only one arrived intact. Thus the German shore defences were ready when the US troops landed laying down machine gun fire from the strong points and murderous mortar, small-arms and artillery fire raining down from the heights overlooking the beach. With no armour the American troops were cut to pieces as soon as the ramps dropped down. Half of those attempting to land never made it to the water's edge, but wave after wave poured forth until a long line of soldiers huddled under the safety of the seawall. The beach ran red with blood.

West of OMAHA beach the shore became precipitous with 100-foot vertical cliffs that stretched for several miles. Midway between UTAH and OMAHA beaches on this vertical shore, a point jutted out into the sea. Perched on this point was the six-gun battery of Pointe du Hoc that could fire 11 miles, sufficient range to rain havoc on both UTAH and OMAHA beaches. To silence this threat, 200 men of the 2nd US Ranger Brigade landed at the base, threw up grappling irons, and scaled the cliffs at 0630 hours. After a fierce fight they captured the battery and destroyed the guns -- a remarkable feat. Pointe du Hoc remains today one of the most vivid reminders of the ferocity of D-Day, for it is still heavily pockmarked with bomb and shell craters and displays the immensity of the fortified gun positions.

Because of the congestion of wounded and wrecked equipment on the beach, landing was halted in mid-morning at OMAHA. Lt Gen Bradley, commander the First US Army, in his book '*A Soldier's Story*' noted,

> "There was due to arrive at noon in the transport area off OMAHA beach a force of 25,000 troops and 4,400 vehicles to be landed on the second tide. However, only a portion of the first wave of 34,000 troops and 3,300 vehicles had as yet gone ashore. Unless we moved both forces ashore on D-Day, the whole intricate schedule of build-up would have been thrown off balance."

A deadlock developed with thousands of the 1st US Infantry Division soldiers pinned down by machine gun fire on the beach while German artillery chased the landing craft to and fro in front of the shore. Finally, the American destroyer USS Thomson steamed dangerously close to shore blazing away. It laid down a concentrated fire on two strong points on the eastern end of the beach and destroyed them enabling troops to break out from the beach, fight their way through the exit and gain the summit. The defending German 352nd Infantry Division, thinned by the bombardments and hand-to-hand combat, slowly succumbed to the American troops pouring onto the summit. Troop and equipment landings proceeded and by the end of the day, the 1st US Infantry Division and the 29th US Infantry Division had taken the bluffs over OMAHA beach. However, the position was precarious for much equipment had been lost, 2000 men were casualties and the rest were exhausted. Any concerted counter-attack by the Germans at that point in time might well have defeated the OMAHA landing.[1]

Whereas OMAHA beach was worse than the pessimistic planners had foreseen, UTAH beach proved to be an easy victory. The landing location was a low and open sandy beach with little habitation, behind which lay a flooded expanse several miles long running parallel to the beach. Connecting the beach to the mainland were five mile-long causeways. At first, sporadic German shore batteries and artillery fire was directed at the beach as the first wave of the 4th US Infantry Division landed at 0620 hours. Battleships silenced the guns within minutes permitting the landing to proceed almost unopposed, enabling the American troops to move across the causeways, establish themselves firmly immediately and connect with elements of the101st and 82nd US Airborne Divisions by nightfall.

The landing at GOLD beach was made at 0725 hours – nearly an hour later than at OMAHA because of a variation between tide patterns at the two beaches. As at OMAHA, the bombing had not destroyed any of the beach defences, but the Navy guns were effective.[2] Just before the landing, the huge German guns at Longues opened up on the fleet but were immediately silenced by HMS Ajax. High seas prevented the launching of the DD tanks at sea, however, the navy personnel brought the ships carrying these tanks right onto the beach and the DDs landed directly, although manoeuvring to accomplish this change of plan meant the tanks arrived after the assaulting troops and the AVREs (Armoured Vehicles Royal Engineers). The fighting was furious from the outset while the troops waited for armour to help them. At one moment, a German strong point with an 88mm gun sitting high on the rise one kilometre from the beach knocked out six British tanks before the gun was destroyed. The tide was unusually high and that made the beach much narrower than planned -- the congestion increased the difficulty of clearing the beach and added to the casualty list, however bit by bit the obstacles at GOLD beach were overcome and by 1030 hours, six exits had been cleared off the beach and many units took the high ground. On three occasions Sgt Maj Stanley Hollis single-handedly destroyed German resistance centres and earned the Victoria Cross for his actions. One group of 300 Commandos which landed at 0950 hours, drove immediately inland and circled, bypassing Arromanches, to capture Port-en-Bessin to the west. By midnight the 50th British Infantry Division held a beachhead that extended 8 miles inland and joined the Canadian beachhead to the east. The casualties on the beaches were about 400 – many fewer than predicted.

The 3rd Canadian Division landed on JUNO beach at 0745 hours, ten minutes later than planned. The DD tanks were successfully landed and immediately started cleaning up the strong points absorbing enemy fire that was much less than expected until after the first wave of troops were ashore and heavy mortar and small arms fire burst out of every bunker and every house, pinning down the troops and making it difficult for the AVREs to start clearing exits from the beach. At the eastern end of JUNO beach a detachment of 500 Royal Marines landed behind the first wave of Canadians, their mission was to wheel left and connect with another group coming from SWORD beach. Just off the coast at this point, three miles of offshore reefs prohibited a landing being made, hence this two-pronged attack. The Royal Marines landed right in front of a strong point and lost half their number almost immediately. The casualty loss rate at JUNO beach in the first three hours was as high as at OMAHA beach, much of which reflected the terrible losses of the Royal Marines. Fortunately at JUNO, the fighting was over after three hours, whereas at OMAHA it went on until late in the day. Slowly the defenders were overcome, but the Marines could not connect with their counterparts from the east. By 1050 hours, JUNO was sufficiently cleared to allow the second wave of Canadian troops to land and drive through the original assault units to achieve the day's objectives, and by noon a considerable portion of the field artillery units had landed and set up. Total casualties for the 3rd Canadian Infantry Division were 950.

The SWORD beach landing was another difficult one The landing started at 0725 hours with the locations of the actual landfall bunched much closer together than planned and the high tide left a beach half as wide. It was this assault force, led by tanks, that was supposed to relieve the airborne troops and go on to capture Caen before day's end, but congestion on the beaches under intense mortar and machine gun fire caused high casualties and delayed the marshalling of armoured units by several hours. Furthermore, the main body of troops was immediately held up by two very heavily fortified points a half-mile inland blocking the whole area. Code-named Morris and Hillman, they were thought to be just large pillboxes, while in fact, each held fifty to a hundred defenders in vast underground bunkers -- much more like forts than pillboxes. It took six hours to overcome them. Between the inability to get the tanks out in front, and the hold-up caused by the two forts, it became apparent by 1500 hours that the 3rd British Division could not take Caen that day. Casualties at SWORD beach ran to 630.

In the afternoon the 3rd British Infantry Division at SWORD ran into a strong armoured force consisting of 40 Mark IV tanks of the German 21st Panzer Division. British anti-tank guns destroyed a half-dozen tanks and stopped the attack, however the remaining Mark IVs backed off and attacked further to the west finding the seam between the British-held area and the Canadian-held area and drove through to Luc-sur-Mer. On the way they had 17 of their tanks knocked out, but they reached the sea before midnight -- just as Hitler and Rommel expected the Panzer divisions to do in response to an invasion. However, with no infantry or artillery support they were shocked to see hundreds of gliders overhead, and fearful of encirclement, withdrew to Caen before morning.

After the next day dawned, the Canadian troops and the British troops moved in to occupy the area where the German tanks had been. Through this action, the eastern part of the lodgement was united from Ouistreham at the eastern end of SWORD to Port-en-Bessin at the western end of GOLD. Although the Canadian and British sectors were one continuous lodgement, there was a large strong point located at Douvres-la-Délivrande, right in the middle between the British and Canadian sectors. It was defended fiercely but the Allied troops surrounded and sealed it off, then moved inland.

A Note About Tanks

The Allies relied upon three basic tanks – the Cromwell and Churchill tanks used by the British Army and the Sherman tank used by American, British and other Allied forces. German divisions were equipped with the standard Mark IV tank, though a few Panzer SS divisions had the more deadly Mark V Panther, or the most deadly Mark VI Tiger tank. The Allied tanks were a match for the Mark IVs, but much inferior to the Panthers and Tigers. The Tiger was massive; its six-inch thick armour plate was twice as thick as a Sherman's, but the Tiger was unreliable and hard to maintain and most important, the

Germans in Normandy had very few of them. That was just as well for the Tiger could only be stopped by an anti-tank gun or rocket-firing aircraft. The Sherman was fast, reliable, very manoeuvrable and had a high gun-turret-traversing speed, so that it could get off shots faster than any other tank, but its armour was much thinner and its 75 mm low-muzzle-velocity gun was inadequate. A Tiger could destroy a Sherman at a range of two-and-a-half kilometres while a Sherman's shells would bounce off a Tiger's armour at point blank range. A few Sherman tanks, fitted with the excellent British 17-pounder anti-tank gun were called Fireflies, and they could battle Panthers and Tigers. Curiously they were never used by the Americans. The armour on Churchill and Cromwell tanks was as thick as the Panther, but the guns they mounted didn't have enough hitting power. Thus overall the Allied armour was no match for its German counterpart.

The Beachhead

At midnight on D-Day, UTAH was a beachhead five miles wide and about as deep, surrounded by many inland pockets held by the dispersed airborne troops. OMAHA was 10 miles further east. It too, was about five miles wide but just a mile deep. The beachhead controlled by the British and Canadians -- GOLD and JUNO -- covered 12 miles in width and was about eight miles deep, however on its east side, a break of about four miles separated the beachhead from that of SWORD. It was into this breach that the 30-odd tanks of the 21st German Panzer Division had struck, before losing half their number, pausing and then withdrawing. Across the whole area 152,000 troops had been landed – 130,000 by sea. In the British/Canadian sector 4,000 tons of supplies had been unloaded, and 6,000 vehicles and 900 tanks had come ashore.

What was the Air Force to Expect on D-Day? Was Dieppe a Model?

When the Canadians hit the beaches at Dieppe in the ill-fated raid of 19 August 1942, the skies above the area witnessed the greatest air battle that had been seen since the Battle of Britain. The aerial fighting started early in the morning and lasted all day long, in wave after wave of encounters. Both sides claimed over a hundred fighter aircraft destroyed, and although the actual German losses were much lower, these high figures were remembered as an indication of the level of losses that could be expected during an invasion.

When pilots asked the OVERLORD planners what kind of air strength they could expect to meet over the Normandy beaches, the answer was 'two thousand sorties a day' – 400 fighters times five or more sorties per day. The planners said that only – I./JG 2, III./JG 2, I./JG 26 and II./JG 26 were in the immediate area, but it was believed that hundreds of additional fighters would be diverted to Normandy within hours of the invasion, in effect doubling or trebling the number of sorties per day. That settled it – the Allied fighters going into battle on D-Day were convinced they would have to fight tooth and nail.

A Word about Luftwaffe Fighter Units

Jagdgeschwader (JG) was the term used by the Luftwaffe to denote a parent assemblage of day-fighter wings. Jagdgeschwader were numbered in Arabic numerals of the form JG 2 or JG 54. Within the parent JG organization there were usually three or occasionally four wings called 'gruppen'. These gruppen were identified by Roman numerals, as in I./JG 2 or III./JG 54. These denoted the 'I' gruppe of the parent JG 2 jagdgeschwader and the 'III' gruppe of the JG 54 jagdgeschwader. Staffel was the German term for a squadron and was identified by Arabic numerals of the form 3./JG 2 or 6./JG 2. Each jagdgeschwader had three or four gruppen, as in I./JG 2, II./JG 2 and III./JG 2 and each gruppe had three or four staffeln, as in 1./JG 2, 2./JG 2 and 3./JG 2 in the gruppe I./JG 2 and 4./JG 2, 5./JG 2 and 6./JG 2 in the gruppe II./JG 2, and so on.

Although on many occasions two or more JG gruppen teamed up on a certain mission, generally each gruppe flew as a separate entity with the same type of aircraft. In Normandy, these were usually either FW 190 A-8s or Bf 109 G-6s. Planned allotment of fighter aircraft was 12 per staffel. Thus a gruppe had 36 aircraft, and a jagdgeschwader 108. Throughout the Normandy Campaign the number of serviceable aircraft in each unit was seldom more than half of this allotment -- the scarcity of pilots, poor serviceability and limited fuel availability accounted for this shortage.

Coastal Command on D-Day

Far out to sea, in the Atlantic, in the North Sea and in the Bay of Biscay, flew the Sunderlands, Wellingtons, Catalinas, Halifaxes and Liberators of No.19 Group of Coastal Command. They had been on high alert for a week before D-Day, and they knew how critical this moment was. 21 squadrons of Coastal Command aircraft guarded the approach from the North Sea to the north-east; 30 squadrons guarded the south-west approach from the Atlantic. Every square mile of the Channel and its approaches was investigated every half-hour. U-boats had to surface each day to replenish air, re-charge batteries and report directly to Admiral Karl Dönitz. From these communications, ULTRA intercepted the information and fed the exact location of U-boats to Coastal Command. Of 35 available U-boats, 16 were despatched by Dönitz to the Channel on D-Day, but 19 Group harried them at every turn. They sank two on D-Day and six others in the following four days. Not a single U-boat got through to the crowded invasion sea-lanes on D-Day, though a couple of E-Boats did.

Heavy Bombing on D-Day

Between 0300 hours and 0500 hours of 6 June, 1056 Lancasters and Halifaxes of Bomber Command dropped 5,267 tons of bombs on selected coastal batteries and strong defensive positions -- losing 11 aircraft and 70 men in the effort. In addition, 2,600 Fortresses and Liberators of the US 8thAF pounded the remaining coastal batteries -- incurring the loss of 14 US bombers and 55 aircrew. The landing forces later reported that the bombing appeared to have had little effect upon the defensive positions at the beaches, but it was not for the lack of trying, for the bomb zone was set far behind the beaches.

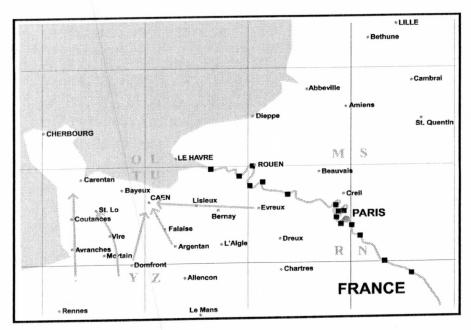

Figure 2 -- Interdiction targets*. Major routes for the Germans to reinforce the Normandy defences (arrows) are shown together with the major bridges over the Seine (squares)*

Not seen by those on the beaches, within a couple of hours of the landing, the bombing and the naval bombardment silenced all but two of the 27 coastal batteries situated the length of the coast.

Medium Bombing on D-Day

Number 2 Group from Bomber Command had been assigned to the 2ndTAF since early in the year. It consisted of 12 squadrons of Mitchells, Bostons and Mosquitos. The role of these squadrons on D-Day was to concentrate on five reinforcement routes that the Germans would have to use to counter the seaborne assault. These routes were:

1. Avranches – Coutances – Lessay (the route up the west coast to Cherbourg)

2. Fougères – Vire – St. Lô (the route from Brittany north to St. Lô)
3. Domfront – Flers – Caen (the route from the south-west to Caen)
4. Argentan – Falaise – Caen (the route from the south-east to Caen)
5. Evreux – Lisieux – Caen (the route from Paris to Caen)

The US 9thAF had 12 squadrons of A-20 and 32 squadrons of B-26 medium bombers. The role of these powerful forces was to bomb all the strong artillery batteries that were situated just behind the coast – to bomb them just after the heavy bombing, and then to go back again and again until the guns were silenced. In addition to the coastal batteries, they bombed four marshalling yards east of the Seine, and hit road junctions and all the bridges along the Seine. They flew 820 sorties during the day.

A note regarding the bombing of bridges

From the beginning of the implementation of the Transportation Plan every bridge across the Seine, L'Eure and Loire Rivers was targetted. When these bridges were destroyed, Normandy and Brittany would be cut off from the rest of Europe. Concerned with how completely this might be accomplished, Operations Research scientists estimated that with the area bombing techniques employed at the time, it would take 600 tons of bombs to destroy a bridge.[3] It was soon discovered that in fact the average was more like 640 tons when dropped from heavy bombers, but it took only 90 to 180 tons when dropped by Typhoons[4] or P-47s – each of which could carry two 500-pound bombs. Nonetheless, this translated into hundreds of Typhoon sorties to destroy a single bridge. With half the carrying capacity, and less stability as a bombing platform, the Spitfire required more than twice as many sorties as would a Typhoon.

Night Fighters

The night of 5/6 June, an armada of transport aircraft and gliders stretched out in three long aerial archways across the Channel, but even before the first aircraft in the stream reached the French coast shortly after midnight, there had been much aerial activity. Two Wellingtons and seven Mosquitos carried out reconnaissance, 36 Bostons and six Mosquitos flew on high-level bombing runs (although the foul weather inland over France caused 21 of these to abort), and 102 Mosquitos patrolled northern France to intercept any night bombers and fighters the Luftwaffe might send up.

All night long, the Beaufighters and Mosquitos of 29, 264, 406, 409, 410, 418, 488 and 604 Squadrons cruised the length and breadth of the coast where the invasion would occur and the sea lanes of the assault fleet guarding against chance discovery of the armada. These flight patterns, worked out to intricately fit the outline of the unfolding invasion fleet, were repeated and repeated until the light glow in the eastern sky signalled the imminent arrival of the day fighters. Three Mosquitos were hit by flak while on intruder missions over France resulting in the death of five of the six aircrew. Two aircraft claimed victories shooting down a Ju 188 and an Me 410.

D-Day Beach Patrols

From first light until last light on D-Day, and for the whole of the Normandy Campaign, the maintenance of air supremacy over the beachhead was accomplished by having fighters continuously in the air. At all times throughout the first three days, three squadrons of US 9thAF P-47s provided cover above 8,000 feet, while six squadrons of RAF or RCAF Spitfires provided low cover below 2,000 feet. That was the plan.

Time	HIGH PATROL			LOW PATROL WAA			LOW PATROL EAA		
430	10	81	313	130	611	501			
520				64	234	345	402	303	350
530	512	513	514						
610				302	308	317	222	349	485
630	22	23	53						
700				403	416	421	441	442	443
730	506	507	508						
750				331	332	66	310	312	313
830	410	411	412						
840				132	453	602	401	411	412
930	10	81	313	303	234	345	329	340	341
1020				130	64	611	402	501	350
1030	512	513	514						
1110				302	308	317	222	349	485
1130	22	23	53						
1200				403	416	421	441	442	443
1230	506	507	508						
1250				331	332	66	310	312	313
1330	410	411	412						
1340				132	453	602	401	411	412
1430	10	81	313	303	234	345	329	340	341
1520				302	308	317	222	349	485
1530	512	513	514						
1610				403	416	421	441	442	443
1630	22	23	53						
1700				331	332	66	310	312	313
1730	506	507	508						
1750				132	453	602	401	411	412
1830	410	411	412						
1840				130	611	501	329	340	341
1930	10	81	313						
2020				403	416	421	441	442	443
2030	512	513	514						
2110				331	332	66	310	312	313
2130	22	23	53						
2200				132	453	602	401	411	412
2230	506	507	508						
2250				130	64	611	402	501	350

Table 4 – Beach patrol. *Please note that the five US 9th AF FGs were the 50th (10, 81, 313FS), 406th (512, 513, 514FS), 36th (22, 23, 53FS), 404th (506, 507, 508FS) and the 373rd (410, 411, 314FS). The 2ndTAF fighter wings were from ADGB (130, 611, 501), ADGB (64, 234, 345), ADGB (402, 303, 350), 131 Wing (302, 308, 317), 135 Wing (222, 349, 485), 127 Wing (403, 416, 421), 144 Wing (441, 442, 443), 132 Wing (331, 332, 66), 134 Wing (310, 312, 313), 125 Wing (132, 453, 602), 126 Wing (401, 411, 412), ADGB (303, 234, 345), 145 Wing (329, 340, 341).*

34

As one group finished its patrol, it was replaced by another. The schedule of squadrons that flew this relentless watch is as shown above. The time at left is the time when the squadron was to be on station conducting the patrol, the High Patrol covered the whole of the assault area, while the Low Patrol was broken into the Eastern Assault Area (EAA) and Western Assault Areas (WAA), separated at Port-en-Bessin. The squadron numbers are shown.[5]

The US P-47s flying from their UK bases could remain on station an hour, but because of their more limited range, 2ndTAF Spitfires could only remain on station for 50 minutes.

The timing of the patrols didn't change, but as it turned out, the weather severely changed the plans. The 6th, 7th and 8th of June saw thick 10/10ths cloud covering nearly the whole sky, with a ceiling varying from 3,000 to 6,000 feet above the ground. In the first three days of the campaign, all the aircraft had to fly under this cloud layer – making for considerable congestion and considerable danger from ground fire. That ground fire came not only from German flak units but also from Allied ships and ground troops with itchy fingers and only recently acquired aircraft recognition skills.

The first patrol aircraft reported off the Normandy coast at 0430 hours in the early morning – two hours before the actual beach assault landings began. The last aircraft reported on station at 2250 hours at night and did not leave the patrol to return to the UK until 2345 hours. During the war, the UK was on double daylight saving time – two hours ahead of Greenwich Mean Time. Sunrise over the Normandy coast 6 June 1944 was 0506 hours British Double Summer Time, while sunset was 2211 hours British Double Summer Time. To be on station at the appointed hour, the first patrols took off from England in pitch darkness about 0400 hours, took up their positions with only a glow in the eastern sky, were relieved of their patrol with the first glimpse of the sun, flew back to England and landed just as the sun's disk appeared. The last patrol of the day took off 10 minutes after sunset, reported on station at 2250 hours, watched the last glow of the day in the western sky, flew their patrol and returned home in total darkness, landing near midnight.

The nine wings of Spitfires from 2ndTAF plus three wings from Air Defence of Great Britain (ADGB) – 36 squadrons for a total of over 450 Spitfires -- flew over 1550 sorties on D-Day. Five FGs of P-47s from the US 9thAF – 15 squadrons, about 200 P-47s flew 773 sorties on D-Day. All the patrols were flown precisely to schedule. Shortly after 0800 hours on D-Day, a 602 Squadron Spitfire crash-landed on UTAH Beach, but American soldiers rescued the pilot. In the early afternoon, a 441 (Canadian) Squadron pilot had his engine cut out when hit by flak and bailed out in the Channel and was rescued almost immediately. A Spitfire of 63 Squadron was shot down while spotting for naval fire. The pilot bailed out and was rescued by the Navy off Cherbourg. In the day, seven Spitfires were lost – four shot down by flak, the remainder due to accident and mechanical failure – but only four were part of the patrol schedule.

A word about Claims and Losses

Any book that deals with aerial combat invariably emphasizes what has often been called the numbers game. Pilots claim many more aircraft shot down than are actually recorded by the opponent as lost. Many have thought this a propaganda trick – and in some cases, such as the daily tallies reported in the British newspapers during the Battle of Britain in 1940, this was a propaganda trick, but several factors must be considered. Firstly, one must believe that the pilots are trying to be truthful – indeed they welcomed corroboration from both their comrades and from ground forces who often watched the battles. Secondly, those interested in motivating budding fighter pilots, saw good reasons to encourage a system that distinguished between 'destroyed', 'probably destroyed' and 'damaged'. Both British and American air forces used these categorizations. Destroyed required a second witness to verify the claim. Probably destroyed often had a second witness as well, but recognized that no one saw an explosion, a pilot bail out, or a crash. Damaged was the category for a hit without any claim that the enemy aircraft could not return to its base and be repaired. The reason it was advantageous to have such a system was that it often took a long time before a good fighter pilot became a great fighter pilot. Having other measures of success like the probable and damaged categories served to recognize pilots in the course of their developing careers.

But there is a consideration that is more important from a military point of view, and that is whether the aircraft was lost or not, and whether the pilot was lost or not. A pilot may see an opponent trailing heavy smoke and appear to be headed for the ground, but the aircraft actually managed to recover sufficiently to get back to base and was repaired. For the attacking pilot's career it may be worthwhile to record what damage he inflicted upon the enemy, but if both enemy pilot and aircraft survive to fight another day, is that a victory from the military point of view? On the other hand, a victim of attack may disappear into cloud with only a slight indication of trailing smoke but crash while attempting to land back at home base killing the pilot. This is a victory regardless what claim was made. Someone might limp home with an aircraft so damaged that it slides to a stop at home base and is immediately written off as junk. This too is a victory for the opponent.

For these many reasons, although this book often mentions claims, it emphasizes the destroyed category and rarely makes reference to any damaged claims. The real measure of the effectiveness of the aerial activity is losses, and so this book tries to concentrate upon losses on both sides – losses of aircraft, and losses of aircrew.

Reconnaissance on D-Day

From first light D-Day, the seven reconnaissance squadrons of the 2ndTAF, the eight reconnaissance squadrons of the US 9thAF and five reconnaissance squadrons of the US 8thAF continuously flew photographic missions and tactical reconnaissance missions reporting enemy positions. During the day the US 9thAF alone despatched 196 reconnaissance sorties and the 2ndTAF flew 194 and lost three aircraft – one of them destroyed by a rocket barrage fired from the in-coming assault forces off JUNO beach. Two other Mustangs were lost throughout the day – one to flak, and one shot down by FW 190s. All three pilots were killed. Notwithstanding this valiant effort, the poor weather, the nature of the Normandy landscape and the Germans' ability to camouflage their positions, combined to frustrate the effectiveness of the reconnaissance, and not much enemy troop movement was revealed. As expected, confusion reigned, and the senior commanders needed an overview.

> "AM Geddes, Senior Administrative Officer (to ACM Leigh-Mallory), ventured forth in a Mustang aircraft with one port-facing oblique camera. He left RAF Station Northolt at 0935 hours, flew the length of all five beaches at about 1000 feet running out of film after GOLD beach, but recording everything he saw. Geddes had been a key contributor to the planning of OVERLORD and so knew exactly what to look for. He returned to Northolt at 1125 hours and reported in immediately."[6]

This report gave the high command their first complete view of the invasion situation on each of the beachheads.

Direct Support to the Army on D-Day

The 2ndTAF had 18 squadrons of Typhoon aircraft and six squadrons of P-51 aircraft to support specific army objectives. Nine Typhoon squadrons were assigned targets of military headquarters, strongly defended localities and enemy batteries. All but one of their assigned targets was reported as destroyed. Three Typhoon squadrons equipped with rockets were assigned to each of SWORD, JUNO and GOLD beaches. The remaining aircraft waited back in England for assignment, however, assignment did not come, so by late morning two Typhoon squadrons were ordered out on armed recces (the term used to describe a sweep in a specific area searching for targets of opportunity). During the day, Typhoons flew 400 sorties – 287 before noon. In the process they claimed the destruction of six tanks, 12 armoured vehicles and 21 trucks (referred to in all reports as motor transport or MT). They also claimed as many again damaged – that is, hit and possibly smoking, but not on fire or exploded. The 342 (Free French) Squadron flying Bostons, laid down smoke screens, one to the east of the assault area, and one to the west. Owing to wind direction the western screen was called off just before completion.

In addition to the 15 squadrons of P-47s the US 9thAF assigned to beach patrol, it had 27 squadrons of P-47s, nine squadrons of P-38s and six squadrons of P-51s. Many of these were assigned to escort duty – escorting troop transport, escorting the medium bombers, and escorting dive-bombing and reconnaissance missions. In addition to these, the US 8thAF had 45 squadrons of fighters available in reserve. Over the mid-Channel sea lanes in daylight hours, 15 squadrons of fighters flew -- mostly twin-boomed P-38s because they were easily identified and were not likely to be unintentionally shot down by trigger-nervous navy gun crews.

The remaining aircraft were assigned to direct army support. Of the 3,040 sorties flown by US 9thAF on D-Day (this includes everything but transport sorties) 592 were flown in dive-bombing and strafing sorties as direct support to the army – most to previously assigned targets, but eight missions were in answer to direct army requests for action. Medium bomber B-26 and A-20 aircraft flew 820 sorties bombing coastal batteries, enemy strong points, many road bridges and four marshalling yards east of the Seine.

Luftwaffe presence on D-Day

Only one wing – 135 Wing, made up of 222 Squadron, 349 (Belgian) Squadron and 485 (New Zealand) Squadron – encountered German Ju 88 aircraft over the beaches. On its patrol at 1110 hours F/L Houlton of 485 Squadron shot down a stray Ju 88 that managed to charge toward the beaches to bomb the congestion there. Four hours later at 1520 hours, Houlton on another patrol, shot down another Ju 88 and shared in a third. In this engagement 349 Squadron also claimed two shot down, for a total of four Ju 88s claimed. A pilot of 349 Squadron, Sgt Van Molkot bailed out of his severely damaged Spitfire and was captured.

Few if any returning Spitfire pilots heard of these encounters. Instead, the disappointing conviction spread throughout the 2ndTAF that no German bomber or fighter aircraft were coming to greet them. This view became folklore when Cornelius Ryan, in his book *The Longest Day*, suggested that only two German fighter aircraft attacked the beaches on D-Day. It was none other than the legendary Luftwaffe ace Pips Priller, Geschwaderkommodore of JG 26, and his wingman who flew this mission. Priller received word of the invasion at his headquarters in Lille (near the Pas de Calais) sent word to his three gruppen to move to the Paris area, and then jumped in his FW 190 and took off. He and his wing man flew 200 miles south-west over Le Havre, dropped down to 50 feet and dashed the whole length of the beachheads, from SWORD to OMAHA. They emptied their ammunition at the landing troops before climbing into the low-hanging clouds and high-tailing it back to an airbase at Creil with almost empty tanks.

This is the story as told by Cornelius Ryan and this has led to the general understanding that there was no other Luftwaffe presence on D-Day. The myth has gone further. Since the Allies quickly established air supremacy in the Normandy skies, it has become commonplace to say that the Luftwaffe was nowhere to be seen in the whole Normandy Campaign.

An anecdote, often quoted but of unknown origin, quotes a captured German soldier saying, "If the aircraft is silver, it's American; if it's camouflaged, it's British; if it's invisible, it's German!" This anecdote has been used to illustrate that the Luftwaffe just didn't show up for the Normandy Campaign. However, if the Allied experience was that the Luftwaffe rarely appeared, the exact opposite was the German experience. Every time a German aircraft took off, it ran into aerial battles. How could this be? How could the Allied pilots lament that they rarely ever saw the Luftwaffe, but the Luftwaffe reported fighting with the Allied aircraft on nearly every mission?

The most often quoted figure regarding sorties flown by the Luftwaffe on D-Day is 319 – more than half of them flown by JG 26 (Don Caldwell, authority on the history of the JG 26, says they flew 172 sorties). The 319 sortie figure includes the Ju 88 bomber attacks on the beachheads, but these were few as the major bombing effort got underway the following day. The only other active jagdgeschwader on D-Day, JG 2, flew about 120 sorties. The 319 sortie figure represents about a dozen serious fighter attacks on the Allied air umbrella. That is quite a substantial effort, even if it does pale into insignificance against the traditionally quoted figure of 14,700 sorties[7] flown by Allied aircraft. However, the massive Allied figure includes all categories of missions, including over 30 squadrons of Coastal Command flying the sea-lanes. A more representative comparison might be the 2,300 sorties flown by the beach patrol aircraft, plus another 1,900 sorties for direct army support, spotting and reconnaissance, nearly 900 sorties of medium bombers and 700 escorting sorties -- a total of 5,800 Allied sorties. A check on the reasonableness of this figure comes by way of 3,040 sorties flown by US 9thAF[8], 2,450 from the 2ndTAF[9] together with an estimated 300 or so flown by US 8thAF and ADGB. Using these figures, the Luftwaffe sorties were outnumbered about 18 to 1. Any Luftwaffe aircraft was 18 times more likely to run into Allied opposition than was an Allied aircraft.

Returning to the actual Luftwaffe presence on D-Day, we find that contrary to *The Longest Day* account, there was a fair amount of aerial combat. In addition to the four attacks on the beaches already mentioned, at least five significant aerial combats occurred – one of which involved as many as 60 combatant aircraft.

Aerial Battles on D-Day

The aerial battles on D-Day were fought from just behind enemy lines to a depth of 100 miles into the Normandy hinterland -- the first aerial battle was fought over Caen at noon. 16 P-47s from the 365th FG of the US 9thAF were attacking ground targets six miles south of Caen when, just minutes before noon, 29 FW 190s from JG 2 bounced them. The commanding officer of JG 2 was a German ace, Geschwaderkommodore Hauptmann Kurt Buhligen. He led a formation consisting of the headquarters element known as Stab./JG 2 plus two gruppen, I./JG 2 and III./JG 2. Diving out of the clouds upon the American P-47s Buhligen shot down one and claimed the first Luftwaffe aerial victory of the Normandy Campaign at 1157 hours. Buhligen had 97 destroyed aircraft to his credit at this date – the P-47 made it 98. One other P-47 was also destroyed.

The remaining P-47s escaped, but within minutes of climbing to altitude, JG 2 spotted eight Typhoons of 183 Squadron attacking a road convoy. The convoy was one of the many bringing the 12th SS Panzer Division to the front from Lisieux. The Typhoon squadron scored a dozen hits on the vehicles before they were bounced by the FW 190s of III./JG2 led by Hauptmann Herbert Huppertz and three Typhoons were shot down -- Huppertz claimed two. Huppertz, Gruppekommandeur of III./JG 2, was another Luftwaffe ace who had a record of 64 destroyed aircraft. These two Typhoons, plus three more he would add before the day was over, brought his total to 69. Another Typhoon was claimed by JG 2, however only five aircraft were actually lost – two P-47s and three Typhoons. Although it is unclear whether the P-47s or the Typhoons were responsible, the Luftwaffe lost one FW 190. All three Typhoon pilots and the FW 190 pilot were killed.

Just after noon, 60 miles away near Le Mans, P-51s of 334th FS, 335th FS and 336th FS of the US 8thAF 4th FG tangled with 10 FW 190s of III./SG 4. This was a German reconnaissance group and there is some indication that several of the German aircraft were being ferried to their base at Laval. In short order the Americans shot down four FW 190s including the kommandeur of the gruppe, Hauptmann Mihlan – although he parachuted to earth unhurt. The American claim of four victories was accurate, but they paid a very high price. A mechanical failure, a collision and heavy flak were all factors in the loss of 10 US P-51s and six pilots.

Several encounters occurred throughout the day, each time with a single claim or single recorded loss. In addition, Allied and German anti-aircraft fire brought down a steady stream of fighters and bombers.

At 1825 hours, JG 2 caught eight Typhoons of 164 Squadron attacking troop convoys entering Caen and shot down one. Huppertz claimed this victory.

The time is uncertain, but probably in late afternoon, in a lucky bounce near Abbeville, 15 P-51s of the 505th FS shot down three FW 190s of the famous I./JG 26. The Americans claimed four, but only three German losses were recorded in the JG 26 history.

At 1900 hours at Laval, there was a repeat of the earlier engagement. German records report that as several FW 190s of III./SG 4 were in the landing pattern, they were attacked by P-51s. It is not certain which American unit this was, but the result was loss of three FW 190s and their pilots.

A series of engagements occurred between 2030 and 2100 hours, centred around the cities of Evreux and Bernay, half way between Caen and Paris. The P-51s of the 487th FS of the 352nd FG of the US 8thAF were bounced by elements of I./JG 2, III./JG 2 and I./JG 26. Three American planes were shot down, however one pilot evaded and lived to fight another day. Huppertz claimed his fourth and fifth victories of the day and the 69th of his career.

A curious encounter occurred at 2045 hours half way between Chartres and Orleans and about 70 miles south-south-west of Paris. A large US 8thAF formation of about 48 P-51s – the 354th FS, 357th FS and 358th FS of the 355th FG – happened upon a great number of Ju 87 Stuka dive-bombers. These Ju 87s were from SG 103 -- a training unit -- and for some unexplained reason, they flew in a large formation hedge-hopping their way from Metz to Le Mans. The 355th FG caught them and claimed 12 aircraft destroyed, one probably destroyed and five damaged with no losses of their own. German records indicate that SG 103 lost at least six Ju 87s, but this figure is probably understated.

By the end of the day the RAF had lost nine Spitfires, eight Typhoons, three Mustangs and three Mosquitos. The US 9thAF lost eight P-47s, two P-38s, two P-51s, and 11 medium bombers; the US 8thAF lost 20 P-51s. This brought the Allied total aircraft losses to 66 – 55 fighters and 11 medium bombers. These figures exclude the loss of 41 troop carrier aircraft or heavy bombers missing and destroyed. Of the 55 Allied fighter losses, only 16 were shot down in combat, the other 39 were lost to flak or were involved in accidents.[10]

The Luftwaffe lost 17 FW 190s and one Bf 109 – 12 shot down in combat, six to flak and flying accidents[11]. Only four Luftwaffe medium bombers are known to have been lost in the Normandy area on D-Day. Total fighters and medium bombers lost numbered 22.

All-in-all the Allies put forth an overwhelming display of aerial might. They launched thousands of aircraft as part of OVERLORD -- the official figure was 14,700 sorties for all categories of aircraft. Total Allied losses for all categories of aircraft on D-Day was reported to be 113 for a total Allied loss rate per sortie of 0.77 of one percent. Of the 113 aircraft lost, 66 were fighters and medium bombers. Whereas the total number of fighter aircraft and medium bomber sorties flown over Normandy on D-Day was estimated at 5800, that represents a loss rate per sortie at 1.1 percent.

However the Luftwaffe figures are far different, with 319 sorties flown and with 22 Luftwaffe aircraft destroyed, the loss rate per sortie is 6.9% -- six times the loss rate of the Allies. If there was to be a battle of attrition in the skies over Normandy, the Luftwaffe fighter and medium bomber pilots had no chance to win it.

Chapter Three – 7 June through 30 June

Not one of the senior German military commanders in the Normandy area was at his post when the alarming reports came in from observers on the coast. The first reports to reach high command were of sighting parachute landings and observing a massive number of attacking ships offshore. The reports were not believed. Allied troops landed by air and by sea, and it was only the local junior officers who realized this was a major assault. Hitler had insisted that his Panzer divisions were not to move until they received orders directly from him, but Hitler was asleep and no one dared to disturb him. It was late in the morning before Hitler and his generals met to determine what response was appropriate, and they all agreed this was a feint – a distraction because they were convinced the real invasion was coming across the straits at the Pas de Calais.[1] Operation FORTITUDE had been remarkably successful.

When the magnitude of the Normandy landing was fully known, a simple calculation should have shown the Germans that a second assault of equal or greater magnitude across the Channel was beyond Allied military strength, but the German high command still didn't believe it. They insisted on holding the German Fifteenth Army in the Pas de Calais area for the entire month of June, however, during the night of 6/7 June they did order the 12th SS Panzer Division to move from near Paris to join 21st Panzer Division at Caen, and they ordered the 1st SS Panzer and Panzer Lehr Divisions from their locations in Brittany into the sector immediately west of Caen. Thus only four panzer divisions were assigned to Normandy -- hardly enough to hurl the invading forces back into the sea.

Expanding the Lodgement

In the Eastern Assault Area, Generaloberst Richter's 716th German Infantry Division manning bunkers all along the invasion coastline had been shattered by the first assault. Eighty percent of its men were casualties. As 7 June dawned, it looked as though there was nothing to oppose the 3rd Canadian Division or the British 50th Division. Both divisions were determined to make up the shortfall in their D-Day objectives. The British 50th Infantry Division took Bayeux and met some advance elements of the 1st US Infantry Division who had broken out of OMAHA beach. This union linked OMAHA beach to GOLD beach. In the eastern part of the lodgement, the 3rd Canadian and 3rd British Divisions consolidated the beachheads of JUNO and SWORD, occupying the ground where the tank squadron of the German 21st Panzer Division had charged to the sea late on D-Day. By occupying this area they surrounded and by-passed the fort at Douvres la Délivrande. This fort was not captured until 17 June. Its capture cost several tanks and a number of casualties, but only after the surrender of its 200 German occupants, was it discovered to be a complex of radar facilities 300 feet below ground. From 6 June to 17 June it had been the only German radar station south of the Pas de Calais to escape destruction, although there is little evidence that it was operational.

The Canadians then set out to attain their D-Day objectives of occupying Carpiquet Airport and cutting off the Caen-to-Bayeux road. They moved off on a single axis without artillery support. Eager troops took Buron just three miles from Caen, and moved on to Authie, knocking out German anti-tank guns as they went. However, because of the failure of their naval coordinator's radio, they lost contact with HMS Belfast which was their heavy gun support, just as they ran into a counter-attack by advanced units of the fanatical Hitler Youth 12th SS Panzer Division. Unlike the 21st Panzer Division that only had Mark IV tanks, the 12th SS Panzer Division had a number of Mark V Panther tanks. The Canadians were driven out of Authie and Buron and badly mauled. Before contact with HMS Belfast was re-established, the Canadians lost 110 men killed, 192 wounded and had 21 tanks destroyed. Belfast's guns restored the balance and Buron was retaken, but the cost had been nearly a third of the losses suffered on D-Day. Further to the west, the Canadians advanced, and while their position was tenuous, an ill-conceived attack by advanced units of the German 12th SS along the Caen-to-Bayeux highway was repulsed at Bretteville l'Orgueilleuse with six German tanks destroyed – five of

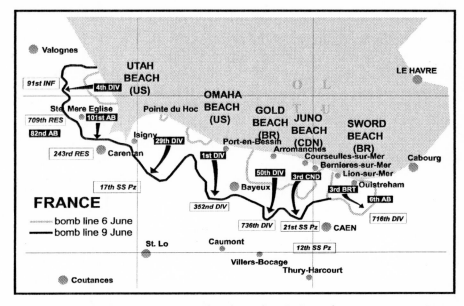

Figure 3 – Bomb line 9 June. *The day after D-Day there was a continuous lodgement from Pointe du Hoc through to Ouistreham – only UTAH was isolated. This was rectified by 9 June when the Allies were firmly entrenched in a continuous lodgement. Unfortunately, the German defence position was rapidly put in place and this bomb line would hold for nearly a month..*

them Panthers. Another attack the next day was again repulsed with seven Panthers left burning. This was an important battle. Had the12th SS been able to get through the Canadian lines, the lodgement may have been shattered, for the 7th British Armoured Division and the 51st British Infantry Division had not yet landed.

The situation in the sector behind OMAHA beach and Pointe du Hoc was much as it was at GOLD and JUNO. Breaking through the seaward defences of the resident elements of the 716th German Infantry Division and the 352nd German Infantry Division caused such high enemy casualties that opposition crumbled. The 352nd fell back fighting a rearguard action while the 1st US Infantry Division advanced 10 miles inland to connect with the 50th British Infantry Division at Port-en-Bessin and inland at Bayeux. At the western end of this beachhead, the 29th US Infantry Division connected up with the Rangers at Pointe du Hoc, taking all the territory between Bayeux and Isigny. They fought a heavy battle at Isigny but managed to take the town after a ferocious bombardment from the battle cruiser HMS Glasgow. That night an advanced unit from the 1st US Infantry Division cut across the swampy ground north of Carentan to link up with the 101st US Airborne Division. Days later on 12 June in a pincer movement, Carentan fell to the 101st US Airborne.

For the 2ndTAF, the major challenge was trying to find where the elements of the 21st Panzer Division and the 12th SS Panzer Division were located. The 21st Panzer had advanced elements in Caen when the assault began. The remainder of its force had passed through Paris days before and by D-Day-plus-one, was moving along the Argentan-to-Falaise route. The 12th SS Panzer had been well east of Paris on D-Day. It was ordered to move to Paris and its main units were now trying to make their way through Dreux and Evreux to Caen. It was known that both had come into Paris by train, but crossed the Seine by ferry and then proceeded by as many secondary routes as possible. The harassment of trains, the destruction of all bridges and the daylight strafing of truck convoys forced the Germans to travel by night. Allied intelligence had a pretty good picture of this situation because of the excellent reporting of the French Underground. All available Typhoon and Mustang squadrons were assigned stretches of connecting road, junctions and key towns and villages where they hunted, attacked and destroyed.

A word about armed recces and maps

A constant stream of squadron-strength missions flew into Normandy from England. Some had specific targets while many sought out targets of opportunity. These latter missions became known as armed recces – armed reconnaissance missions. They were defined only in terms of a geographic zone, such as Lisieux/Bernay/L'Aigle or St.Lô/Vire/Coutances. Some had a specific target to be attacked first, such as dive-bombing the bridge at T.9439 near Conde,[2] followed by a free-ranging search and destroy mission. The dive-bombing armed recce was often accomplished by sending half the squadron with 500-pound bombs, and all with extra fuel and full ammunition. The mission would start with the flight across the Channel, cross the coast into Normandy before dropping their extra fuel tanks and attacking. If it were a Spitfire squadron, six aircraft would fly high cover – about ten thousand feet over the target area – while the other six aircraft dive-bombed. The bombing aircraft would approach the target in line astern formation at about eight thousand

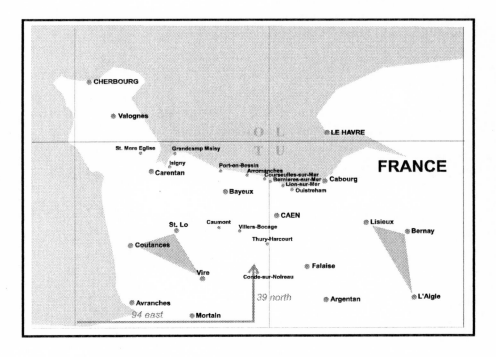

Figure 4 -- Armed recces. The map shows two typical target areas for armed recces. Note the 100-kilometre square entitled 'T' Map references such as T.9439 refer to 94 kilometres east and 39 north as shown.

feet and fly until the starboard wing tip covered the target. The Spitfire pilot would then peel off and dive at a sixty-degree angle keeping the target just over the nose. At three thousand feet he would pull out, count to three and release the bomb. Judging the exact steepness at 60°, controlling dive speed from going off the clock and pulling out at exactly 3,000 feet when the altimeter was whirling like a spoke in a bicycle wheel, were extremely difficult. Since the placement of the bomb depended upon strict control of these factors, it is easy to see why the Spitfire was not a very good platform for dive-bombing. It was also hazardous. By the time the third Spitfire had completed its run, there was little doubt that the anti-aircraft gunners on the ground knew exactly where the next attacker was coming from. It was a daunting challenge to be fourth, fifth or sixth, diving at a target whose defending gunners had refined their aim to hit your 500-pound bomb before you dropped it.

As soon as six bombs were dropped the whole squadron would strafe, or if the flak were too intense, would go off to look for other targets. Though an unstable platform for dive-bombing the Spitfire proved an excellent strafing vehicle. Despite the risks, most Spitfire pilots enjoyed the dive-bombing and strafing missions.

A note about rocket-firing aircraft

Of the 18 squadrons of Typhoons, 11 were configured for rocket-launching – called RP (rocket projectile) Typhoons – while seven were configured for bombs – called Bombphoons. Bombphoon pilots often flew the same pattern as Spitfires did, and with greater success, for the Typhoon was a much more stable bombing platform. However, they also employed several different bombing techniques such as skip-bombing and flat trajectory bombing. More often than not, a Typhoon attack was a rocket attack followed by strafing with the four 20mm cannon of these powerful aircraft. These rocket attacks were highly regarded by the Allies and highly feared by the Germans though their accuracy was often questionable. On several occasions – such as the march on Cherbourg, and the German counter-attack at Mortain – it was believed that rocket-firing Typhoons turned the tide of battle. The British rockets fired from Typhoons were launched on a rail that guided them nearly to the point where the rocket had sufficient speed to rely upon its small fins for flight stability. The 9thAF added rockets to their P-47 aircraft in August, but the American rockets were slung under the wings like bombs, with no guiding rails to improve the trajectory. Consequently, they were much less accurate. Because of this, the Americans, unlike the British, relied on the rocket hardly at all. In the Normandy Campaign, the Americans launched only 13,960 rockets, while the 2ndTAF launched 222,500 – nearly 16 times as many.

The Bomb Line

The pattern on the ground below the pilots was now very clear and everywhere evident. There was a bomb line that indicated where the Allied troops faced the German defenders. The bomb line was lit up frequently by artillery and mortar barrages as each side jockeyed for position. But when viewed from the air, the bomb line was not characterized by gun flashes and bursts so much as by the contrast in activity. Behind the bomb line on the Allied side trucks, tanks, bicycles and people moved about freely, often clogging the arteries of the crowded lodgement area. Fields were often just as congested -- now all the equipment that had clogged southern England was clogging the beachheads of France -- trucks, ammunition, medical supplies, equipment, food, materials for constructing airfields, tents for new arrivals, field hospitals – all the material needed to feed and care for a large army. A few fields were still under cultivation and appeared wide open and peaceful, but many large tracts were bulldozed, levelled and cleared to create airstrips – the first two were available for emergency landings on the evening of 7 June. This busy, seething activity stopped at a point – this point was the bomb line.

On the other side of the bomb line, the roads were empty. Whenever a vehicle appeared, it darted warily between points of cover – under trees or beneath overhanging canopies of netting. For when a vehicle appeared for longer than a few minutes, there was bound to be an Allied aircraft that spotted the movement and dove down to strafe or bomb. Almost every German general who fought in Normandy left testimony of how profoundly this condition affected the conduct of the German defence. Their best weapon, said one general was bad weather, for then the Allied aircraft couldn't fly. They testified that complete air supremacy made them move anything during daylight at great peril, the only safe way was to move everything at night. And after an intense night's effort to redistribute tanks, guns and soldiers, extreme efforts were made to ensure no telltale tank tracks or carelessly discarded equipment was left about to betray where the military equipment was hidden. Even when German units were highly concentrated, their skill at camouflage could make a field full of dug-in tanks and bristling with machine guns look empty from the air. On the Allied side of the bomb line it was very evident that a huge army was scrambling about; on the German side it looked as though no one was there.

Bringing up German troop reinforcements

On D-Day, several Panzer divisions were ordered to make their way to Normandy to reinforce the defenders. Normally, these units prided themselves on quick mobile response to a military initiative – they were, after all, the heart of the famous German Blitzkrieg. In their glory days they had burst into Holland and Belgium, and overrun everything, travelling over 300 miles in 10 days. But Allied air supremacy in Normandy changed all that.

Getting the Panzer Lehr division into the battle line illustrates what air supremacy did. The Panzer Lehr was a crack division – one of the few panzer divisions in Western Europe at full strength in June 1944. Its base was Chartres, 100-miles south-east of Caen. The afternoon of 6 June it was ordered to move to take up a position a little west of Caen to join in a planned counter-attack against the British in the central part of the Allied front. We now know that the Germans planned compressing three of the most powerful and prestigious panzer divisions into the sector between Caen and Bayeux, and through counter-attack push the Allies back into the sea. The Panzer Lehr got ready to pull out of Chartres the night of 6 June. At 0530 hours on 7 June, the lead column of tanks and trucks, just starting out, was attacked by Typhoons and many vehicles set on fire. Several convoys broke off from the main body to take different routes to Caen. Throughout the day Typhoons, P-47s and Mustangs took turns flying through cloudy and wet conditions, searching for the snaking convoys and attacking every convoy route they could find. In that one day alone Panzer Lehr lost 130 trucks, five tanks and 84 self-propelled guns. The disruption this loss of equipment caused compelled them to travel only by night, and driving in the dark over damaged bridges on their route slowed progress to a crawl. In addition the 2ndTAF had Wellington bombers drop parachute flares during night-time hours, to help Mosquitos strafe and bomb the columns of trucks and tanks. It took Panzer Lehr until 11 June before the forward part of the division was in place in the line alongside 12th SS Panzer Division. And when Michael Wittmann (part of the advance units of the Panzer Lehr) single-handedly stopped the attack upon Villers-Bocage 13 June, he did so with only four of the lead tanks out of the battalion's complement of 45 Tiger tanks. It took more than eight days to move the Panzer Lehr division at minimum strength, the 100 miles from Chartres to Caen. We don't know how long it was before the whole 18,000-man division was in place at full strength – probably another week. In contrast to Panzer Lehr's 100 miles in 15 days, Patton raced two whole armoured divisions of his 3rd US Army a hundred miles from Avranches to Le Mans in less than 3 days.

On 12 June, Field-Marshal Rommel sent a letter to Field-Marshal Keitel, Commander-in-Chief of the German Army. It said[3]:

> "The enemy has complete command of the air over the battle zone and up to 100 kilometres behind the front and cuts off by day almost all traffic on roads or by-ways or in open country. Manoeuvre by our troops on the field of battle in daylight is almost entirely prevented, while the enemy can operate freely….. Neither our flak nor the Luftwaffe seem capable of putting a stop to this crippling and destructive operation of the enemy's aircraft."

Bringing in Luftwaffe reinforcements

On D-Day morning, no German fighter gruppen were located in the immediate vicinity of the landing beaches, although two of the three gruppen of JG 2 and two of the three of JG 26 were close enough to make combat appearances right after the invasion got underway. Like their Allied counterparts, the Luftwaffe fighter gruppen were experienced at moving quickly from one airbase to another. They had a two-fold task – not just to move closer to the battlefield, but to move to an obscure grass-field base where they could find trees under which the aircraft could be hidden. Within days the following gruppen were moved into an arc from Beauvais to Paris to Le Mans. (The number of aircraft quoted are those that were actually available; the number of authorized aircraft for each unit was half as much again – 36 aircraft per JG gruppe. The only units at full authorized strength were I./JG 5 and II./JG 5.):

No.aircraft	Type	Gruppen
56	FW 190	I./JG 1 and II./JG 1
30	Bf 109	III./JG 1
30	FW 190	I./JG 2, and III./JG 2
11	Bf 109	II./JG 2
32	Bf 109	II./JG 3 and III./JG 3
72	Bf 109	I./JG 5 and II./JG 5
25	FW 190	I./JG 11
30	Bf 109	II./JG 11
48	FW 190	I./JG 26 and II./JG 26
21	Bf 109	III./JG 26
63	Bf 109	I./JG 27, II./JG 27 and III./JG 27
14	Bf 109	II./JG 53
14	FW 190	III./JG 54
15	FW 190	III./SG 4

*Table 5 -- **Luftwaffe reinforcements**. The German fighter aircraft known by Allied pilots as the Messerschmitt 109, or 'Me 109', was actually designated by the Germans as 'Bf 109' because of the aircraft manufacturing plant that produced it. ORBs and Combat Reports all refer to Me 109s, while the proper designation Bf 109 appears elsewhere in this book.*

Wednesday 7 June -- D-Day-plus-one

Weather on the day after D-Day was a repeat of D-Day. The heavy cloud broke up before midnight and the sky became quite clear after midnight over the continent – clear enough for 61 Mitchells and 129 Mosquitos to patrol the sea lanes and the approaches to the battleground, while another lot of 49 Mitchells and 122 Mosquitos bombed key targets without loss. But as dawn approached, the heavy cloud structures that had clung to England's south coast moved across the Channel and began to sock in the lodgement area. Visibility was good, but the ceiling – as with D-Day – was low and becoming lower as the morning progressed. By mid-morning, when activities would normally be at their height, all armed recces were cancelled awaiting better weather. An improvement an hour after noon saw both the Allies and the Germans unleash their aerial power, but then unfavourable conditions set in again and it was about four in the afternoon before activity resumed. In spite of this on-again-off-again day of fighting, 7 June, became the most fiercely contested day in the skies of the whole Normandy Campaign.

Allied troops fought furiously from one end of the total lodgement area to the other. In the Cotentin Peninsula, the American army fought to bring the widely scattered airborne troops into cohesive units, while the defending German troops scrambled to hold firm. The whole base of the peninsula was sprinkled with small pockets of Allied or enemy troops – only the UTAH beachhead and the captured town of Ste. Mère Église were sizeable holdings. Further east, the Americans still had a very tenuous hold on OMAHA beach. The landing of new troops and supplies was building up the strength of their position, but German 88 millimetre guns miles away laid down a withering fire on the beach. In addition to the beach patrols, the US 9thAF was asked to provide continuous fighter-bomber support to search out and attack the enemy guns that were bombarding OMAHA. P-47s of the 365th, 366th and 368th FGs were selected. They flew 35 squadron-strength missions and provided at least one squadron over the Bayeux-to-Isigny area at all times during daylight hours of 7 June. The nine squadrons flew four missions apiece dropping bombs and strafing. They destroyed five gun positions. This was what the tactical air force did best – destroy obstacles in the army's path, and it did the trick, for all the last echelons of the US 1st and the US 29th Infantry Divisions were safely landed at OMAHA beach on the day after D-Day. The difficulties encountered in the landing at OMAHA beach had resulted in a full one-day delay in getting these units ashore.

Shortly after 0600 hours, a large force of over 40 FW 190s from I./JG 2, III./JG 2 and II./JG 26 launched a sweep between Bayeux, Caen and Evreux. South of Caen they came upon the Typhoons of 245 Squadron attacking the rail junction and the road south to Falaise. One Typhoon was shot down and claimed by Hauptmann Josef Wurmheller, Staffelkapitän of 7./JG 2. This was Wurmheller's 98th claim of his career. He is notable because he was a young pilot at the time of the Dieppe raid and scored eight victories on that one day. After many months on the eastern front, he returned to the western front flying with 7./JG 2. The very next day (D-Day-plus-two) his Gruppekommandeur would be killed and Wurmheller would take over III./JG 2, but he would not survive the Normandy Campaign.

Between 0600 and 0700, the three squadrons of the Polish 133 Wing flying Mustangs, were on the prowl. They passed over Evreux on their way to Argentan where 315 Squadron and 306 Squadron bombed the train station while 129 Squadron provided high cover. Before the bombing they shot up a few roads and when near Evreux happened upon a handful of FW 190s from II./JG 26 and claimed one victory. On the way back from Argentan they again met elements of I./JG 26 and II./JG 26. In the two engagements, 133 Wing lost four aircraft. while the Germans lost two. Two Allied pilots evaded, one was killed, one was captured. S/L Lapka was one of the evaders -- he got back to England several weeks later. One German pilot was killed while the other parachuted to safety. I./JG 26 had just taken up residence the previous evening at their new base of Boisy-le-Bois about 50 miles north-west of Paris, half-way to Rouen. This was their first mission of intervention.

Three hours later, at 1000 hours, re-armed and refuelled at their home base at Coolham in the UK, the Polish Wing was back to dive-bomb the marshalling yard at Dreux. After bombing the target they spotted 10 Bf 109s of III./JG 1. They flew into the gaggle of German aircraft and claimed four victories, although the German gruppe recorded only three aircraft lost with two pilots killed and one pilot surviving by parachute.

Every Allied wing not committed to patrol duties was dispatched throughout the day hitting key centres – just as 133 Wing did. With the extra demands placed upon the US 9thAF to support OMAHA, the US 8thAF filled in by sending two FGs of P-51s and two of P-47s to fly armed recces. The day was not characterized by any large swirling battles, but rather with a continuous succession of smaller skirmishes where two or three victories were recorded on either side.

The three squadrons of 126 Wing of the 2ndTAF had just come on station to patrol the Eastern Assault Area that morning. They flew four of these patrols on D-Day and were back at it today for the first time and in none of these patrols had they seen a single German airplane. At 0840 hours they were turning to start their first leg of the patrol between Port-en-Bessin and Cabourg when they came upon more than 30 Ju 88 bombers of NJG 2 flying through the forest of barrage balloons mounted over the ships[4]. 401 (Canadian) Squadron charged into them and shot down six Ju 88s in a matter of two minutes. W/C George Keefer got the first one. Keefer had flown with 274 Squadron in the Desert Air Force where he was credited with four destroyed, two probables and eight damaged -- this claim gave him ace status. Later that same day, 401 Squadron accounted for two more Ju 88s destroyed – much to the envy of every other Spitfire pilot of the 39 squadrons assigned to beach patrol, for they had still not seen the enemy. And at the same time, Keefer claimed a FW 190.

In the next hour, encounters occurred at Dreux, Paris, Caen and Rouen as P-51s and P-47s of the 8thAF and the six wings of Typhoons roamed and clashed with several of the gruppen that had appeared in the battle area. Gruppen of each of JG 3, JG 5, JG 11, JG 27 and JG 54 made appearances to join JG 2 and JG 26. On D-Day we noted the presence of several of the Luftwaffe aces – Buhligen and Huppertz of JG 2 and Priller of JG 26. On D-Day-plus-one these aces scored again, but several other aces came forth as well – we have been introduced to Hauptmann Wurmheller of III./JG 2 who claimed his 98th, but there was also Leutnant Kempf of III./JG 26 who claimed his 60th, Hauptmann Weiss of III./JG 54 who claimed two to bring his total to 102 and Hauptmann Weissenberger,

Gruppekommandeur of I./JG 5 who claimed five on the day, to bring his career total to 180.[5] Still another ace was Hauptmann Weber of III./JG 1 with more than 30 claims. In a battle with the 133 Polish Wing shortly after 1015 hours, Weber was shot down and killed. This was the first of a long list of German experten to die in Normandy.

The battle tapered off in one place or another as heavy rain clouds marched across the battlefield. Another notable encounter occurred around 1600 hours near Beauvais when the experienced P-47 pilots of the 353rd FG of the 8thAF fought a moderate force of Bf 109s from III./JG 1 and II./JG 11. In a wide-ranging milling battle, the Americans claimed nine victories and the Germans claimed three. However, when the chips were counted, the Americans returned all their fighters to the UK while the Germans recorded five losses – two killed, one safe and two unknown as to whereabouts.

Though somewhat dampened by heavy downpours and thick cloud, the fury continued until the onset of darkness. The last large battle to occur was again centred at Caen and saw the matching up of two squadrons of P-47s of the 373rd FG of the 9thAF against the Bf 109s of III./JG 3. The battle lasted just six minutes. Again the Americans flew home without a loss while the Germans recorded eight losses – four were killed, two taken prisoner and the fate of the other two unknown.

When the losses were tallied up at day's end, the Allies had lost 89 aircraft -- 45 USAAF and 44 RAF fighters and fighter-bombers. Thirty were US P-47s (23 from the 9thAF and seven from the 8thAF), 18 were Spitfires and 17 were Typhoons. The break-down between those shot down in aerial combat as compared to those shot down by flak is interesting – 36 of the 44 RAF, and 37 of the 45 USAAF aircraft were destroyed by flak. 25 RAF aircrew were killed, while four became prisoners of war. Eight who were missing, evaded and returned within days. Equivalent figures for the USAAF are not available, but would be similar.

The Luftwaffe had lost 71 aircraft – 36 Bf 109s, 22 FW 190s and 13 Ju 88s. Two German units, II./JG 11 and III./JG 3 lost 11 and 10 aircraft respectively on their first day in Normandy. It was clear that whereas the FW 190 continued to perform as a very worthy adversary for Spitfire IXs, P-47s or P-51s, the Bf 109 was considerably inferior as an instrument of war for anyone other than the experten like Weissenberger of I./JG 5, or Huppertz of III./JG 2. The problem for the Luftwaffe was that of the 24 gruppen operating in France, 13 were Bf 109 gruppen. A further point of vulnerability was the reconnaissance squadrons who flew the superior FW 190, but flew them in recce roles. The reconnaissance gruppe III./SG 4 lost seven FW 190s on D-Day and lost seven more on D-Day-plus-one.

If aircraft losses are the measure of the severity of the struggle, the day after D-Day proved to be the worst day for fighters of the whole Normandy Campaign. The Allies lost 89 aircraft; and the Luftwaffe lost 71 for a total of 160 aircraft destroyed in the one day. To put these figures in perspective, the actual losses on 19 August 1942 at Dieppe -- often referred to as the Greatest Air Battle of the war -- were Allies 118 and Luftwaffe 48 for a total of 166 aircraft destroyed. The greatest air battle had only six more aircraft destroyed than 7 June 1944.

From five miles behind the beaches to 100 miles inland, P-47s, P-51s, P-38s, Typhoons and Spitfires roamed, usually in squadron-strength. All 18 squadrons of Typhoons from 2ndTAF flew at least three missions on that day. In all, 2ndTAF Spitfires, Typhoons and Mustangs flew 2,360 sorties 7 June – as many as they flew on D-Day.

Pilot Skill Level

We noted how many German super-aces appeared in the air battle. The skill level of the pool of German pilots was not homogeneous but rather, presented a dramatic contrast. The killing of so many good pilots in the first six months of 1944 left most gruppen with a smattering of super-aces, a small number of experienced but not yet expert pilots, and the vast majority with but a few hours flying experience. These latter had been desperately pressed into service without sufficient training. With the clashes in June killing off some experts and some semi-experienced pilots, the mix between pilot geniuses and pilot dunces became extremely exaggerated. By August Allied records report many cases of new German pilots thrown into battle so prematurely that when faced with an enemy aircraft they just rolled over and bailed out.

By contrast, the Allies presented three different pictures of skill level. Least skilled of the three services was the US 9thAF. Almost half of the squadrons had only been formed two or three months before D-Day and the pilots were just starting to get enough actual combat experience to allow them to survive. The 9thAF had a few aces and a small number with four or three claims. However, the pilots were well trained and it was only a matter of time until they became fully experienced.

The RAF and Commonwealth squadrons had a lot of new pilots, but almost all of them had many months of combat experience flying over France, and every squadron was liberally sprinkled with veterans who were returning for a second tour after proving themselves in places like Malta and Italy. Amongst their ranks were aces like W/C Johnnie Johnson with 28 victories, W/C Kingaby with 20, S/L McLeod with 15, W/C Harries with 14, S/L Le Roux with 12, S/L Horbaczewski with 11 and perhaps 20 or 30 aces with five or more victory claims. Skill level in these RAF squadrons was homogeneously distributed between aces and fledglings.

Except for Eagle Squadron veterans[6], the US 8thAF did not have the benefit of returning veterans bringing experience from a prior tour, but they had something just as good. In the bitter fighting before and after Big Week in February the fighter pilots of the US 8thAF had learned the hard way. Every day was a tough fight – a life-or-death struggle that taught rapidly how to survive and overcome. They had among their ranks many aces like Capt Gabreski with 25, 2Lt Johnson with 25, Col Zemke with 13 (Zemke added two more claims on 7 June), Maj Blakeslee with 10 and a large number of other aces. Skill levels in these squadrons were homogeneously distributed as well.

As the Normandy Campaign progressed, the Allied pilots became stronger and more homogeneous in the range of pilot skills that they exhibited. Included in the ranks were experts, semi-experts, partial experts, experienced pilots and a handful of newly arrived rookies. Meanwhile the Luftwaffe drifted into having a smaller and smaller handful of experts and a larger and larger mass of rookies.

Thursday 8 June

The high cover and low cover patrols over the beaches continued to be flown at wing-strength from 6 June through 10 June, but the total number of sorties flown declined. Whereas 1550 Spitfire sorties were flown on D-Day, that total dropped to 1230 on 7 June and to 1030 the following day. The weather was certainly the foremost factor in this reduction, but the small number of German attacks of the beaches during daylight hours was an equal factor. The Germans settled for a policy of attacking the beaches at night and using their meager day-fighters where they could do the most damage – interdiction of Allied attacks upon key points. After 10 June the Allied wing-strength patrols were cut to two-squadron patrols, and a week later, cut to single squadron patrols.

The Luftwaffe reacted at first by putting bombs on their FW 190s in the hope of bombing the beachheads, but they could not get through, and so by 12 June all Luftwaffe units were ordered to take the bomb racks off and concentrate on shooting down Allied fighters. The tactics employed consisted of waiting until needed, and then throwing 40 fighter aircraft from several gruppen against the Allied fighter-bombers -- particularly the Typhoons. This occurred when extraordinary support was needed by the German army. The remainder of the Luftwaffe effort consisted of reconnaissance flights and bombing the lodgement every night with as many Ju 88s as they could muster – although after the first few days this was more often in twos and threes than larger formations. The Luftwaffe flew about 400 sorties in a twenty-four hour period – only half in the form of fighter sweeps.

Skirmishes started early on 8 June. In the middle of the night Mosquitos of 29 Squadron destroyed two Ju 188s, but lost two Mosquitos – one from 29 Squadron and another from 605 Squadron. All four Allied aircrew in the Mosquitos died. After the sun came up the fighting continued.

Between 0600 hours and 0630 in the Caen/Bayeux area, four Luftwaffe gruppen tangled with the low level beach patrol of 135

Wing, and with Typhoons of 266 Squadron and P-51s of the 339th FG. One FW 190 from III./JG 54 and two Bf 109s from III./JG 3 were destroyed by 349 Squadron and 485 Squadron -- all three German pilots died. As this battle ended, III./JG 26 came on the scene, lost one of its Bf 109s to a P-51 of the 339th FG, but in turn shot down one P-51 and an unwary Typhoon from 266 Squadron.

Dogfights spread evenly from Cherbourg in the west over the sprawling beachhead and on to Rouen. Two of these skirmishes were of particular significance. Around 0945 hours, just south of Caen the Gruppekommandeur of III./JG 2, Hauptmann Herbert Huppertz was killed. Huppertz was the German pilot who claimed five victories on D-Day and another on D-Day-plus-one. His total after four years of flying was 70 claims. Along with Weber killed the day before, he was the second German super-ace to be killed in Normandy. A Staffelkapitän (a squadron commander) from III./JG 2 was also killed. Huppertz was immediately succeeded by Hauptmann Wurmheller. The result of the loss of these two key pilots put the gruppe out of action for a week. The successful Allied unit is believed to have been the 374th FS of the US 8thAF's 353rd FG. One American pilot was shot down and captured.

The second significant battle occurred around 1530 hours between Bayeux and Caen. 135 Wing was once again on beach patrol, when it ran into about 30 Bf 109s of III./JG 3. Whereas in the morning it was 485 and 349 Squadrons that made claims, this time it was 485 and 222 Squadrons of 135 Wing. The result was the destruction of four machines of III./JG 3. This brought the total losses for the gruppe on that day to six machines and the total for the two days -- 7 and 8 June – to 16. No losses were sustained by 135 Wing.

Before the afternoon was gone, another significant event occurred. Deep into Brittany, near Rennes, the Gruppekommandeur of I./JG 11, Hauptmann Simsch, took off from his base in deteriorating weather. He spotted a small formation of P-51s from 339th FG of the US 8thAF and immediately attacked not realizing that the whole FG was in the vicinity – the others hidden by clouds. Attacking from above, the 503rd FS and 505th FS swept down. They shot down Simsch, his wingman and two others in the first encounter, however, in the mêlée that followed three Americans were shot down in retribution. But

Simsch was dead. In that day I./JG 11 lost five fighter aircraft and their commander. Adding another five losses the previous day, left the gruppe with only 15 available FW 190s – less than half strength.

For the day, the Germans lost 30 aircraft and 15 pilots were dead or missing; the Allies lost 28 aircraft and 16 pilots were killed. But the difference was that the Germans had lost Huppertz and Simsch.

A note about flak

The German military planners relied upon anti-aircraft guns to an ever-increasing degree as the war rolled on. This reflected the burgeoning problems of a diminishing capability of the training system to produce pilots, and the diminishing capability of industry to produce aircraft fuel. Steel production and aircraft manufacturing grew stronger in the face of Allied bombing, but pilot training and oil production did not. Anti-aircraft guns were the alternative.

The Germans employed several standard anti-aircraft guns throughout the war, including 20 mm and 37 mm guns that were referred to by Allied pilots as medium flak -- pilots generally referred to small-arms fire as light flak. The maximum vertical range for this flak was 6,000 to 7,000 feet. The far deadlier heavy flak was almost always 88 mm guns. These truly remarkable weapons served as anti-tank guns as well as anti-aircraft guns. This gun had a very high muzzle velocity, deadly accuracy and a range as high as 32,000 feet. However, since the accuracy of the 88mm fell off dramatically over 10,000 feet, many

Figure 5 -- 88 mm. The powerful German 88 mm gun served equally well as an anti-aircraft as an anti-tank weapon.

(private collection)

pilots flew regularly above 8,000 feet to avoid the lighter flak[7], and above 12,000 feet to avoid the heavy flak. The Allies had no equivalent flak gun to counter this splendid weapon. By the time of the Normandy Campaign, the Germans had developed even more potent 105 mm and 128 mm guns, but most of these were employed in the defence of the Fatherland.

In the years between 1942 and 1944, the Germans increased their flak strength in Western Europe from 3,900 heavy and 9,000 medium and light guns, to 10,600 and 19,400 respectively. This build-up of flak continued with greater emphasis upon the heavy guns until by early 1945 there were 12,000 heavies and 20,000 medium and light guns.

Friday 9 June

The weather on 9 June was the worst so far, grounding all aircraft until early evening. This was part of the reason three unfortunate incidents occurred. A wing of Spitfires left RAF Station Tangmere at 2020 hours and flew across the Channel to take up their station over the lodgement at 2050 hours. It was an attempt to resume the policy to have six squadrons of Spitfires over the beaches at all times. As they approached the shore at OMAHA beach, Royal Navy ships opened anti-aircraft fire. The ceiling was only 800 feet, so the sailors must have felt the aircraft came in upon them too fast and too low. Air controllers radioed the ships to stop firing and directed the wing to once more approach the shore. Again the naval fire started. They blazed away with anti-aircraft guns and set one 403 Squadron Spitfire on fire causing it to crash near Cherbourg. The pilot was severely injured and remained in a Cherbourg hospital under German care until Cherbourg fell to the American forces 29 June. The navy anti-aircraft gunners seriously damaged three other 403 Squadron Spitfires and slightly damaged the Spitfire of the W/C (Flying) – Lloyd Chadburn.

That was not the only case of friendly fire that evening. A half-hour earlier over St. Lô, two US 9thAF P-51s of the 107th Tactical Reconnaissance Squadron were shot down by intense fire from US ground forces. And at 2040 hours, two other P-51 pilots of their sister squadron – the 109th -- were shot down by Allied naval anti-aircraft fire off UTAH Beach. As the evening wore on, two more Spitfires were shot down by US ground forces flak around the Carentan/Isigny area. Only one of the two pilots survived. Urgent orders flew around immediately, attempting to halt these private wars between the different Allied ground, sea and air services.

The Germans lost 18 aircraft while the Allies lost 11 on that day. In the first four days of fighting the Germans lost a total of 142 aircraft while the Allies lost 192.

Another gift from ULTRA -- Saturday 10 June

Sometime during 9 June, code-breakers at Bletchley Park picked up an intercept through ULTRA that indicated that General von Schweppenburg, commander of Panzer Group West, had moved his headquarters to a position 12 miles south of Caen, at the Chateau de la Caine. Any time a headquarters could be located was good news, but the Allies didn't realize how good this news really was. Only later was it learned that from here Panzer Group West planned to direct a major blow to drive the Allies back into the sea. The German Army was about to counter-attack with its four mighty panzer divisions – 21st Panzer, 12th SS Panzer, Panzer-Lehr and the recently-arrived 17th Panzer Grenadier Division. Panzer Group West, unaware that their location was known, set up tents and spread trucks and half-tracks about in the orchard next to the chateau.

The 2ndTAF was immediately instructed to act upon the ULTRA intelligence. On 10 June they despatched 40 Typhoons from 121 Wing and right behind them, 60 Mitchell medium bombers from 137 Wing and 139 Wing. The Typhoons went in with rockets and the Mitchells followed with 500-pound bombs. The orchard and the tented area where the mobile headquarters had been set up, were completely saturated with bombs and rockets. Photo reconnaissance pictures that afternoon confirmed that everything in the orchard was destroyed and the chateau received many hits. Immediately after the raid it was not known whether the raid was successful or not. The entry in the 2ndTAF ORB stated;

"There were indications that the HQ of a panzer division was located and 2 Group put on a medium level of attack with Mitchells (and Typhoons). 2 Group was convinced it was a successful mission. This remains to be proved." [8]

Within days ULTRA intercepts confirmed that 18 senior German officers, including von Schweppenburg's Chief-of-Staff and Chief-of-Operations were killed at the chateau. The remnants of the headquarters that survived the attack were immediately withdrawn to Paris. The hopes of organizing a serious coordinated counter-attack was set back by three weeks; the hopes of throwing the Allies back into the sea vanished. This was not an example of winning a battle, but it was definitely an example of aerial activity spoiling a battle plan before the battle got started.

Saturday was a fine day with good visibility and the Allies conducted air operations from sunrise to sunset. The 2ndTAF recorded 1106 Spitfire sorties flown on patrols and cover, 152 naval spotting sorties, 392 Typhoon sorties on 25 missions hitting tanks, gun positions, headquarters positions, 71 Mitchell bombing sorties and 110 Mustang sorties flown on 14 separate armed recces. The US 9thAF flew similar missions and in the same level of effort. Together the Allies flew over 3,500 sorties compared to about 470 Luftwaffe sorties.

10 June saw several large aerial battles develop. After four incidents when single victories were claimed or lost, two gaggles of aircraft confronted each other in the skies south of Caen at 1035 hours. About 25 P-47s of the 389th FS and 390th FS of the 366th FG of the US 9thAF met nearly 40 Bf 109s from II./JG 3 and III./JG 3. In a wild whirling tangle through cloud from 9,000 feet to ground level the P-47s shot down five Bf 109s and anti-aircraft immediately claimed two more. The Americans lost four P-47s. Every one of the German pilots was killed or was declared missing. The 9thAF was learning fast.

A horrendous aerial battle occurred in the airspace near Lisieux between two o'clock and two-thirty. A force of over eighty FW 190s and Bf 109s from four gruppen – I./JG 27, III./JG 27, IV./JG 27 and II./JG 26 ran into three squadrons of P-47 Thunderbolts. The American forces were the three fighter squadrons of the 78th FG of the US 8thAF. In the battle that followed, the Luftwaffe pilots claimed nine P-47s shot down, however American records show only two losses. Luftwaffe records indicate nine Bf 109s from III./JG 27 and IV./JG 27 went down in flames -- a decisive victory for the Americans.

Another air battle raged near Lisieux about 1800 hours when elements of the 365th FG of the 9thAF attacked II./JG 26 and III./JG 26. After a furious 20 minutes both sides broke off after running out of ammunition. Each side lost three aircraft – a draw.

At 2115 hours over Evreux the last big battle of the day saw two squadrons of P-51s and two of P-47s from the 359th FG and 353rd FG respectively try to feast on 30 Bf 109s of the II./JG 3 and III./JG 3. Four Bf 109s were shot down, but in the low-flying scrum, very accurate flak took out four P-47s and one P-51. Another P-51 was shot down in the combat. It was a six-to-four victory for the Germans.

In the course of the day, the Allies lost 60 fighters and fighter-bombers including 23 P-47s and 12 Spitfires, while the Germans lost 32 aircraft 25 of them Bf 109s.

An interesting note for this date appears in the Operations Record Book for the headquarters of the 2ndTAF at Uxbridge;

> "The first R & R strip (refuel and re-arm B.3) is reported ready and use of it may be made for refuelling and re-arming fighters employed on cover. ALG B.2 which was also practically completed to 1200 yards, could not be occupied owing to the limited advances made by the 2nd Army, and so it was agreed that the opportunity should be taken to extend this ALG to 1500 yards which would delay its availability until 13 June, but would then render it suitable for operating Typhoons."[9]

Advanced Landing Grounds (ALGs)

In North Africa the RAF found it had to leapfrog from base to base in order to keep the short-range fighters close enough to the front lines and because of this the first Servicing Commando Units (SCUs) were formed in early 1942. By spring 1943 6 SCUs had been formed, their soldiers, trained to land on foreign soil with assaulting troops, and proceed to the planned locations of new Advanced Landing Grounds (ALGs). They brought their own trucks laden with tents, ammunition, fuel and defensive gear including anti-aircraft guns and machine guns. Each SCU comprised two officers and 148 men including cooks and equipment for providing food to aircrews. Every member of the SCU had to have combat training, know how to drive and repair the trucks, how to land from all kinds of landing craft, how to operate anti-aircraft guns, and how to service a great variety of aircraft. The more skilled tradesmen were taught to become specialist in one type of aircraft.

Figure 6 -- Sommerfeldt track. *A crew of an Airfield Construction Group are seen here starting to lay down the Sommerfeldt tracking for the runway of a new ALG in Normandy.*

(Imperial War Museum CL 708)

The SCUs landed at JUNO and GOLD beaches early 7 June together with the 12th, 23rd, 24th, and 25th Airfield Construction Groups (ACGs) -- Royal Engineers of Montgomery's army. The task of an ACG was to construct an entire airfield, complete with runways, access roads, hangars, water system, communication system, and space provision for crews, ammunition dumps and maintenance facilities. Each ACG was composed of a command company, two companies of sappers, two companies of pioneers and one company of mechanical and electric engineers for a total of 800 men. Each ACG carried with it a lot of material and equipment – bulldozers, scrapers, rollers, and steel netting called Sommerfeldt tracking. They levelled a field, lay the steel tracking, set up markers and set up such fundamentals as the electrical system, latrines and the communication system.

While the ACG unit was building the airfield, the SCU unit was defending the place and setting up anti-aircraft guns, fuel dumps, ammunition dumps, the facilities to re-arm and refuel fighters, parts storage and a maintenance depot. When the base was ready to receive aircraft, the engineers moved on to another location but the SCU stayed. Individual aircraft or whole squadrons would land and be re-armed and refuelled entirely by the SCU. Before a wing moved from England to take up permanent residence at the new ALG, one of the advance echelons from the wing would move in with the SCU and work with them. On moving day, the aircraft would be ferried in and set in permanent dispersals, and the other pilots and ground crew would be flown over by transport. When the full complement of wing personnel were permanently moved in to the base, the SCU moved on to set up the next ALG. Two of the ACGs and four of the six SCUs landed in the early hours of D-Day-plus-one.

The American airfields were built by Engineer Aviation Battalions (EABs). They were a combination of engineer and servicing commando. The first EABs landed 9 June. They started 12 airfields and seven of them were operational by the end of the month. Though differently organized, both British and American builders worked well with each other, and the truly amazing thing is that 25 ALG airfields were built in a little more than a month. Four were completed before 10 June, and 17 before 30 June. When completed, each ALG handled a wing of nearly one thousand people, 54 to 72 aircraft, spares, fuel, food, a dozen anti-aircraft guns, 200 trucks, kitchens, messes and a small village of tents.

The first emergency runways were open for use 7 June – the day after D-Day. ALGs in the British sector were designated with a 'B' as in B.1, B.2 etc.; those in the American sector were designated A-1, A-2 etc. Two days after completion of the emergency runway saw completion of B.2, B.3, B.4, B.6, A-1 and A-3. These were the fully furnished landing strips that would become operational bases in France in just a few more days. By 8 June, 3537 personnel and 815 trucks had been landed to build the British ALGs. By 10 June, three more runways were serviceable. Early in the day, aircraft of 303 (Polish) Squadron and 130 Squadron became the first Allied squadrons to be refuelled and re-armed in France. Later in the day, Johnnie Johnson's 144 (Canadian) Wing of the 2ndTAF was the first to land in full wing strength and be serviced in France. In the next ten days:

> 144 (Canadian) Wing (441, 442 and 443 Squadrons) flying Spitfires moved to ALG B.3 Ste. Croix-sur-Mer permanently 15 June

> 127 (Canadian) Wing (403, 416 and 421 Squadrons) flying Spitfires moved to B.2 Bazenville 16 June

> 126 (Canadian) Wing (401, 411 and 412 Squadrons) flying Spitfires moved to B.4 Beny-sur-Mer 18 June.

The American squadrons came too:

> 368th FG (395th, 396th and 397th FSs) flying P-47s moved to A-3 Cardonville 19 June

> 366th FG (389th, 390th and 391st FSs) flying P-47s moved to A-1 St. Pierre du Mont 20 June

Some airfields, such as B.5 le Fresne-Camilly and B.6 Coulombs, though completed soon after D-Day, were still under constant enemy fire and so moving there had to be delayed. As a result, other airfields were hastily built closer to the coast. When the Great Storm struck 21 June, nine squadrons of Spitfires and six squadrons of P-47s operated on French soil. When operating out of the UK, these squadrons could only spend an hour over France if they were to retain enough fuel to get home, now operating out of France only a few miles behind the front lines, they could spend two hours or more on armed reconnaissance flights dive-bombing and strafing. The Allied air war was stepped up a very large notch.

Between 21 June and the end of the month more British and Commonwealth units arrived:

124 Wing (181, 182 and 247 Squadrons) flying Typhoons, moved to B.6 Coulombs;

122 Wing (19, 65 and 122 Squadrons) flying Mustang IIIs moved to B.7 Martragny;

143 (Canadian) Wing (438, 439, and 440 Squadrons) flying Typhoons moved to B.9 Lantheuil;

35 Recce Wing (2, 4 and 268 Squadrons) flying Mustangs and Spitfires moved to B.10 Plumetôt along with 184 Squadron flying Typhoons;

125 Wing (132, 453 and 602 Squadrons) flying Spitfires moved to B.11 Longues-sur-Mer.

In this period more Americans arrived as well:

354th FG (353rd, 355th and 356th FSs) flying P-51s moved to A-2 Criqueville;

48th FG (492nd, 493rd and 494th FSs) flying P-47s moved to A-4 Deux Jumeau;

371st FG (404th, 405th and 406th FSs) flying P-47s moved to A-6 Beuzeville;

50th FG (10th, 81st and 313th FSs) flying P-47s moved to A-10 Carentan;

365th FG (386th, 387th and 388th FSs) flying P-47s moved to A-7 Azeville.

Sunday 11 June

The weather was terrible with much heavy fog on the south coast of England, and heavy, low cloud covering the Channel and northern France. Only two clearing breaks occurred in the course of the day -- one in the first part of the morning and the other in late afternoon. As a consequence, aerial activity by both sides was much reduced from the previous day. Still, Hauptmann Lang of II./JG 54 recorded his 147th claim when he shot down a Lysander near Caen.

Both adversaries over-claimed in the one fair size aerial battle of the day. Luftwaffe records show that the Bf 109s of I./JG 5 and the FW 190s of I./JG 26 led by Geschwaderkommodore Priller of JG 26, attacked two squadrons of P-38s and claimed the destruction of seven of them. Priller claimed one of these – his 99th victory. This action occurred about 1520 hours between Montdidier and Beauvais, 50 miles north of Paris. At that time and place the 338th and 343rd FSs of the 55th FG of the US 8thAF recorded eight claims. In fact the Germans lost three Bf 109s and a FW 190 – four aircraft not eight. The Americans lost three P-38s not seven.

At day's end the Germans recorded 10 aircraft lost while the Allies lost 27. 12 of the Allied losses were due to flak, two losses of both aircraft and pilot occurred when two Spitfires of 229 Squadron, returning to England, crashed in very dense fog on the Isle of Wight.

Monday 12 June

The ORB for 2ndTAF had this to say:

"On this day we took over part of the responsibility for armed reconnaissance in the Cherbourg Peninsula so as to free some of the 9thAF long range fighter-bombers for operation further inland beyond the range of our Typhoons. AVM Broadhurst, Air Officer Commanding 83 Group, discussed the build-up of his squadrons on the other side. It was decided, for the time being, to operate squadrons from the ALGs commencing on 13 June 1944 but returning the squadrons to England in the evening as AVM Broadhurst does not consider them safe during the night owing to enemy activity. Part of the available space of the ALGs will be utilized for Typhoons so that he can have a striking force immediately available, and in view of the very limited enemy air activity in day time, the need for fighters as such is not as great as we had foreseen during our planning."[10]

Although the weather deteriorated late in the day, it was a pretty fair day for aerial activities. The summary of 2ndTAFs operations carried out on 12 June were typical and consisted of:

> "-- 1149 Spitfires were employed on escort, spotting, cover and sweeps
> -- 54 Typhoons attacked radar installations near Le Havre
> -- 238 Typhoons on armed recces attacked crossroads at T.9268, tanks, trucks and troop concentrations on Cherbourg Peninsula
> -- 73 Typhoons on support calls attacked road convoys at Beauzeville and Jouigny
> -- 2 Typhoons were on air sea rescue
> -- eight aircraft and five pilots are missing
> -- 34 Mustangs provided escort for Mitchells and Bostons
> -- 67 Mustangs on armed recce attacked railway viaduct at T.7158, train at R.3370, roads around Caen and wood at Q.6970
> -- eight Mustangs on support calls attacked motor transport at Jouigny Reconnaissance wings flew 183 sorties
> -- 72 Mitchells made a daylight attack on 21st Panzer Division in Forêt de Grimbosq. four aircraft and 13 crew are missing from this operation
> -- 24 Bostons made the rear echelon of the above attack."[11]

Dogfights started early at 0605 hours with JG 2, JG 54 and JG 27 tangling with the P-47s of the 353rd FG of the US 8thAF in the area between Bernay, Evreux and Dreux. Two of the German aces were in this battle. Major Kurt Buhligen Geschwaderkommodore of JG 2 claimed his 102nd victory and Hauptmann Meyer of IV./JG 27 claimed his first 3 victories in Normandy for a career total of 21. However the Americans acquitted themselves well with Col Duncan claiming three and other American pilots claiming six others while losing seven P-47s. Actual losses were nine for the Germans – six of them killed -- and seven for the Americans, three of them killed.

About ten in the morning, the 72 Mitchells and 24 Bostons referred to above bombed the last elements of the 21st Panzer Division that were relocating into position in the Forêt de Grimbosq – a heavily wooded area to the south of Caen. Mustangs of 122 Wing covered the operation, but no opposition came from the Luftwaffe.

Half an hour later the sky was full of warriors. Between Caen and Lisieux there appeared about 60 FW 190s and Bf 109s from JG 2 and

JG 27 greeted by the 72 P-47s of the 366th FG and the 368th FG of the US 9thAF. Starting at 11,000 feet the engagement broke into several cork-screwing spirals of descending aircraft jockeying for firing position until they got down to 2,000 feet where some escaped and others were destroyed. Survivors climbed to gain position and then started another spiralling scrum -- they swirled and swarmed for twenty minutes. Hauptmann Wurmheller shot down two, but Capt Hendricks of the 397th FS, who had no credits to his name, shot down four FW 190s, and two other American pilots claimed two apiece. In all, the Germans lost five FW 190s and seven Bf 109s while the Americans lost five P-47s. The 9thAF was indeed learning fast.

At noon, 315 (Polish) Squadron flew escort to bombers attacking the Alençon area. After the bombing raid, the Polish Mustangs split up into wide-ranging sections looking for action. Four Mustangs led by S/L Horbaczewski spotted seven FW 190s eight miles south of Sees, south-east of Paris, and bounced them. The aircraft were from I./JG 11. In one pass four of the seven were shot down without loss to 315 Squadron. Horbaczewski scored his 12th victory claim.

Two other aerial combats were significant that day. Two Spitfire squadrons flying the high altitude Mark VII version – 131 Squadron and 616 Squadron -- were escorting bombers. The mission was to bomb marshalling yards at Le Mans, when they were attacked by Bf 109s and FW 190s. The Spitfire fighter escort jumped in, shot down three FW 190s and claimed another when it collided with a Bf 109. Without inflicting losses on the Allies, the German force from III./SG 4 lost five aircraft.

While the RAF squadrons were tangling at Le Mans, another battle was shaping up 80 miles to the north-east. Between Evreux and Dreux the P-47s of the famous 56th FG of the US 8thAF came out of cloud to face a large gaggle of Bf 109s from II./JG 3 and III./JG 3. Leutnant Zimmermann of II./JG 3 recorded his 23rd victory and LCol Francis Gabreski of the 61st FS claimed two bringing his career total to 26, however, whereas Gabreski's claim was probably legitimate for the German units recorded six aircraft lost, Zimmermann's claim is clearly overstated for no aircraft was lost by either the 61st FS or the 62nd FS.

For the whole day the Luftwaffe lost 50 aircraft while the Allies lost 43.

Night of the 12th and 13th of June -- the V-1 Menace

After midnight 12/13 June the weather improved greatly and 80 Mosquitos patrolled and a few bombed, but between them they claimed seven Ju 88s and Ju 188s without loss. However, this night was not noted for shooting down Ju 88s, rather it signalled the introduction of Hitler's new terror weapons – the first of the dreaded 'V weapons'. The first V-1 unmanned jet aircraft was launched upon London the night of 12/13 June, bringing into play a whole new phase of the battle.

Early in 1943, the Allies became aware of the German development of two weapons of terror – weapons intended to bring the British populace to plead for peace. Intelligence reports gave general descriptions of the size and power of the first of these – the V-1 pilotless bomb – while, the second, the rocket-powered V-2, was still shrouded in mystery. In August 1943, Churchill ordered a major bombing attack upon Peenemünde and this was successful enough to delay the development program by half a year, but by February 1944, aerial photography and reconnaissance sightings reported many compact launching sites located in the Pas de Calais area and in Belgium. Each suspected launch site had a ramp shaped like a hockey stick or a ski-jump and two or three small buildings for storage and flight preparation. The sites, dubbed 'No-ball' targets, were bristling with anti-aircraft batteries. Operation CROSSBOW was introduced to destroy the V-1 launch sites, starting with area bombing by heavy bombers, but this did not prove effective. So it fell to the bomb-dropping Typhoons and Spitfires, and later to the P-47s and P-38s to try to destroy the V-1 sites -- seven squadrons of fighters and fighter-bombers were assigned.

In 12 and 13 June, 120 V-1s were launched with about 30% reaching London. Hitler's goal was to get that figure up to 300 launchings per day, and had he been able to do this, the whole course of the war may well have been altered. The V-1 was an ingeniously simple device that could be mass-produced cheaply. It proved a very difficult opponent even though it was unmanned and flew straight-and-level, for it was very fast and very small and to get in close enough to shoot it down meant being close enough to be caught in its 1000-pound bomb blast. Between 13 June and 5 September, 9,017 flying bomb V-1s were launched. Less than a quarter – 1,771 -- were shot down by aircraft. Tempest and Comet fighters proved most successful; anti-aircraft gunners and balloon cables were equally effective – 1,690 destroyed. But the only truly effective way to stop them was to capture the sites from where they were launched. By 5 September, most of the V-1 launch sites had been overrun by Allied troops, but by that time over 9,000 flying bombs had been launched, 2,340 of which got through to London. The civilian casualties were about one per V-1 launched, but to that total must be added the aircrew losses in Operation CROSSBOW – those amounted to another 3,000.

Breakout Attempts

Now the Allies tried a threefold attack. In the east the Canadians and British attacked just west of Caen, but were repulsed by the 12th SS and 21st Panzer Divisions. In the west the 4th US Infantry Division, reinforced by the 82nd US Airborne and the 90th US Infantry Division drove straight across the Cotentin Peninsula cutting off the port of Cherbourg. In the middle of the line the US 1st Infantry Division, the 50th British Infantry Division and the 7th British Armoured Division, drove due south against the German 352nd Infantry Division and the 17th SS Panzer Grenadier Division, to capture Caumont.

Defeat at Villers-Bocage

It was a part of this drive in the middle that caused a turn for the worst. On 11 June, the Allies noted that the advanced elements of Panzer Lehr Division moved up to the front in a very uneven way. There was a unique opportunity for the 7th British Armoured Division

– the famous Desert Rats – to drive deep into a gap between two positions held by the German Panzer Lehr Division. They withdrew from the line five miles south-east of Bayeux, and in a wide sweeping arc sent an armoured regiment through Caumont to take the key crossroads town of Villers-Bocage. They completed this sweeping operation without opposition -- it seemed like a great victory. This particular town was pivotal because the Allies planned an airborne assault to the south-east that would strike deep into the flat country to the south-east of Caen. When that happened, Villers-Bocage would be the jump-off point to relieve the airborne.

However, victory was not to be. Four huge Tiger tanks of the German Panzer Lehr Division approached Villers-Bocage just after it was first occupied 13 June. Commanding this small squadron of tanks was Oberststurmführer Michael Wittmann – a veteran tank commander who earned the iron cross while fighting in Russia. Without hesitation, Wittmann in the single Tiger tank that was working well, approached the town from the east, lumbered down the road and picked off tanks and half-tracks at will. He knocked out 25 vehicles – more than half of them British Cromwell tanks -- before his Tiger tank was disabled by an anti-tank shell and Wittmann and his crew escaped on foot. Later that day and the following day, the whole British Armoured Regiment was killed or captured by units of the Panzer Lehr Division. The attack had backfired, but though they had decimated the British end-run, the Panzer Lehr could not break the British and American stranglehold in the Caumont area. Michael Wittmann who appeared so dramatically onto the stage of the Normandy Campaign, was killed unceremoniously in his Tiger tank a month later on 8 August in a little town between Caen and Falaise where the Canadian cemetery stands today.

Tuesday 13 June

Tuesday dawned clear and bright over southern England, but it was cloudy over the Normandy beaches and so heavy in the Paris and Le Mans areas as to ensure no flying at all. This bleak day was not only noted for the beginning of the V-1 campaign and the humiliating defeat at the hands of Wittmann at Villers-Bocage, but it was also noted for several other key events.

In the early hours before dawn, a mid upper gunner of 419 (Canadian) Squadron in his Lancaster bomber risked his life to free a burning and trapped rear gunner. When it became evident that he could not free him, the mid upper gunner jumped out of the aircraft, but with clothes on fire he died before he landed. His name was P/O Andy Mynarski and he was Canada's only Victoria Cross winner in Bomber Command.

In those same early hours, Mosquitos of 147 and 141 Wing flew 80 sorties patrolling the corridors through which the Germans were infiltrating two new SS Panzer divisions – the 9th and 10th. They attacked road and rail targets throughout Normandy. In the course of their efforts, they shot down three Ju 88s and four Ju 188s without loss. As sunrise approached their efforts were curtailed by rapidly deteriorating weather conditions over the Channel and over France. By dawn, Normandy was covered in thick cloud. Only one aerial encounter occurred. Eight Mustangs of the Polish 315 Squadron left their base at Coolham in fairly good flying conditions. At 0705 hours they were flying high over the cloud near Caen, when they came upon seven FW 190s of II./JG 26. In a single circling collision of the two gaggles of fighters, the Poles shot down three enemy aircraft without loss.

In the afternoon amid total cloud cover, 127 Wing was flying a two-squadron beach patrol. The wing leader, W/C Lloyd Chadburn, directed 416 Squadron to follow him in responding to a ground controller's report of bogeys to the west. They found no enemy aircraft and attempted to rejoin 421 Squadron five miles north of Caen. The two groups met in thick cloud and before evasive action could be taken, Chadburn and F/L Clark of 421 Squadron collided in a fiery flash. When Chadburn's aircraft came to rest on the ground, he was pulled to safety by British troops at Benouville, but he was so badly injured that he never regained consciousness and died within hours. Clark died in the explosive collision. As with the Germans' loss of Weber, Huppertz and Simsch., Chadburn's loss was an enormous blow to the RAF.

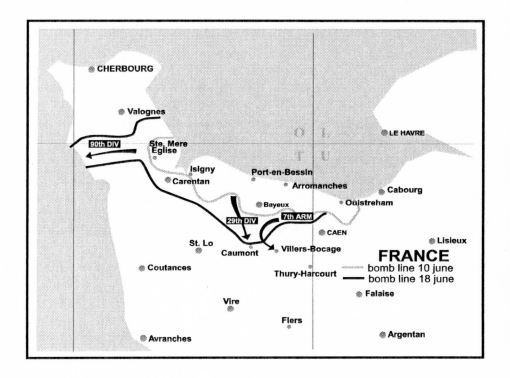

Figure 7 -- Bomb line 18 June. *Caumont was taken 13 June, but that day and the next, a brigade of the 7th British Armoured Division suffered a serious defeat at Villers-Bocage. A week later, the recently-landed 90th US Infantry Division joined a US force that charged across the Cotentin Peninsula cutting off the port of Cherbourg.*

For the day, the Allies lost 18 aircraft, while the Luftwaffe lost 19 – seven of which were claimed by the early Mosquito raids.

Wednesday 14 June

In the wee hours of 14 June, 40 sorties by Mosquitos pounded the rail centres at Mézidon just east of Caen, and at Vire. They also bombed three ammunition dumps and hit selected crossroads. In the course of this action they shot down two He 177s and a Ju 88 for the loss of one Mosquito of 21 Squadron.

The day was clear and fresh at the outset, and sun and cloud alternated throughout the day. A large formation of 8thAF B-17s was stretched out between Rouen and Paris -- the target was the Paris area. They were escorted by US 9thAF P-47s and US 8thAF P-38s. Near Rouen the P-47s were bounced by II./JG 54 and Hauptman Lang shot down three to bring his total to 150. In all, six P-47s went down in flames. Then as the bomber force neared Paris, JG 26 and JG 27 struck, but the P-38s of all three squadrons of the 55th FG were ready and promptly shot down five Bf 109s, killing three German pilots. Three P-38s were destroyed with two pilots killed. East of Paris a final battle developed between II./JG 26 and the 364th FS of the 357th FG, in which the American P-51s shot down two FW 190s. In the several battles that stretched from Rouen to east of Paris and took half-an-hour the Americans lost nine fighters and three B-17 bombers, while the Germans lost five Bf 109s and two FW 190s. Hapless IV./JG 27 lost only one Bf 109 this time. Only two days earlier, IV./JG 27 lost 11 aircraft -- had it not been for the receipt of fresh reinforcements, they would not have been able be in the air this day. The reinforcements had come by way of a unit intended to operate in Normandy, JG 77, which was broken up and fed into two decimated jagdgeschwaders primarily JG 27.

Typhoons were everywhere, flying support missions as the American 29th Division thrust into Caumont in concert with the British 50th Division on their left flank. Typhoons flew 551 sorties throughout the day. All the Spitfire wings were out in force as well, flying escort to medium bomber raids and patrolling the beaches and front. They flew 668 sorties.

When the sun set both sides counted the cost. It had been another pretty expensive day with the Allies losing 31 aircraft while the Germans lost 24.

Thursday 15 June

The good flying weather of the previous day continued throughout the night and into the early hours of the day. Under a bright half-moon Mitchells and Mosquitos carried out 84 sorties as they attacked the railways and roadways. They shot down five Ju 88s.

The sun came up at 0450 hours and ground crews everywhere prepared for a busy day. At 0640 hours the Norwegian 132 Wing, led by W/C Berg, flew a sweep into the Lisieux area. A Spitfire of 331 Squadron was hit by flak and the pilot killed, but the remaining 35 Spitfires carried on and blew right through elements of JG 2 and JG 3 who opposed them while one other unidentified Spitfire squadron pitched in. The RAF units pulled off a coup. The Germans lost seven aircraft -- four FW 190s of JG 2 and three Bf 109s of JG 3. Berg's 132 Wing lost only the one Spitfire shot down by enemy flak.

Twenty minutes later, a large force of 8thAF B-24s attacked Chartres and were met by the combined force of JG 26. 40 FW 190s of I./JG 26 and III./JG 26 and 25 Bf 109s of II./JG 26. JG 26 lost three while managing to shoot down two B-24s and one P-51. One B-24 was claimed by Oberstleutnant Pips Priller.

Another dogfight occurred at 0820 hours near Laval, this time between the P-51s of 380th FS and a mixed force from JG 11. It ended in similar results. Although early in the morning, it was beginning to look like this was an unlucky day for the Luftwaffe, but the weather stepped in to stop further activity. After 0900 hours heavy rain and wind settled in and halted aerial activity throughout the morning and half the afternoon.

As the weather cleared, 10 Dakota aircraft and the Spitfires of 144 Wing appeared and landed at B.3 Ste. Croix-sur-Mer. This was the day that the first full wing moved to France. W/C Johnnie Johnson brought his three squadrons -- 441, 442 and 443 Squadrons -- from their base at Ford in southern England to B.3. The Allied fighter aircraft were here to stay.

In the evening, 12 Spitfires of 421 Squadron took off on the last patrol of the Eastern Assault Area before returning to the UK. They had operated out of B.2 Bazenville all day. Unlike Johnson's pilots they were temporary guests not ordered to officially move until the next day. Just outside Bayeux they tangled with 30 FW 190s and Bf 109s. In the mêlée they shot down eight Bf 109s but lost one pilot. The German Gruppen were I./JG 27 and III./JG 27. The German records confirm this victory but they claim three Spitfires destroyed. In fact they were right, for although two Spitfires were severely damaged, the two pilots returned safely to base, but after crash-landing had their aircraft promptly written off as unrepairable. This combat is described in much greater detail in the second part of this book.

As the day progressed Typhoons flew over 327 sorties, Mustangs flew 103 sorties and Spitfires (including the aerial combats recorded here) flew 613. In addition to this, reconnaissance wings flew 139 sorties, naval spotting accounted for another 119, and Mitchells and Bostons flew 61. It was a busy day. The losses were comparable to the previous day – this time slightly in favour of the Allies. However, for the two days, the totals were just about even. In two days the Allies lost 54 aircraft – 50 fighters and four medium bombers – while the Germans' lost 55 – 45 fighters and 10 medium bombers. These figures do not include the 10 B-17 and B-24 heavy bombers lost by the US 8thAF.

Friday 16 June

The clear weather came to an abrupt end shortly after midnight. Heavy cloud and rain moved into France blanketing Normandy and shutting down all aerial activity until three in the afternoon. At 1735 hours over Lisieux, a III./JG 26 pilot shot down a Typhoon from 438 Squadron as it attacked a motor convoy -- the pilot evaded and returned within a week. A few other skirmishes took place but little was left of the day.

This day it was 127 Wing's turn to move to France and settle in at B.2. The next week would see more Spitfire squadrons, the first Typhoon squadrons and two USAAF wings of P-47s move to France. Air supremacy over France was ratcheted up still another notch.

For 144 Wing, it was a day of happiness and sorrow. In the early evening W/C Johnnie Johnson shot down a FW 190 to bring his career total to 29. But before the victory could be celebrated in the officer's mess, word was received that four Spitfires of 443 Squadron had been bounced, all four destroyed and the S/L and two of his pilots killed under circumstances that were totally unknown at the time. Only one pilot survived, evaded and returned weeks later to tell what happened. F/L Don Walz hid out until 13 August when he was liberated by American troops and then rejoined his old squadron to describe what had happened.

Saturday 17 June

Saturday 17 June started as cloudy but dry. Over Caen the P-47s of the 513th FS, 406th FG tangled with the FW 190s of II./JG 2. In a furious fight six FW 190s and three P-47s crashed and burned. Two other tussles broke out wherein a couple of aircraft from each side were shot down, but by 0800 hours it started to pour and all flying was suspended except a minimal beach patrol activity. By noon the worst of the weather was over and aerial engagements resumed.

At 1310 hours near Caen and at 1335 hours near St. Lô, two quick clashes between US 9thAF P-51s and P-47s resulted in the loss of 10 German aircraft – four of them with no information regarding the aircraft or the pilots, one parachuted to safety but five resulted in the death of the pilots. The Americans lost three – all missing and presumed dead.

At 1435 hours over Evreux the P-38s of the 367th FG fought with the Bf 109s of I./JG 3 and III./JG 3 in a pretty even match that saw both sides lose three aircraft. From that hour until pitch black, skirmishes occurred from Carentan and Caumont to Alençon and Dreux. The finally tally for the day was 43 Allied aircraft lost compared to 33 Luftwaffe aircraft.

Sunday 18 June

Sunday was very unsettled and although the usual patrols were flown and the usual dive-bombing of bridges and other targets went on, only three minor skirmishes took place. In each the Allies were bested and the Luftwaffe shot down a total of five aircraft without loss. Losses were 21 for the Allies – 16 to flak – and 15 Luftwaffe losses all due to flak.

Monday 19 June

About 0330 hours in the early morning of Monday 19 June the wind came up and it blew solidly. Apart from weather reconnaissance flights hazarded from time to time and a handful of shipping patrols over the sea lanes, there was little flying by either adversary.

Tuesday 20 June

Curiously enough, although the Canadian wings were placed on readiness and had all operations suspended, they flew a surprising amount that day. Driving rain and a fierce wind greeted the aerial planners that morning. The storm was heaviest near Paris. But shortly after 0700 hours there was a pronounced clearing in north-western France and in the area near Argentan. Into these two pockets cut like doughnut holes in a wild storm, poured the P-47s of the US 8thAF near Montdidier, P-38s of the US 9thAF and RAF Mustangs of 122 Wing near Argentan.

At 0700 hours the full 78th FG clashed with the Bf 109s of I./JG 3 and III./JG 3 in the skies between Montdidier and St Quentin. In a 15-minute battle that involved over 70 aircraft the Americans claimed three Bf 109s, but lost one of their own shot down and killed. Records are not clear as to whether any P-47s were severely damaged; perhaps this was one of those cases when the American pilots brought their Jugs home ridden with holes. The German force claimed five, but lost four. Three of the four German pilots shot down were killed. Of the fourth there is no identification or clarification of his fate.

Between Argentan and Falaise, the P-38s of 401st FS of the 370th FG performed two successful bounces. The first occurred shortly after 0800 hours on their inbound flight, when they burst through the cloud upon the FW 190s of II./JG 1 and shot down and killed a German pilot without loss. Three-quarters-of-an-hour later they clashed with the sister-gruppe I./JG 1, in a bounce that turned ugly. As they circled and milled about two P-38s were sent crashing to earth, as were three FW 190s. Both US pilots died, while the Luftwaffe pilots parachuted to safety. Nonetheless the score was four to two in favour of the Americans.

Shortly after this engagement near a place identified as Dessau, the P-51s of 380th FS of the US 9thAF claimed four Bf 109s and two FW 190s destroyed for a loss of one of their number. It is uncertain as to who the adversary was.

After 0830 hours the fury of the storm invaded all of France and the Channel. Then in mid afternoon another break provided some clearing through Rouen to Evreux. This occurred between 1600 hours and 1800 hours. Flying from their base at Funtington Church in the UK, the two Mustang squadrons of 122 Wing, 19 Squadron led by S/L Loud and 122 Squadron led by S/L Lamb ran into a gaggle of FW 190s of III./JG 54 led by the Gruppenkommandeure Hauptmann Weiss and accompanied by Hauptmann Lang – both pilots with over 100 victories. Lamb claimed one victory and his pilots shared another but they lost a pilot, P/O Schofield, who parachuted and evaded capture. The German pilots claimed that around 1615 hours they shot down eight P-51s – four of them claimed by Hauptmann Lang. These claims are hard to understand. There was the P-51 mentioned in the previous paragraph, lost at 0920 hours, and there is a record of another P-51 – this one from the US 8thAF -- shot down by flak about 0920 as well. But apart from these two and Schofield's Mustang, no other P-51s were lost on the twentieth of June. What are we to make of the claim of eight?

One other engagement took place in the evening with the time being uncertain and the place thought to be Caen. The Polish Spitfire 317 Squadron is thought to have fought the FW 190s of II./JG 51 and shot down two of them. One Spitfire was shot down -- the pilot landed within Allied lines. One of the German pilots parachuted to safety but was made a POW, while the other one died.

Shortly after this battle the storm reached a fury that was described as the worst that anyone could remember.

The Great Storm – 19 June to 21 June

In the two weeks since D-Day, the Mulberry at OMAHA and the one at Arromanches had become the two biggest ports in Europe. Between them, they were handling 12,000 tons of supplies and 2500 vehicles each day. In addition to the Mulberry harbours, five Gooseberries were built with sunken ships off each landing beach, acting as breakwaters to permit unloading directly onto the beach. This brought the total unloading capacity from 12,000 tons to over 30,000 tons per day.

The Great Storm blew for three days and three nights with such strength as had not been seen for 80 years or more. The storm struck the south of England, the Channel and the French coast in the early hours of 19 June and raged throughout the day. But on Tuesday 20 June, just as it had done before D-Day, two slight breaks in morning and afternoon opened up before the storm resumed. Then by that evening it blew up again this time even more furiously for the next 36 hours. It was a gale that was compared to the one in 1588 that destroyed the Spanish Armada. Offloading came to a standstill and then the structures began breaking up. When the storm abated 21 June, the Normandy coast was littered with hundreds and hundreds of craft thrown up beyond the beach. The storm damaged the Mulberry at OMAHA beach to such an extent that it was considered irreparable, and was cannibalized to repair the Mulberry at Arromanches. It took superhuman effort to try to make up the lost ammunition and supplies, but the troops working at the docks did it. The peak unloading rates rose to pre-storm levels within a day and went on to a level half again as high as planned -- Arromanches Mulberry actually achieved 11,000 tons in one day.

Needless to say, there was very little flying until the storm abated, but Luftwaffe Ju 88s took off in lulls in the storm and bombed the landing beaches the nights of the 20th and the 21st, and the 8thAF reported 16 aircraft crashed after being lost in fog and bad weather.

Thursday 22 June

Some days were loaded with contrasting episodes -- 22 June was one of those days. About 0600 hours 12 Spitfire Mark Vs of 402 Squadron flying out of Digby in the United Kingdom, came low over the beaches on patrol. A group of trigger-happy anti-aircraft gunners shot at the Spitfires over GOLD beach. Three aircraft were shot down in flames, one of the pilots killed. Luckily the other two pilots survived.

The 2ndTAF was asked to send all their Typhoons to help the American drive to capture Cherbourg. USAAF P-38s and RAF Typhoons and Mustangs were ordered to swamp the German defences in the Cotentin Peninsula. They did a splendid job, and helped the break-through that led to the capture of Cherbourg 29 June. Some have seen this as another case where the aerial ground support was the key ingredient in breaking through the German defences. In later years, the armchair generals will argue how effective aerial ground support really was, and when they do, they'll refer to the drive up the Cotentin and the defence of Mortain as two examples of success or of misrepresentation.

At noon, four squadrons of rocket-firing Typhoons – 174, 175, 181 and 198 Squadrons – attacked the northern half of the assault area concentrating on artillery and flak positions. One Typhoon was lost. The Mustangs of the Polish Wing -- 129, 306 and 315 Squadrons -- strafed following the Typhoon attack. Three Mustangs were lost and only one pilot survived. But their efforts were much appreciated by the ground forces and the American troops advanced.

German flak in the Cotentin was concentrated and extremely accurate. Eight P-38s of 367th FG and two from the 474th FG were shot down by German flak over Cherbourg. Only one pilot escaped, one was taken prisoner and the others died.

Well south of Caen, about 30 Bf 109s from III./JG 26 ran into several squadrons of P-47s from 365th FG at about 1400 hours. Their battle took them drifting to the south, and as the fighting continued, a squadron of P-47s from 368th FG joined in and before long Bf 109s and FW 190s from JG 2 and JG 26 and Spitfires from 144 Wing pitched in as well. The resulting donnybrook ended with 20 German machines destroyed versus four P-47s, and W/C Johnnie Johnson got his 30th victory claim while his force suffered no losses. For the Germans, the tragedy of that day was amongst the many who died was Gruppekommandeur Hauptmann Joseph Wurmheller.

Weber, Huppertz, Simsch and now Wurmheller ... and for every Gruppekommandeur who fell, two Staffelkapitän perished beside them. Considering the way the abilities of the Luftwaffe units were being stretched between super-aces and rookies, this situation was moving from the discouraging to the disastrous.

The rest of the day progressed with few aerial engagements but much activity in ground attack roles that resulted in staggering losses to the Allies because of anti-aircraft fire – fully 35 aircraft were shot down by flak. Nonetheless, the clash that occurred between 1400 hours and 1419 hours stands out as a turning point of the day, and perhaps of the campaign. After the loss of Wurmheller the final outcome was no longer a question but a certainty. Losses on 22 June were Luftwaffe 29, Allies 50. But in the 29 was Wurmheller, and of the 50, 35 were by ground fire.

Friday 23 June

Friday started a bit cloudy but began to clear early and turned out to be a lovely day. The early cloudiness delayed the start of things but by 1140 hours, 125 Wing could claim a confirmed victory, and by noon the Polish 133 Wing escorting B-17s to bomb the German airfields one more time, ran into Bf 109s of III./JG 3. In a desperate all-out fight the Polish pilots destroyed six of their adversaries and prided themselves with losing only four of their own – one killed, two POW and one evaded. However, this is one of those cases where the end result differs from the reported or claimed. When they limped back to base four aircraft were listed as Cat B and two were upgraded to Cat E – that is, four aircraft were severely damaged but thought could be repaired at base, but upon reconsideration, two were scrapped. Final score – six Polish aircraft lost, one pilot killed, two

POW one evaded two got back to base, six Luftwaffe aircraft lost, two pilots killed and four safely returned to base. It was a draw.

As the afternoon progressed, JG 26 and JG 54 bested the 2ndTAF, the ADGB and the US 8thAF in three engagements where six Allied aircraft were shot down. However in the evening the Canadian squadrons of 127 Wing and 144 Wing reversed the process and shot down eight confirmed aircraft while losing just one.

When the day was over the Luftwaffe had lost 24 while the Allies had lost 34.

Saturday 24 June

A furious battle occurred 24 June near Dreux when the three squadrons of Mustangs of 122 Wing – 19, 65 and 122 Squadrons -- were on an armed recce when they engaged JG 26 and JG 54, about 35 FW 190s. The result was even, for ignoring claims and going to losses, 122 Wing lost four aircraft but only one pilot was killed while three evaded and returned to their units. Amongst the Germans, four aircraft were lost, one killed and three returned to fly again. Had we listened to claims, the Germans claimed 10 shot down, four lost, the British claimed five victories, four lost. Hauptmann Lang claimed four victories in this dogfight, and Hauptmann Matoni claimed another one. But with only four lost ... one of their lifetime records is out by at least one.

Around noon, two squadrons of the Polish Wing – 306 and 315 Squadrons – were flying an armed recce in the Paris area. They were being led by W/C Skalski. Squadron records indicate that they encountered 40 or more FW and Bf 109 aircraft. In a free-wheeling dogfight they claimed six victories. Skalski had the distinct pleasure of out-manoeuvring two Bf 109s into colliding with each other thereby recording two aircraft destroyed without firing a shot. It is difficult to place any Bf 109-equipped unit in the area at that time of day. The best candidates are II./JG 3 and II./JG 5, both of whom had teamed up together that day, and I./JG 2 and II./JG 2 flying FW 190s and Bf 109s respectively. But between all four units only three Bf

109s were recorded as lost. In any event, one Polish pilot was shot down and killed.

Total losses for the day were 35 for the Luftwaffe and 24 for the Allies – just the reverse of the preceding day.

Operation EPSOM

Immediately after the Americans broke through to the coast sealing off the Cotentin Peninsula, Montgomery called on the Allies to launch assaults that would take Cherbourg and Caen. It was to be a double-barrelled attack, and it was to begin 22 June. For the Americans, this was just a renewed effort to take Cherbourg, and this is exactly what they did. For the British and Canadian troops the taking of Caen required a new assault plan – one that featured a main drive by reinforcement units. The Great Storm delayed the landing in France of the 15th Scottish Infantry Division, 43rd British Infantry Division and the 11th British Armoured Division, and that in turn led to Operation EPSOM – as the attack upon Caen was to be called – being delayed until 25 June.

Operation EPSOM was a frontal assault launched in daylight with air support only as requested. It was intended to puncture a hole in the German defences between Caen and the American salient at Caumont. When the hole was widened, three divisions spearheaded by the 11th Armoured Division were intended to drive deep into the countryside to Thury-Harcourt – maybe even to Falaise -- and when this drive got underway, the plan called for the 3rd Canadian Division to launch an assault to take the western outskirts of Caen and the 3rd British Division to take the eastern outskirts. It began well. On a clear day with puffy summer clouds, the 43rd British Infantry Division attacked on a 3-mile-wide front and captured the town of Rouray. The following day, 26 June, the recently landed divisions drove deeper into enemy territory leap-frogging the 43rd and crossing the Caen-to-Villers-Bocage road. But the Germans had been reinforced as well with the Panzer Lehr Division moving into the central part of the front 13 June, 2nd SS Panzer Division joining them and immediately to the east, the 9th SS Panzer Division and the 10th SS Panzer Division, recently arrived from Russia, moved into the line between Panzer Lehr and the 1st SS Panzer Division. The attack by the 15th Scottish, 11th British Armoured and 43rd British Infantry came to a halt against the strengthened defence by this wall of Panzer forces. The British units fought their way to the banks of the Odon River, tributary of the Orne, but could go no further. During this attack, the heaviest fighting was between the 15th Scottish Infantry Division and the 2nd and 9th SS Panzer Divisions. Elsewhere along the line, the Germans counter-attacked but the British forces held firm.

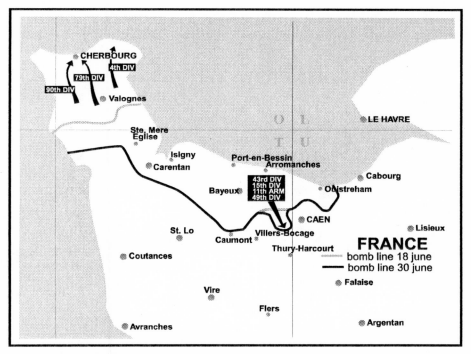

Figure 8 -- Operation EPSOM. The newly arrived British divisions tried an attack 25 June that slammed into seven panzer divisions defending the eastern part of the lodgment. EPSOM made little progress. Three American divisions fought continuously from 22 June, and completed the capture of Cherbourg 29 June.

Starting late on 25 June and continuing through 27 June, the weather was extremely changeable, heavy downpours interspersed with bright sun and strong winds. The weather caused some air support to be called off, and made military movements on the ground difficult. Notwithstanding, fighting all along this new front was fierce, with the British consolidating their gains and holding their ground. The 11th British Armoured Division renewed its attack 28 June by crossing the Odon River and driving two miles to the south-east towards a strategic position called Hill 112. But the Germans were now in defensive control, and the 10th SS Panzer and the 1st SS Panzer blunted the drive and when British supporting forces could not be moved past the defending Germans, the 11th British Armoured Division withdrew from the hill to a position just over the Odon. Operation EPSOM came to a standstill.

Sunday 25 June

Operation EPSOM called for air support only as needed. The 2ndTAF flew 746 fighter and fighter-bomber sorties (416 of them from bases in Normandy) in aid of the assault. Unfortunately, it was another day with heavy cloud and a low ceiling. This condition was devastating for aircraft because to fly low enough to hit targets the army wanted removed meant exposing the aircraft to the intense light flak from the defending German troops.

At 0700 hours, the three squadrons of P-38s of the 370th FG of the US 9thAF still flying out of Andover in the UK, attacked bridges in the Lisieux area when they were bounced by about 40 enemy aircraft – a mix of Bf 109s and FW 190s of I./JG 2, II./JG 2 and III./JG 2. They caught the American P-38s in a dive out of the sun and shot down seven P-38s (German records claimed fourteen) in a matter of six minutes. The furious dogfight that followed ended with the downing of twelve enemy machines in retaliation – five FW 190s and seven Bf 109s. The P-38 was an aircraft of great contrasts. In Europe it was not considered a success because of its sluggish attributes in turns and rolls and slow rate of climb. But it was fast, was a much better performer at high altitude and had a powerful sting – with four 50-caliber machine guns and a 20-millimetre cannon firing through the nose. In the hands of a good pilot it was a very worthy adversary, and in the South Pacific it was a favourite. Hence the outcome of a successful bounce that destroyed seven P-38s was followed by revenge in the form of 12 Luftwaffe aircraft shot down.

At 1100 hours in the Dreux and Evreux area 24 P-47s of the 365th FG attacked an equal number of FW 190s. The victory went to the Americans by downing 11 while losing only one P-47.

Apart from those large battles a few skirmishes broke out that in total netted 18 Allied aircraft lost versus 38 Luftwaffe aircraft -- 23 of them as a result of these last two battles.

Monday 26 June

The weather helped both sides recover from the pressures of the previous few days. Alternating bouts of sunshine with heavy showers and unpredictable winds, kept aircraft grounded for the better part of the day. The Allies lost only three aircraft, while the Luftwaffe lost 13 – all aircraft falling to flak.

Tuesday 27 June

With continuing bad weather – low ceiling and intermittent and sometimes driving rain – the Typhoons answered 17 calls for support from the British forces, while the Mustangs hammered bridges and all staging areas behind the lines. A heavy bomber attack was flown that evening to support Operation EPSOM, but with little visibility and fear of hitting Allied troops, the raid was aborted. The momentum of the assault had been slowing down, and when the air raid didn't materialize operation EPSOM ground to a halt.

Spitfires experienced a fairly productive day as they picked away at the German units in a series of skirmishes from morning to night. 453 Squadron of 125 Wing, and 442 Squadron of 144 Wing were the principal actors. In the 442 dogfight near Evreux, F/L Dowding claimed two victories bringing him to ace status. In the course of eight different clashes the Germans lost 15 aircraft (at least three due to flak) while only three Spitfires were lost.

At 2000 hours around Paris, three US FGs had some frenzied excitement in a battle with the unlucky Bf 109s of I./JG 27 and II./JG 27. It started with the P-47s of the 350th and 351st FSs of the 353rd FG bouncing I./JG 27 and III./JG 27 near Épernay. They claimed two, when suddenly LCol Gabreski and his 61st FS, 56th FG, followed by the 62nd FS jumped upon the Bf 109s. Seven German aircraft were shot down including Hauptmann Sinner of I./JG 27. Gabreski got one to bring his total to 27. However, four of the German pilots, including Sinner, parachuted to safety. In the same area, and possibly in the same dogfight, the 352nd FG lost one P-51, although the details of the timing are not known.

In the course of 27 June, the Luftwaffe lost 28 aircraft – 21 of them Bf 109s -- while the Allies lost 18 – nine for 2TAF and nine for USAAF.

Wednesday 28 June

Weather broke the day into three parts -- morning 0600 to 0900 hours, midday 1130 to 1230 hours and late day 1700 hours until dark. Heavy cloud and blowing rain marked the shutdown periods and clearing but not sunny intervals marked the periods between.

This day turned out to be the day not just for Spitfires, but for Canadian Spitfires. Of the nine wings of Spitfires in 2ndTAF, only three of them were Canadian. The three wings were 126 Wing led by W/C Keefer, 127 Wing led by W/C Buckham and 144 Wing led by W/C Johnson. First blood of the day went to 403 Squadron of 127 Wing at 0600 hours when it met II./JG 11 – each side scoring one.

At 0927 hours near Caen, 443 Squadron of 144 Wing shot down three JG 2 FW 190s with no loss. This was very satisfying and redeeming to the pilots of 443 Squadron for just 12 days earlier, four of their aircraft had been bounced by FW 190s and everyone shot down and killed except one Spitfire pilot who lived to tell the tale.

Between 1120 and 1130 hours 416 Squadron of 127 Wing shot down three Bf 109s over Caen on beach patrol, while 442 Squadron of 144 Wing got four in the Villers-Bocage area. All seven Luftwaffe losses were at the expense of JG 26.

Fifteen minutes later, 401 Squadron of 126 Wing moved into the Caen area and shot down two Bf 109s of Stab./JG 27. And twenty minutes after that, sister 411 Squadron scored three at the expense of IV./JG 27. At 1700 hours after the cloudy and rainy hiatus, it was 416 Squadron that again downed a II./JG 53 Bf 109, while fifty miles away, 412 Squadron of 126 Wing despatched another Bf 109. At 1730 hours 421 Squadron of 127 Wing scored three. Three hours later, between 2030 and 2130 hours, 412 Squadron and 401 Squadron of 126 Wing destroyed six more Luftwaffe aircraft. Among these last F/L Kennedy scored one that raised his career total to 11.

At day's end the Luftwaffe had lost 29 aircraft – all but one shot down by the Canadians. The Allies lost eight aircraft – three being Canadian, one shot down, one due to mechanical failure and one lost to flak.

Taking Cherbourg

Only in the Cotentin Peninsula, with the drive to take Cherbourg was there any positive action along the Allied front. The 4th US Infantry Division that landed at OMAHA beach together with the 82nd and 101st US Airborne Divisions and the 90th US Infantry Division were joined by the 79th US Infantry Division. Then while the Airborne Divisions held the line to the south, the other three US infantry divisions drove north towards the tip of the peninsula. It was at this point in time that the Great Storm struck Normandy. For American ground operations the high winds and driving rain turned the countryside into a muddy quagmire, and hampered the assaulting troops. The Germans too were hampered, but the big difference was air power. For the Allies, air power was a most important weapon in their armoury, and the Great Storm brought aerial activity to a dead stop. Without air support the American drive withered and waited. The storm raged from the nineteenth to the twenty-first of June. As it waned, the Americans resumed their assault 22 June, and massive aerial support from the 2ndTAF helped them to drive north. After bitter fighting and 6,000 casualties, the Americans took Cherbourg 29 June. It had been demolished by the Germans and required several weeks of repairs before it was to function again as a major seaport[12].

Thursday 29 June

Whereas the Wednesday aerial dogfight action had been monopolized by the Canadians, Thursday became a more usual day with everyone making claims. Two air battles of moderate size stand out. The first occurred at 0710 hours over the Lisieux area, when the P-47s of the 411th FS of the US 9thAF 373rd FG were pitted against the Bf 109s of the ill-fated IV./JG 27. The win was never in doubt as five Bf 109s fell from the sky, while all the American machines returned to base.

The second dogfight is a curious one. German records document the loss of six Bf 109s in an aerial battle in the Evreux area about 1150 hours. To offset these six losses, claims of five P-47s shot down – including three claimed by Oberstleutnant Rödel bringing his career total to 97 -- were recorded by the Germans. It seems difficult to believe this was just imagination, but there is no record for that time and place – either 29 June or the days before and after – of 8thAF or 9thAF claims or losses by any American P-47. Not far from Evreux, at Bernay, a P-51 aircraft of 15th Reconnaissance Squadron claimed shooting down one Bf 109 at 1155 hours with no loss, but how does one explain five claims and six losses recorded by the Luftwaffe?

Losses for the day were Germans 22, Allies 14.

Friday 30 June

The last day of June became another day for the Canadian Spitfire wings. 126 Wing scored four, 127 Wing scored six and 144 Wing scored six – a total of 16 of the 23 aircraft the Luftwaffe lost that day. Details of the six victories claimed by 127 Wing can be found in the second section of this book. Total Allied losses for the day were 14 –

two of which were Canadian machines. The Germans lost 23 – 20 of which were Bf 109s.

Stalemate

As June came to a close, the Allied lodgement was one continuous band of Normandy countryside from the west coast of the Cotentin Peninsula in a deeply dipping line through to the outskirts of Caen. In this limited space 23 Allied divisions consisting of 860 thousand personnel and half a million vehicles were jammed, with ammunition and supply dumps everywhere. In addition, 17 air bases had been built populated by 55 squadrons of fighters and fighter-bombers. The Germans realized they could not dislodge the Allies; the Allies realized that their frontal assaults were ineffective against German Army units well versed in defence occupying positions that gave enormous advantage to the defender. Conventional military wisdom requires a numerical advantage of at least three-to-one for an aggressor to overcome a defender. Opposing the Allies, but with excellent defensive positions developed, were 22 German Divisions, of which 12 were Panzer Divisions. But whereas the Allied divisions received replacements[13] after they incurred casualties, the German divisions did not. At the outset of the invasion, only a few Panzer Divisions, such as the Panzer Lehr or the 12th SS Panzer Hitler Youth, were at full strength. But by the end of June, all except the most recent arrivals had been badly mauled, and were very short of equipment and ammunition.

June

The month of June saw skirmishes in which both Allied pilots and Luftwaffe pilots exchanged losses, but the attrition for the Allies was greater than the Luftwaffe. The 2ndTAF lost 322 aircraft, the US 9thAF (the principal invading force) lost 255 aircraft, while the US 8thAF (intervening only occasionally) lost 125. Total Allied losses were 702 fighters, fighter-bombers and medium bombers -- 56 more than the 646 lost by the Luftwaffe.

The Luftwaffe concluded that the loss rate on combat missions was running 20 to 30 percent, and that three German aircraft were being lost for every Allied fighter loss. If German losses were three-to-one in aerial combat, the effects of flak more than evened the match.

Taking information from all our sources suggests that Luftwaffe fighters and fighter-bombers flew about 8,000 sorties in June, compared to about 99,000 flown by the Allies. Earlier, it was noted that the Allies flew 18 times as many sorties on D-Day as the Luftwaffe. These totals for the month suggest that in June the Allies flew at a slightly reduced advantage -- 12 times more sorties. Using these figures with loss figures quoted above indicates a loss rate per sortie of 8.0 percent for the Germans versus a loss rate of 0.7 percent for the Allies.

Chapter Four – Caen and the Break-out

As July dawned, both sides paused to count the gains and losses. Operation EPSOM had yielded only five miles of gain, not a quarter of the distance to Thury-Harcourt, and the cost had been high, the British suffering 4,000 casualties, 2,300 of them from the 15th Scottish Infantry Division. Since it had not resulted in a break-out, the actions for the British and Canadian divisions had to be re-planned to capitalize upon the salient that had been created by EPSOM.

New Air Bases

In the first week of July two new ALGs were completed in the British sector, and six in the American sector. With the new airstrips came 20 new squadrons of fighter-bombers and reconnaissance aircraft. For every aircraft operating on the continent, the increase in flying time over the front lines was double that of operating from the UK bases. The number of ALGs built was truly astounding. At the end of the Normandy Campaign 18 British and 19 American bases were in operation – sufficient to accommodate over 1900 fighter, fighter-bomber and reconnaissance aircraft.

Goering's Answer to Aircraft Losses

The losses of British and American pilots and aircraft was high, but replacement was immediate[1] – usually the next day – and the Allied squadrons were thus always at full strength. The Luftwaffe situation was the exact opposite. Arrivals of new replacement aircraft for the Luftwaffe came in a trickle – one or two new aircraft at a time to replace ten or more lost. The only way German gruppen could keep up was to absorb the pilots of sister gruppen and take over their aircraft.

Veterans who commanded staffeln, gruppen, and geschwader were being lost at an alarming rate, and could not be replaced. The situation led Reichsmarschall Goering in early July, to insist that senior Luftwaffe officers not fly unless accompanied by a minimum number of aircraft – six for a staffelkapitän, 15 for a gruppekommandeur, and 45 for a geschwaderkommodore. These were the men who scored the victories. Since it became more and more difficult to assemble enough aircraft to support the senior commanders under these new rules, the quality of the Luftwaffe fighting force declined further. Luftwaffe fighter sorties that numbered about 400 per day in June began to decline to half that level by the end of July while the size of gaggles of enemy aircraft got bigger.

Saturday 1 July

The weather at the end of June had been pretty good and was accompanied by the frantic and ferocious battles that were concentrated on the 23rd through the 30th, however the new month brought mostly adverse weather that haunted the first half of the month.

Weather prohibited operations until late in the day when a fairly sizeable battle developed at 1940 hours in the evening, between the P-47s of all three squadrons of the 78th FG of the 8thAF and the Bf 109 of II./JG 11. In this engagement the Americans had lost one P-47 while the Germans lost four Bf 109s, but unfortunately, two P-47s had collided upon take-off to go off on the mission, so final score might be more accurately considered three to four.

Despite the weather, 2ndTAF managed to fly 88 sorties on armed recces, 28 sorties on army support missions, 225 sorties on front line and beach patrols, 81 sorties on escort, and 32 sorties for reconnaissance and naval spotting.

The aerial losses of fighters, fighter-bombers and medium bombers were beginning to see-saw with the Luftwaffe losing 11 for the day; the Allies just six.

Break-out in the Cotentin

On 2 July the Americans initiated an attack designed to win manoeuvring room south of Carentan. In this area they were hemmed in by marshy land criss-crossed by causeways. Further west and to the south, the land was higher and broken up with valleys and plateau where bocage fields abounded. The attack began on the right near the sea with the 82nd Airborne, 79th and 90th Infantry Divisions. It widened eastward with the 1st and 4th Divisions, while the whole front pivoted on St-Lô where the 29th and 30th Divisions were engaged.

German forces in the battle zone constituted remnants of no fewer than 12 divisions including the 17th SS Panzer Grenadier and part of the 2nd SS Panzer. Only the latter unit had tanks and these were Mark IVs -- there were no Tigers or Panthers in the American sector. Unlike the Americans, the Germans had plenty of room to manoeuvre and good communications for making a flexible defence, and their greatest advantage lay in the hedgerows, which were everywhere, hampering offensive action and limiting the use of tanks. The hedgerows had been built hundreds of years earlier by digging roads and piling the dirt either side and some were up to ten feet high and hard as concrete. Bushes and trees grew along the embankments and the combination of the hard gritty Norman soil and tangled roots made the hedgerows very tough to penetrate. Norman farms had been divided and divided again with each succeeding generation so the fields were small. Fields stretched out endlessly in every direction while the hedges lent themselves to dug-in emplacements and concealed strong points, difficult both to locate and to attack and the sunken roads were excellent killing zones when a concealed tank suddenly swung out into the road. This landscape was known as bocage country.

The American efforts to take ground gained only a few miles before the determined German defence caused it to bog down by 4 July. But the failure only caused a more determined and effective plan to be devised.

Sunday 2 July

In a clear morning sky, 411 Squadron of 126 Wing started the day by trading single losses with the FW 190s of II./JG 26 near Lisieux. The German pilot was killed but the Canadian managed to evade capture.

A prolonged downburst brought flying to a halt in mid-morning, but by 1500 hours 403 Squadron was flying a front line patrol near Caen when its Spitfires tangled with a large force of over 50 Bf 109s from I./JG 27, IV./JG 27 and II./JG 53. Just as the dog-fighting became serious, a squadron of P-47s heading for the Caumont area joined the fray. The German gruppen claimed six victories, but neither the US 388th FS nor 403 Squadron recorded any losses, while the Germans lost six – five pilots were killed.

While this fight was underway, ten miles to the north-east at Cabourg, two squadrons of Spitfires from 125 Wing – 132 Squadron and 602 Squadron -- attacked the FW 190s of II./JG 26. In this tussle Sub Lt Pierre Clostermann -- a Free French pilot flying in the RAF – shot down a FW 190 bringing his career total to seven. Clostermann went on to become one of France's top aces.

Figure 9 -- FW 190*. The Focke Wulf 190 was as good a fighter aircraft as any. This I./JG 26 aircraft is seen being hidden in the trees after returning from a mission. The base is Boissy-le-Bois, half way between Rouen and Paris.*

(Bundesarchiv)

Two hours later, two Spitfire squadrons – 401 and 411 of 126 Wing – bounced the Bf 109s of III./JG 3 and dodging through cloud that aided and hindered, they shot down four enemy aircraft killing their pilots. F/L Hap Kennedy of 401 Squadron recorded his 12th career victory in this engagement, but the squadron lost a pilot who was killed in action.

Getting in on the action at 1950 hours was 65 Squadron of 122 Wing when they downed three Bf 109s of III./JG 27. Half-an-hour later at 2030 hours 453 Squadron of 122 Wing, and at 2050 hours 441 Squadron of 144 Wing each recorded victories without loss. All of these dog-fights occurred between Caen and Falaise. The three squadrons recorded three, two and three victories respectively over a variety of gruppen that included JG 27, JG 2, JG 26 and JG 54. Three of the German pilots were killed and one taken prisoner while the other four parachuted to safety. Only one Allied pilot was lost – temporarily, for he evaded capture and returned to his unit a week later.

This day's action was contrary to the rule for the Germans lost 21 aircraft while the Allies lost only five – one of which was shot down by flak.

Monday 3 July

Rainy Monday. Normandy woke up to a soggy, rain-soaked countryside that shut down flying much of the day and it was well after supper before aerial activity took place and although it was intense, the 400 sorties undertaken by 2ndTAF were uneventful except for some moderate success achieved against three bridges and two railway stations. US 9thAF concentrated on the supply centres at Alençons and Argentan.

Tuesday 4 July

Much better weather greeted the opposing air forces on Tuesday. A few light showers did nothing more than slow things down at times, but it was an extremely active day for the 2ndTAF which stepped up activity from the 400 sorties flown on Monday to well over 1400 sorties on Tuesday -- all the local bridges and main arteries near the lodgement area were the prime targets. US 9thAF prime targets were the bridges of the Seine and Loire rivers since, in the month since the invasion began, the Germans had repaired or partially repaired 16 bridges across these two river systems.

The first aerial battles occurred at 1410 hours in the sky between Coutances and St. Lô, in the Cotentin. The three P-47 squadrons of the 406th FG US 9thAF swooped down on about 20 FW 190s of I./JG 1 and shot down three German aircraft. The first bounce took only a minute or so but in the aftermath, 513th FS lost one of its flight leaders.

Figure 10 -- Bf 109. *While Willie Messerschmitt designed the German fighter, Bayerische Flugzeugwerke was the company that manufactured the aircraft, and so it was designated the Bf 109. All Allied aircrew knew it as the Me 109. This one belonged to II./JG 3. It is being hidden under trees at a base called Sours just outsides Chartres.*

(Bundesarchiv)

Shortly afterward, in the area between L'Aigle and Lisieux, vigorous attacks by the FW 190s of II./JG 26 and the Bf 109s of III./JG 26 led to the claim of six Allied aircraft destroyed – a P-47, a Spitfire and four P-38s. JG 26 lost one of its pilots in this battle. However, it is unclear what Allied units were involved. Two P-38 squadrons of the US 8thAF were escorting heavy bombers near Laval, almost 100 miles south-east of L'Aigle and the records show that two P-38s of the 434th FS and one of the 435th FS were shot down by anti-aircraft fire in the Laval area. Unfortunately, the time this occurred is not recorded.

At 1800 hours over Caen, 411 Squadron of 126 Wing shot down three Bf 109s of IV./JG 27 killing two of the German pilots.

60 miles to the east and 20 minutes afterwards, the full 56th FG of the US 8thAF flew into the Evreux area surprising 14 Bf 109s of II./JG 2, but were then being set upon by a combined force of nearly 40 Bf 109s from III./JG 2 and all three gruppen of JG 27. It was an ambush of P-47s by Bf 109s – no FW 190s were around -- that broke into two huge scrums with the 62nd FS of the 56th taking on the fourteen Bf 109s of II./JG 2, while the 61st FS and 63rd FS took on III./JG 2, I./JG 27, III./JG 27 and IV./JG 27. In the first battle the Americans destroyed 10 of the 14 Bf 109s – Lt Bostwick claiming three and two others claiming two apiece. In the second battle the Americans lost one but shot down five of the German aircraft – three of these losses being absorbed by IV./JG 27 which had lost three aircraft only 30 minutes earlier. In this huge aerial battle nine German pilots were killed.

This battle bears light on two revealing elements of the aerial war the Luftwaffe was waging. First was the marked inferiority of the Bf 109 G-6 compared to the FW 190 A-8. These were the two most common models serving the Germans, but it was evident that the Bf 109 was no match for its adversaries except in the hands of the most capable pilots. The second point to note is the unbelievably unfortunate record of IV./JG 27. This gruppe flew into Normandy late on D-Day with 24 Bf 109s. In the first five days they lost 13 aircraft, received some replacements and lost 12 more in the following four days. Temporarily held back to re-group and restore morale for a week, they started attacking again on 21 June. In the 10 days following they lost 34 Bf 109 aircraft. As noted, they lost six aircraft on this day and they would lose 10 more before sunset on 7 July. Before they were mercifully recalled to Germany 3 August, they had lost 98 Bf 109s. And theirs was not the worst record amongst the gruppen – II./JG 3 lost 116 Bf 109s in Normandy and III./JG 3 lost another 93. The tragedy of IV./JG 27 is that they served only two months in France while the two gruppen of JG 3 served the whole three months of the campaign. Of the 23 jagdgeschwader that served in Normandy only four had fewer than 50 aircraft destroyed, nine had between 50 and 60 destroyed, and the remaining ten over 60.

How do these losses compare to those of the Allies? About 36 wings of Commonwealth and 36 wings of US fighters and fighter-bombers served in Normandy: one wing lost 59 aircraft, another lost 50. Thus 70 wings had fewer than 50 losses, two between 50 and 60, and none over 60. One third of all Allied wings lost fewer than 20 aircraft.

Five other small encounters occurred throughout 4 July all with one or two victories and the day had more than its share of aircraft lost to flak. At final count the Luftwaffe lost 38 aircraft, the Allies 23.

Wednesday 5 July

An hour after midnight, in total darkness at B.11 Longues-sur-Mer ALG, a single FW 190 half-heartedly strafed and dropped a bomb near the dispersal area for 132 Squadron causing no damage. One indication of Allied air supremacy in Normandy is that although 37 Allied airfields were plainly visible in the fields of Normandy, only this rather ineffective German attack and three others are recorded. By comparison, the German airfields clustered around Paris and every other airfield from Rennes in Brittany to Cambrai near the Belgian border, were repeatedly bombed by medium and heavy bombers.

When the sun came up on 5 July it brought typical Normandy weather – rain showers and clear spells brewing up or dying down in a matter of minutes. The number of Allied sorties decreased to about a third of what was normal.

At 0910 hours 24 P-51s of the 351st FG of the US 8thAF went on an armed recce in the area between Evreux and Gisors, south-east of Rouen. They bounced 20 Bf 109s of I./JG 5 and destroyed four while losing one of their own and a second to ground fire.

An hour-and-a-half later east of Caen 9thAF's aircraft – the 362nd FG -- got into a dogfight with Bf 109s and FW 190s of JG 2, JG 27 and JG 53 that drifted westward ending over Caen. After losing two P-47s the Americans bounced back and shot down three Bf 109s and two FW 190s. Two other Bf 109s were brought down by anti-aircraft fire.

It was becoming another discouraging day for the Germans. At about 1600 hours between Rouen and Evreux, two FGs of the US

8thAF traded blows with the whole JG 2 jagdgeschwader. The Americans destroyed four while losing two. And at about 1900 hours the Spitfires of 441 Squadron dove out of the sun and shot down five FW 190s of I./JG 11 when they caught them near Alençons. The day ended with 39 German losses versus 19 Allied losses.

Thursday 6 July

Fighters and fighter-bombers of the 2ndTAF flew 1097 sorties this day while Boston and Mitchell medium bombers flew another 77 sorties hitting fuel dumps in Chartres and Argentan.

There wasn't a cloud in the sky until noon and aerial battles started at 0615 hours and carried on through the day. None was very large nor very decisive and the day ended with 27 aircraft lost by the Luftwaffe, 20 by the Allies. The only notable happening of the day occurred at 0849 hours ten miles south of Cambrai when Hauptmann Weissenberger claimed two victories over P-38s, bringing his career total to 187. It is true that the 434th FS of the 479th FG of the US 8thAF – flying P-38s -- was operating in the area, for they claimed the destruction of a Bf 109 at 0900 hours at Valenciennes, but it is also true that they recorded no losses. Sometimes inability to match a claim with a loss results from confusion as to the day, but in this case neither the day before nor the day after reveal any similar missions involving P-38s.

Friday 7 July

The bomb that was dropped on B.11 Longues-sur-Mer 5 July, did no damage other than to awaken all the airmen. In a copycat raid early in the morning of 7 July, another attack occurred. This time it was on B.6 Coulombe – two miles south of the last attack – and this time it was a little more serious when a FW 190 dropped a bomb and fired a few strafing rounds, but as it left, experienced a secondary explosion that rocked the airbase. The bomb hit a Typhoon and a rocket stowed nearby fired and flew into an ammunition truck, blowing it to smithereens, killing two ground crew and injuring several others. The sound of the explosion was heard for miles around.

The day dawned rather poorly, but lightened up by noon and was a half decent flying day after that, notwithstanding the 2ndTAF flew only 600 sorties – less than the really busy days. The heroes of this day came from 126 Wing when, on their turn to fly beach and front line patrols they encountered German aircraft six times. The Canadian Spitfires of 401, 411 and 412 Squadrons scored victories at 1000 hours, 1140 hours, 1405 hours, 1710 hours, 2005 hours, and 2300 hours. In all they claimed 12 victories, but German records confirm only seven. The Canadians lost only one pilot who was shot down, evaded capture and returned to the squadron in August.

The total losses for the day were 16 German aircraft and 10 Allied.

A Note About Heavy Bombing

Those who have lived through a heavy bombing raid describe the abject terror it causes. Huddled in a foxhole, one hears a 'karump' a few hundred yards away, feels the shudder as it shakes the ground, just as another explosion – much closer this time – shakes the ground more violently. Shrapnel and debris fly over the open face of the foxhole and one listens to the whistle of the next bomb, which is surely headed directly here. Another explosion well past the foxhole provides relief for the briefest of moments as other sticks of bombs are blasting their thunderous staccato to right and to left. A half-hour of this pulverizing assault leaves one shocked, petrified and terror-stricken to the point of immobility.

Figure 11 -- Allied chiefs. Gen Bernard Montgomery, AM Arthur Coningham and Lt Gen Miles Dempsey are seen here discussing operations of the army and the air force.

(News Services)

The assaulting troops who landed on D-Day were told that this is what would happen to the shore defences -- the bombing would leave the Germans totally incapable of fighting. However when the day came, all landing parties agreed that the bombing seemed to have had no effect because most of the bombs fell well inland, none of the coastal pillboxes were destroyed and the Germans were ready with a warm reception. A month later, when first used in conjunction with an artillery barrage, the role of carpet bombing became better appreciated and its effects better understood.

After the war, many German field commanders who fought in Normandy were questioned about the effects of the bombing. The consensus among them was that whereas in the first month the great number of casualties resulted from hand-to-hand fighting and aerial attack, later it was the carpet bombing that caused more than half the casualties. The mistake the Allies often made was to be too slow to capitalize upon the confusion and stunned condition of the German troops immediately after the bombing.

Figure 12 -- Rommel. *Generalfeldmarschall Erwin Rommel is seen here with his entourage inspecting a unit of the 21st Panzer Division near Caen shortly after D-Day.*

(Bundesarchiv)

Dissension among the German Generals

During this period the German high command was severely shaken. First of all, Hitler was so outraged at the loss of Cherbourg that he ordered Gen Dollman, commander of the Seventh Army, to commit suicide and the same day 28 June he ordered von Rundstedt and Rommel to report to him in Berlin. Hitler was not at all pleased with his generals, and holding to the belief that the main attack of the Allies would be at the Pas de Calais any day, he insisted they stiffen the resolve of every German soldier to stand and fight until death.

Within a week Caen fell with a great loss of life on both sides and in the west, the American forces were building up so fast that they appeared likely to pour out anytime. The German high command saw the situation deteriorating quickly and 12 July, when Generalfieldmarschall von Kluge took over command of the Seventh Army he reported to Hitler that the situation was grim. On 15 July, Rommel wrote to Hitler that after witnessing the build-up of American forces, he was convinced the Axis defences must soon crack. Thus when von Rundstedt confessed defeatism, and urged him to make peace, Hitler flew into a rage at his generals dismissing von Rundstedt and appointing von Kluge Commander-in-Chief of the whole Army in the West. The 16 July, Rommel told his new superior von Kluge that to date his Army Group had lost 97,000 men and obtained only 6,000 replacements and that though 250 tanks had been destroyed only 17 had been replaced. In a cruel twist of fate, it was the next day that Rommel's staff car was strafed by a Spitfire, Rommel severely injured, and though later recovered, played no further part in the Normandy Campaign.

The attempt upon Hitler's life occurred 20 July, when a bomb exploded under the table at one of his meetings. Hitler, in a blind fury, had several of his generals rounded up and shot and now assumed that anyone not in full agreement with him was his enemy. On 24 July, the day of the first carpet bombing of St. Lô, von Kluge told Hitler that the front would soon break and that lack of mobility would inhibit the Army's ability to maintain organized ground operations. Von Kluge took his own life 18 August and Rommel poisoned himself in October when Hitler accused him of being one of the traitors who tried to kill him.

Saturday 8 July

The nocturnal aerial activity by both sides continued, interrupted only when weather would not permit. Each night a handful of German Ju 88s made their way from bases near Rennes, Chartres or Amiens to fly over the beaches and bomb the endless stream of supplies flowing to reinforce the Allies. Each night Mosquito bombers and night-fighters shot down some of the Ju 88s and in some cases escorted night bombing raids by the RAF bombers. The 2ndTAF records show that 8 July was a typical night with 98 Mosquito sorties flown before dawn and 25 Boston medium bombers dispatched to bomb train depots. The Mosquitos claimed two Ju 88s destroyed, but they lost one of the two attacking aircraft when debris from an exploding Ju 88 knocked out an engine. The Mosquito pilot was killed, but his navigator parachuted to safety.

The night was often the time when the US 9thAF called out its B-26s to bomb airfields, marshalling yards or ammunition dumps and in the early morning hours of 8 July, 32 B-26s from 322nd Bomber Group in conjunction with a large heavy bomber attack by RAF Lancasters, was sent to bomb a V-1 Control Centre in the Abbeville area. At this time the V-1 assaults were at their peak. The German defences were ready and night fighters of I./NJG 301 claimed 20 Lancasters and six B-26s. In fact it was more damaging, the 322nd Bomber Group had 9 bombers shot down, two returned but were write-offs at home base, and two other seriously damaged by flak. The mission was a disaster.

The weather was not great, but this day was the launch date for Operation CHARNWOOD – the assault upon Caen -- and the 2ndTAF had its marching orders. It sent out 213 Typhoons, 65 Mustangs and 259 Spitfires to attack specific bridges, junctions, staging areas and defensive centres. Another 150 Spitfires flew front line patrols. Most of these activities were unopposed by the Luftwaffe.

At day's end, the Germans had lost just four aircraft and the Allies 19.

Operation CHARNWOOD

The new plan for the Caen area called for a probing attack by one brigade of the 3rd Canadian Infantry Division to take Carpiquet Airport to the west of Caen, to be followed by a massive carpet-bombing, and that in turn, by an attack by 3rd Canadian Division, 59th British Division and 3rd British Division to take the city of Caen. Unlike earlier operations, this time air support and naval support were key parts of the plan as the firepower of HMS Rodney and HMS

Belfast were added to the British and Canadian artillery to soften up the defences prior to the assault.

One brigade of the 3rd Canadian Division started the assault 4 July and completed it the next day, at great loss. On the evening of 7 July, a broad rectangular bomb drop zone three-quarters-of-a-mile wide and two miles long was laid out by pathfinders across the northern part of Caen. To avoid bombs falling on Allied troops, the bomb drop zone was three miles ahead of the Allied lines in the area of the German support artillery. In 40 minutes, 800 Lancaster bombers of RAF Bomber Command dropped 3,000 tons of bombs. This was the third time the Allies had used heavy carpet bombing as an offensive precursor of a ground assault -- D-Day was the first, EPSOM at the end of June was the second occasion -- it was to become a regular feature of future Allied offensives. The bombing caused great devastation to the city of Caen and it turned out to be a double-edged sword; Canadian troops later complained that the ruins created excellent defensive positions for the Germans, resulting in much higher casualties in mopping up Caen than needed to be.

Early on 8 July, the 59th British Division and the 3rd British Division crossed the start line and drove south towards Caen. The 3rd Canadian Division fought in Buron – the site of the first bloody encounter with the 12th SS Hitler Youth Panzer Division one month earlier – in a brutal repeat struggle that lasted all day. For the Canadians, Buron became known as 'Bloody Buron' and in the days following came discovery of the atrocities that were chronicled in the War Crimes Tribunal in Nuremberg after the war. Over 100 Canadian soldiers were murdered by the fanatical Hitler Youth after being taken captive.

When finally all three divisions had secured their immediate objectives, they moved into the outskirts of Caen. In the next two days there was savage house-to-house and room-to-room fighting that has been likened to the desperate struggles that occurred at Stalingrad or Ortona. By 11 July, Caen was in Allied hands, but only to the river in the centre of town, for the bridges across the Orne River were destroyed and German defensive positions on the other side of the river were virtually unassailable. Losses to both sides were appalling.

In the infantry battalions, losses of 25% were the rule, not the exception.

Sunday 9 July and Monday 10 July

During the night of the 8/9th, Mosquitos and Bostons bombed the Seine bridges and hit the railroad marshalling yards at Mézidon and Argentan. The skies continued to be socked in most of the day with a few brief clearing spells. Dodging in and out of the weather, the 2ndTAF sent 366 Spitfires, Typhoons and Mustangs on specific army support sorties or armed recces while 269 sorties were flown on patrol or escort duty.

At this point the Operation CHARNWOOD assault came to a halt in the gloomy weather, having achieved the taking of the rubble heap that was Caen and smoothing out the front line. The Luftwaffe hardly made an appearance during these three days when the flying was very tricky, but the need for army support so great. Two small aerial battles occurred on Sunday and none on Monday, and the total losses for both days were respectively, four and five for the Luftwaffe, and eight and six for the Allies. The losses were almost all due to flak and included accidents upon landing and one instance of a Spitfire hitting a barrage balloon.

Tuesday 11 July

This day Allied soldiers were able to walk in Caen without being hit by snipers, although just across the river, defending destroyed bridges and crossing points, the German Army lobbed artillery and mortar shells into the rubble-strewn city. A solid ceiling hung at 1,000 feet over the whole of Normandy and light rain in the morning became driving rain before noon. The Typhoons continued to attack tanks and artillery positions and Spitfires managed 108 sorties on armed recces, but the flying was tough going and the results rarely observed. A few Luftwaffe aircraft made a showing over the front but six were shot down by anti-aircraft fire. Nine Allied aircraft suffered a similar fate. In total the Luftwaffe lost 12 aircraft, the Allies 14.

Wednesday 12 July 1944

Wednesday was a bit better. At 0950 hours over Le Mans, 12 P-51s of the 382nd FS of the 9thAF's 363rd FG screamed out of the morning sun and bounced about 20 FW 190s of I./JG 11 shooting down three and then disappearing.

Over Mortain at 1405 hours, a Spitfire of 412 Squadron flown by F/L Banks, in a chance encounter, fired on a solitary Bf 109 of IV./JG 27. The Bf 109 exploded and crashed killing its pilot. It was flown by Hauptmann Meyer – an up-and-coming ace with 21 victories to his credit. This was the fifth German super-ace to fall in the Normandy Campaign. Banks went on to six claims in Normandy and a career total of nine victories.

At 1430 hours near Dreux, the FW 190s of I./JG 26 and III./JG 54 shot down five P-47s of 367th FS and 366th FS of the 358th FG 9thAF whilst sustaining only one loss. One of the victors was Hauptmann Weiss of II./JG 54 who claimed two of the five and brought his career total to 112 and another well-known super ace, Leutnant Kemmethmüller of I./JG 26 claimed two as well, bringing his career total to 82.

Half an hour later the Mustangs of 19 Squadron were dive-bombing when they were attacked by the Bf 109s of III./JG 1 near Caen. The Germans knocked down two Mustangs, but the pilots of 19 Squadron turned around and shot down four Bf 109s. When they got back to base, another Mustang was a written off, so in this engagement it was four losses to three for the Allies.

At 1800 hours 416 and 421 Squadrons were just starting out on an armed recce to Chartres when they met the Bf 109s of II./JG 3. They shot down three – although the Luftwaffe squadron records name only one of the three. There was one Allied loss and one damaged but repairable Spitfire.

The score for the day was pretty even at 16 and 15 for the Germans and Allies respectively.

Thursday 13 July

True to form, there was a window of good flying weather in the early morning and then a miserable wet and windy day through to late afternoon, however the air was much warmer. It felt as though there might be a hot summer after all.

Around 1815 hours the Typhoons of 146 Wing led by W/C Baldwin were returning from a rocket attack at Pont l'Éveque, intending to refuel at one of the ALGs before returning to their base at Hurn in the UK. Out of a vertical pillar of cloud flew some 40 or more Bf 109s of III./JG 1 and I./JG 5 – the latter led by their super-ace Hauptmann Weissenberger. The Typhoon could be a pretty tough customer at lower altitudes when clean of rockets or bombs. Baldwin tore into the Germans, and in a swirling dogfight that lasted about 15 minutes, three Typhoons and three Bf 109s went down in flames. Weissenberger claimed two – his 17th claim in the Normandy Campaign, and the 192nd of his career. Baldwin claimed one, his 3rd in Normandy and 16th of his career.

This was the only large engagement of the day that saw the destruction of eight Luftwaffe and six Allied machines.

Friday 14 July

It turned warmer and though showers persisted, both sides flew missions all day. In the afternoon six dogfights occurred.

Since the Ju 88s had little success in bombing Allied ships as they unloaded at the Normandy coast, the Luftwaffe resorted to flying further out to sea dropping mines. At 1320 hours, 416 Squadron was flying an anti-mine-laying patrol off Cabourg when it met the Bf 109s of II./JG 2 and promptly shot down two.

An hour later at 1415 hours, four aircraft of 411 Squadron on front line patrol clashed with a large formation of 40 or more FW 190s of I./JG 11 and I./JG 1. In spite of the odds, they waded in and shot down three before beating a hasty retreat.

From Paris I./JG26 was searching for American fighter-bombers when, near Alençon, they broke out of cloud and dove down on two squadrons of P-47s from 358th FG. Executing a perfectly timed firing pass they shot down four P-47s, but before they climbed back into cloud, the Bf 109s of III./JG 26 and I./JG 27 joined the ruckus at their cost as one of I./JG 26's FW 190s was shot down, as were one Bf 109 from II./JG 26 and two from I./JG 27. Both sides lost four aircraft.

While this battle was underway to the south-east, three Spitfires of 416 Squadron still flying mine-laying patrols, attacked a mixed force of JG 5 aircraft and shot down three Bf 109s before disappearing into cloud.

The next battle involved another clash between 416 Squadron – this time at full 12-Spitfire strength. They attacked another mixed gaggle of FW 190s and Bf 109s belonging to JG 1 and I./JG 5. They claimed three shot down, but German records show only two, with two others succumbing to flak.

The last dogfight of the day went to the P-38s of 55th FS and 77th FS of the US 8thAF's 20th FG. Returning from a long-range escort mission, they met a FW 190 equipped unit just recently thrown into the fray – III./JG 77. Lack of experience cost the newcomers two aircraft, although both German pilots parachuted to safety.

Saturday 15 July

Saturday was socked in from first light, clearing only about nine in the evening. Some limited flying by brave souls went forth, but for the most part both sides waited for a clearing. The day's total losses of four and five for German and Allies respectively reflects this wash-out kind of a day.

At this point in mid-July it is interesting to compare the profile of aircraft losses for the two sides. In the first two days of the Normandy Landings, the Allies lost 155 fighters, fighter-bombers and medium bombers compared Germany's 93. For a time this difference – at first 60, but soon rising to nearly 100 more aircraft lost by the Allies than by the Luftwaffe – persisted. For instance on the eighteenth of June, just before the Great Storm, total cumulative losses were 476 for the

Allies and 365 for the Germans. But then things evened out a bit, and at the end of June, it was 702 Allies, 646 Germany; now by the middle of July, it was neck-and-neck at 877 Allied losses, 874 German losses.

	Allied Aerial Losses	German Aerial Losses
6 June thru 18 June	476	365
19 June thru 30 June	226	281
1 July thru 15 July	175	228

Table 6 -- Losses 15 July. Allied and German aircraft losses totaled 877 and 874 respectively by the end of July, notwithstanding the uneven pattern exhibited by the two protagonists.

Sunday 16 July

In the morning there was heavy cloud here and there with lots of sun too and this continued all day, but surprisingly, it was a day of very little aerial activity

In the twilight gloom in the vicinity of Vire south of St. Lô about 2010 hours, 12 aircraft of 403 Squadron tangled with nearly 50 Bf 109s of JG 3 and JG 52. Killed in this engagement was another ace -- Leutnant Friedrich Wachowiak who had 86 victories to his credit. Losses on 16 July were 17 to seven in favour of the Allies and Wachowiak's loss brought to six the total number of German super-aces killed.

Monday 17 July

There was heavy fog on Monday morning – fog that grounded all aircraft until the after noon. On the many bad weather days, squadrons could still carry out mine-laying or beach patrols because though forced by the cloud base to fly under a thousand feet, they were away from German flak, and by now the Allied naval gunners were starting to behave themselves. On this day, the fog was so thick that even beach patrols were out of the question until the fog lifted. When it did lift, all manner of aerial mission took off.

A large formation of B-26s of the US 9thAF hit the fuel dumps at Rennes accompanied by P-38s, some of whom carried napalm bombs for the first time and this day recorded another first – P-47s were fitted with rockets and sent out to do the same kind of damage as their Typhoon cousins.

The first dogfight of the day occurred as the clearing came about 1500 hours. Elements of three different FGs of the US 9thAF were attacking ground targets near St. Lô when they were bounced by the FW 190s of I./JG 11 and the Bf 109s of II./JG 1. The battle was a furious one that ranged south to Vire and north to Isigny as circling fighters tried to gain position over their opponents. At the end of the 30-minute engagement the Americans lost three P-51s – all from 353rd FS 354th FG, while two Bf 109s from II./JG 1 and four FW 190s from I./JG 11 were sent crashing to earth. Four of the six German pilots were killed. Claims for the American victories were made by 355th FS (P-51s), 365th FS (P-47s), and the 508th FS (P-47s).

Major Klaus Mietusch had 71 victories to his credit, nine of them having been chalked up since D-Day. At 1550 hours, in his Bf 109 G-6, he led a sweep by III./JG26 in the area between Caen and Argentan when he ran into a squadron of Spitfires believed to be 602 Squadron from 125 Wing. In the engagement S/L Le Roux claimed two Bf 109s, bringing his career total to 22 victories while Mietusch claimed one Spitfire, but had two of his pilots shot down and killed, two others injured and he was forced to crash-land back at his base thereby sustaining injuries. Despite his injury, Mietusch took off immediately afterward and claimed a Spitfire destroyed at 1640 hours, and indeed that correlates in time and place with a 403 Squadron Spitfire that was so seriously damaged that its wounded pilot got home only to have the aircraft written off. However, Mietusch was so weak from his injury that he was sent to hospital that evening and remained there for many weeks. Another super-ace was lost to the Luftwaffe – and one who could fight anyone from his Bf 109.

It was while returning from the bounce of Mietusch's Bf 109s by S/L Le Roux's Spitfires that 602 Squadron came upon a staff car with a motorcycle escort on the roads north of Flers. They attacked killing the driver, sending the staff car into the ditch and seriously wounding the occupant.[2] The occupant was none other than Generalfeldmarschall Erwin Rommel and the attack resulted in a severe concussion for Rommel and although he recovered slowly with time, he was never active again in the war and committed suicide in October.

About 1935 hours the other two Spitfire squadrons of 125 Wing – 441 and 453 – tackled the FW 190s of III./JG 54, and the Bf 109s of III./JG 26 – without Major Mietusch leading them. The 125 Wing pilots shot down three FW 190s and two Bf109s without loss to themselves. This brought the daily loss of Luftwaffe fighters and fighter-bombers to 20, while the Allied air forces lost 13.

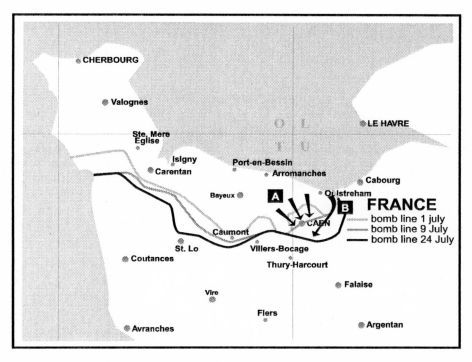

Figure 13 -- Bomb line 24 July. In the American sector to the west, progress was slow but continuous as the line was pushed south. In the British sector it was stalemated and forced ahead at great cost by Operation CHARNWOOD (A) 8 to 9 July, and by Operation GOODWOOD (B) 18 to 21 July. At this point in the campaign, the whole line was poised for a breakout.

Operation GOODWOOD

The first orders for the launch of an all-out attack of British armour aimed at driving through to Falaise were issued 13 July. Montgomery was under considerable pressure from Eisenhower, Churchill and the Air Chiefs to open up the flat country to the south-east of Caen. Original OVERLORD planning saw this as the best place to build the vital air bases the Allies would need. Instead, the Allies had been crowded into the bulging lodgement area, building air bases in every field that wasn't already piled high with equipment, fuel, ammunition, food or medical supplies.

By this time the eastern flank of the lodgement had been reinforced by the 79th British Armoured Division, the Guards Armoured Division, the 59th and 53rd British Infantry Divisions, the 2nd Canadian Division and much of the 4th Canadian Armoured Division. The Germans now realized they no longer needed forces in the Pas de Calais and moved several Fifteenth Army divisions south to join the defence. They had eight Panzer divisions and the remnants of nine Infantry divisions against the British and Canadians in the east, and three Panzer divisions and seven Infantry divisions opposing the Americans in the west. These forces were designated as the Fifth Panzer Army and the Seventh Army.

The Americans launched continuing drives to break out in the west, but between 7 July and 15 July they only managed to advance the bomb line by a few miles at a high cost in casualties -- this was the cost of fighting in bocage country. However, the fact that disturbed the German High Command most was that the port of Cherbourg opened up on 16 July. With a huge port the build-up of Allied material began to grow by leaps and bounds. Then on 18 July, the 29th and 2nd US Infantry Divisions pushed their way to the outskirts of a totally obliterated St. Lô.

Tuesday 18 July 1944

The morning of 18 July was clear and bright. Bombers of all types – heavy, medium and fighter-bombers -- dropped 7700 tons of bombs on selected targets along the 20-mile front north-east and south-west of Caen. The full weight of naval bombardment and massed artillery followed and then four armoured divisions flooded the flat country to the south-east of Caen, driving south with 600 tanks. The British and Canadian start line for Operation GOODWOOD was the Orne River. Crossing at the Pegasus bridges captured on D-Day, the British 7th Armoured Division, 11th Armoured Division and the Guards Armoured Division formed one massive force of tanks that turned right and smashed five miles south and west into German held territory parallel to the Orne River. The 3rd Canadian and 3rd British Infantry Divisions supported them. At the same time to the west of Caen, the newly arrived 2nd Canadian Infantry Division crossed the Orne in the face of intense opposition and spread out to link up with the British armour.

The tank battle was fierce, and although Typhoon rocket-firing aircraft redressed some of the difference against German Tiger and Panther tanks, the shootout cost the British 200 Sherman and Cromwell tanks and 1500 men in the first day alone. The second and third days of Operation GOODWOOD went from bad to worse as the 2nd Canadian Division was badly mauled while attempting to attack uphill at Verrières Ridge against a German defence of well entrenched machine gun and mortar posts and the tank slaughter continued. Casualties were 60% among some units -- throwing more troops in to bolster the attack drove the casualties even higher. Several companies were completely wiped out.

Heavy rain began on 20 July and worsened the next day. The Typhoons were grounded. In a deluge of rain and mud over a smoking battlefield, Operation GOODWOOD ground to an inglorious halt in driving rain 21 July at a cost of 6100 casualties, and 400 tanks -- although many were later repaired. The total gain moved the bomb line about nine miles at its deepest.

The first day of Operation GOODWOOD, the 2ndTAF flew 492 sorties in army support, 185 on armed recces, 817 on escort and patrol, and 156 spotting and reconnaissance.

Aerial encounters occurred in the early evening and were situated well south and well east of the raging armoured ground clash. At 0920 hours near Alençon, the P-47s of 388th FS 365th FG clashed with the Bf 109s of II./JG 3 and III./JG 3. Eight Bf 109s were destroyed while four P-47s were shot down.

Farther east near Evreux, three squadrons of P-38s of the 474th FG of the 9thAF plowed into a combined force of FW 190s and Bf 109s from a motley group of five different jagdgeschwaders when gruppen from JG 5, JG 54, and JG 1 were joined by II and III./JG 26. The P-38s claimed 11 enemy aircraft shot down – seven by the 428th FS and two each by the 429th FS and 430th FS. The Germans claimed they destroyed 12 P-38s, but when the shouting was over, the 474th FG recorded only four losses while the German units recorded a total of nine aircraft lost. Six of the nine German pilots were killed. Three of the American pilots were also killed.

Without knowing the details, there is evidence of a group of Spitfires claiming five more victories – no time or place is known. This is mentioned here only because IV./JG 52 – a new unit just introduced into the Normandy Campaign two days before -- recorded that it lost four of its Bf 109s to Spitfires on this day. Two of the German pilots were killed in the action.

By far the greatest aerial activity on this day was in the ground-to-air war. German flak units shot down two P-38s, six P-47s, one P-51, two B-26s, one Spitfire and 10 Typhoons. Total losses for the day were 21 for the Germans all due to aerial combat, and 33 for the Allies -- 11 due to aerial combat; 22 due to flak.

Though not appearing over the battlefield by day, the Luftwaffe did its best by night. During the hours of darkness the Luftwaffe mounted 103 sorties against the Allied front line positions and the Allied landing places at the Mulberry, the other beaches, and the newly opened port of Cherbourg.[3]

Wednesday 19 July

With the dawn came a change to more Normandy-like weather, although the heavy cloud and poor visibility of the morning gave way to clearing in the midafternoon. This change in weather severely curtailed Allied ground support of the armoured drive of Operation GOODWOOD and again the Luftwaffe failed to make an appearance over the front. The much quieter day in the air was a rank contrast with the ferocious struggle on the ground where the assault was losing momentum.

At 2020 hours east of the battle area, the Typhoons of 266 Squadron were attacking ground targets when the Bf 109s of I./JG 5 and of II./JG 3 set upon them. Although the German pilots claimed many times the number, only three Typhoons were shot down – all pilots killed. A tactical reconnaissance Mustang from 168 Squadron was also shot down, though its pilot parachuted to safety. The Germans lost two Bf 109s in the engagement.

Thursday 20 July

Trying to keep the assault going, Bomber Command sent its Lancasters to hit the German defensive positions while 226 Spitfires escorted them. Typhoons flew 121 support sorties while 93 Spitfires, 40 Typhoons and 30 Mustangs flew armed recces. Three Spitfire wings leapt into the air in early afternoon, and recorded victories. At 1300 hours near Argentan, 401, 411 and 412 Squadrons of 126 Wing shot down eight FW 190s of II./JG 1 with no loss of their own. Five pilots were killed and one taken prisoner.

At 1540 hours south of Argentan, 132 and 453 Squadrons of 125 Wing scored two victories while testing cannon. W/C Geoffrey Page claimed one Bf 109 from II./JG 3, bringing his Normandy total to five and his career total to 11.

Ten minutes later over Caen, 443 Squadron bounced a gaggle of FW 190s and chased two of them to Lisieux before claiming victories

-- one each for S/L Wally McLeod (his 20th) and for F/L Larry Robillard (his 7th).

But things were not going well on the ground. As the weather deteriorated so did the fortunes of Operation GOODWOOD. Heavy rain and thick cloud moved in, grounded the Typhoons, battered the coast and drenched the land. It was another large storm like the one that struck a month earlier causing such havoc.

Friday 21 July

Everything was grounded by the ferocious storm.

Saturday 22 July

The storm appeared to have ended by Saturday morning, but then a heavy rain set in and continued all day. Even beach patrols were cancelled at 1000 hours after flying a mere 22 sorties.

Sunday 23 July

Rain at some times blowing heavily, continued all night and by first light it was clear this was no day to begin a new assault. Operation COBRA against St. Lô was planned to begin this day, but like D-Day it was delayed one day.

Monday 24 July

The weather was still not good the following day, but the bombers of the US 8thAF took off in worsening conditions anyway. Most were called back, but 350 heavy bombers continued on to their targets and dropped bombs on St. Lô in less than satisfactory cloud conditions thereby inflicting many casualties on US troops because the bombing was 2200 yards short of the target. They hit troops of the 30th Infantry Division – one bomber actually dropped its load on the airbase of the 404th FG, at A.5 Chipelle killing four, wounding 14 and destroying two P-47s. But these casualties were nothing compared to the number of dead and wounded soldiers of the US 30th Infantry Division. It was the heavy bombers of the US 8thAF this day, but it was to be the B-26s of the US 9thAF the next day.

In a day of very moderate aerial activity, two large dogfights took place. The first started at 1420 hours between Caumont and Vire, the P-47s of 509th, 510th and 511th FSs of the 9thAF's 405th FG happened upon the Bf 109s of II./JG 2 attempting a rocket attack on American positions while the FW 190s of III./JG 2 were flying cover. The Americans waded in and shot down two Bf 109s and five FW 190s. When I./ JG 27 tried to intervene, they lost three more Bf 109s. In all, seven German pilots were killed and three became prisoners of war. No P-47s were lost.

An hour later two patrolling Spitfire squadrons – 12 aircraft of 412 Squadron and four aircraft of 453 Squadron -- approached Caen from different directions. They met and found themselves flying directly over 20 Bf 109s of JG 3. They promptly dove and dispatched seven of them to the ground in flames. On this same mission a Spitfire of 453 Squadron was shot down by the friendly fire of a P-47 and its pilot was killed.

Operation COBRA

The day GOODWOOD ended, Bradley presented a plan for Operation COBRA – the American break-out through St. Lô. Hurriedly, Montgomery ordered the Canadians to launch an assault concurrent with COBRA to ensure no German armour would be diverted the moment COBRA began. Operation COBRA was planned to begin 23 July with the now-standard carpet bombing by heavy bombers of the US 8thAF. But heavy rain caused a delay of one day.

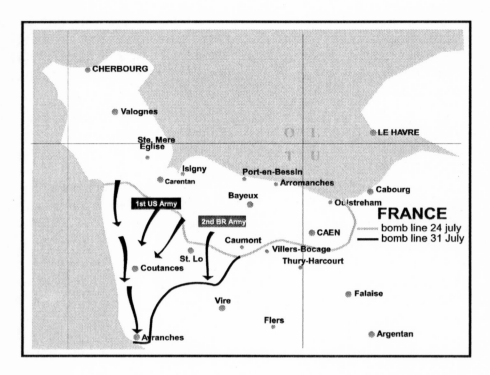

Figure 14 -- Bomb line 31 July. *The full weight of the US First Army burst through crumbling German defences west of St. Lô 25 July. Three armoured divisions and seven infantry divisions drove south. They took Coutances 28 July and entered Avranches 31 July. Meanwhile the British break-out paralleled it driving half way to Vire by 31 July and meeting the Americans at Vire 6 August.*

Tuesday 25 July

Operation COBRA actually began at first light. Eight groups of fighter-bombers strafed an area 7000 yards by 250 yards for half an hour -- the planes flew one group after another, with one squadron after another -- each squadron separated by three minutes attacking alternately the eastern area and the western area. Then 1507 B-17 and B-24 heavy bombers of the US 8thAF dropped 3300 tons of bombs saturating an expanse one-mile wide and five-miles long, followed by seven more groups of fighter-bombers strafing, bombing and napalm bombing as well. The timing for this was H-Hour – 1100 hours, when the troops began to advance. Immediately, 42 B-26s of the US 9thAF inadvertently dropped their loads short of the bomb line and killed 102 and wounded 380 troops of the 30th US Division.[4] Between the two days' bombing by friendly forces, the 30th Infantry Division incurred 700 casualties.

The assault began after the bombing. At first it looked as though the German defence would hold, but by noon some American troops had outstripped the defensive positions far to the west and found they had punctured the German lines. The German defenders were confused and disorganized after the bombing, and it became apparent to the American field officers that the air strikes had destroyed the German communication system.

Meanwhile, at the eastern end of the Allied line, the Canadians mounted an attack called Operation SPRING intended to ensure that no armour was diverted from the Caen sector to reinforce the sagging St. Lô defence. Every available fighter and fighter-bomber from the USAAF and 2ndTAF patrolled along the front south and east of the action and created a curtain to ensure no enemy aircraft appeared over St. Lo – and none did.

A wing of Spitfires was at Rouen and Pont l'Éveque, where it destroyed five Bf 109s from JG 1 and JG 5. In this engagement Hauptmann Weissenberger claimed two Spitfires bringing his total to 200, but only one Spitfire was lost by 127 Wing. A wing of RAF Mustangs – 122 Wing – was at Dreux taking on and destroying more Bf 109s of II./JG 3. And at Paris the 357th FG of the US 8thAF shot down two more Bf 109s of III./JG 26. All of these engagements occurred between 1100 hours and 1200 hours.

In the afternoon, the P-47s of the 407th FS of the US 9thAF hammered JG 1 FW 190s over Lisieux while two other FGs were holding the line at Alençon and south at Laval and Rennes. Sporadic clashes of aircraft occurred in the late afternoon and evening from Evreux, L'Aigle and Argentan, and they all served to keep the Luftwaffe away from the ground fighting. Losses for the day were 26 for the Luftwaffe, 25 for the Allies.

The American forces broke through the German lines west of St Lô and headed for Coutances. It was the first time since D-Day that the German defences had been completely severed.

Wednesday 26 July

The weather was much improved and all along the Allied lines a steady stream of fighter-bombers went forth to hit everything that could be an obstacle to the advancing army units. The US 9thAF flew 56 eight-aircraft armed recces as well as supporting the troops. The 2ndTAF flew 36 squadron-strength Spitfire armed recces while 224 Typhoons flew army support missions and another 220 Spitfires flew patrols. This was an all-out effort; this was the break-out.

Over Avranches at 1430 hours, the 353rd FS of the 354th FG, attacked JG 27 and destroyed nine Bf 109s while losing just one of its P-51s. Other engagements occurred over Argentan and Chartres, but like the preceding day very little of the aerial fighting was over the advancing American troops.

Thursday 27 July

Weary pilots bombed, strafed and fought until darkness and then were up at the crack of dawn to start again. At 0700 hours between Caen and Falaise, FW 190s and Bf 109s of JG 1, JG 26 and JG 54 – over 70 aircraft – clashed with 416 Squadron Spitfires and 122 Squadron Mustangs. For nearly 35 minutes the confusing whirl of aircraft ebbed, flowed, spiralled down and climbed for height and position. The moment it ended, the two Allied squadrons counted the burning wreckage of seven German machines and one of their own. Five FW 190s had been sent down in flames, as had two Bf 109s. In this engagement Oberstleutnant Ihelfeld, Gruppekommodore of JG 1 claimed a Mustang bringing his career total to 121.

An hour later 401 Squadron shot down three Bf 109s near Lisieux. After that it was US 366th FG's turn at St. Lô, then RAF 441 Squadron's turn at Vimoutiers, the US 508th FS at Granville, RAF

442 Squadron at Lisieux, and so it went until darkness fell and day-fighter activity came to an end.

Finally the aircraft filtered back to their bases and landed in total darkness. The day had been true to form, this time with the Germans losing aircraft to Allied pilots while Allied pilots were brought down by German flak. In the three days of intense fighting over the St. Lô break-out, 68 German and 75 Allied aircraft had been destroyed. Of the Allied losses, 51 were brought down by anti-aircraft fire; of the 68 German losses only 10 were brought down by Allied ground gunners. So in aerial combat it was 58 German losses compared to 24 Allied losses.

Friday 28 July

It rained Friday morning, but quickly cleared around noon and returned Normandy to the long-overdue summer weather.

When the German defence line crumbled, Bradley seized the opportunity to pour his 2nd, 3rd and 4th US Armoured Divisions through the breach with orders to drive their tanks to Avranches 35 miles away. He instructed them to keep continuous pressure on the enemy so that the German forces could not regroup. By 28 July the armoured forces were 15 miles into German-held territory capturing Coutances, and three days later the 4th US Armoured Division drove into Avranches nearly unopposed.

Pockets of decimated German units were everywhere, but their communications were destroyed and their efforts disorganized. About 1510 hours the three squadrons of the 405th FG were released from the armed recce missions they were supposed to be flying because they had found a large concentration of German vehicles under the overhanging trees and hidden in the many valleys that laced the countryside around the small village of Gavray. They established a continuous attack, squadron after squadron strafing and bombing for 15 minutes each for six hours until darkness brought the activity to a halt. In that period they claimed 400 vehicles and 12 tanks destroyed.[5]

By late afternoon the Luftwaffe began appearing. Miscellaneous sections of JG 2, JG 3, JG 26 and JG 52 flew into the battle area and were met near Vire by two squadrons of the 354th FG. Seven Bf 109s were shot while 355th FS lost one P-51 and its pilot.

Far to the east over Lisieux at 1900 hours, six Spitfires of 416 Squadron of 127 Wing were on patrol when they engaged III./JG 54 and sent three FW 190s to the ground. An hour later another six Spitfires from 416 on the succeeding patrol, met and destroyed another FW 190.

Saturday 29 July

Now came the British break-out. Wheeling several armoured divisions around in a great right hook, the British units struck south parallel to, but further to the east of Bradley's troops racing south towards Avranches. The British objectives were the town of Vire and the tactical advantage of Mont Pinçon, the highest peak in Normandy. The 2ndTAF flew 384 sorties in support of this action.

There was only one small aerial battle far to the east at Evreux. There the Mustangs of 65 Squadron of 122 Wing shot down a Bf 109 but lost one of their own in exchange.

Sunday 30 July

The weather continued to be lovely. American and British troops rushed to maximize their gains while the German defensive machine was reeling from the break-out. Armed recces were sent to every bridge and marshalling yard, medium and heavy bombers pounded fuel dumps and ammunition dumps in Rennes, Le Mans, Chartres and Evreux and reconnaissance flights doubled in intensity to try to detect where the German might stiffen their defence or mount a counter-attack. And to protect all this activity, a myriad of patrols and escort sorties were flown over the whole Normandy landscape.

This Sunday saw three tussles of consequence. In the first at 1430 hours at Avranches, the P-47s of 81st FS exchanged victories with two gruppen of JG 1 as the Germans gave up three FW 190s and managed to destroy two P-47s. The second occurred between Avranches and Montagne at 1530 hours, Canadian Spitfires and American P-47s teamed up to send two FW 190s down in flames. The Canadian victory earned S/L McLeod of 443 Squadron his 21st claim.

In the third engagement the results are very confusing with three gruppen recording the loss of aircraft but at a time and location that doesn't seem to fit with anything. It is also possible that some of the seven aircraft – four Bf 109s and three FW 190s were shot down by flak. But for the day, the Germans lost 13 while the Allies lost 20.

Monday 31 July

Early in the morning Bradley's armoured units entered Avranches took control of the city and prepared for further penetration. Before the day was out, Lt Gen George Patton was given command of the Third US Army, while Omar Bradley commanded the First US Army and retained overall command of both. Patton, now with four armoured divisions and as many supporting infantry divisions, was turned loose and the next day sent his 4th US Armoured Division charging into Brittany. The great break-out was a fait accompli; the great end-run was about to begin.

For Hitler and the German high command the final blow was about to come. Patton was considered by Hitler to be the Allies' most accomplished general. Whereas Montgomery was seen as brilliant, he was thought too ponderous; Patton was seen as brash, impulsive and forever aggressive – just the kind of general to make a stampede across Europe and into Germany. It had been Patton, continuously reported in Kent waiting with a huge army to cross at the Pas de Calais, who caused Hitler to hold his Fifteenth Army there.

By the end of July the two opposing air forces had lost nearly the same number of fighters, fighter-bombers and medium bombers. The Luftwaffe had lost a total of 1097 in Normandy – 646 in June and 451 in July. The Allies lost 1110 – 702 in June and 408 in July. The US 8thAF fighter and fighter-bomber activity was much reduced in July. The breakdown of Allied losses is as follows:

	2 TAF	US Ninth	US Eighth	Total
6 June thru 30 June	322	255	125	702
1 July thru 31 July	193	186	29	408
Total	515	441	154	1110

Table 7 -- Losses 31 July. *Overall aircraft losses between the Allies and the Germans were 1110 to 1097. Within the Allies' groups, the American losses were only slightly higher than the British losses.*

Chapter Five – Mortain and the Falaise Pocket

German Counter-attack

Hitler's reaction to the American breakout combined with the failure of the British and Canadians to gain much of an advance south of Caen, was almost predictable. He believed his eastern flank was secure and immediately ordered von Kluge to gather as much armour as could be mustered, form a new unit and drive due west, straight through the American lines north of Domfront, through Mortain and Avranches to the sea. By so doing, the German Army would cut off

Figure 15 -- P-47. The Republic P-47 Thunderbolt was the mainstay fighter of the USAAF until the P-51D came along. These P-47s of 81st FS of the 50th FG of the US 9thAF were located at A-10 Carentan.
(National Archives and Records Administration)

Patton in the south from Bradley in the north and Patton's army, without supplies or reinforcements, would have to surrender. Hitler refused to believe this could not be done – any questioning of the assault's success was treason. Von Kluge knowing the weaknesses of his army, thought this attack was doomed to failure, however, at the same time that von Kluge received the order to attack Mortain, he received word that Hitler believed him to be part of the murder conspiracy. Von Kluge was in an impossible position, he could do nothing but order the attack and implore his commanders to execute the order promptly and completely.

Tuesday 1 August

The weather in late July had been delightful with much welcome sunlight and warm summer temperatures. Of course there was a price to pay. When the rain stopped, the dust on the runways of the ALGs in France once again rose in billows 30 to 50 feet high, and the noses and throats of all airmen took on the permanent grittiness they had remembered from June. After a week of clear sunny weather came the sultry part of a Normandy summer -- 1 August dawned with heavy, muggy ground fog that reduced visibility to nearly zero, and left one with the thought this is going to be a sticky one. By noon the fog had lifted, but everywhere was a haze nearly as devastating to pilots' visibility. No one could fly until afternoon.

At 1445 hours near l'Aigle, there was an encounter between the 357th FS and 358th FS of the US 8thAF's 355th FG and two units of JG 1 – Stab./JG 1 and III./JG 1. Two Bf 109s of III./JG 1 were shot down, although only one claim was made by the Americans. Hauptmann Ihlefeld shot down a P-51 of the 358th FS claiming his 123rd victory, and three pilots of III./JG 1 each claimed a P-51 victory. But the records are contradictory, for the 357th did lose three P-51s, but their records show one lost due to mechanical failure and two to flak. From whatever source, the net result was four Americans shot down, three of whom died and one evaded -- two Germans shot down one died the other's fate is unknown.

This result was reversed an hour later when at Tours, well south of Le Mans, 12 P-51s of the 353rd FS of the 9thAF shot down four Bf 109s of I and IV./JG 27. One of the successful Americans, Lt Anderson became an ace by claiming his 5th victory.

Nineteenth Tactical Air Force

The nature of the campaign had shifted. While Bradley's First Army moved ahead pushing the Germans back, Patton's Third Army was to try an end run. The US 9thAF was split into two parts to permit the Nineteenth Tactical Air Force – an identifiable component of the 9thAF from the beginning – to support Patton's driving armoured push to take Brittany and drive east to Paris. Leading the differentiated US 19thAF was Brig Gen Otto Weyland. With this change in command came a change in ground support methodology. Both the 9thAF and 2ndTAF had been trying to develop a method of placing air force personnel – preferably pilots -- in with army counterparts in command vehicles at the battle scene. The idea was to develop direct, on-the-spot, ground control by radio contact between the command vehicle and aircraft immediately overhead. For all kinds of reasons the idea had never worked in the static confines of the Allied lodgement, but with Patton's impending race to drive his armour deep into German-held territory, it was mandatory that it be made to work -- he had to be assured that his flanks were secure, and that he knew what was waiting around the next bend. The 19thAF P-47s gave him this power.

Wednesday 2 August

It was the start of a pattern – Wednesday's weather was a repeat of Tuesday's. Indeed, the first 10 days of August would see this pattern recur most mornings. The ground fog was so dense that it was 1400 hours before operations could get seriously underway.

Two minor skirmishes occurred around Argentan and both saw Spitfires trading victories with the Luftwaffe.

Thursday 3 August

At this point in the aerial battle of Normandy, there was a nearly comic interlude. After trying to bomb and mine Allied ships with little success, the Germans tried to launch a small fleet of miniature submarines against the congested shipping spread out across the Channel to the Allied lodgement. The 2ndTAF was called upon to team up with the Navy to deal with the new menace. Suddenly, on 3 August amidst the continuing accumulation of dry statistics in the headquarters daily log at Uxbridge – statistics that repeated endlessly the number of sorties flown by each category of aerial operation – a curious item was almost buried;

> "29 Mitchells attacked Serqueux marshalling yards, 24 Mitchells attacked Abancourt. From the UK 139 Spitfires escorted Halifax bombers of Bomber Command to bomb three No-ball targets, 34 tactical reconnaissance sorties were flown. From France 132 (Squadron) Spitfires destroyed 6 midget submarines out of 16." [1]

The story behind this rather bizarre entry is told in the ORB for 125 Wing.

> "Quite a considerable amount of excitement added spice to the first series of low patrols flown by 132 Squadron from 0634 (hours). The spice no less than the presence of German midget submarines and human torpedoes attempting to attack our shipping in the sea from the Orne Estuary. On this first patrol 132 (Squadron) made attacks on 11 of the midget subs and claim them destroyed. Further patrols yielded a further bag of five more midget subs. No human torpedoes were seen but some of our smaller vessels were seen unloading depth charges in the area and on the 1126 (hours) patrol flown by 453 (Squadron) no more of these Hun nuisances were reported, but the Navy was seen liberally sprinkling the infested area with depth charges." [2]

Note how Headquarters never gets it right – 16 midget subs destroyed while HQ only gives the hard-working front-liners credit for six of them.

In the American sector, General Patton was plunging deep into enemy territory and the US 19thAF soon learned to have on-the-spot support P-47s peeking around the next bend and advising the racing tanks of Patton's armour when to slow down, and where the next resistance point would be.

At 1130 hours the Spitfires of 401 Squadron tackled the Bf 109s of II./JG 3 and sent four down in flames.

After a quiet afternoon, at 1900 hours the 379th FS of the 9thAF bagged a FW 190 and a Bf 109, and at 1930 hours F/L Lindsay of 403 Squadron shot down a Bf 109 – his 5th in Normandy and the 6th of his career.

Friday 4 August

In the after-midnight hours before the ground fog set in, the Germans renewed their effort to hit Allied shipping and ammunition dumps. This brought out the night-fighting Mosquitos of 140, 141 and 147 Wings which claimed the destruction of five Ju 88s, for the loss of three Mosquitos. Two RAF aircrew members were killed, the other four landing safely.

The increased number of reconnaissance flights reported more activity on the German side of the line – particularly in the area around Caumont and Flers. As yet unconfirmed to the Allied High Command, Hitler had made up his mind to counter-attack through Mortain to Avranches, and what the recce pilots were seeing was the assemblage of armour from the eastern part of the German defence line deployed to the western part.

The morning haze lasted well into mid-afternoon. This naturally curtailed much aerial battle activity, but several hurriedly-arranged bombing missions attacked army designated targets and on barges, bridges and other conveyances spanning the Seine. The 2ndTAF flew 873 sorties; the US 9thAF flew over one thousand. At days' end the Luftwaffe had lost 12 aircraft, the Allies 19.

Saturday 5 August

Again the early hour activity was quite intense with four Ju 88s claimed by Mosquitos while losing just one. The Americans ground forces advanced south and took Mortain.

Flying above the heavy blanket of fog, P-38s of 429th FS 474th FG, found a bit of a hole near Compeigne north of Paris and through the hole, far below them were a dozen FW 190s of II./JG 1. Diving from the sun they shot down two in one pass before the German formation dispersed and disappeared into the haze.

But it was not a day of dogfights, rather a day of bombing targets that were critical for the tactical requirements of the army or for the logistic counter-move -- the ever-increasing efforts of the Germans to launch their counter-attack.

Sunday 6 August

Sunday was another day of heavy ground mist that hid everything until noon. A few hundred feet in the air the visibility was satisfactory, but if one ever got up, one could never land. This condition was a great help to the German army as it hurriedly assembled as much armour as it could to launch the assault against Mortain. Sensing an impending counter-attack, the 2ndTAF and the 9thAF sent out every available Mitchell and B-26 to bomb ammunition dumps at Alençon through the cloud, the marshalling yards at Mézidon and assumed tank concentrations at Argentan and Domfront.

Figure 16 -- Typhoon. *This is a Hawker Typhoon 1b of 193 Squadron at its base at Hurn in the UK. It is about to be armed with rockets for a sortie over France.*
(Canadian Forces Photo PL42738)

Heavy bombers from the US 8thAF and RAF Bomber Command hit Paris and its suburbs with massive raids. These raids attracted a large crowd of German fighters -- between 1215 hours and 1230 hours, the Bf 109s of III./JG 26 attacked and destroyed seven RAF Lancasters and Halifaxes, while four other gruppen – the FW 190s of III./JG 54 and the Bf 109s of I./JG 5, II./JG 3 and II and III./JG 1 shot down 11 US 8thAF B-17s and B-24s. The Norwegian 132 Wing, consisting of 127, 331 and 332 Squadrons, flying escort to the bombers waded into the German fighters and claimed three, but the bombers must have defended themselves well for a total of nine German fighters were destroyed – six Bf 109s and three FW 190s. Amongst the German pilots shot down this day was Leutnant Mors of I./JG 5. He claimed a B-17 – 60th of his career – but then had to bale out of his severely damaged machine. He was unhurt and immediately returned to his unit.

Two-and-a-half hours later over Dreux, the P-47s of the 512th FS traded victories with the Bf 109s of II and III./JG 3 – the Germans losing three while the Americans lost one.

But for this day most Allied activity centred upon armed recces and army support missions. Typhoons gave much support to the British troops holding Mont Pinçon while Mustangs shot up hundreds of barges transporting troops and supplies across the Seine.

That afternoon, Allied headquarters received an ULTRA intercept that confirmed that the German counter-attack would consist of portions of over five armoured divisions led by the mighty 2nd SS Panzer Division, that the assault would begin during the night of the sixth and seventh and targetted against Mortain.

Monday 7 August

During the night of 6/7 August, four German divisions attacked east of Mortain.[3] Von Kluge's 2nd SS Panzer division had a fearsome reputation of achieving fanatical victories and was near full strength. His 1st SS Panzer Division was depleted but still formidable, while two infantry divisions, the 116th German Infantry and the 2nd German Infantry were reinforced with additional armour from what was left of the Panzer Lehr division.[4] The Germans struck at Mortain and drove ten miles into the American lines. They did so in thick ground fog that was as effective as a smoke screen. The American 30th Infantry Division who bore the brunt of the attack fell back but left a large force holding Hill 317 in Mortain completely surrounded by German tanks. They called for aerial support from the rocket-firing RAF Typhoons, but nothing could fly in the fog. At first it was feared the fog would completely foil the Typhoons, but at noon the fog miraculously lifted and the 2ndTAF Typhoons attacked and destroyed somewhere between 40 and 80 German tanks.

Back at 2ndTAF Headquarters at Uxbridge this is the way they saw it;

> "On the morning of the 7 August, it was evident that the Germans had decided to mount an all out counterattack to attempt to cut through the American supply artery feeding the whole of the

Brittany and south campaigns at the narrow Avranches gap. It was a desperate bid which, if successful, would have had a serious effect upon the whole American sector, and upon the strategy of the whole Western Europe Campaign. It was soon obvious that the German counterattack was a full scale effort as the remnants of five Panzer divisions were engaged, consisting of an estimated strength of 250 tanks. Obviously the Hun had drawn upon all available armour to launch the 'last fling' counterattack in the western sector and the relatively thin American ground strength in this area required the use of maximum tactical air strength to blunt the German cutting edge of attack.

"Air Marshall Coningham of 2nd TAF conferred with the Ninth USAAF and it was agreed that the RAF tank-destroying rocket Typhoons should deal exclusively with the tanks and armoured concentrations, whilst the American fighters and fighter-bombers should operate further afield to prevent the enemy aircraft from interfering and also to destroy transport and communications leading up to the battle area.

"The weather for once was favourable. It was the first occasion in Normandy when the air forces had the opportunity of striking at a real German armoured concentration. It was also a situation that required speed and flexibility of air striking power. Here was an imminent fluid battle in which the use of sledge-hammer blows by heavy bombers was not practical. No fixed positions existed to be obliterated, it was a battle of armoured columns striking with speed and mobility. The TAF Typhoons adopted (a) shuttle-service and as the day developed it was evident that air history was being made. As the tempo of the attacks increased so did the morale of the tank crews diminish, and at the height of the battle it was being noticed that the Germans were not waiting to stand our fire. The sound of the Typhoons approaching was enough to make them abandon their tanks and scamper as fast as their legs would carry them and as far from their armour as they could.

"By mid-afternoon there was so much dust and debris in the battle area that the Typhoons could not operate. Advantage was then taken of the flexibility of the TAF force. A small enemy counter was developing in the British sector east of Vire, and the Typhoons were switched to that area. Very speedily they disposed of five tanks and broke up the threat. By this time they were able to resume their tank destruction in the Mortain area and continued the offensive until dusk. When they saw the American armour and anti-tank screens engage the spearheads of the German columns the Typhoons then struck at the middle and the rear elements of the enemy.

"The total statistical assessment of the RAF rocket-firing Typhoons was, 89 tanks destroyed and 56 probably destroyed, a total of 145. In addition there was the claim of 56 damaged. The day's score in enemy motor transport was 104 flamers, 47 smokers and 81 damaged. Of much greater significance was the overall result. The Allied Tactical Air Forces had not merely blunted the edge of the enemy counterattack. They had effectively destroyed its strength and purpose."[5]

Soon after the battle, a British Operations Research team went to the scene to chronicle results and measure the effectiveness of the attack. They found that more tanks were abandoned than were destroyed and of those destroyed, more were attributed to anti-tank gunfire than to rocket fire. There have been many who have used this evidence to belittle the effectiveness of the rocket attack by Typhoons, but as shown in the 2ndTAF report, those facts were known at the time. The Typhoons were so feared by the German tank crews (especially the less-experienced ones) that they abandoned their tanks and ran as soon as they heard the engine of a Typhoon. When a few tanks were abandoned or destroyed, no vehicle in the armoured columns could move, and rather than wait to be picked off by anti-tank guns, more tanks were abandoned. No matter how one looks at it, the Typhoons broke up the massed armoured attack, and the defeat of that attack spelt the loss of the battle of Mortain, and ultimately the battle of Normandy for the Germans.

While the Typhoons attacked the German armour, the USAAF true to commitment, headed off German aircraft before they got too close. At Chartres, the P-47s of 396th FS, 368th FG, shot down three Bf 109s of II./JG 26 at 1510 hours, and the P-51s of 353rd FS, 354th FG, shot down three more that had managed to get all the way to Domfront.

Another battle between the P-47s of 379th FS and III./JG 51 resulted in two FW 190s destroyed at Le Mans at 1555.

At 1925 hours at Chartres, the FW 190s and Bf 109s of I./JG 26, II./JG 3 and I./JG 1 suffered a loss of six aircraft at the hands of the 411th FS and 412th FS of the 373rd FG. In all these battles the Americans lost seven aircraft shot down, but they lost twice that number to flak. RAF losses to flak were five Typhoons, four Spitfires and a Mustang.

Just before midnight of this day a thousand RAF bombers blanketed the area south of Caen with 3,462 tons of bombs and this was followed by the advance of the armour of the First Canadian Army. A new assault, called Operation TOTALIZE, was launched.

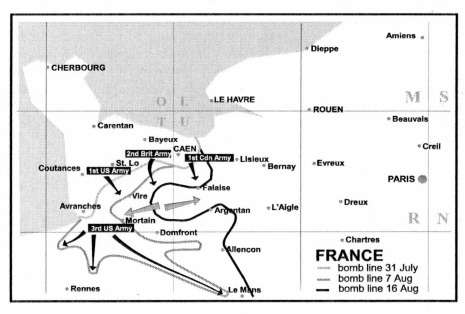

*Figure 17 -- **Bomb line 16 August**. Patton sent forces into Brittany to take Brest and Rennes and turned the rest east. By 7 August when von Kluge counter-attacked at Mortain, Patton was near Le Mans. When the counter-attack failed, the Allies began to tighten the noose.*

The German Defence

To this point in time the German defence plan had been excellent. In the west where the Americans had to fight field-by-field through

145

the bocage country, a small number of defenders could hold much larger forces at bay. In the east in the valley of the Orne and south-east of Caen, the land was rolling and much more open. It was the kind of country that allowed ample manoeuvring room for tanks and artillery-supported troops. Immediately south-east of Caen was a series of three ridges that stretched -- each higher than the one before -- across the route to Falaise. The first was Verrières Ridge that had a well-defined reverse slope and was riddled with abandoned mine shafts. It stretched two or three miles to either side of the main road. Beyond Verrières was a second ridge and beyond that a third between Caen and Falaise, with each ridge offering a reverse slope upon which the Germans concentrated their artillery and heavy mortars. They laid out artillery aiming points, mortar concentration points and machine-gun fields of fire for first, second and third lines of defence. If a part of a line should sag or crumble before an Allied attack, the next defensive position behind it was already in place and ready to swing into relief. Looking south from Caen the country to the south seems flat, but looking back towards Caen in the north, every ridge afforded an excellent view of any action made by the British and Canadian forces.

In addition to well thought out positions, the Germans had 40 Tiger tanks and 50 Panther tanks ready to throw into any engagement that might threaten the defence.[6] They also had 1600 field guns and mortars and three brigades of Nebelwurfers. These latter were large multiple-barrelled mortars with six to ten barrels capable of firing rocket-powered projectiles several miles. The projectiles were huge – some weighing 280 pounds. The Allied troops called them Moaning Minnies from the swoosh upon firing and a wailing sound in flight. They landed with the impact of large artillery shells, and were very demoralizing.

This was the defensive set-up against which the frontal assault of the Canadians and British was hurled, holding them in check for fifty days. In hindsight however, once the Allies had broken out at St Lô, the best move for the Germans would have been to fall back – perhaps to the Seine – and set up a similar defensive line. The attack at Mortain was a useless waste of dwindling German armour that doomed both the German Seventh and Fifth Panzer Armies to destruction.

The German position in Normandy was hopeless. Von Kluge, in a decision that flew in the face of Hitler's orders, sanctioned the withdrawal of non-combatant German units on 10 August. For the first time since D-Day the flow of men and materials across the Seine reversed.

Reorganization

Throughout the Normandy Campaign it had been the intention of the planners to have one major airborne assault that would leap-frog well behind enemy lines and create a great move forward. Those who follow the account of the Allied conquest of north-western Europe know that this eventually was tried at Nijmegen, Eindhoven and Arnhem. It had been intended to use this tactic to bypass the defences at Caen and push into the flat country south-east of that city, however after the sound thrashing at Villers-Bocage and particularly after the disappointment of Operation EPSOM, leap-frog airborne plans were temporarily forgotten. Now, sensing victory in Normandy, the military planners guessed that the Germans would likely fall back well north of Paris, so perhaps the leap-frog idea was still a good one. US Lt Gen Brereton was given the job of forming a new First Allied Airborne Army by taking over all the troop-carrying wings from the 9thAF. His replacement as the new commander of the US 9thAF was Maj Gen Hoyt Vandenberg.

Tuesday 8 August

After the usual morning mist, Tuesday became a scorcher. The German counterattack had been stopped but not driven back, and there was ferocious fighting that carried on for four more days. However the initiative had passed from German hands to the Americans.

To the south, Patton's Third US Army entered Le Mans. Aerial activity continued to be armed recces and specific army support targets; aerial encounters were piece-meal and of little consequence. But the effort now had two foci – Mortain and the road to Falaise. Aerial losses were low -- 14 and 13 for the Germans and Allies respectively.

Wednesday 9 August

Wednesday was another muggy scorcher like Tuesday. On the ground, the Germans tried one last time to gather their troops and push forward to Avranches but their armour was half gone and the communications and coordination were lacking. By day's end they obtained permission to withdraw.

If anything, the army support was stepped up a notch and 350 Typhoon sorties in army support and an additional 147 on armed recces. Over 100 sorties were flown by Spitfires and Mustangs against barges and other vessels on the Seine.

There was just one aerial battle of consequence when, at 1800 hours, the P-47s of 378th FS, 362nd FG, battled JG 26 and JG 54 over Chartres and bested them by destroying two FW 190s and two Bf 109s without loss to themselves.

Thursday 10 August

The tenth was the day that the Germans started pulling back their forces from the aborted attack at Mortain. They made one more assault, but since they could see no chance of victory, they fell back. It was a beautiful sunny day, but German commanders felt none of the inner warmth that was experienced by their enemy.

The Commander-in-Chief of the Allied Air Forces, ACM Leigh-Mallory issued the orders that US 9thAF would now operate south of the line Vire-Argentan-Dreux-Mantes-Arras-Boulogne – while the 2ndTAF would operate north of the line. The 19thAF would devote all its attention to the speeding armoured columns led by General Patton, with a particular eye to enemy flanking movements.

At this time the Mustangs of 122 Wing and 133 Wing were directed to the Seine to sink barges, while the six Typhoon wings were directed to re-visit all the bridges and road junctions, they still had time to fly 315 sorties in support of the army. 106 Spitfires flew escort to Lancasters bombing all the known fuel dumps in and around Paris.

Operation TOTALIZE

A reorganization of Allied forces gave Canadian Lt Gen Crerar command of the First Canadian Army comprising British, Canadian and Polish units. Although exhausted from the pounding they received at Verrières Ridge and the surrounding towns, a new initiative was being planned for this new army. Three separate exercises – EPSOM, CHARNWOOD and GOODWOOD -- had failed to gain ground on the way to Falaise, and the price for each had been a great loss of life. Now Crerar ordered one of his corps commanders, Lt Gen Guy Simonds – a man with a reputation for innovative planning -- to launch a new attack to be called Operation TOTALIZE. Simonds concluded that the massed armour of Operation GOODWOOD had failed because there was no infantry to counter the expertly placed enemy anti-tank gun positions. By contrast, the other assaults had been launched with insufficient armour. Simonds decided that a large armoured attack had to be launched by troops protected by armoured vehicles. He ordered the howitzers to be stripped from Priest tanks and turned into armoured troop carriers. With the gun removed, these Priest tanks were immediately dubbed 'Unfrocked Priests'.

Simonds also changed the pattern of the attack. Up until now, all infantry attacks had been preceded by a devastating bombardment by heavy bombers followed by several hours of intense field artillery. Only after this period did the assault troops pour across the start line. But in every case, the temporary demoralization caused by the bombing, diminished during the period of the artillery barrage, so that as the troops started out across the start line, German artillery reigned down on them, and the German infantry was ready to fight. This time Simonds planned a heavy carpet bombing throughout the night with the assault launched right after the bombing. Artillery would come into play only well after the assaulting force was past the start line.

The day after the Germans attacked Mortain, Operation TOTALIZE was launched. After midnight, the morning of 7 August, 2300 bombers from USAAF 8thAF and RAF Bomber Command pounded the area. As the central part of the carpet bombing strip was cleared by virtue of the bombers shifting to the extremities right and left, the tanks and armoured troop carriers started out before dawn. Their goal was not just to take Verrieres Ridge, but to punch through it and over-run the second ridge line of defence as well. Part of the 2nd Canadian Infantry Division moved in their armoured carriers with the 4th Canadian Armoured Division tanks and part of the 51st British Infantry Division with the 1st Polish Armoured Division tanks. The two battle groups attacked either side of the Caen-to-Falaise road. On the extreme flanks were the 53rd British Infantry Division and the 49th British Infantry Division. The German opposition consisted of 277th German Infantry Division, 89th German Infantry Division, 12th SS Panzer Division, 85th German Infantry Division and 276th German Infantry Division. The Germans had 40 Tiger tanks and 50 Panthers.

The 2nd Canadian Division attack soon broke the stranglehold the Germans had placed on the Verrières Ridge and May-sur-Orne sector. The 53rd British Infantry made sizeable advances to the west, as the whole front moved towards Falaise. In six days of fierce fighting Operation TOTALIZE gained a mile a day in the middle and two miles a day on the western flank. The eastern flank pivoted around the start position. By 13 August, the momentum stopped with the attackers still five miles from Falaise.

Elsewhere on 13 August, Bradley pushed the Germans back from Mortain and took Domfront. Patton's two armoured Divisions were deep into Brittany while his main force swung east of Le Mans and north to Argentan – only 18 miles from the Canadians. And significantly, it was 13 August that Hitler reluctantly agreed to a withdrawal of German forces back to the River Seine.

Figure 18 -- B-26. *The Martin B-26 Marauder was nicknamed 'the Widow Maker' but was highly regarded by its crew members for being sturdy. This one is from the 450th BS of the 322nd BG, 9thAF.*

(National Archives and Records Administration)

Friday 11 August

Another gorgeous summer day. 22 Typhoon sorties and 120 Spitfire sorties were flown on armed recces along the whole length of the British sector.

Daily aircraft losses in these early days of August were running about 10 a day for the Germans and twice that level for the Allies – very little of it due to aerial combat. On this day for instance, the Luftwaffe lost nine – three of them victims of Mosquito night-fighters – while the Allies lost 15, all but one a victim of flak.

Saturday 12 August

Four armies now formed the 'C' shaped jaws of a vice. To the north-east, the First Canadian Army under Crerar, to the north the Second British Army under Dempsey, to the west the First US Army under Bradley, and to the south, the Third US Army under Patton.

The US 9thAF sent 60 B-26s each carrying 4,000 pounds of bombs to drop on all 40 cross-roads in the area south of Falaise. The order of the day was fighter-bomber attacks, armed recces and close support to the army, while the medium bombers of the US 9thAF and of the 2ndTAF continued to hammer the supply and ammunition dumps.

Sunday 13 August

Advance units of Patton's Third US Army reached Argentan, but they were ordered by Bradley to stop while his First US Army drove through Domfront aiming at Vire and Argentan. Meantime Dempsey's Second British Army tightened the noose in the interior and Crerar's First Canadian Army bled their way south to Falaise.

At 0825 hours, eight P-51s of the 382nd FS, 363rd FG, attacked 12 FW 190s of I./JG 26 near Le Mans and shot down five of them without loss to themselves. Lt Webster was awarded three of the victories.

A half-day later at 2015 hours, the 382nd FS was to taste success again, this time over Alençon. The squadron mounted 16 P-51s against nearly 30 Bf 109s from II./JG 3 and III./JG 3 and the Germans took a hammering as they lost seven aircraft in 15 minutes of battle. For the day, this squadron had shot down 12 enemy aircraft killing all but two of the German pilots. The Americans had lost no one.

From the headquarters of the 2ndTAF came this summary of activities.

"The First Canadian Army's big push towards Falaise, which opened on the night of 7/8th August, initiated a week of the most sustained activity by TAF since D-Day. ... Over the period of one week, TAF flew a total of 8665 sorties, an average of over 1200 daily."[7]

Monday 14 August

Only a few battles in the Normandy Air War involved US P-38s, but each was a humdinger. This day saw 24 P-38s of 392nd FS and 393rd FS of the 367th FG 9thAF meet the FW 190s of I and II./JG 2 and the Bf 109s of III./JG 2 -- the whole JG 2 jagdgeschwader, or what was left of it. In the hot summer skies, the two sides circled and clashed for 12 terror-filled minutes. Two P-38s went down in flames but so did seven FW 190s and one Bf 109.

The story of JG 2 is typical of the stressed conditions the Luftwaffe operated under in Normandy. Two of its units, I and III gruppen flying FW 190s, had been fighting in Normandy since D-Day. II./JG 2 flying Bf 109s, joined them 15 June. I./JG 2 was withdrawn 11 July after losing 36 FW 190s, leaving only seven in operating condition. They gave them to III./JG 2 and returned to Germany to regroup. I./JG 2 returned to the battle 4 August and then saw it through to 28 August, a week after the other two gruppen had been withdrawn to Germany. In the whole campaign, JG 2 lost 121 FW 190s and 69 Bf 109s.

Tuesday 15 August

This was one of those hot sticky days that started with haze, became more unbearable as the day wore on and ended in a thunderstorm that didn't improve the humidity situation at all.

The Third US Army entered Chartres and found itself only 60 miles from Paris.

A series of dogfights started at 0815 hours with a Bf 109 shot down by S/L Loud, the commander of 19 Squadron of Mustangs -- it was his 5th. At 1130 hours 19 Squadron was back, this time teamed up with its sister squadron 122. They bounced the Bf 109s of III./JG 1 over Paris and shot down three, losing one of their number, but their day was not over. Shortly after noon, 19 Squadron and 122 Squadron were back again near Chartres. They started to battle the FW 190s of I and II./JG 26. Each side had suffered a loss when the battle was joined first by III./JG 26, and then by two squadrons of P-47s, the 411th FS and 412th FS of the 373rd FG 9thAF. The P-47s promptly sent four German aircraft down in flames but in turn lost four of their own. The final score was five lost by each side – one Mustang and four P-47s for the Allies and four FW 190s and one Bf 109 for the Germans.

For the day, the Allies lost 19 aircraft while the Luftwaffe lost 13.

Wednesday 16 August

This day became a notable one for the 354th FG of the US 9thAF. About 1630 hours 32 P-51s of the 353rd FS and 356th FS of the 354th FG bounced about 45 Bf 109s of II./JG 11 and III./JG 27 ten miles south-west of Paris. In a battle that continued for nearly 30 minutes, 11 Bf 109s were shot down while two P-51s were lost. The Americans claimed 14 victories, but only 11 Bf 109s were written off the books that day. But the day was memorable for the US pilots because Lt John Bakalar claimed three, while Lt Charles Koenig claimed two making him an ace, and Lt Kenneth Dahlberg also became an ace by claiming three.

Thursday 17 August

One aerial battle stands out with interest. It occurred between 1915 and 1930 hours near Lisieux. The Typhoons of 266 Squadron and 184 Squadron were flying very low, attacking military vehicles when I and II./JG 2 pounced upon them and shot down a Typhoon from each squadron. The ruckus was noted first by the Spitfires of 401 Squadron travelling west after an armed recce at Bernay, and by 416 Squadron travelling east to hit roads near Lisieux. The 24 Spitfires rapidly avenged the loss of the two Typhoons by shooting down two FW 190s and two Bf 109s. One of the Typhoon pilots was killed, but all four of the German pilots died. No Spitfires were lost.

Once again the subject of human torpedoes comes into the record. The Polish 131 Wing had been operating out of the airbase at B.10 Plumetot for two weeks. In a morning patrol to the Cabourg area, one of the pilots spotted something – a perspex bubble moving in the sea. The Spitfire attacked with cannon and the mini-submarine sank. Breaking into sections the Spitfires found and destroyed two more human torpedoes four miles off shore and sank them. Soon after, an additional three were sunk.

Friday 18 August

Intelligence data concluded that 3,000 German motor vehicles and 1,000 horse-drawn vehicles were moving through the pocket between Trun and Chambois. The 2ndTAF reacted quickly.

"At the request of the army, 2ndTAF commenced its operations today by attacking targets well to the east of the gap area, as it was felt that the closeness of the two army thrusts and the general constriction of the salient would make any extensive air operations there excessively dangerous for our own troops. As a result the fighter-bombers sought out targets in the Evreux to Bernay area and also attacked Seine barges. On the railway line between Lisieux and Bernay two trains were discovered which on closer examination were revealed to be carrying tanks. These were heavily attacked, explosions were seen and at least three of the tanks were destroyed.

"By midday reconnaissance had shown that the gap situation was materially changed. A tremendous concentration of vehicles was seen east of Trun and it was quite evident that the enemy panzer divisions were on the point of fleeing north-east towards the Seine. The programme was instantly changed and 2ndTAF went on the attack. Shuttle-service attacks were made by Spitfires, Mustangs and Typhoons and the whole of the effort was directed onto the Trun to Vimoutiers area, where the panzers, all idea of taking cover gone in their panic, were driving frantically up the road. It was a non-stop operation. The aircraft poured their ammunition to the last round into the 'sitting targets', returned to base, reloaded and set off again to continue the destruction."[8]

While the 2ndTAF was flying a non-stop shuttle service strafing the area between Trun and Chambois until ammunition ran out, several notable aerial battles were fought further afield.

The Polish Mustang squadron 315 was off on an early morning sweep of the Cormeilles-Romilly region about 50 miles south-east of Paris. It was officially designated Rodeo 385. The squadron was led by their veteran S/L Eugeniusz Horbaczewski, affectionately called 'Dziubek'. En route to the target and flying at 8,000 feet, they spotted 12 FW 190s taking off from a grass airfield seven miles north-east of Beauvais. Two sections of 315 Squadron peeled off to attack them, but at that moment 24 other FW 190s were seen to be forming up at 3,000 feet below and a little to the east. The Polish squadron, with the advantage of height and the sun at their backs, dropped their extra fuel tanks and attacked. As they dove, they noticed another group of FW 190s several miles away. Never mind, there was time. The adversaries were the top-guns of the Luftwaffe – II./JG 26. Horbaczewski was the first to get two bursts away on the first four FW 190s taking off from the airfield. Two of them crashed to the ground in flames. The rest of the lead section shot down three other FW 190s. Red section then climbed to join their comrades who had bounced the 24 FW 190s forming up thousands of feet below them. In the battle that followed, Horbaczewski shot down another FW 190 and the whole squadron claimed another nine. This all occurred between 0810 and 0825 hours. In all, 315 Squadron claimed 16 on this outstanding occasion – the largest number of claims by a single RAF squadron in World War II.

Official German II./JG 26 records attest to nine losses while claiming that five Polish Mustangs were destroyed, but the real figures are something else. It's possible that two more FW 190s should be included in the actual loss figures. Two were lost by I./JG 2, although the time is uncertain. There was only one 315 Squadron P-51 lost – that of Horbaczewski. The three FW 190s that he claimed from this encounter raised his career total to 16 victories and 1 shared. Adding the machines from I./JG 2, the final score was 11 FW 190s destroyed versus only 1 Spitfire, but for the Allies, losing Horbaczewski was a severe loss.

That was not the only aerial encounter of the day, indeed perhaps the largest had not yet taken place. But first, the 512th FS of the 406th

FG 9thAF, shot down three Bf 109s without loss at Dreux at 0945 hours. In the afternoon a tussle with the 367th FS of the 358th FG, near Chartres, appears to have resulted in four Bf 109 losses – although some of those may have been due to flak. A battle near Lisieux between 65 Squadron and both III./JG 1 and I./JG 11 resulted in one loss to the Allies and three to the Luftwaffe.

Then came the biggest battle of the day. Near Beauvais between the hours of 1930 to 1945, claims and losses were truly staggering. The following German units were involved – the FW 190s of I./JG 2, and the Bf 109s of II./JG 3, III./JG 3, III./JG 26 and III./JG 27. Between them, they claim to have shot down 13 P-51s. Some of their number, like Major Dullberg of III./JG 27 claimed the 45th of his career, and Leutnant Zimmermann of III./JG 3 claimed his 27th. They met up with the P-51s of the 334th FS, 335th FS and 336th FS of the 4th FG of the US 8thAF. This was the FG that eventually produced Blakeslee, Gentile, Beeson, Godfrey and Hofer -- five of the 25 top-scoring US aces. While the Americans only claimed seven victories, their victory was greater for the Germans recorded 11 losses and while the Germans claimed 13 victories the Americans only had nine losses. In all, 20 machines were destroyed. The Americans lost six pilots killed, two evaded and one prisoner of war, while the Germans lost six killed, two prisoners of war, one safe, the fate of the others unknown.

That day the Germans lost 34 aircraft, the Allies lost 55.

The Falaise Gap

The moment the Germans attacked Mortain, Bradley suggested to Eisenhower and Montgomery a giant pincer movement that might be sprung to catch the whole German army in Normandy. By having the British/Canadian/Polish force take Falaise, and having Patton swing east and then north through Argentan, the remnants of the German Seventh and Fifth Panzer Armies might be trapped and destroyed. All agreed.

The Canadians took Falaise on 16 August, while to the south, thousands of Germans streamed through a gap between the villages of

Trun and Chambois. To the west, all the remaining German units in Normandy were encircled in a pocket that was 20 miles long and eight miles wide. Pressure from all sides compressed the pocket into a mere 10 miles long and four miles wide by 18 August. To escape, all the Germans in that collapsing pocket had to be squeezed through the two-and-a-half mile wide gap between Trun and Chambois which became known as the Falaise Gap.

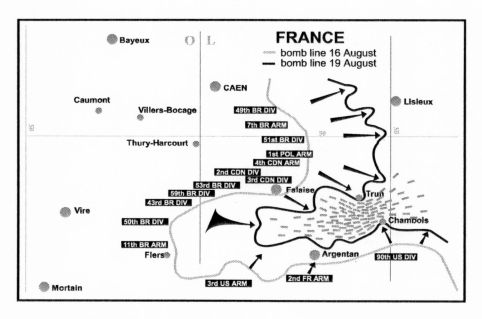

Figure 19 -- Bomb line 19 August*. This is the Falaise Gap through which the remnants of the Seventh and Fifth Panzer Armies fled like frightened bulls as they crossed the valley of the small Dives River running between Trun and Chambois. Behind them lay wrecks and corpses. The escape route was still open 19 August, but slammed shut 21 August.*

Into this compressed killing ground on 18 August the aircraft of the 2ndTAF flew round-the-clock sorties strafing and bombing the endless stream of vehicles, horses and soldiers. The slaughter was appalling -- tanks on fire, smoking trucks, dead horses bloating in the August heat, and everywhere the buzz of flies and the stench of death. Large groups of fleeing soldiers held up white flags in an attempt to surrender to the aircraft, but amongst the streaming flow of machines and men were many strong fighting elements desperately trying to survive. Spitfires, Mustangs and Typhoons exhausted their ammunition, flew back to base to re-arm and returned to shoot up anything still moving. The 1st Polish Armoured Division pushed right through the stream of fleeing Germans, and on 20 August, occupied a position on the hillside of Mont Ormel to the east of Chambois. They were on the edge of the streams of fleeing German troops shelling them with their tanks. Fierce local battles erupted here and there. Confusion and gunfire were continuous well into the night as German units tried again and again to dislodge the Poles, but to no avail.

That night the Luftwaffe tried to drop supplies to the fleeing army, and a plan was devised to assemble an assault unit to break out while a Panzer division attacked from the Seine in order to break into the pocket. At St. Lambert-sur-Dive, half-way between Trun and Chambois, a Canadian unit under Maj David Currie was surrounded by the fleeing hordes and fought in all directions. For his actions, Currie won the Victoria Cross.

All through 20 August and into the early hours of 21 August, German soldiers walked and ran to escape. The expected break-out and relief effort by the Panzers didn't materialize. The end was near. By nightfall on 21 August, Bradley's troops were shoulder to shoulder with British troops in the west. The Canadians had relieved the surrounded Poles and met Patton's 90th US Infantry Division at Chambois. The Falaise Gap was closed. Everywhere were surrendering German soldiers -- the Canadians captured 12,000; the US 90th Division took 4,000 on 21 August alone.

Saturday 19 August

After the furious bloodbath of Friday, Allied units were expecting a continuation. But the weather had other plans. Heavy cloud started moving in from the west early in the morning. It spread scattered showers and then turned into a heavy downpour. By noon it blanketed all of Normandy and had reached Paris.

Before everything was closed down by the weather, there was intense activity in the pocket near Vimoutiers where ground fire brought down at least nine Typhoons. A bit to the east of this were two running aerial battles, one moving from Dreux in the direction of Paris, the other moving from Bernay in the direction of Rouen. Both occurred between 0845 hours and 0915 hours, and both attracted an unusual combination of players. A roving group of Bf 109s of II./JG 27 and FW 190s of I and III./JG 2 appear to have started the show by shooting down a Typhoon of 609 Squadron. It was claimed by Oberleutnant Lemke – his 70th. The Germans were soon engaged by a patrol of eight P-47s of the 404th FS 371st FG and at least two squadrons of P-47s of the 406th FG -- the 512th FS and 513th FS. East of Dreux, two FW 190s were destroyed. The battle lasted almost half an hour of chasing and hiding in clouds, but it ended west of Paris with a count of four Bf 109s and four P-47s shot down.

The second running battle saw 401 Spitfire Squadron of 126 Wing tackle the Bf 109s of II and III./JG 3 east of Bernay and then, joined by the P-47s of 387th FS, chase them to Rouen. Five Bf 109s were destroyed, the last crashing at Elboeuf six miles south of Rouen. The Allies lost one Spitfire and one P-47 in the exchange.

All in all the adversaries lost 19 and 23 aircraft – German and Allied respectively -- before the weather closed the day down about noon.

Sunday 20 August

Sunday was the reverse of Saturday. The sky was wild and wet early in the morning but started to clear by noon. It was however a deception, for when it was looking like a return to good weather in late afternoon, the skies deteriorated until by the time darkness set in the wind was up and the rain was coming down in torrents as another great storm slammed into north-western France.

What aerial action there was occurred between 1500 hours and 2000 hours. II and III./JG 3 were in the Dreux area about 1545 hours when they tangled with the P-47s of the 378th FS, 365th FG, and in one large scrum lasting ten minutes six Bf 109s went down in flames and two P-47s burned on the ground with them. Lt Matte of the 378th FS claimed four Bf 109s destroyed.

At 1920 hours just west of Paris, the Mustangs of 19 Squadron and 65 Squadron of 122 Wing were on a rampage when 19 Squadron bounced 24 FW 190s of I./JG 11 and shot down four. One of the pilots claiming a victory, F/L Collyns, became an ace but was himself shot down and killed. 20 minutes later, closer to Rouen, it was 65 Squadron that shot down three FW 190s. The pilots of 65 Squadron claimed four including three claimed by F/L Burra-Robinson bringing him to ace status.

The day ended with a downpour that ushered in another great summer storm.

Monday 21 August

Neither side could fly in weather like this. In the early evening a patrol of eight Bf 109s of I./JG 1 tried to fly a reconnaissance mission over the front lines, but had to fly so low under the ceiling that they lost four aircraft to Allied anti-aircraft fire. Only one of the four pilots survived.

Canadian and Polish troops connected at Mont Ormel and the Falaise Gap was closed. In an area marked off as the four-mile road between Trun and Chamboise, and extending to the heights at Mont Ormel – roughly an equilateral triangle four-miles on each side –as many as ten thousand corpses rotted in one giant coffin.

Figure 20 -- P-51. The North American P-51D Mustang was originally designed to British requirements then modified to the configuration shown above and with a Packard-built Rolls-Royce Merlin engine became the most amazing long-range fighter. This one is from 380th FS of the 363rd FG at A-15 Maupertus.
(National Archives and Records Administration)

Tuesday 22 August

The storm wore itself out by midday and within two hours two big dogfights broke out. In a desperate bid to get opposing aircraft in the air, the Luftwaffe threw a new unit into the fray. III./JG 76 made its first appearance in Normandy this day over Paris and promptly lost nine of the 20 Bf 109s it committed to battle. Only one pilot managed to parachute to safety. The victors were the P-51s of the 355th FS and 356th FS of the 354th FG, which suffered no loss.

Between 1400 and 1430 hours, 75 miles to the east at Chalons, the P-47s of the 365th FS and 366th FS, 358th FG, shot down five Bf 109s of 20 that rose to meet them. One P-47 was lost and its pilot killed.

Five hours later near Amiens the P-38s of 393rd FS and 394th FS 367th FG, destroyed six FW 190s while losing one P-38 and its pilot.

Wednesday 23 August

Heavy cloud and a low ceiling persisted until mid-morning and the weather remained unsettled throughout the day. The Luftwaffe planned one large operation, hoping to attack the several bridgeheads that had spanned the Seine, but it delayed until early afternoon. Nearly 80 German aircraft consisting of about 30 FW 190s of I./JG 2, and II./JG 26 and 50 Bf 109s from II./JG 11 and III./JG 27 were ordered to the attack. At 1330 these aircraft were no sooner in the air when they ran into 19 Spitfires near the village of Senlis outside Paris for the only major engagement of the day. The Spitfires of two squadrons of the Canadian 127 Wing, shot down 13 German aircraft - four FW 190s and nine Bf 109s. Included in those shot down was Hauptmann Siegfried Bogs, Staffelkapitän of 3./JG 2. The Canadians lost three Spitfires – all three pilots being killed.

Thursday 24 August

Though bad weather again kept most Allied and German aircraft on the ground the Germans lost three aircraft while the Allies lost five – all eight shot down by flak.

Friday 25 August

D-Day-plus-one, 7 June, was the day that saw the greatest number of aircraft – both Allied and German destroyed in the Normandy Air War. Friday 25 August turned out to be the second bitterest day fought in the air over Normandy. It was also the day that Allied ground forces entered Paris and at 1515 hours accepted the surrender of the German commander there.

The day dawned bright and clear, a lovely warm summer day with good visibility. At about 0930 hours, the 354th FG sent out its three squadrons of P-51s on concurrent sweeps. The 355th FS swept Rethel, and near Reims, spotted 35 FW 190s at low altitude. The

163

enemy aircraft from I./JG 11 were flying to a new base further north. The P-51s attacked and the Germans responded by scrambling the Bf 109s of their sister-gruppe II./JG 11. But whereas the Germans then had numerical advantage, the Americans had the first bounce. Disregarding the claims on both sides I./JG 11 lost four FW 190s while 355th FS lost two P-51s.

The 356th FS was sweeping the area near Beauvais when it spotted enemy aircraft on an airfield. A strafing attack claimed the destruction of 10 FW 190s on the ground. The third squadron of the 354th FG – 353rd FS – saw nothing then nor on the other two sweeps of the day. However, the other two squadrons of the group were not yet finished for the day.

An intelligence report furnished by the Maquis, indicated that a new gruppe consisting of 40 FW 190s, had moved into a small base near St Quentin called Herpy-l'Arlésienne. As part of the continuing round of dive-bombing enemy air bases, the 367th FG flying out of A-11 St Lambert, despatched three squadrons of P-38s to bomb this air base and two other bases near to it. Their 35 aircraft dive-bombed the first two and arrived at Herpy-l'Arlésienne at 1245 hours, just as the FW 190s of II./JG 6 were taking off. II./JG 6 was a new gruppe that had arrived in France only on 22 August, after being re-constituted in Germany. They had only one or two experienced fighter pilots – and what experience they had was on night-fighter operations. They climbed into the P-38 formation and fought for their lives. The FW 190 A-8 was a superior aircraft to the P-38 J in almost every performance measure except firepower, top speed and range, however in the hands of an inexperienced pilot, a FW 190 was no match for an experienced pilot flying an inferior aircraft. In a battle that lasted 20 minutes, the two sides traded blows until burning aircraft careened from the sky. Capt Blumer of the 394th FS of the 367th FG, claimed five FW 190s destroyed – making him an instant ace. Both sides made claims higher than actual, but in the end the 367th FG lost seven P-38s – six shot down on the spot and one that crashed upon returning to base. The Germans recorded the loss of 15 aircraft – two pilots were wounded and four were recorded as killed in action, the remaining nine were recorded as missing. For II./JG 6 this battle earned them the unfortunate Luftwaffe record as the gruppe with the greatest number of aircraft lost in one engagement in the whole war. Both sides broke off at 1315 hours

It is not known whether any part of that aerial battle spread in the direction of Beauvais about 60 miles to the west-south-west, but one half hour later after bombing three air bases in the Peronne area near

St Quentin, the 30 P-38 of two squadrons of the 474th FG engaged about 50 enemy fighters. The 428th FS and 429th FS were up against elements of the FW190s of I./JG 26, II./JG 26 and the Bf 109s of III./JG 76. This last gruppe had been thrown into the battle poorly prepared like II./JG 6, and had been in France for only a few days. The battle raged for 40 minutes. Hauptmann Emil Lang, the Gruppekommandeur

Figure 21 -- Lang. Hauptmann Emil Lang of II./JG 26 was credited with 28 victories in Normandy -- the highest score of any pilot.

(Bundesarchiv)

of II./JG 26, claimed three P-38s raising his career total to 170 victories. The 474th FG reported 11 P-38s failed to return to base, while the two JG 26 gruppen

recorded six FW 190s lost, III./JG 76 recorded the loss of 12 Bf 109 aircraft. Not only were the statistics in the American favour 18 to 11, but among those shot down and killed were Hauptmann Albrecht of Stab III./JG 76 and Hauptmann Prang the Staffelkapitän of 12./JG 76. Both were experten pilots -- Albrecht had 25 victories to his credit.

Throughout the afternoon, P-38s and P-47s of the 365th FG, 367th FG and 370th FG combined to make two ground strikes. In the first of these, 12 aircraft were claimed destroyed on the ground, and in the second, 21 aircraft were claimed destroyed on the ground. In both cases the greater number were Ju 52 transport aircraft massing to evacuate troops.

The last major encounter of the day occurred at 1850 hours when 25 P-51s from the 356th FS and 357th FS of the 354th FG, bounced

25 Bf 109s of II./JG 11. They immediately shot down three. However, they were then bounced by 30 FW 190s and Bf 109s of II./JG 26 and III./JG 1 respectively. This time, the Germans got the edge, shooting down four P-51s while losing only three.

For the day, Luftwaffe records show the loss of 49 fighter aircraft – the number lost on the ground is unknown. The Americans recorded 27 fighters lost, all in aerial combat, while the British forces lost 11, all to flak, except one Typhoon of 164 Squadron claimed by the Gruppekommandeur of II./JG 53, near Rouen at 1925 hours. However, the big news of the day was the performance of the 9thAF P-38s, that had not been stellar performers in Normandy until this day when they set one new record -- the 367th FG destroying 15 enemy aircraft at a cost of seven P-38s -- and then breaking the record again as 474th FG shot down 18 at a cost of 11 of their own.

Saturday 26 August

At 0830 hours the P-47s of 352nd FS of 353rd FG of the US 8thAF claimed shooting down a FW 190 at Charleroi near the Belgian border and a little after 0845, the Spitfires of 602 Squadron 125 Wing, claimed two FW 190s near Gournay, but lost two aircraft over Rouen due to flak.

At 0900 the Spitfire squadrons of 421 and 416 Squadron, both from 127 Wing, and on parallel armed recces to Gisors and Gournay, arrived and between them claimed three FW 190s shot down but lost two Spitfires. I./JG 26 and II./JG 26 both claimed victories in the Beauvais/Rouen area between 0917 and 0919 -- Hauptmann Lang claimed his 171st and 172nd.[9] The time is uncertain, but it appears that the three FW 190s lost by II./JG 6 at Rouen occurred at this time too. The Spitfire squadrons lost four and the Germans lost five.

Another air battle over Rouen involved 329 and 341 Squadrons from 145 Wing, at 1415 hours. The two Spitfire squadrons lost three aircraft and these are thought to be the three victories claimed by I./JG 26 and II./JG 26 over Gisors.

Between 1445 and 1507 hours, and between Paris and Rouen there are claims and losses that can only be lumped together. The 313th FS of 50th FG 9thAF claimed three Bf 109s and lost two P-47s over Rouen, while a gaggle of II./JG 26 flying FW 190s and III./JG 26 and II./JG 53 flying Bf 109s were all in the Rouen area where they lost three Bf 109s and two FW 190s and claimed shooting down three P-47s. Meanwhile 453 Squadron of 125 Wing claimed three Bf 109s at Paris for no loss to them selves. In terms of losses it was Germans five versus Allies two.

All the other losses of the day were to flak --- the US 9thAF lost a P-47, a P-51, and a P-61 to flak, and the 2ndTAF lost three Typhoons and eight Spitfires to flak mostly in the area south between Rouen and Evreux.

Sunday 27 August

This day would see the withdrawal of seven jagdgeschwaders, leaving only three to fight one more day. This winding down resulted in only two aerial engagements. At 1420 hours over Rouen, 19 Squadron Mustangs shot down a Bf 109 of I./JG 4 killing the pilot. At almost the same time over Paris, the P-47s of the 506th FS claimed two Bf 109s destroyed and several more unconfirmed. However, they lost four P-47s and their pilots. In the final analysis, I./JG 2 and I./JG 11 recorded five FW 190s lost.

Monday 28 August 1944

The Air War in Normandy was all over but the shouting -- all Luftwaffe units withdrawn to bases in Germany -- and although three Bf 109s were shot down near St. Quentin and two others brought down by anti-aircraft, they were the last losses or claims until aerial battles began to occur over Belgium and Holland. The Allies lost 15 aircraft all due to flak

Summary of the Air War in August

During August the US 9thAF dispatched 9,142 medium bombers, of which 34 were lost and 1,032 damaged. Fighter-bombers and reconnaissance aircraft of 9thAF flew 12,305 sorties and lost 123 aircraft while claiming 98 in the air and 63 on the ground. Fighter-bombers of 19thAF flew 12,292 sorties, lost 114 aircraft while claiming 163 in the air and 66 on the ground. Both air forces claimed to have destroyed a total of 4600 vehicles, 470 tanks 245 locomotives and 3000 railroad cars.[10] In addition, the US 9thAF flew 6,400 sorties.

The 2ndTAF summed up it August activities in Normandy as follows:

"August has been the greatest month for the Allies as it has been the most disastrous for the German Army which, now broken, demoralized and decimated has left the scene of its defeat in Normandy and is fleeing across the Low Countries.

"August has also been the greatest month for the 2ndTAF, which can claim as its share in the victory 10,500 of Germany's sorely needed transport and 850 of its tanks. The Typhoons and Spitfires maintained a consistently high daily score in these victims but had two sensationally successful days, the first on August the 7th when the Hun mounted a counter-offensive near Mortain and lost 135 tanks to the Typhoons; the second on 18 August when, the enemy making his most desperate attempt to withdraw in force from the Falaise Gap, the whole of 2ndTAF's strength was turned on to the concentrations of transport with the result that they knocked out a minimum of 3,000 vehicles.

"Of 2ndTAF's total of just over 26,000 sorties for the month, 12,590 were armed recces, the missions which have made daylight travel a terror to the enemy.... Towards the end of the month, over a period TAF paid particular attention to the Seine, where they initiated a programme of attacking ferry crossings, jetties and barges. 179 such attacks were made by formations of Typhoons, Spitfires and Mustangs. Locomotives and rolling stock were attacked 130 times. There were occasional brief periods of strong enemy air reaction, which resulted in a score of 77 destroyed and 46 damaged."[11]

Based upon these figures, USAAF and 2ndTAF reconnaissance, fighter-bombers and fighter aircraft flew a total of over 66,100 sorties in August -- about 2400 a day. The Luftwaffe vacated the Normandy skies after 28 August 1944.

The Normandy Air War

Whereas the Luftwaffe had 21 jagdgeschwader operating in France in June, that number decreased as decimated units were sent back to Germany to regroup and occasionally sent back to the fray, but the number fell continuously until in August it had been reduced to about 12. Without having actual data regarding the number of sorties flown by the Luftwaffe during the Normandy Campaign, we can hazard a guess based upon the estimated number of aircraft available, availability and the extent to which poor weather cut into flying time. The day after D-Day, 380 fighter and fighter-bomber aircraft were flown into Normandy to augment the 48 that had been available on D-Day, thereby trebling the possible number of sorties per day. Assuming 60% availability and 30% reduction due to weather and an average of nine replacement aircraft a day, the losses incurred would still only permit a 400 sorties per day figure in June, 450 to 500 in July and 250 in August. In total it is estimated the Luftwaffe flew 36,000 sorties in the Normandy Campaign.

The Allied aerial offensive effort was at an all-out-effort level of 5800 sorties per day on D-day, but declined dramatically the rest of June, although with the continuing presence of 8thAF sorties provided 99,000 sorties in June -- over 3900 per day. In July both the 8thAF redirection to its strategic bombing roles and the diversion of seven RAF wings to counter the V-1 threat, dropped the Allied average sorties per day to about 3100 per day. The total number of Allied fighter, fighter-bomber and medium bomber sorties in Normandy is estimated at 261,000.

The Allies lost 1639 aircraft in the campaign while the Luftwaffe lost 1522 as shown here:

	2ndTAF	9thAF	8thAF	Allies	Luftwaffe
at 30 June	322	255	125	702	646
at 31 July	515	441	154	1110	1097
At 31 August	769	652	218	1639	1522

Table 8 -- Losses 31 August. Comparative figures of the total cumulative losses of fighters, fighter-bombers and medium bombers throughout the Normandy Campaign.

Thus the final loss rate for the Allies in the whole campaign was 0.6% per sortie, down from the 1.1% on D-Day, while the Luftwaffe loss rate of 4.2% per sortie was also down from the 6.6% encountered on D-Day, but the relationship between the two remained the same -- the German rate was six times the Allied rate.

The Allied Experience of daily losses

The pattern of average daily aircraft losses shows a contrast that in some ways describes the whole Normandy Air War. After the spike in number of aircraft lost on D-Day-plus-one the average number of losses dropped down consistent with a learning curve through June and became pretty flat figure at the level of 12 losses per day through the whole month of July and August, rising to a peak when the Falaise Gap was closed.

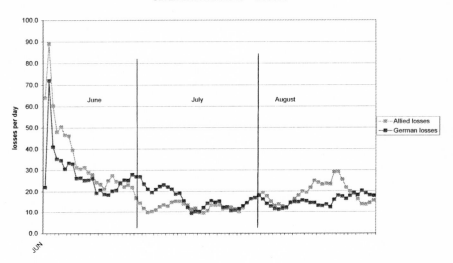

SEVEN-DAY AVERAGES -- LOSSES

Figure 22 -- Losses per day. Because the day-to-day number of actual daily losses jumped around so much, this graph shows the seven-day trailing average number of losses for the Allies and for the Germans covering the period 6 June through 28 August when the last aerial battles were fought over Norman soil.

The Luftwaffe Experience

The Luftwaffe experience was different. After D-Day-plus-one, average losses dropped faster than the Allied experience probably reflecting the difference between the performance of the numerous super-aces in the Luftwaffe compared to the newly tested Allied pilots. However when it dropped to the level of 20-losses-per-day in the third week in June, it rose again in a hump that carried over into mid-July. What caused the increase? Within the first few days of combat in Normandy the Luftwaffe lost Weber, Simsch and Huppertz -- all super-aces. Within 20 days they had lost or had seriously injured nine other officers at the Hauptmann level including Joseph Wurmheller who had 102 victories to his name. The only way to contain the situation was to recall six jagdgeschwader in the first two weeks of July and set limits on the number of accompanying pilots there must be depending upon rank (Goering's dictum). The jagdgeschwader were not replaced, indeed four more were removed before July was out. The Germans dropped their average loss rate by taking out players. When the loss rate settled down to about 15-per-day, that amounted to about a 4% loss rate per sortie.

Victory in Normandy

On 18 August, von Kluge took his own life – he had been replaced 16 August and ordered to return to Berlin. The final collapse of the German Seventh Army and the Fifth Panzer Army was startling. Ten thousand Germans were killed, while somewhere between 20 and 50 thousand escaped -- many during the days before Falaise fell. The early escapees were mostly non-combat troops and staff officers. They were the ones who got out at von Kluge's command before the gap was closing. Those who were nearly trapped but got out through the gap, took their clothes and little else leaving their equipment when they started to flee, abandoning their vehicles when attacked from the air or having their horses shot from under them, and then fleeing on foot -- often at night. Only a handful of tanks, trucks or field guns crossed the Seine.

It is estimated that over 40 thousand prisoners were taken while closing the gap, bringing the total number captured in Normandy to 200,000. Altogether, German troops killed and missing in Normandy totalled 400,000. Allied killed and missing were 73,000 -- 84,000 including those killed before D-Day[12]. For twenty miles through the Falaise Pocket there was a trail of every conceivable form of refuse, wreckage and carnage, and on all the small roads in the vicinity of Trun and Chambois a count revealed the remains of 3,040 vehicles. By any measure the defeat of the German Army in Normandy was a stunning Allied victory.

According to the official RAF history, the total aerial effort that contributed to this victory was shared equally by the Americans and the RAF (British and Commonwealth forces). Between 6 June and 31 August 1944 the Americans flew 183,400 sorties and the RAF (including all commands) flew 206,000 sorties. The USAAF lost 2,065 aircraft, while the RAF lost 2,036 aircraft. USAAF casualties were 8,536, while RAF casualties were 8,138.[13]

David Clark

PART TWO –
A Canadian Wing in the
Normandy Air War

Heavy bombing became a standard feature of each new assault in the Normandy Campaign. This photo taken from 29,000 feet 12 June 1944 shows a box of six B-24 Liberators of the US 8thAF flying over Normandy.

(Wilfrid Laurier University LCMSDS 304/4067)

David Clark

Chapter Six – Background

From the first days of the formation of the 2ndTAF, nine wings had been set aside to form a nucleus called No. 83 (Composite) Group commanded by AVM Harry Broadhurst. The nine wings were grouped three to a sector. One of these sectors – No. 17 (Canadian) Sector -- was commanded by RCAF G/C Bill MacBrien. Everyone had a nickname and MacBrien preferred the nickname 'Iron Bill' but the irreverent airmen usually referred to him as 'Tin Willie'. Before D-Day, the three wings under MacBrien's command were 126 Wing commanded by W/C George Keefer consisting of 401, 411 and 412 Squadrons, 127 Wing commanded by W/C Lloyd Chadburn consisting of 403, 416 and 421 Squadrons and 144 Wing commanded by W/C Johnnie[1] Johnson consisting of 441, 442 and 443 Squadrons. This is the story of the Normandy Campaign fought by the second of these -- the pilots, ground crew and Spitfires of 127 (RCAF) Wing.

How to become a Tactical Air Force

The three squadrons of 127 Wing had each been selected as candidates for the new 2ndTAF early in 1943. The first exposure of the members of the wing to what was foreseen as their ultimate method of operation occurred when the squadrons began living under canvas in August when they moved away from the red brick buildings of RAF Station Kenley, to camp and fly from first one and then another small grass airfield in Kent. Everything from maintenance and field operations to medical and officer's mess facilities was housed in tents, but that did not deter the wing flying daily over France and the Lowlands on escort missions or armed recces. At one point the two W/Cs managed a room in a fine country manor, but that quickly changed and soon they too were under canvas. Along with the tents came trucks – about 200 of them for each wing, for this new tactical air force of which they were to be a part, had to learn to move within days to follow the front line troops. The wing consisted of about 800 airmen, and the plan was that upon a day's notice half would pack up part of everything, drive to a new location and set up shop. The second half of the wing would follow the next day when the aircraft themselves moved to the new location. The moves to two different Kent grass airfields and back to RAF Station Kenley in 1943 were practise runs. Although the young men took to living out in the open readily, there was much relief for pilots and ground crew when, with winter approaching, the wing took up indoor quarters once again in the warmth and luxury of RAF Station Kenley.

Figure 23 - Chadburn. *W/C Lloyd 'Chad' Chadburn, DSO and bar, DFC and bar is seen here in Canada early in 1944 while on a bond promotion tour. He is chatting with F/L Jimmy Sinclair MP.*

(Canadian Forces Photo PL24257)

The three squadrons of 127 Wing came together for the first time in February 1944, when 416 Squadron rejoined the other two. In March, each squadron was rotated through a special ground-attack school to teach the pilots dive-bombing and strafing, then when all had been trained, they prepared to relocate closer to the south coast.

In April 1944 they moved from the comfort of indoor accommodations at Kenley to tents in the fields around RAF Station Tangmere in East Sussex. Each move had made them more adept, and by the time they were established at Tangmere, they were reasonably ready to make 'the big move' when shortly after D-Day they would move to France. Techniques had been perfected – certain trucks were modified to operate as operations rooms, communication centres and squadron commander offices. Every wing had two W/Cs – one known

Figure 24 -- Brown. The base commander of B.2, W/C Mannifrank Brown, is seen here watching a take-off or landing from the command vehicle at mid-field. He has a Very pistol beside him to signal the pilot.
(Imperial War Museum CL94)

as W/C (Flying) and the other as base W/C. The W/C (F) was expected to lead nearly every mission and to be the senior officer for pilots, while the other W/C ran everything except the actual fighter operations. W/C Lloyd Chadburn (known affectionately as 'Chad') was the W/C(F) for 127 Wing while W/C Mannifrank Brown ('Brownsie' or 'Father Brown') was the base Wingco. Chad had the back of a covered truck fitted out as an office; Brownsie went one better, he had a trailer (what the British called a caravan) outfitted for his trek in style across the continent. Aircrew likened it to the King's Coronation carriage, or to Montgomery's private rail car.

The Months of Waiting

Everyone knew 1944 was the year for invasion of the continent, however the first five months of the year had been a wash-out for the eager pilots. On the 21 January – before 416 Squadron had joined 403 and 421 in 127 Wing – there was an encounter with the enemy when P/Os Claude Weaver, DFC, DFM and bar, and Hart Finley of 403 Squadron brought down a couple of FW 190s. Weaver's career came to an end just one week later when, with 12 kills under his belt from Malta and north-west Europe, he was killed in action over Amiens. He was an excellent fighter pilot and his was the first loss of the invasion year for 127 Wing.

On 8 March, a Ranger mission was laid on for 403 Squadron to sweep the areas of Evreux, Paris and Creil. The aircraft attacked a barge and a tug in the Seine, setting them on fire and added some burning army trucks to the tally, but intense flak brought down F/L Dave Goldberg who crash-landed but evaded capture and F/L John Ballantyne who crashed and was killed. Ballantyne had earned a DFM for his action in Malta on his first tour and had started his second tour with 403 Squadron only in January. He is buried in the Military Cemetery at St. André-de-l'Eure in France.

Before March ended, two other 403 Squadron pilots lost their lives – F/O Richard Dennison was killed in a flying accident 18 March, and F/L George Pennock was shot down by flak on the 25th. Both are buried at Brookwood Military Cemetery in Surrey.

In April and especially May, the number of operations was increased until 127 Wing flew round after round of dive-bombing attacks on targets in France and flew escort missions to medium bombers knocking out rail facilities and bridges -- all part of the Transportation Plan aimed at destroying France's communication system. When they returned from these missions, they celebrated in the officer's mess tent, chatted it up in the dispersal tent or took their aches and sniffles to the medical tent. April was a cold and wet month, but just as everyone was becoming wretched with the perpetual damp of sleeping out, a lingering, deliciously warm and kindly May saved them. Health rebounded quickly -- now all they needed was action.

Some long overdue victories came on 7 May, when an aerial battle resulted in F/Ls Doug Lindsay and John Hodgson of 403 Squadron each destroying a FW 190. The very next day F/Ls Paul Johnson and Hank Zary of 421 Squadron destroyed a Bf 110 in the air, a Ju 88 on the ground and with two other pilots, damaged two more Ju 88s on the ground. The month started to look a bit more promising on 19 May when Lindsay and Hodgson repeated their feat destroying two more FW 190s. Unfortunately, in this action F/O Robert Smith was hit, baled out over the Channel but died. Since his remains were not recovered, he is commemorated on the panels at Runnymede Memorial on Panel 248. That same day a 421 pilot – F/L Dick Henry -- was hit by flak over Neufchatel and parachuted into the arms of the German army. At a cost of one life and one prisoner of war, the wing had six victories in May, but the month was not over, and the biggest show had yet to be staged.

On 21 May, 12 squadrons of Spitfires assembled at Hawkinge on the coast of Kent just across from Calais, to fly a massive train-busting operation called Ramrod 905, intended to confirm the Germans' belief that the invasion would take place at Calais. 144 Spitfires swarmed over France arousing fearful displays of heavy flak but causing terror along the railway lines destroying 17 trains and damaging twice that number, however the effort was bought at the price of 21 aircraft and 20 pilots lost. 403 Squadron lost F/O Tommy Bryan who parachuted and evaded capture; 416 Squadron lost F/O Sten Lundberg who parachuted but was taken prisoner; 421 Squadron lost F/O Jimmy Davidson, who was also taken prisoner and F/L Ralph Nickerson who evaded capture.

The next day it was victory time again -- 416 Squadron's turn this time. On 22 May, F/L Bill Mason and F/O Al McFadden brought down FW 190s while P/O Bill Palmer and F/L Pat Patterson shot down Bf 109s. Ten victories in May – the boys were just aching for action, and they believed D-Day and the invasion of Europe were going to be the time when it all would happen. However, all was not roses, on 29 May, P/O Harry Boyle ran into the tail of F/O Stanley William Smith as they taxied. Boyle was injured, but Smith died and is buried at Brookwood Cemetery.

In the first two days of June, 127 Wing lost two more pilots. On a train-bashing armed recce just off the Somme River, P/O Joseph Rolland Guillot, who had been with 416 Squadron less than a month, reported engine trouble and crashed into the sea. He is buried in Calais War Cemetery. The second day of June, F/L John Hodgson who had just recently destroyed two enemy aircraft was brought down by flak and killed. He is buried at St. Pierre Cemetery, Amiens.

Figure 25 -- 403 Squadron. Back row: F/O Brannigan, F/O Hodgson, F/L Coles, F/L Southwood, Sgt Chevers, F/O Preston, F/L Goldberg, F/O Gordon, F/L Pattison. Middle row: F/O Foster, F/O Middlemiss, F/O Lambert, F/L Dover, S/L Grant, W/C Johnson, F/L Ogilvie, F/O Dowding, P/O Browne, P/O Gray. Front row: F/O Logan, P/O Thornton, P/O Wilson, Sgt Barnes, F/O Matthews, W/O Moulinette, Sgt MacKinnon -- taken at Kenley September 1943.
(Canadian Forces Photo PL19718)

The weather was so favourable in May that the airmen got to swim in the Channel and to sunbathe whenever time permitted, and as they got dark brown and healthy looking they grew more impatient for the balloon to go up. The invasion was coming, but when?

What Would be Needed in France?

The plan called for each wing to have its own Advanced Landing Ground, or ALG, that engineers would build while other personnel would operate until air force operational units arrived. The Royal Engineers would have to clear a runway, bulldozing through several hedgerows at each airstrip, level the field and lay down a mesh of Sommerfeldt tracking – a sort of heavy wire mesh secured by long staples driven into the ground. Then they would have to set up an electrical system, build a voice communication system, build latrines, lay out taxiways, locate aircraft dispersal areas, set up tent areas, build bomb and ammunition dumps and clear a parking lot for 200 vehicles. In the meantime there had to be a group of soldiers to defend the airstrip, man the anti-aircraft guns and service aircraft of many types, because experience from North Africa taught everyone that before an airfield became permanent home to a wing, a steady stream of different kinds of aircraft would seek refuge or require refuelling and maintenance. The men who performed this early servicing were called Servicing Commandos and they had to be as adept at stripping down a Merlin engine as they were at routing out German snipers. Both engineers and Servicing Commandos would come ashore as soon after the initial assault as possible. Supply personnel would also have to be there to provide the steel mesh, petrol, oil, ammunition, spare parts, water trucks, tools, tents, food and medical supplies – first for the advanced guard, and later for the progressive build-up of the wing. Echelon by echelon, the wing personnel were to cross the Channel until the full complement of nearly a thousand personnel were there at the ALG.

What Was it Like to Fly a Spitfire?

In the 1930s and 1940s every young boy's dream was to fly the world's most famous fighter aircraft – the Supermarine Spitfire. Even before the war started, a steady stream of young Canadian, American, Australian, New Zealand and South African boys found their way to Britain to join the RAF, and in most cases their goal was to become a fighter pilot and fly a Spitfire. When the war started, the stream became a torrent of those joining the Air Force and entering the British Commonwealth Air Training Plan – the programme that trained 131,000 air crew in Canada alone[2] to staff the RAF, RCAF and other Commonwealth air forces. Bill Olmstead who flew in the Mediterranean and in Normandy, eventually leading 442 Squadron, wrote a book entitled *'Blue Skies – autobiography of a Canadian Spitfire Pilot'*. He tells of the first time he sat in a Spitfire.

> "My attachment to this aircraft was instantaneous and total. With my parachute strapped to my back, I stepped onto the left wing root, moved up one short pace, and entered the cockpit through the open hatch door. With some shifting I positioned myself in the metal bucket seat moulded to accept the parachute pack, which then acted as a comfortable cushion. The Sutton harness straps were positioned over my shoulders and hips to hold me securely in position. My body seemed to fill the cockpit space completely, putting the controls within easy reach. I looked at the throttle and pitch control quadrant mounted ahead of the hatch with trim tabs and radiator regulators immediately below. The doughnut-shaped control column moved easily in every direction. I noted the gun button was in the OFF position. Directly in front of my eyes were the major flying control instruments, the air speed indicator, the altimeter, the directional gyro, and the turn and bank dial, all neatly centred, allowing the pilot to look forward at all times. Every instrument detailing the condition of the engine or the fuselage was easy to read and reach. About fifty different knobs, switches, dials, buttons, tabs, and controls were to be my constant guides in the future, and I was determined to understand them completely."[3]

Figure 26 -- Spitfire cockpit.. *The circular object at bottom centre is the control column complete with button for firing guns. Clockwise from bottom left are; throttles and trim, radio and oxygen, gunsight (top centre above flying instruments), engine instruments and landing gear. The gyro compass is immediately in front of the control column.*

(author's photo)

The Spitfire had a mystique about it that is often said to have been totally unwarranted. Some point out that the mystique began because the first versions of this proud lady won the Schneider Trophy in the 1930s, while others state the mystique began in the Battle of Britain when the Spitfire got all the credit while the humble Hawker Hurricane did all the work. Some point out that it took nearly twice as long to build a Spitfire as it did to build a Hurricane just because of the designer's nearly complete disregard for considerations of ease of manufacture and of course, this made the Spitfire much more difficult to repair than a Hurricane. This they say made it a spoiled thoroughbred. Oh there were so many reasons why the Spitfire was said to be undeserving of its reputation – until one flew one. For those who flew the Spitfire the praises could not be greater. Here is the engine starting procedure:

> Fuel Cock – ON
> Ignition Switches – OFF
> Throttle – ½ to 1 inch OPEN
> Propeller Speed Control Lever – FULLY FORWARD
> Supercharger Switch – AUTO NORMAL
> Carburettor Air Intake Filter – CLOSED
> Priming Pump – PER TEMPERATURE
> Ignition Switches – ON
> Starter and Booster Coil Buttons – PRESS SIMULTANEOUSLY

Here's Bill Olmstead's description of starting up, taking off and flying a Spitfire.

"I primed the engine and gave the thumbs up sign to the 'Erk' (mechanic) to give the engine power from his electric cart. The Merlin caught immediately with a cough and a stutter, which quickly smoothed into a quiet, throbbing burble as I throttled back. The machine vibrated slightly, seeming to come alive suddenly in response to the engine's song of power, a very distinctive and easily identifiable sound. I hooked up the oxygen tube and plugged in the radio cord after closing the hatch door. At my signal the wheel chocks were removed, freeing the aircraft to move forward. Slowly moving ahead, I found there was no forward vision on the ground, the view being completely blanked out by the long nose and the broad engine cowling. By bursts of the throttle and shoves on the rudder pedals and brakes, however, the nose could be swung from side to side, which allowed me to see enough to keep the aircraft on the taxi strip without 'pranging' some obstruction.

"At the down-wind end of the runway I ran the engine up to test the magnetos. No serious drop. I was ready for and received permission from flying control to take off. I made a last quick check of the brakes, trim, flaps, contacts, pressures, undercart, and radiator, ensuring everything was in order. I opened the throttle smoothly. The engine responded with a deep-throated roar typical of the Rolls-

Royce Merlin and the Spit accelerated rapidly. Christ, how it accelerated! I could scarcely believe how quickly the machine gathered speed with the pressure forcing my whole body tight against the contoured seat. As more power was added there was a strong tendency for the aircraft to swing to the right, and I countered this by increasing pressure on the left rudder pedal. Faster and faster, the tail up now as the control surfaces gained effect with the increasing speed. After what seemed a short take-off run, the Spit freed itself from the ground at 100 mph. My speed built up rapidly as I moved the wheels-up lever. Within a minute the aircraft was clean, responding instantly to even the lightest touch on the controls."[4]

Those who flew her had great affection for her. One who also described the beautiful Spitfire was Hugh Godefroy, who flew with 403 Squadron, rose to command that squadron and eventually became W/C (Flying) of 127 Wing until he was succeeded by W/C Lloyd Chadburn in April 1944. In his book *'Lucky Thirteen'*, Godefroy covers a bit of the same ground as Olmstead, but gives us some additional insight into the feeling of flying the Spitfire.

"When the engine was properly primed and switched on ready to start, a push on the starter button fired a cartridge which turned the engine over. There were four cartridges in the starter drum, and if you failed to start with the fourth cartridge, the drum had to be re-loaded by the ground crew. The small landing flaps were activated by compressed air. They had two positions, up and down.....Because of the small rudder surface the Spitfire had a rudder trim that had to be put in the full right position on takeoff to keep it straight. To prevent the aircraft from skidding in flight, thus throwing the bullets off the line of sight, the rudder trim had to be adjusted at different speeds. The beautiful elliptical wings were stressed to withstand a sustained nine Gs, and a short snap of up to twelve. The aircraft would shudder very noticeably well in advance of a stall, useful when flying by the seat of your pants in combat. Because of the very small coolant radiator, the Spitfire was prone to heating up when taxiing or idling on the ground. This had to be taken into account when planning formation takeoffs so as to get all the aircraft into the air before engine temperatures went off the clock. Once in the air with the wheels up, the Spitfire was superlative."[5]

Figure 27 -- 416 Squadron. *Top of aircraft: F/O Tafuro. Back row: F/S Greenman, F/L Mason, F/L Patterson, F/O Cuthbertson, F/O Borland, F/O McFadden, F/L Noonan, S/L Green, F/L Prentice, F/L Campbell, F/O Gould, F/O Harling, P/O Farquarson, Front row: P/O Palmer, F/O James, F/S Boulais, F/O Fraser, W/O McCrae, F/O Rainville, F/L Hayworth, F/O Lundberg, F/S Maranda, F/O Eskow, F/O St Georges, P/O Scott taken February 1944.*

(Canadian Forces Photo PL26651)

Airfields like Kenley and Tangmere had wide concrete runways and wide parallel stretches of grass runway so that a squadron could take off on the runway in waves of four aircraft line abreast, or even six or more aircraft line abreast using the grass surface. Airfields like B.2 in France had runways much reduced in width limiting take-off to a maximum of two aircraft at a time -- more often one-at-a-time. Thus a squadron commander had to climb to a specified altitude after take-off and circle while his squadron formed up into a complete 12 aircraft squadron. In the case of wing-strength missions, the wait was longer as each of three complete squadrons had to form up. The formation would usually be two squadrons separated by perhaps a thousand feet of altitude and about a quarter-of-a-mile apart, with the third squadron flying perhaps three to five thousand feet higher. While the lower squadrons searched for targets, the high squadron watched for intruding enemy aircraft.

Squadron formations had undergone many changes since early in the war and by 1944 almost always consisted of three sections of four aircraft each flying in what was called 'finger four' formation. In most cases the sections were called 'red', 'blue' and 'yellow' but occasionally more exotic colours were chosen. The name finger four referred to the relative position of the four aircraft of the section viewed from above -- each was placed like the fingernails of an outstretched hand. The first section, red section, consisted of the squadron commander centre with a number two pilot flying 300 feet behind and to one side. The other two aircraft flew at the opposite side and behind. All four aircraft would fly at different altitudes 50 feet above or below one another. Looking down on the section one would see, from left to right, Red 2, Red 1, Red 3 and Red 4. If viewed head-on, the section would look to be in a slight 'vee' shape. As they flew along, each pilot could see the other three pilots in the section, and the space between aircraft was large enough to let them search for enemy aircraft rather than concentrate on keeping the right distance apart. It was in turning the section to attack that this formation proved so flexible. Rather than wheeling all four aircraft in the same formation – forcing the inside man to slow down while the outside man had to fly flat-out – the pilots just crossed over, that is, they switched over at the same altitude each was flying at and turned in such a way as to have the top view change from a right hand to a left hand. They could do this without changing speed. Red section as a whole flew in the middle, ahead of blue section 200 yards higher and to the right, while yellow section flew 200 yards lower on the left.

> "With the sections staggered in height, with the lowest being on the sun side and the highest on the up-sun side, we always had a cross-over view that largely eliminated the possibility of surprise. Our loose and wide-flung formation meant that 12 pairs of eyes were constantly searching the sky for the enemy while, at the same time, each man was able to see all our aircraft clearly."[6]

A variation on the finger four was called the 'fluid six'. On a dive-bombing mission, the custom was to have six aircraft carry 500-pound bombs, while the other six flew escort. It was to accommodate this situation that fluid six came into being. This was a finger four formation with one more pair – a lead pilot and his wing man – added on the side next to the formation leader's wing man.

Figure 28 -- 421 Squadron. *Back row: F/O Grigg, F/L Grant, F/L Gilmour, F/L Clark, F/O Smith, F/L Paterson, F/L Johnson, S/L Conrad, F/L McElroy, F/L Zary, F/O Warfield, F/L Thorne, F/O Murray, F/L Wilson. Front row: F/O Tetroe, F/O Curry, F/O McRoberts, F/L Stronach, F/O Bamford, F/O Driver, F/L Drope, F/O Brandon, F/S Saunders, F/O Calvert, F/O Cook -- June 1944.*
(Brandon collection)

In finger four or fluid six they would cruise on their way to a target or returning -- at the target was a different matter. In a strafing attack, they would often break into pairs flying line abreast, into sections line abreast or sometimes form a single line of wingtip-to-wingtip aircraft. In a dive-bombing attack, they would fly line astern at 6,000 feet, wait until the right wing tip of the lead aircraft covered the target and then peel off to the right, dive at 60-degrees, hold speed to 300 mph and release the bomb at 3,000 feet just at the start of the pull-out -- the second aircraft would repeat the operation and so on. When attacking a convoy of vehicles, one aircraft was detailed to take out the lead vehicle and another to take out the last vehicle. With the convoy stopped and men scurrying for cover, the rest of the squadron could attack at its leisure. When the squadron got into a dogfight, the sections immediately broke into pairs with each lead man attacking an enemy aircraft and each wing man trying to stay with his leader, continuously striving to keep his rear clear while the leader concentrated on his target.

Learning how the Spitfire acted in combat, and what tricks the enemy usually employed, was the skill that separated the aces from the sprogs (the Air Force term meaning a rookie pilot), and the survivors from the victims. As was so clearly learned in World War I, the first aim was to be between your adversary and the sun. The second tried and true lesson was to get on the enemy's tail. The head-on attack was another fundamental manoeuvre to learn to perfect. A major lesson was how to suddenly 'break' when an enemy got on your tail by means of a sudden turn, a sudden dive, a deceleration or sometimes a well-timed slide to one side. However with each combatant trying to get on the tail of his adversary, each throttled back and tried to turn in a tighter circle than the other, often entailing ever tighter diving turns with both aircraft nearly at right angles to the earth, cork-screwing ever downwards often to treetop level.

After completing one tour and before taking over as W/C (Flying) of 127 Wing, Hugh Godefroy was temporarily assigned to testing the performance of a captured FW 190. His intriguing job was to fly the Spitfire Mark IXb in simulated dogfights against the FW 190 and compare the performance and handling of each machine.

"But the things I discovered about the comparative performance of the Spitfire IXb proved invaluable to me in the next two years. In level flight and high speed the 190 flies slightly nose down. With a higher wing loading than the Spitfire, the 190's maximum rate of climb was attained at an airspeed of about 240 miles per hour. The Spitfire IXb's maximum rate of climb was attained at 160 miles per hour. Thus, if you were foolish enough to try to follow the 190 in full throttle at the same angle, you would soon find that he was above you. On the other hand, if you pulled away and held the Spitfire at an air speed of 160, you would climb at a much steeper angle and end up with a height advantage.

"Below 20 thousand feet in level speed runs there wasn't much in it either way. But once above 20 thousand feet, the Spitfire IXb's second blower kicked in, giving it the advantage.

"If Jamie Rankin, who was flying the 190, followed the favourite German technique of flicking over on his back and going straight down, he would pull away from me in the first two or three thousand feet. After that the Spitfire IXb could gradually catch him. Jamie never tried to tun inside me in the Spitfire. Both of us knew that wasn't possible. That was an advantage all British fighters enjoyed. At the end of the trials I came to the conclusion that I would still prefer a Spitfire IXb."[7]

Again and again in the combat reports quoted in the pages ahead, we will read cases illustrating Godefroy's point about the better diving characteristics and turning ability of the Spitfire, when we read how the Spitfire caught up with a diving enemy aircraft, or how it turned inside its German opponent.

The lessons that can only be learnt in combat also included some of the classic manoeuvres developed by expert pilots in both World Wars. There is the 'loop' known to everyone who has ever watched an airshow. Another is the quick 'breaking turn' where a pilot drops his wing to vertical position and rapidly turns through 90° before righting. Still another is the 'barrel roll' in which a pilot flicks over on his back while climbing slightly and then does a roll over as he rights himself and climbs slightly to resume his original direction. One famous manoeuvre is called the 'Immelmann' after the World War I German ace who perfected it. The pilot pulls up quickly into a steep climb, follows it as though in a loop but flicks out at the top of the loop to normal flight attitude going in the opposite direction. The reverse of this is the 'split-S' in which a pilot flips on his back, dives vertically and pulls out quickly travelling in the opposite direction in normal attitude. Other manoeuvres perfected to become favourites of some pilots are the 'skid' and the 'wing over'. In the skid, the pilot dips a wing slightly, applies strong opposite rudder and loses a bit of altitude, but appears to noticeably skid to one side or another. In the wing over, a pilot pulls into a steep climb, enters into a near stall, applies full rudder to yaw the aircraft in a cartwheeling turn, and enters into a dive almost along the course of his climb.

The pilots who became super-aces learned how to accomplish these tricky manoeuvres by instinct and to get themselves into and out of advantageous positions at will. Because these skills appeared only to come with actual combat, the death rate among young pilots newly introduced to combat was at its highest and if a new pilot could stay out of trouble for his first few combats he might survive; if not he became a statistic generally accompanied by the statement, "he had only been with the squadron for two weeks."

In addition to performing these manoeuvres instinctively, and having excellent eyesight to spot trouble before anyone else, a pilot had to perfect the art of 'deflection shooting'. This is the familiar problem of shooting at a horizontally flying bird -- and knowing how far ahead and how much above the horizontal one must aim so that bullet and bird meet. But compared to this simple example, the fighter pilot had to develop this ability in three dimensions from attitudes that might entail firing when he was upside-down and at speeds that varied from zero (flying behind) to 600 mph (flying head-on). This ability was the hardest to master – only a handful of aces became really expert at it.

Figure 29** -- **The Spitfire Mark IXb. *This clipped-wing version of the aircraft was never flown by 127 Wing but was purchased by John Paterson (an ex-421 pilot) shortly after the war. He painted it in 421 Squadron colours, flew it and eventually contributed it to the Canadian War Museum in Ottawa. Note the 421 Squadron code AU.*

(promotion photo)

Wing and Squadron Organization

Whereas, in the early years of the war, a fighter squadron was a self-contained unit, by 1944, the evolution of 2ndTAF required that whole airfields move with the advances of the army. A wing structure was introduced consisting of three squadrons supported by centralized services, where squadrons were reduced from about 140 personnel[8] to 35 personnel -- 29 pilots and six support officers -- while maintenance, cooking, flight control, intelligence, communication and transportation were concentrated in the wing organization. Each fighter squadron was allotted 18 Spitfires plus a small light plane to ferry men or materials, usually a Tiger Moth or an Auster. The optimum size for operational strength for a fighter squadron was 12 – originally two flights of six aircraft, but later three sections of four aircraft. Add an aircraft or two for training, an allowance for aircraft temporarily out of service for unscheduled repairs and those taken out for scheduled maintenance, and the usual total was 18 aircraft.

The squadron commander held the rank of S/L. He had two senior officers reporting to him – the commander of 'A' flight and the commander of 'B' flight -- both at the rank of F/L -- and he had several other administrative officers reporting to him – an Adjutant, a Medical Officer, an Engineering/Technical Officer and an Intelligence/Operations Officer and two clerical personnel. These were usually of F/O or Sgt rank. All the other pilots reported to one or other of the two flight commanders.

Early in the war, pilots were generally F/Ss or P/Os. As they became more proficient they were promoted to F/Os. A tour of duty was 200 operational hours. By 1944 many pilots were on a second or even third tour of duty gaining promotion over the years. While in 1942 it was very rare to find more than the two F/Ls in a squadron (the leaders of 'A' Flight and 'B' Flight) and to find many sergeant pilots, by 1944 every squadron had five, six or more F/Ls and most of the other pilots were F/Os.

Only the flight commanders and senior pilots were assigned their own aircraft, while others shared an aircraft. A crew chief and a team including an armourer, an instrument and electrical specialist, an engine mechanic and an airframe mechanic were assigned to each aircraft and other unassigned ground crew helped out with special servicing requirements such as installing extra fuel tanks and bombs, or with special maintenance requirements such as an engine change.

The official identification of RAF aircraft was a serial number which, after late 1941, consisted of two letters and three numerals, such as MJ887 or MK472 -- most of the Canadian Spitfire Mark IXbs being in the MH, MJ, MK, ML or NH series. Each squadron had its own unique two-letter (or one-letter-plus-a-numeral) call sign, those for the squadrons of 127 Wing were:

403 Squadron – KH

416 Squadron – DN

421 Squadron – AU

443 Squadron – 2I (443 Squadron joined 127 Wing, 14 July 1944)

In addition to the squadron code, each individual aircraft carried a single letter painted on the side of its fuselage after the squadron code in the form KH-N or DN-B. The general practice, though not all squadrons followed it, was to have the S/L's aircraft given the A letter, the flight commanders given B and D and then the remaining 15 aircraft assigned other letters. The letters O and C were rarely used. This system worked well, for even in the confusion of battle a pilot could catch a glimpse of E or K streaking by and quickly know which comrade it was. When an aircraft was sent to a repair depot or written off (the official term used was SOC -- stricken off charge) a new replacement aircraft would be painted up with the replaced identity letter.

Wing commanders were allowed to have their initials painted on the fuselage instead of the usual two-letter squadron code and single-letter aircraft code. Thus W/C Lloyd Vernon Chadburn flew a Spitfire with the code LV-C painted on its side, W/C George Keefer flew GC-K and W/C James Edgar Johnnie Johnson's aircraft carried JE-J.

Chapter Seven – D-Day and the days until the move to France

On 17 April, 127 Wing personnel arrived at RAF Station Tangmere just 15 miles east of Chichester in West Sussex and found the place very crowded, for in addition to a couple of fully resident squadrons, there were six visiting squadrons of Spitfires. Three belonged to 126 Wing and the other three to 127 Wing.

The 108 Spitfires of the six squadrons were painted with broad invasion stripes only the day before D-Day. It had been a frantic last minute effort with every available hand painting the one-foot-wide white-black-white-black-white stripes on each wing by the wing root and on the fuselage just aft of the aerial mast. At midnight of 5 June, all pilots and key wing personnel were assembled in the briefing hall in the officer's mess to receive their instructions as to what was expected of them on D-Day. The long anticipated Second Front was about to open -- the day of action and of glory was at hand.

All spring long the conjecture flowed; with every member of aircrew and ground crew harbouring his own opinion as to when it would be. A lot of betting took place. Only the handful of the top secret inner circle knew -- and they couldn't tell on pain of death. As the nervous babble of the assembled crowd in the officer's mess quietened down, W/C Brown mounted the stage while outside, the assemblage could hear the rumbling roar of hundreds of four-engine aircraft filling the night sky flying nearly over the base. You could have cut the excitement with a knife.

Shortly after midnight the morning of 6 June, S/L Robert Whalley, Administration Officer at 127 Wing Headquarters, was at Old Sarum north of Salisbury preparing an echelon of 127 Wing personnel and their vehicles to move to France soon after D-Day. No one told Whalley that this was D-Day. No one had to; he found out by witnessing it. Here is what he wrote for the 127 Wing ORB:

"6 June – During the early hours, most persons were awakened to hear a roar of planes overhead and the increased activity over anything previously heard, brought many out of their beds to see

Figure 30 -- Whalley. *As the senior Administration Officer of 127 Wing, S/L R L Whalley wrote the 127 ORB for W/C Brown's signature, and so become the chief narrator of this part of the book.*

(McElroy collection)

what was happening. A great armada was passing overhead and by the light of the moon, which occasionally appeared between breaks in the cloud, we saw a scene which warmed and excited our hearts. The planes were heavy bombers; behind each of which we made out the outline of a glider. There were hundreds of them and they took over an hour to pass by. All the aircraft were flying in formation, using their navigation lights, and the long line stretching across the sky for as far as the eye could see, was one of the most magnificent and thrilling sights most of us had ever witnessed. The aircraft seemed to be climbing up the ridge to the north of us, and with their various coloured lights, it appeared as slow light flak ascending into the heavens. We didn't know it was D-Day, but many of us guessed that this was the initial assault. News at breakfast confirmed the fact that the Second Front, so called, had begun. We are supposed, providing the operation goes to plan, to land on the continent on D-plus-seven – less than one week to go. Each succeeding news broadcast was received by persons who crowded around the wireless. We were itching for information and knew so little. The OC (Officer Commanding) 'B' Echelon, S/L Whalley, announced the invasion to the wing parade at 0900 hours. The cheer that went up warmed many hearts. Everybody seemed keen and this keenness should go a long way to making this a successful venture."[1]

Meanwhile, back at Tangmere, each of the three squadron adjutants in 127 Wing made entries in their individual squadron ORBs. Perhaps the one from 421 Squadron prepared by F/O Lloyd Hennessy best summed up what everyone was thinking:

> "6 June – D-Day. Yes it has finally arrived. Squadrons all briefed for the big show late last night and everyone on readiness ever since dawn. As a result, most personnel spent a sleepless night wondering and waiting for the push to start. However, we were doomed to disappointment as far as enemy aircraft opposition went. The squadron carried out four patrols between dawn and dusk, and not a living thing was sighted in the air except apparently thousands of Allied aircraft all making their way towards Hitler's European Fortress. Returning pilots report that the Channel seems to be full of sea-going craft of all shapes and sizes, apparently everything is going well."[2]

The briefing ended at about 0130 hours in the morning and the pilots were up and ready for action by 0600. Each of the three squadrons of 127 Wing flew four wing-strength patrols on D-Day for a total of 138 sorties. Though they were tired from such a long day, and extremely disappointed because they had seen no action, the pilots of 127 Wing were sure it was just a matter of time before the Hun, as they called him, would appear.

S/L Whalley, still at Old Sarum on 7 June -- D-Day-plus-one -- wrote this entry for the 127 Wing ORB:

> "During the night and day, hundreds of aircraft passed overhead. Despite poor weather in this area, the operation continued. We are all anxiously waiting for news of successes by our own squadrons. Unfortunately, only the wireless and newspapers are giving us any idea of what is happening. All personnel turned in their English currency for French francs and invasion money. Bathing parades were organized for all ranks. The MT (motor transport) section was busy assisting with the waterproofing of our vehicles. By 1700 hours the stage (of the preparation procedure) allocated to this area was completed, and vehicles were run back to their hard standings. Other units in this same camp received their movement orders for 8 June. We won't be moving until June 9th at least. Main HQ 83 Group challenged the MT section to a game of soccer and we won.

Others of our personnel played softball – many spent the day catching up on their correspondence. The meals are good and the camp, is very efficiently run. So far we have had no casualties on sick parades, the general health being excellent. Censorship of all mail continued, and a number of officers were kept busy with this duty. Our first incoming mail was received and distributed."[3]

Early losses

The OVERLORD planners predicted a certain number of losses of fighter pilots as part of the initial D-Day assault, however, apart from the losses that occurred when one of the landing craft was sunk, 127 Wing did not lose anyone. This was not to be for long.

The day after D-Day, on the second patrol of the day a little before 1300 hours, F/L Johnny Drope of 421 Squadron was flying with his squadron just off UTAH beach when he reported the engine of his MJ554 running roughly. S/L Wally Conrad advised Drope that it would be too risky to try to land on the beach because of the congestion of troops and vehicles, instead he advised Drope to bale out. W/C Lloyd Chadburn agreed. Drope rolled his ailing aircraft over, slid out of the cockpit of his Spitfire and pulled the rip chord. Nothing happened. His parachute failed to open and Drope fell from 2,000 feet with his unopened parachute streaming behind him, hit the surface of the Channel waters and sent a plume of water higher than that made by his Spitfire when it crashed minutes later. It occurred in plain view of the whole wing and everyone was appalled. Drope was an excellent pilot and a very affable and loved team-mate who seemed to know someone in just about every one of the Canadian squadrons. His remains were recovered immediately and F/L William John Drope was later buried at Bayeux Cemetery.

At 1940 hours, with the squadron still smarting from the senseless loss of so popular a pilot, the fourth and final patrol of the day took off. The pattern of the day was to have squadron-strength flights with an extra spare position. 13 aircraft would take off and if all the other aircraft were in the air and functioning normally, the spare would return to base. This evening F/O Robert Grigg was flying spare for 421 Squadron. After forming up a few miles over the coast and starting out across the Channel, Grigg bade his friends good-bye and turned his aircraft NH183 back to return to Tangmere. About five minutes after his departure he gave a Mayday signal indicating his aircraft was going down. Pilots from Tangmere were sent out for an intensive search before nightfall set in, but there was no sighting of Grigg nor of any wreckage. Considering the time the Mayday signal was heard, the pilots figured Grigg was about 10 or 12 miles off St. Catherine's Point. F/O Robert Jackson Grigg is remembered on panel 246 at Runnymede Memorial in Surrey.

This was most shocking and disconcerting. Two pilots were lost through freakish accidents and 127 Wing had yet to see an enemy airplane.

The following day – 8 June – was to be a day like D-Day and D-Day-plus-one. The wing flew four wing-strength patrols over the Western Assault Area. At about 1230 hours, as 416 Squadron wheeled around completing a leg of its patrol, the squadron was subjected to a blast of enemy flak. P/O Bob Maranda was hit and had to bale out of MJ929 over the waters off UTAH beach. The navy was alerted and it was assumed Maranda would be in the water only a matter of minutes while the wing pilots watched his parachute float down to the Channel waters, but after it hit he was seen struggling with the parachute release. When the navy boat reached him, Maranda had drowned, pulled under by his parachute. P/O Joseph Cyril Robert Maranda is remembered on panel 251 at Runnymede Memorial in Surrey.

When the 7th and 8th of June brought 140 and 114 sorties but still no enemy opposition, the pilots of 127 Wing were becoming very frustrated and confused by the senseless death of three of their number. To provide variety but no relief from their feelings of disappointment and frustration, the weather socked in 9 June bringing a ceiling that hung a mere 200 feet of over the Channel. It rained heavily all day until suppertime. The only activity of the day was a wing-strength patrol that took off at 2020 hours in cloudy gloom – but at least with a bit better ceiling of about 800 feet -- however, 800 feet was not enough. As the 36 Spitfires flew in towards OMAHA beach, Royal Navy ships opened up with a blistering anti-aircraft barrage and

403 Squadron took the heaviest beating from this friendly fire, as the squadron record tells it:

"9 Jun – Even the birds are walking today – dirty weather. But at about 2020 hours we were on our way again on a patrol over the beachhead. The ceiling was down to about 800 feet and as we came in over OMAHA beach our navy let everything they had go at us. We immediately got out of the way and called Research who told us to come in again as it would be alright this time. So in we went again, this time flying line astern and with our navigation lights on, but still those trigger twitchy guys of the navy let us have (it) a second time. Those guys must really be blind, because of all the aircraft that have been seen most in this show, the Spit most certainly has. So away we go again, giving Research hell, and prepare for a third go, and sure enough the navy cut loose with everything they have a third time, hitting four of our kites causing F/L E C Williams' aircraft to disappear, nothing more being seen of him. P/O Kelly was slightly wounded but landed his aircraft safely at Tangmere and taxied over to the ambulance at flying control. F/O Thomson and F/O Shapter's aircraft were hit but the pilots themselves were uninjured."[4]

F/L Bill Williams' aircraft MJ827 came down on the Cotentin Peninsula west of UTAH beach. He was seriously injured, captured by the Germans and taken to a hospital in Cherbourg, staying there until Cherbourg fell 29 June, when he was liberated by American soldiers. P/O Ed Kelly's aircraft MJ952 was slightly damaged, and Kelly was reported to be slightly wounded. His slight wound turned out to be from a Royal Navy 50-calibre bullet that passed through the seat armour, seat and parachute and took away part of his rump necessitating him sleeping on his stomach for a very long time! The other two squadrons were much farther from the Royal Navy ships and received no damage from the navy flak.

Building B.2 Bazenville

The plan to operate out of France entailed many co-ordinated actions. A small group from the administrative part of the wing was to form an advanced party referred to as 'A' Echelon. They would cross the Channel with the last wave of assaulting troops late on D-Day and be there from the beginning, helping out as best they could the company of engineers who were to build the airfield and the servicing commandos who were to defend it and service aircraft. Many years later Bill Mason, who was a F/L in 416 Squadron at the time, described the beginning of this process:

> "I have a friend here in Victoria, Alexander Hamilton, past CEO of Canadian Forest Products and Domtar Ltd. Alex was the chief Engineering Officer for 127 Wing for most of the war. On 5 June, Alex as chief technical officer, along with 28 RCAF personnel including an intelligence officer, two padres, and a medical doctor boarded LCTs (landing craft, tank) in the Thames estuary awaiting the call. On 6 June Alex arrived at the beachhead (near Courseulles-sur-Mer) which had been secured by the North Shore Regiment of Nova Scotia. Alex's instructions were to proceed to Bazenville and confirm the suitability of the designated B.2 site and also investigate the possibilities of utilizing the Caen airport at Carpiquet."[5]

The Allied plan for D-Day included the taking of Caen by the British 3rd Division by the evening of 6 June. Had that been accomplished, the large concrete-runway airfield at Carpiquet just outside Caen would have been a prize, for although it might be damaged by retreating Germans, and would likely still be under artillery fire, it could be turned into a valuable base for the Allies. The airstrip proposed to be located at B.2 was intended to be a repair and re-arm airstrip, with a shorter runway than a regular ALG and not as well equipped. Mason continues:

Figure 31 -- 416 pilots. *Back row F/L Pat Patterson, F/L Bill Mason and F/O Sandy Borland. Front row: P/O Bill Palmer, F/L Dick Forbes-Roberts and F/O Al McFadden taken at Tangmere 30 May 1944.*

(Canadian Forces photo PL30229)

"The latter (Carpiquet airport) had not been taken and work on the B.2 site went ahead with RAF Commandos bulldozing and laying 5000 feet of steel runway matting. They hoped to complete the strip by D-plus-two, but this was thwarted by a damaged Liberator which tore up a third of the matting when it pranged (crash-landed). Nevertheless it was finished by D-plus-three and operational by D-plus-four, i.e. available with petrol for refuelling, ammunition, etc. Incidentally, the medical staff crossed the Channel on the same day under the command of Dr MacArthur but unfortunately they were torpedoed but all survived." [6]

Three LCTs were torpedoed by a couple of E-Boats that broke through the defences and streaked across the invasion route late on D-Day. One of these was the LCT that carried some 'A' Echelon staff and some equipment and materials. The chief Medical Officer for 127 Wing was S/L Cam MacArthur -- the senior 127 Wing officer in the group. He was accompanied by technical officers and intelligence officers.

"They, apparently, had an interesting time .... One party, led by S/L MacArthur was torpedoed on the way across. Fortunately, none of our personnel was missing, though one officer, F/L McNab, Intelligence, suffered minor burns. All the equipment on board went down. Several of the officers transferred to other shipping coming over, and some airmen returned to England. A number of airmen of 3207 and 3209 Servicing Commandos, who were on board, went down with the vessel." [7]

The loss of some of the material has left a strange scar in the form of a lapse in the continuity of 421 Squadron's ORB. Each squadron showed some variation in the way it kept its records, but generally the rule was that each aircraft serial number was recorded when the aircraft was flown. 421 Squadron's ORB conformed to this rule from its inception in 1942 right up until the end of March 1944, and resumed again in June 1944, but in the intervening months of April and May, each flight was recorded showing only the aircraft code, that is, A, B, D, etc. Although nowhere stated, it seems the April and May records went down with the LCT. Confronted with that loss, the only way the adjutant could reconstruct the ORB details was to consult with each pilot's flight log book knowing that pilots rarely if ever recorded serial numbers in their log books, but they always recorded aircraft codes. Hence the strange discontinuity of the records.

3209 Servicing Commandos bore the heaviest loss when the LCT went down, for no unit records have survived. The loss of several men and the equipment, set the schedule back considerably, but it is remarkable how quickly others recovered.

> "6 June -- Five Airfield Construction Groups were phased in to land on the beaches on D- Day. All the Groups got ashore between 12 and 36 hours behind schedule owing to the rough seas, which delayed the work of the rhinos and small craft. The landing of the preloaded stores was even more delayed and this fact affected the whole weeks work.

> "7 June – No. 16 Group started work on B.2 on this day and had a strip ready for tracking by 9 June." [8]

No. 16 Airfield Construction Group of the Royal Engineers was assigned to build B.2. While they built it, No. 3207 and No. 3209 Servicing Commandos units provided the protection and support. The Servicing Commandos (reduced in number after the loss of the LCT) landed shortly after midnight 7 June along with the engineers. While the engineers unloaded their bulldozers and graders, the Servicing Commandos unloaded cranes and truckloads of tools. Together they built runways, dispersal areas, communications facilities, landing lights (and the power facilities to light them), set up and manned anti-aircraft guns, maintenance bays plus the many other camp requirements. The airfield was bulldozed to even it out (the south-west end was 20 feet higher than the north-east end), and was covered with Sommerfeldt wire mesh. Construction was started just after midnight D-Day and would have been completed by 9 June, if the B-24 hadn't ripped it up. B.2 first serviced the 36 aircraft of 127 Wing on 11 June, and the wing moved in fully on 16 June.

Another team was busy at work at B.3 Ste.Croix-sur-Mer, only a mile-and-a-half away. The plan had been to first construct an Emergency Landing Strip (ELS) at which aircraft in trouble could set down, then a Refuelling and Re-arming strip (RR) and finally ALGs to which wings were to move, and from which they would operate. Because Caen was not captured, and because the lodgement was thereby so restricted in size, plans had to be hurriedly revised and all available sites in the lodgement turned into ALGs. What eventually became B.2 and B.3 ALGs were supposed to have been the ELS and the RR.

The Servicing Commandos worked hard. In one day they serviced 77 Spitfires, one Mustang, two Thunderbolts and four Typhoons. All this while the only 127 Wing personnel in France were the 'A' Echelon people. The second group to go over, 'B' Echelon, left Tangmere on 5 June and proceeded to Old Sarum to go through the sausage machine – a process of waterproofing all the vehicles and preparing the drivers and other members of the echelon for the trip across the Channel. S/L Whalley was in charge of this 'B' Echelon group and that is why the narrative in the 127 Wing ORB follows him through Old Sarum. This group travelled in two LCTs -- one under the command of S/L Whalley the other commanded by F/L Singer, a technical officer. They left Old Sarum at 0650 hours on 14 June and landed in France just around midnight. Though separated at the landing point both groups made their way to B.2 where they were re-united with the 'A' Echelon. Here is Whalley's colourful description of what they did and what they found when they got there:

"The convoy departed at 0100 hours (14 June) and headed for Normandy, arriving off Mike/Nan Beach, west of Courseulles-sur-Mer at 1030 hours. The American craft in which we were travelling, dropped anchor some two miles off shore, and we waited for naval instructions to beach. While waiting off shore, persons watched the 'battle wagons' of the Royal Navy – HMS Rodney and HMS Warspite, as well as a number of unidentified craft, send salvo after salvo inland in the general direction of Caen. Altogether, the day was interesting to most of us. All sorts of craft went backwards and forward with their loads and on various missions. Aircraft patrolled the beaches during this waiting period. We received orders to beach at 2040 hours, anchor came up and into shore we went. The tide was well up and eight feet of water confronted us. It must be noted that this applies to the craft occupied by S/L Whalley's party. F/L Singer's party was nowhere to be seen. It was since ascertained that he landed several miles to the westward, but that conditions were similar. The tide was not favourable for landing our vehicles until 2230 hours. Just as we started to run the first vehicle off the ship, Jerry appeared, and the AA (anti-aircraft guns) opened up. Nothing was dropped near us, but the craft beached next to F/L Singer's received a direct hit. As a result, the landing on that beach was considerably accelerated. We followed our party inland through the Transit area and into Assembly. The last vehicle arrived 0030 hours (night of 14/15 June), necessitating our remaining there overnight.

Nobody, or very few, had any sleep but remained on their vehicles. The almost continuous drone of enemy aircraft overhead and the, or so it seemed to us, terrific barrage put up by the AA was deafening. We were in France and no one knew what lay ahead. We left the Assembly area at 0800 hours (morning of 15 June) and proceeded in convoy with 17 Sector to B.2 ALG. There, we were greeted by those of our advance party who had come over earlier. The day was spent in organizing our camp. Most persons turned in very early for a good night's rest, but only after digging themselves a good slit trench. The Hun's butterfly bombs were landing on some nights too close for comfort, and a small number of persons had already received injuries. We had hoped to sleep, but few did. As the last fighter disappeared from the area because of darkness, Jerry appeared. He started off his activity by dropping two 1800 kilo land mines just off the airfield; one landing on the outskirts of Bazenville. The following hours of darkness realized numerous explosions in the vicinity, but the continuous bark of our own AA was the main cause of sleeplessness. No person was injured."[9]

The final move of the balance of 127 Wing personnel, the last of the trucks and the aircraft and pilots themselves would occur two days later -- 16 June.

Continuing operations

On 10 June, two of the advanced landing grounds were sufficiently completed that they could receive patrolling aircraft and re-arm and refuel them. That changed things considerably. Instead of taking off from Tangmere with 90 gallons of extra fuel to extend their flight time to over two hours -- a half hour to cross the Channel, an hour on patrol and a half hour to get home – they could double the length of their patrols. After Johnnie Johnson's 144 Wing proved the workability of this replenishment routine, W/C Chadburn took 403 Squadron and 421 Squadron to France early on 11 June. They flew a 90-minute patrol of OMAHA and UTAH beaches starting at 0830 hours, and then landed at B.3 Ste.Croix-sur-Mer. After re-arming and refuelling they patrolled once again for an hour and then returned to Tangmere arriving home at 1040 hours. They did it a bit differently on 12 June. Both 403 and 421 took off at 1125 hours and flew to

France under Chad's guidance, but whereas Bob Buckham and his 403 Squadron returned to Tangmere with Chad, Wally Conrad landed his 421 Squadron at 1320 hours at B.2 after completing an extra patrol. Though the record is unclear, it appears 421 did another two patrols before returning to Tangmere. The narrowness of the lodgement left the Germans well within artillery range of the first few airstrips. For this reason AVM Broadhurst forbade any of his day-fighters from spending the night on the continent as originally planned.

Tuesday 13 June was to be a more elaborate affair than the previous two days. It was decided that 403 could now have a day off while 416 and 421 spent the whole day in France. They flew to Normandy early in the morning, flew four patrols throughout the day, each time returning to B.2 or B.3, and flew back to Tangmere that night. It was intended to be a dress rehearsal for the day – now ordered to be 16 June – when 127 Wing would move to France and make B.2 its new permanent home. Little did the planners know what a tragedy was about unfold.

The Loss of Lloyd Chadburn

At 0730 hours 13 June, Chadburn, 12 aircraft of 416 Squadron led by F/L Dave Prentice and 12 aircraft of 421 Squadron led by S/L Wally Conrad took off from Tangmere. Immediately after take-off, F/L Pat Patterson of 416 experienced engine trouble with MJ770 and turned back to base. Less than a half-hour after take-off F/O Robert Murray of 421 Squadron, had the engine of his MJ235 act up. When he dropped out of formation he was already two-thirds of the way across the Channel so two pilots from his yellow section, F/L Roger Wilson and F/O John Hamm, were detailed to catch up with Murray and escort him back to Tangmere. Unfortunately, Murray never made it back but died in the Channel. It is unclear whether he was trying to bale out when he was much too low, or whether he was trying to ditch, but in any event when the searchers discovered him he was dead and hopelessly entangled in his parachute. F/O Robert Wilson Murray is buried at Brookwood Cemetery, Sussex.

The rest of the wing (now reduced to 21 aircraft) proceeded to France, patrolled several trips around the circuit of the Western Assault Area and landed at B.2. 421 Squadron must have done one more trip, for it landed 25 minutes after 416 landed. Both squadrons were on the ground at 0955 hours. An hour later there was a scramble and all 21 aircraft took off at 1110 hours. It was obviously a frightening prospect to think they might be surprised while lined up in the open on the ground. After finding no bogeys Conrad's logbook contained the entry,

"Scramble B.2 – F/A" – (air force parlance for 'fuck all.'),

the aircraft landed at 1130 hours. It was cloudy in France – between 7/10ths and 10/10ths cloud covering the sky throughout the day. At noon the aircraft of both squadrons took off to patrol the Eastern Assault Area. According to 416 Squadron ORB, it was on this patrol that Flight Sergeant Bill Saunders crash-landed ML292 upon take-off. Saunders was not hurt and the aircraft was a Cat B, that is, it could be repaired there at B.2.

After an uneventful patrol, the two squadrons landed at 1400 hours for a two-hour layover. There is some evidence that 416 landed at B.2 while 421 landed at B.3 -- a mile-and-a-half to the north-east of B.2. At 1645 hours the two squadrons were off again for a patrol of the Eastern Assault Area. F/L Bill Mason of 416 Squadron, after consulting his log book recalled the following:

> "While patrolling near Caen, 416 was vectored to some bogeys -- the air controller's term for unidentified aircraft. Chad went with 416. They found nothing. When Chad and 416 Squadron attempted to re-unite with 421 they approached each other in cloud, and Chad collided with F/L Frank Clark."[10]

Clark's aircraft NH415 exploded immediately upon impact while Chadburn's MJ824 must have spun down and landed at the little town of Bénouville beside Pegasus Bridge five miles north of Caen. After his aircraft hit the ground, British troops pulled Chad out of the cockpit, but he was so badly injured that he never regained consciousness and died within an hour.[11]

There is a contradiction regarding the time this occurred. The patrol that took off at 1200 hours, landed at B.2 at 1345 hours. According to the 421 ORB, Clark took off with this patrol and did not return – suggesting the collision occurred some time between 1230 and 1300 hours. At 1645 hours there was another patrol. It was on this patrol – according to Mason's log, and as recorded in the 416 ORB, that the collision occurred. Chadburn's official biographer contends that Chad died that evening and that the accident occurred around 1700 hours. Conrad's flight log disagrees. He was the S/L of 421 Squadron which on this day was code named Lovebird and Clark was his wingman, flying about 200 feet from his wing. Against the 1200 hours patrol, Conrad's log book has the following entry:

> "W/C Chadburn collided with F/Lt Frank Clarke (sic) Lovebird Two over Caen. Both killed."

Whatever the correct time, it was a shocking thing to happen. Chadburn was one of the most revered of Canada's new young air force elite. He had been one of the first graduates from the British Commonwealth Air Training Plan to attain squadron command rank. Socially, he was an affable man who enjoyed the friendship and respect of those who served under him and technically, he was renowned for his sense of the dynamics of an aerial battle -- the sense of when and how to commit his sections or squadrons -- today called situational awareness, but in World War II recognized as an uncommon ability. He was also said to have had an uncanny sense of where home was, many times astounding his squadron by telling them to follow him, then leading them down through thick cloud invariably breaking out over home base. Squadrons and wings – including a couple of American groups -- immediately expressed their shock and their sorrow at the loss of this fine commander. W/C Lloyd Vernon Chadburn, DSO and bar, DFC and bar, C de G avec Palme, L d'H, is buried at Ranville Cemetery near where he crashed. F/L Frank Joel Clark is buried in Bretteville-sur-Laize Cemetery ten miles south of Caen. Both Chad and Frank had sons. Chad's son was born three months after he died. Frank's son was 18 months old, but Frank had not seen him since he was six months old.

This accident had two important effects. First, it caused the powers to be to rethink the succession plan and this led to a restructure of all 2ndTAF fighter wings. Second, it so incensed 421 Squadron that certain members like Johnny McElroy -- who had been Clark's tent-mate -- became highly motivated. Since D-Day, 421 had lost four pilots and their wing commander without having shot down a single Hun and they were now loaded for bear, ready to redeem the squadron's pride. Their chance occurred two days later.

Aftermath of the death of Lloyd Chadburn

The night of 13 June found the personnel of 127 Wing divided and confused. The advanced guard 'A' Echelon had been in France for a week working with the engineers and the servicing commandos to be ready for the rest of the wing. They heard of the tragedy as soon as it happened. 'B' Echelon with half the trucks, half the supplies and equipment and over 200 airmen – including S/L Whalley -- was at Old Sarum, and did not hear about the tragedy for a couple of days. The remainder of the wing was at Tangmere. They heard about the tragedy by suppertime.

Figure 32 -- Buckham. In his first tour of duty W/C Bob Buckham flew with 416 Squadron and was credited with six enemy aircraft destroyed. He became squadron commander of 403 Squadron in October 1943 and by D-Day he was close to the end of his second tour. Upon the death of Lloyd Chadburn, Bob Buckham was promoted to replace him as W/C (F) of 127 Wing..

(McElroy collection)

The evening of 13 June S/L Bob Buckham, squadron commander of 403 Squadron, was informed of his promotion to W/C to replace Chadburn. Buckham served in that capacity for just one month. Many years later, Hugh Godefroy wrote in his book '*Lucky Thirteen*' about the appointment. Godefroy had been Buckham's superior only months

211

before and knew him well. When told his tour was up, Buckham is reported to have accepted the decision without comment, but when he was ordered to fly back to 83 Group headquarters in England, he refused telling his superior, G/C Bill MacBrien, "Bill, I'm not flying over that Channel one more time. You'll have to send me over in a boat."[12]

In recent years it has been called Post Traumatic Stress Syndrome, but in World War II it was still called Shell Shock, or as the airmen called it the twitch. No human being can withstand continuous strain for very long and it was the duty of every squadron commander to watch his men for changes in behaviour after prolonged exposure to the stress of flying in combat or through flak. Some pilots suddenly began to hang back from danger, others plunged into danger recklessly, still others had more subtle symptoms; inability to sleep, severe nightmares, withdrawal or the opposite, excessive nervous chatter. Airmen could suddenly exhibit this kind of shift in behaviour, just as they could suddenly develop stomach ulcers. The commander had to be continuously aware of the point when one key player of his team could begin to endanger the lives of the others.

Figure 33 -- McElroy. *F/L John McElroy flew in Malta earning a DFC after destroying 8 enemy aircraft. After a leave he joined 421 Squadron on his second tour in January 1944. McElroy led the successful patrol 15 June.*
(McElroy collection)

Whereas this effect has been known to suddenly strike individuals, senior officers knew that it could strike groups as well. Morale – that curious element that can turn ordinary people into giants or giants into pygmies -- is always a key ingredient of a group's performance. A sudden traumatic event can trigger in large numbers of people a lack of belief in one's leaders, disbelief in one's certainty to win, doubt and despondency. The violent death of Lloyd Chadburn was such an event -- as was the violent death of

Frank Clark. Among the many groups, fragmented and shocked by this event, some felt leaderless, some felt the wing had fallen apart, some like Bob Buckham felt a burden thrust upon him, and some like Johnny McElroy felt so angry he was ready to take on the world.

Luckily, Wednesday 14 June was a day of light workload. 403 Squadron flew an uneventful sweep to Paris without meeting opposition and landed at B.4 Beny-sur-Mer. There they sat around on standby from 1300 hours to 2100 hours before going on another uneventful sweep on their way back to Tangmere. Bob Buckham -- controlling his fear of a Channel-crossing for one more day -- led his squadron for the last time. 416 Squadron flew a similar pattern, sweeping Montdidier and landing at B.2. After a day of standby, they too flew a patrol on their way back to Tangmere. As for 421 Squadron, they flew a two-aircraft convoy patrol early in the morning and then 12 aircraft on Ramrod 1001 – escorting 15 Mitchell medium bombers to Conde-sur-Vire just south of St. Lô. There was no party for 127 Wing that night in the Tangmere mess.

Combat Thursday 15 June

It had been a very typical June day for both southern England and for Normandy. From sunrise it had alternated between cloudy and clear over the south coast of England, clear over the Channel but cloud building into heavier cloud with two layers at 3,000 feet and 6 to 7,000 feet over France. All three squadrons flew an uneventful patrol leaving Tangmere at 0845 hours and returning at 1100 hours. Other wings had flown the front line patrols earlier – indeed, 127 Wing met 132 Wing as they replaced them on station – but as they left France, conditions were getting pretty bad. There wouldn't be another front line patrol until the weather cleared up. The wing got safely back to base and was then placed on readiness at Tangmere. Ground crews kept 36 aircraft fuelled, armed and ready to go, but it was the late afternoon before flying weather again returned. Headquarters sent word that 125 Wing had just been dispatched to fly a front line patrol and that 127 was to fly the succeeding one.

The three squadrons of 127 Wing took off from Tangmere, six aircraft at a time, starting at 1855 hours. The 36 aircraft formed up over Selsey Bill and flew across the Channel, making landfall at Port-en-Bessin about 1930 hours. The sky was now clear of cloud but hazy over the Channel. Inland over France the weather was spotty with a pronounced haze and a lot of lingering cloud. Freddie Green, squadron commander of 416, flew as wing leader on this patrol until the three squadrons split up over the beaches, after which they patrolled under individual squadron command.

A week had passed since D-Day and all three Canadian wings had been in a drought. W/C George Keefer's 126 Wing had one good day when they tussled with the Ju 88s over the beaches the day after D-Day, and just two days ago, two of Johnnie Johnson's pilots each got a Bf 109 -- but that was it. Canadian pilots were not doing well while 127 Wing pilots were doing nothing at all. They were fed up. The order had come through a couple of days before that they were to move to France tomorrow –16 June -- so when they landed back at Tangmere this night it would be for the last time. They hoped things would get better when they were permanently in France.

From Port-en-Bessin the three squadrons split up – 416 taking the western part of the lodgement from OMAHA through to the Cotentin Peninsula, 403 taking the middle part from OMAHA to Caen and 421 taking the eastern part Caen to Cabourg. S/L Freddie Green led his own 416 Squadron, while F/L Hart Finley led 403 Squadron and F/L Johnny McElroy led 421 Squadron. Nothing much was happening in the western sectors but there was a lot of flak around Caen where the pilots could catch an occasional glimpse of some attacking Typhoons. 421 Squadron patrolled for 10 minutes, seeing nothing else.

In the meantime, 20 Bf 109s of I./JG 27 led by Hauptmann Rudi Sinner, took off at 1830 hours from their base at Vertus near Épernay, 60 miles east of Paris and about 200 miles east of the beaches. Their mission was to intercept fighter-bombers and at about 1950 hours they reached the Caen area. As 421 swung towards Caen on its patrol, ground control reported bogeys nearby at higher altitude causing the pilots to jettison their auxiliary fuel tanks and swung into action. Under these evening conditions the squadron of Spitfires, flying lower, went unseen against the dark and haze of the land under them, but the Germans flying between clouds were silhouetted against the light sky. F/L Johnny McElroy picks up the story in his combat report:

"We were patrolling (the) area north-east of Caen when 20 plus Me 109s were sighted at 12,000 feet to 14,000 feet. We broke (up) into them. I got on the tail of a Me 109, which began to climb. At 100 yards range and with 15° deflection I opened fire and I observed some strikes on the fuselage. He broke and disappeared into cloud."[13]

At the first clash the neat finger four sections broke up into pairs, but often while bobbing and weaving, individual aircraft became separated as F/L Bill Stronach relates in his combat report:

"I was flying Yellow Four on patrol with 421 Squadron near Caen at approximately 6,000 feet when 109s were reported 15,000 feet over Caen. We climbed into them and in the confusion I lost my number one. Picked out a 109 and fired a short burst at 1000 yards, then followed him down shooting and closed in. Final burst approximately 300 yards at 20° deflection. I saw strikes, then smoke and fire from the engine. He turned on his back and dove in from 2,000 feet approximately four miles south-east of Caen."[14]

As the aircraft circled around trying to shake each other off, individual struggles developed with opponents trading altitude for position. F/L John Paterson wrote:

"...yellow section climbed to join rest of squadron and we got into a large gaggle of enemy aircraft at 13,000 feet. I fired at a Me 109 from about 350 yards with 15° to 20° deflection, strikes were observed on cockpit and wing root followed by smoke and flame. I orbited and saw him crash. I followed the gaggle around again and picked another 109 firing from 400 yards down to 250 yards. I saw strikes on his wing root, engine and cockpit again followed by smoke and flame. The enemy aircraft was trembling and flicking and on fire when last seen going down."[15]

F/O Bill 'Cookie' Cook was leading blue section as they climbed to attack the Bf 109s of I./JG 27. In his combat report he described his victory as follows:

"20-plus Me 109s were reported at 14,000 feet. I climbed up into one and he started a gentle dive to starboard. I fired one burst from about 400 yards which missed then I closed to about 200 yards and firing with about 15° to 20° deflection and saw strikes around wing roots from astern. Glycol or white smoke poured out and he rolled over on his back. My number two, F/O Warfield saw him crash into a field saying he went in at about an 80° angle."[16]

F/O Willie Warfield, who had followed Cook through this encounter, submitted his own claim. His description captures the exhilarating experience of turning, flick-rolling and diving always lower to gain speed and to out-manoeuvre the opponent -- diving until at tree top level the fight becomes a test of nerves:

"I was flying Blue Two behind Blue One as he attacked an Me 109. Two Me 109s bounced us from six o'clock and I broke 180° port. Blue One broke into sun. Both 109s turned with me but one flicked out, the other spiralled down but I managed to keep with him after completing four rolls. This 109 dove to the south of Caen and it took me approximately eight to 10 miles to close with him. I opened fire approximately 600 yards at 0° to 5° deflection, corrected and immediately the 109 streamed coolant from the port side. I fired my second burst from 300 to 400 yards with 0° to 5° deflection, a long one and strikes appeared all over the 109 which finally disintegrated. When I broke off attack another 109 was on my tail so I steep-turned through trees about 10 feet off the deck and was cutting him off and getting into position to fire when he either flicked in or hit a tree, and catapulted into an open field and exploded. No one was about to confirm either, but my camera was on throughout the first attack and before I was able to attack the second Me 109, I was able to take a cine film of it crash into the ground. Also a picture of the first 109 that crashed into a wood, setting trees and undergrowth on fire. The attack commenced about 1200 feet and ended up at zero feet and I probably attained 450 mph closing on the first Me 109."[17]

In this battle, F/O Jack Bamford distinguished himself with the feat of destroying three enemy aircraft at one time. Here is his combat report.

"We were patrolling (the) area north-east of Caen when 20-plus Me 109s were sighted at 12,000 to 14,000 feet. We broke into them. I turned starboard and came up from below firing 500 to 250 yards at four or five enemy aircraft which were flying in tight formation somewhat resembling a beehive. I strafed the group from the leader back but no strikes were observed. I turned violently to starboard and one appeared to break port and I immediately fired a burst into him from about 250 yards with 20° to 30° deflection. He flicked over and spun as I continued to fire into him. The enemy aircraft began to pour black smoke and stream glycol. My number two, F/S Wallace saw the enemy aircraft explode and burst into flames.

"Again I broke violently starboard, and saw a 109 underneath me. He tried to take evasive action and I fired into his port side from about 250 yards, closing down to 100 yards with a deflection of 30° to 0°. Black smoke began to pour from him and he began to go down apparently out of control. As he was going down I was breaking and I noticed an airstrip and balloons below me.

"On completion of the patrol I landed at 144 Wing airfield and was told that an enemy aircraft was seen to go down just east of the field. S/L Browne of 144 Wing saw the enemy aircraft going down and confirms that this aircraft was the one downed by me.

"I broke starboard again, climbed into the sun for a short time, then turned again and dived sharply down. An Me 109 crossed beneath me and so close that the border lines on his crosses were clearly visible. As he half-flicked and went down I followed him and when nearly astern, I opened fire from 500 yards closing slightly later, firing all the time. I followed him down until I was nearly on the deck, only breaking up in time to narrowly miss hitting an armoured vehicle. As I climbed up I could see smoke and dust rising from the ground where the enemy aircraft had apparently crashed."[18]

Figure 34 -- Bamford. F/O Jack Bamford shot down three Messerschmitt Bf 109s in the engagement near Caen 15 June. He was immediately recommended for the DFC, but. unfortunately he was shot down by anti-aircraft fire and taken prisoner 27 June before the award came through.
(Canadian Forces Photo PL19719)

Pilots who have experienced a dogfight like this invariably comment that for a terrifying few minutes the world is filled with aircraft zooming across one's path, blazing tracers cutting lines around one seemingly from nowhere, smoke and oil splatters appear on the windscreen -- all of this accompanied by blackouts in high speed turns and shouts in the radio headsets. And then, they all say, one finds oneself virtually alone – the sky empty of aircraft. A few

217

smoking crash sites, a few black or white smoke trails left by disabled aircraft, and the radio beckons everyone to form up at 10,000 feet over some locality – that is all that is left. Into the quiet that follows the scrum comes the chatter of excited voices: counting heads, asking where each member is, commenting on the state of damage sustained and comparing external observations of each other's damaged aircraft.

By this time the other two squadrons of the wing realized there had been a dogfight and Freddie Green called for the wing to form up over Port-en-Bessin and to head back across the Channel to Tangmere. The Spitfires flown by McElroy MK472 and F/L Benton Gilmour MK687 were so badly riddled that they had to nurse them to one of the advanced landing grounds. McElroy crash-landed at B.2 while Gilmour crash-landed at B.3. Four pilots of blue section accompanied them down and stayed overnight at one or other of the two ALGs.

A half-hour later, back at Tangmere the ground crew and other waiting pilots watched 28 Spitfires circle and land -- eight were missing. They counted them again and observed with pride that the red tape that covered gun ports had been blown away from the 421 aircraft. That meant there had been a battle. As the aircraft landed and taxied to a stop, the word spread quickly, first as to losses -- F/O Dick Reeves of 403 Squadron flying MK974 had been hit by flak and seen to bale out over Allied lines north of Caen; his parachute had opened and he was seen to land safely. The pilots of 421 said that no one knew what happened to F/O Lorne Curry or his aircraft MK941 -- after the initial contact with the enemy he had not been seen again.

The intelligence officer, F/L Henry Martin gathered all the pilots at the dispersal hut, listened to the accounts and made notes as they were related to him. After a radio exchange with the intelligence officers at B.3 and B.2, the facts concerning the claims and the losses were ironed out and typed out a day later. McElroy's Spitfire MK472 was wrecked in the crash-landing and he was lucky to be alive for it was a write-off. Gilmour's Spitfire MK687 was so riddled that it too was headed for the scrap pile. The final results were chronicled as 10 enemy aircraft destroyed and one damaged. Bamford was awarded three Bf 109s destroyed, Paterson awarded two destroyed, Warfield two destroyed, Stronach one, Cook one and McElroy one. F/L Charlie

Grant was awarded one Bf 109 damaged. Application was immediately made for the DFC to be awarded Bamford and a bar to his DFC for McElroy.

They suffered only one loss – F/O Lorne Franklin Curry. Lorne was a tall westerner who liked to play the part of the strong, tough cowboy, but he had the westerner's sociability about him and was a friend to everyone. His family moved to Windsor, Ontario as war started, and so technically his home was Windsor – but Lorne considered himself a Saskatchewan boy. He had been with the squadron since January 1944. He is buried at Bretteville-sur-Laize Cemetery. The other pilot who was seen to bale out over France was F/O Dick Reeves of 403 Squadron. Reeves was also from Windsor. He made his way back to Allied lines without incident and returned to the squadron in its new French home 20 June unhurt and ready to fly.

For the enemy, I./JG 27 claimed three Spitfires destroyed, one credited to each of Unteroffizier Czermy, Feldwebel Sturm and Oberfähnrich Winkler, and they recorded six losses only four of whom are named – Feldwebel Günter Hass wounded, Unteroffizier Josef Mehler missing, Unteroffizier Heinz Klein missing and Leutnant Erich Gerstner wounded. Two other aircraft are recorded as missing, but with no information as to the names or fate of their pilots.

So to sort out the losses, 421 Squadron had one aircraft shot down and one pilot killed, but had two aircraft so badly damaged that they were written off. Final score, three aircraft lost and one pilot killed. For I./JG 27, six aircraft were lost of which two, perhaps four of the pilots were killed.

The night of 15 June there was a great party in the officer's mess at RAF Station Tangmere celebrated by all 100 or so officers of 127 Wing – with the exception of two who were missing and six who sat in slit trenches trembling as the nightly roar of continuous flak shattered any attempt to sleep. They undoubtedly questioned the wisdom of staying overnight in France and missing what everyone knew would be 'one hell of a good thrash.'

Friday 16 June 1944 – Moving Day

The pilots who stayed over at B.2 that night had the company of 'A' and 'B' Echelon and the miserable experience of having to dig a deep foxhole, find something to partially cover it, and try to get some sleep while everywhere there was the rain of falling shrapnel from the anti-aircraft guns. The ground in Normandy had a peculiar grittiness about it that made it very hard to dig into, and the effort of digging raised a very fine powdery dust that got into eyes, ears and nose. The next day – Saturday 16 June -- the Spitfires of 127 Wing took off from Tangmere for the last time and flew to B.2. Trucks crossed the Channel in LCTs, and in the afternoon, 10 Dakotas ferried the remaining aircrew and ground crew of what had been called 'C' Echelon. When the retinue arrived the whole wing was once more united. Then followed a mad day of unpacking, setting up tents, digging foxholes and for the organizers, getting everything from telephones to latrines working, as reported by each adjutant.

"Our squadrons carried out uneventful patrols during the day but arrived during the evening to stay. The wing is now led by W/C R A Buckham DFC, successor to the late W/C L V Chadburn DSO, DFC, killed in action June 13th. W/C Chadburn's grave has been found, and Sector, it is understood, are placing a cross on the grave. Enemy activity during the night was somewhat less but the terrific din of our own barrage allowed few persons to sleep until daylight. No bombs were dropped on the airfield. It appears the Hun's activity is directed, in the main, against shipping on the beaches. The beaches are only four miles away and the balloons can be seen from any part of this camp. The airfield construction unit have moved off to another location, but have left a small party for runway and maintenance purposes. The pilots spent the day digging in and laying out their camp."[19]

"Today we did two convoy patrols. We escorted a cruiser to the beachhead, which proved an uneventful patrol. Today we saw the airlift party, including the squadron adjutant F/O A Birchnall, the clerk Cpl W G Codner, our technical Sgt S G Williams, and the remainder of the Wing HQ's personnel left behind to service our aircraft, leave for France in a flight of 10 Dakotas, which took off from RAF Tangmere at 1415 hours, and when we joined them on landing strip B.2 near Crépon, France, we learned that they had an uneventful trip. Our new CO arrived from 402 Squadron today S/L E P Wood. The squadron's Spitfires landed at the landing strip in France about 2200 hours. We spent the night, five and six to a tent, with just a small visit from the Hun."[20]

"The airlift party landed in France today and weren't very impressed with conditions that existed. Most of the boys got right to work and put up their tents and dug slit trenches to provide shelter from anti-personnel bombs which Jerry has been dropping around about. The pilots arrived later in the evening, and spent the better part of the night putting up tents and watching the fireworks as the Hun came to pay one of his frequent visits."[21]

"The day for our own invasion of the continent has arrived. The airlift party took off at 1415 hours in 10 big Dakota transport aircraft and set down at B.2 at 1520. The Daks were escorted by Spits from our wing, but it proved to be a very uneventful flight. Everyone quite busy at B.2 setting up tents and digging slit trenches and getting organized generally."[22]

S/L Ed Wood, known to everyone as 'EePee' joined the wing to lead 403 Squadron to replace Bob Buckham who was now the W/C (Flying) of 127 Wing.

Chapter Eight – Operating from France

B.2 Bazenville

The airstrip and small town of tents known as B.2 was the home of 127 Wing from 16 June until 27 August. The countryside in the immediate vicinity of B.2 was a flat plateau about 140 feet above sea level, etched by the valleys of several small streams as shown below.[1]

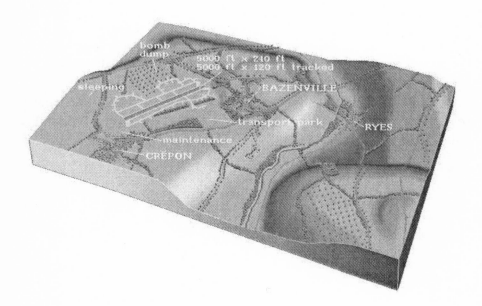

Figure 35 – B.2. *Advanced Landing Ground (ALG) B.2 Bazenville as seen looking south. It was a small village in its own right that accommodated 845 airmen at the end of June 1944. The main runway, shaded dark grey, was 5000 feet long and 210 feet wide, with a strip 120 feet wide covered in Sommerfeldt mesh tracking. Taxiways and dispersal areas to park the Spitfires surround the airstrip (the vertical dimension is exaggerated by a factor of ten).*

(author's drawing)

Mature trees lined the streets of the nearby villages of Crépon, Bazenville and Ryes and the roads connecting them and a small wooded tract covered much of the servicing area and motor transport parking area, but apart from these bits of wooded area and some surrounding apple orchards, the airfield itself was located in wide open fields. The bomb dump and sleeping areas were in an apple orchard. A small stream, called the Gronde, ran through Ryes and entered the sea just east of Arromanches. The road through Crépon continued two miles in a north-easterly direction through the village of Vers-sur-Mer to the sea. It was this road the landing parties took to reach the site of B.2.

A photograph taken in June 1944 looking south-west (a little bit more to the left than the diagram on the preceding page) shows the openness of the countryside and the airstrip.

Figure 36 – B.2 photo. An aerial photograph of B.2 probably taken before it was occupied 16 June 1944. The photographer was looking south-west. The town of Crépon is in the foreground, while some of the scattered buildings of Bazenville, including the spire of the parish church, are in the top right background
(Canadian Forces Photo).

The three Canadian ALGs -- B.2, B.3 and B.4 -- were very similar, and very close to each other with all facilities set up in tents or in trucks with adjoining canopies. The following remarks are how a Spitfire pilot, Bill McRae of 401 Squadron, recalls the sleeping arrangements at his ALG at B.4 Beny-sur-Mer – four miles east of B.2. McRae's squadron was part of the Canadian 126 Wing led by W/C Keefer. They moved into B.4 just two days after 127 Wing moved to B.2.

"Beny-sur-Mer was about two miles from the beach and eight miles from the front line at Caen. When we arrived we found our tents already set up in a line, with a larger mess tent at one end and the usual primitive latrine and shower facilities right out in front. Behind our line of tents was a stone wall, on the other side of which was a newly started cemetery. Our first chore was to set up our cots, four to a tent. The first night we realized that something would have to be done to protect ourselves against the red hot fragments of our own flak that came raining down on us. The Germans were dropping flares to illuminate the beachhead in an attempt to find targets to bomb, and this brought a fierce response from our anti-aircraft gunners. One of my tent mates and I took the jeep to a former German radar post and removed a number of long 2x8-inch planks. We dug a trench in the floor of our tent, lowered the canvas beds into it, head-to-head, then laid the planks across the top. On top of this we put sand bags, the whole set-up covering each of us from the head to about our shins. With this arrangement we had no trouble sleeping, even with the flak sizzling down, sometimes through the tent. Although sometimes lit up, our field was never bombed and as far as I know we had no airman casualties."[2]

The first squadrons to land in France did so on 10 June. They touched down during the day and returned that night to UK bases covered in a fine flour-like dust. The dust created at least two problems. The first problem was that the blue-grey air force uniforms started to resemble the field grey colour of the German troops. It was definitely a life-shortening pursuit to wander about France in RAF blue-grey covered in Normandy dust. In no time at all airmen switched into khaki uniforms. The dust was also critical in other serious ways. Engines seemed particularly prone to extreme wear as a result of the ingestion of the very hard but very fine Normandy grit. Great efforts were made to find suitable filters to protect the engines, but the ground crews and pilots, with dry dusty mouths, and gritty nostrils and hair, knew very well the problem was not an easy one to fix. Armourers found the dust caused guns to jam and working parts to wear excessively. Bill McRae relates;

> "The armourers had their work cut out for them to keep the dust from infiltrating through the empty cartridge ejection chute and yet use a covering that would give way when the empties were ejected."[3]

Luckily, there was rain – frequent rain showers -- that turned the Normandy dust into Normandy mud. The landing strips, covered as they were with steel mesh, were bad enough, but as seen in the

photograph, the strip was surrounded with taxiways that were just plain dirt. Back in the wide grass fields or concrete runways in England, the standard procedure for a Spitfire pilot was to waddle out to his take-off position swinging back and forth to catch glimpses of what was ahead. The long nose of the Spitfire cut off all visibility straight ahead – the fish-tailing waddle served to let them know where they were going. In Normandy, this became a serious problem because the taxiways were not only narrow – narrow enough to ensure one could not waddle up to the take-off runway – but also dusty. Bill McRae goes on to describe this problem.

Figure 37 -- McRae. F/L Bill McRae flew Spitfires with 401 Squadron of 126 Wing stationed at B.4 in Normandy.
(McRae collection)

> "The single taxi track was too narrow to allow the usual zig-zag taxi procedure and there was a rash of accidents with aircraft taxiing into the one ahead. Eventually this problem was solved by having an airman ride the wing to give hand signals as we taxied out and back. Incidentally, victims of these accidents invariably were sent on the dreaded 'course' at Sheffield from which they never returned to the

squadron. It mattered not how well you had served, pilots were now a dime a dozen and you could be quickly replaced."[4]

What about the primitive arrangements for ablutions? The engineers created men's and later women's latrines – usually at opposite ends of the camp – but they were always very primitive. There were showers but for baths, a canvas device had been devised that held some water but little else. Beds were canvas cots as Bill McRae recalls:

"The canvas bed had been my lot for a year before that, so Normandy did not require much adjusting."[5]

83 Group Control Centre (83GCC)

The day after D-Day, trucks were off-loaded at the Mulberry at Arromanches bearing powerful radio and radar equipment and trucks specially outfitted to contain the tracking tables and other paraphernalia of a full-fledged ground control unit. On 10 June, one ground control unit was set up in the British sector and another in the American sector. The one for the British sector was located at B.2. and was designed 83 GCC. This centre controlled and monitored every aircraft of the 2ndTAF, and through cooperation with the army intelligence sources, identified the location of the current bomb line at all times.

"Once the initial echelon of 83 GCC had started to operate ashore, the control of fighters over the bridgehead was gradually transferred from the fighter control ships (there was one at each beach on D-Day) to 83 GCC, which became the master control for the bridgehead in conjunction with the 9thAF fighter control squadron which was set up in the American area. The two control centres were able to operate as effective parts of a single machine, thanks to the excellent teamwork between the commanders of the British and American control centres."[6]

So much has been written about the dissension that appeared to prevail between the British and the Americans at high levels, that it is worthy of note how completely integrated were the two ground control centres. They were in touch with each other from the beginning, and the progressive control extended to each by the high command marched in parallel.

"Direction of air-ground cooperation was in the hands of headquarters 9thAF through 17 June with control being provided by the Senior Air Representative on board the USS Ancon, 6 to 10 June, and then by the 70th Fighter Wing, which became established at A.2 Criqueville, 9 to 11 June. On 10 June, 9thAF was charged with operational control of all fighter-bombers at its headquarters at Au Gay close to Headquarters First US Army (FUSA). A further and more significant step in the provision of continental controls was taken at midnight 17/18 June when Headquarters 9thAF, in conjunction with FUSA, assumed responsibility for designating bomb lines."[7]

With 83 GCC located only a stone's throw from the B.2 airstrip, the administrative people of 127 Wing had direct access to the latest intelligence regarding the conduct of the Normandy Campaign.

Saturday 17 June

The night after the move to France was a typical one. The German Ju 88s came over at 2330 hours when it was dark and bombed the beaches sporadically until just before dawn. That introduced the new arrivals to the regular evening ack-ack that kept them up all night and frightened them every time a bomb was heard to explode a mile or so away. Occasionally Allied night-fighters flew into the area to the south but they were careful to avoid the heavy Allied flak concentration around the beaches. After falling off for an hour after the bombers left, the new arrivals were eager to dig their slit trenches a foot deeper and to scrounge additional sand bags. All the digging raised dust everywhere for it hadn't rained in several days, even though it was still cloudy.

The forecasters view that there would be no clearing until afternoon led the 127 Wing planners to arrange just one two-squadron armed recce for late in the day. 403 Squadron provided four aircraft to share readiness, but beyond that had the day off.

With that encouragement, F/L Hart Finley and F/L Andy MacKenzie of 403 Squadron livened up the base by riding around on two fine horses recently liberated from the retreating Germans. They were German cavalry horses left abandoned when the defenders in the area had to retreat in the face of the Allied landing. Great fun ensued by embarrassing a couple of pilots who decided they should learn to ride. In the days that followed other pilots acquired German cavalry horses as well. A week later an observer noted, "the camp is beginning to look like a dude ranch."

Three pilots of 421 Squadron liberated a German 75mm field piece, borrowed Wally Conrad's jeep to haul it to the fields next to the airbase, and proceeded to fire off a test round. Not only did they scare the hell out of everyone with the firing, they received verbal hell from Wally when he learned that they had stripped the gears of his jeep through hauling the heavy load. It was decided that the pilots should limit their collection of memorabilia to helmets and Lugers.

416 Squadron and 421 Squadron were preparing for the evening armed recce, but at 1515 hours they were scrambled to check out some bogeys. The bogeys turned out to be American P-47s, but while returning to base, F/O Jim Flood was hit squarely by light flak. With great difficulty he managed to nurse his aircraft back to the base. He was unhurt. Another scramble was sounded at 1900 hours, this time it was four Spitfires from 403 Squadron. South-west of Caen they ran into a dogfight as Spitfires were circling and battling with FW 190s. It turned out to be 310 Squadron tangling with III./JG 54 led by the veteran Hauptmann Robert Weiss. As the four pilots from 403 Squadron joined the mêlée W/O Art Clenard's aircraft MK570 was hit and he had to dive out of the fray to find a field to crash-land. The Germans claimed three Spitfire victories in this encounter, but only one was lost – Clenard's. It was dusk, and although he was behind enemy lines, Clenard hid until the middle of the night and then made his way to the front held by the British 50th Infantry Division. The soldiers bandaged his wounds and got him back to B.2 the following morning, but he was sent off to No.52 Field Hospital for more complete dressings.

An armed recce by 416 Squadron at 2020 hours proved uneventful, however a group of pilots and ground crew made their own armed recce into Bayeux in the afternoon and evening where they partied on wine and champagne. When they returned and reported the success of their foray, they had many more followers ready to try it the next night -- the boys had found a replacement for Chichester, their previous watering hole in Sussex.

Sunday 18 June

Sunday was windy, cloudy and riddled with scattered showers. An uneventful scramble, a weather recce and a late night sweep that was called back because of poor visibility was all the action the wing saw. However, the lethargy brought on by duff weather was relieved late in the evening with the arrival of a keg of beer brought in by 416 Squadron attached under the fuselage of a replacement aircraft flown in from the UK.

That night the wind howled, for Normandy was about to witness the three-day event that became known as 'the Big Storm'.

The Big Storm Monday 19 June to 21 June

There was no flying on Monday 19 June but the supply of beer provided excitement enough. One younger member of the 416 team enjoyed it so much he careened around in a jeep acting as though he was, as one adjutant wrote, "Lucky Teeters."

We have already described the Big Storm that blew up 19 June, trashed the Mulberries 20 June, and only blew itself out 21 June. Apart from one very dicey scramble the afternoon of the 21st, there was no flying by 127 Wing for those three days.

Thursday 22 June

Even the day after the storm, the weather was sufficiently unsettled to permit operations only when clearing occurred late in the day. Four uninteresting armed recce bombing missions were flown in the evening of 22 June.

Pilots were well aware of the mixed results they obtained when sent on bombing missions. Sometimes they joked about how hit-and-miss these operations were. But sometimes the pilots got lucky, as the 403 Squadron ORB relates:

> "On the second show our squadron went to bomb a woods in which an ammunition dump was reported to be. We had hits in the target area but little happened. P/O Scott had two hang-ups and when his bomb finally released itself it landed in a woods. A terrific flame and grey smoke filled the sky, so perhaps our do was more profitable than we realized."

Friday 23 June

The day before, had started off with the last lingering cloud from the storm, but then turned sunny and clear. Friday dawned a beautiful clear summer day, but as so often happens in Normandy in the summer, heavy cloud and rain moved in quickly around 0900 hours and moved out just as quickly by mid-morning. After that it cleared up and promised to be a good flying day.

At 0500 hours 421 Squadron sent six aircraft south to Alençon on a weather recce. They reported 3/10ths cloud at 6,000 feet with good visibility except for the ground fog. 403 Squadron flew an armed recce soon after and reported heavy solid cloud moving in, however it didn't stop them from destroying seven trucks, two motorcycles and a staff car on the little side roads to the east of the Caen-to-Falaise highway. They reported 30 to 40 tanks moving towards Caen in the Trun area but did not attack because they were nearly out of ammunition.

Soon there was a downpour and the squadrons waited it out. 421 Squadron was kept on immediate readiness. Ground control radar detected some bogeys east of Caen and six aircraft scrambled to meet them. They took off at 1145 hours. Climbing up through two layers of cloud they burst out at 7,000 feet to find seven FW 190s attacking two reconnaissance Mustangs. In saving the Mustangs and chasing away the FW 190s, F/O Scotty McRoberts got in a couple of good bursts and claimed a damaged.

The day was uneventful for 416 Squadron who flew an armed recce around 1430 and a patrol around 1900 hours, but there was action for 403 Squadron. After taking off at 1615 hours, they broke into two groups of six – red section led by F/O Doug Orr and blue section led by F/L Mac Gordon. F/S Ken Harvey's aircraft ML248 developed engine trouble so he turned back leaving blue section with five aircraft. Red section patrolled the western area and blue section patrolled the eastern section of the lodgement area. A half hour after take-off, blue section ran into 15 FW 190s of III./JG 54 heading straight for them about 300 feet below. The German formation was led by Gruppekommandeur Hauptmann Robert Weiss – the same opponent they had battled six days earlier. Weiss was a baby-faced pilot who had claimed six victories in Normandy and a career total of 106. Flying as the second in command of the group was Leutnant Alfred Gross who had just been promoted to command 8 Staffel of III./JG 54. Just three hours earlier Leutnant Gross had shot down a Spitfire of 229 Squadron bringing his claims in Normandy to four, and his career total to 50. Although half the German pilots had little or no experience, III./JG 54 had more than half a dozen high-scorers, but this day the best of them all, Geschwaderkommodore Hauptmann Hubert Lang, was not with them.

By contrast, the two F/Ls, Mac Gordon and Pete Logan, had distinguished themselves in dive-bombing and attacking ground installations since the beginning of the year, and they both had claimed a couple of damaged aircraft, but they had claimed no kills. Logan's real name was Pierre LeCoq. When advised by an intelligence officer that it may be a disadvantage to use that name if he were ever shot down in France he changed his name to Peter Logan. This had happened back in April.

The story of what happened at this encounter with III./JG 54 begins with Pete Logan's combat report.

*Figure 38 -- **Logan, Beurling, Hodgson.**. This photo, taken in the fall of 1943, shows Pete Logan when he was still F/O Pierre LeCoq. He is shown on the left together with F/L Buz Beurling and F/L John Hodgson. By the time of Normandy, Beurling was back in Canada and Hodgson was killed in action -- shot down by flak 2 June 1944.*

(LeCoq collection)

"Five aircraft of 403 Squadron led by F/L Gordon were flying a patrol east of Caen at about 2,500 feet when from 12 o'clock and about 300 feet below we saw 12-plus FW 190s flying towards us. They were carrying either bombs or jet tanks and these were dropped before the ensuing engagement began. We broke up and around and I got on the tail of one and from about 300 yards fired a 2-to-3-second burst with 20° deflection. I saw strikes on the fuselage and wing roots. The enemy aircraft poured black and white smoke and half-rolled and went straight down from about 2,000

232

feet. I was unable to follow him as by this time I had four FW 190s on my tail.

"I broke up and then down again getting behind another 190. I fired a burst with 15° to 20° deflection and saw some strikes on his starboard wing. When my guns ceased firing I discovered later that my guns had jammed."[8]

Here is Gordon's account of the action:

"We were flying east at a height of 3,000 feet when approximately 15 FW 190s were sighted flying towards us from head-on and around 300 feet below us. We passed each other then broke around. The 190s also broke around and a dogfight ensued. The enemy aircraft were using a defensive circle and it was almost impossible to get anything more than a 1-to-2-second bursts at four or five of them but observed no results. The defensive circle formed by the enemy aircraft had now been broken and I managed to get onto the tail of a 190. He was breaking tightly to starboard and I gave him a short burst from 200 yards range giving him full deflection under my nose. No strikes were seen. I closed to about 100 yards and gave him another 2-second burst allowing full deflection. I saw a group of strikes on his tail and the port half of his elevator and stabilizer broke off. He slipped over to port and started to go down apparently out of control and I broke up into another 190 who was attacking me. F/L Logan saw the attack and part of the enemy aircraft blown away. After returning to base we established the vicinity and time of the combat as U.1372 at 1640 hours. Later in the day the Second Army reported two FW 190s as going down in flames in the same vicinity and at the same time.

"I followed the second 190 who half-rolled onto the deck and headed east. After a long chase I closed to about 200 yards and from line astern I fired but only my machine guns were working. After a short burst they ran out. The 190 began to pour black smoke and he almost went into the deck clipping about 10 feet off a tall tree. However he regained control and continued at a much reduced speed still smoking. As I was out of ammunition I broke off the attack."[9]

The Second Army Headquarters confirmed that two FW 190s came down in flames at U.1372 just east of Caen, about 1640 hours. Both Pete Logan and Mac Gordon were awarded one FW 190 destroyed and one FW 190 damaged. JG 54 lost Unteroffizier Otto

Venjakob who was listed as FTR (failed to return) and Unteroffizier Willi Zim who was killed. Hauptmann Weiss claimed two victories in this aerial battle bringing his total to 108, and an Unteroffizier Zeller claimed another. However the only record of damage recorded for 403 Squadron on that date was one Spitfire that was repaired at the airfield – not serious enough to be sent to a repair depot.

Figure 39 -- Gordon. *F/L M J 'Mac' Gordon was a stalwart with 403 Squadron, and had been since July 1943. He would go on to a record of four destroyed and one shared.*
(Canadian Forces Photo PL19718).

With the long summer evenings, the day still had a lot of flying to be done – and some excitement to be had. An hour after the Gordon and Logan victories, two aircraft of 421 Squadron were scrambled to find a bogey near Caen, but found nothing. An hour after that, seven aircraft from 416 Squadron flew an uneventful patrol. As the day was winding down, 403 and 421 Squadrons took off. The aircraft were clean – that is, no extra fuel tanks – and they were off to sweep the roads south of the lodgement area. Led again by Gordon, Logan and F/L Doug Orr, 403 Squadron struck off due south to sweep Flers, Vire and back to Villers-Bocage and Caen. Led by S/L Wally Conrad, F/L Paul Johnson and F/L John McElroy, 421 Squadron headed south-east to hit the road from Caen to Falaise and on to Argentan. The sun was quite low in the sky at 2100 hours when the 24 Spitfires took off but with double daylight-saving time in force -- and this just two days after the longest day of the year -- it would not set until 2210 hours.

Pilots of 421 Squadron were the lucky ones. The German formation they tangled with consisted of FW 190s from III./JG 2 and I./JG 1. This was the enemy in the main engagement, however, one of the combat reports mentions another force of enemy aircraft -- eight Bf 109s. This unit has not been identified, but the most likely candidate would be III./JG 3. We start the description of the main aerial battle with the account of F/O Al 'Brandy' Brandon:

"During the course of a cannon recce with 421 Squadron of the Caen/Argentan area we ran into 15-plus FW 190s near Le Merlevault. We were flying at approximately 2,500 feet and the enemy aircraft but slightly higher. The 190s broke (from the) cloud on our port. We turned into them. I gave the leader an ineffective squirt and then followed through cloud after several. I saw two 190s above me and heading south ducking in and out of cloud. I took after the last one and closed from 1,000 to 500 yards and gave him a squirt. Smoke poured from the port side of the enemy aircraft. I followed down through cloud and gave him another burst but had no cannon. I returned home alone."[10]

When the two opposing forces met, 421 Squadron was spread out with each section flying line abreast of the others so that the distance from one side to the other was probably a third of a mile. F/L John McElroy was undoubtedly the closest section to the German formation when they stumbled upon each other. Here is his report:

"Near Le Merlevault I called a break when I saw approximately 18 FW 190s emerge from cloud at five to six o'clock. A general dogfight ensued. I managed to get behind two 190s. I fired a 6-second burst from 400 to 300 yards with 25° to 15° deflection at the trailing enemy aircraft. I saw no strikes but a little black smoke came from the port side of the engine. The enemy aircraft pulled up in a tight turn, went over on his back, flicked five or six times and went straight in from 1,500 feet exploding as he hit the ground about three or four miles north of the town. F/O Warfield saw the combat and saw the enemy aircraft crash. I also saw another FW 190 go down and explode on (the) ground about four miles west of me. In between these explosions I also saw a cloud of dust rising which might have been caused by an aircraft crash-landing."[11]

F/O George Mayson had joined the squadron just two weeks earlier. This was his 10th operational flight with 421 Squadron, but he had not seen any action to date. Here is his report:

"I was flying Yellow Two with 421 Squadron on a cannon recce in the Caen/Lisieux/Argentan area when we ran into about 15 FW 190s. We were flying at about 2,000 feet in a westerly direction. The enemy aircraft came from six o'clock and slightly above. My

Figure 40 -- Johnson. F/L Paul Johnson DFC was an American from Connecticut who joined up in Canada. He was flight commander of 'A' Flight in 421 Squadron, and became an ace before he was killed 18 July 1944.
(Canadian Forces Photo PL19719)

number one and I followed two 190s into cloud. I lost my number one in the cloud. I got onto the tail of the 190s and opened fire on the one to my port side. I fired from 500 to 400 yards range with 20° deflection. He went over on his back and went in at 40° angle crashing north-west of Le Merlevault. This aircraft was seen to go in by F/L McElroy. As I was pulling up I saw a parachute coming down through cloud. I was near enough to identify his dress as a brown flying suit and would identify him as an enemy airman. I also saw two or three fires burning around the north and the east side of the town, presumably burning aircraft."[12]

F/L Paul Johnson tells his story:

"In the vicinity of Merlevault we were attacked by 15-plus FW 190s and eight-plus Me 109s from six o'clock. We broke immediately to engage. After tooling about for some time I saw two 190s climb into cloud. The cloud layer had a base of 3,000 feet and extended to a top of 4,000 feet. I went up through cloud and emerged from it directly behind four FW 190s. I closed to about 100 yards and directly behind the trailing 190 and gave him a burst. I followed him down through cloud again and saw him crash just north-east of the town of Merlevault. As I followed my FW 190 down, I saw another FW 190 go down in flames to the east of the town. I also saw a Spitfire apparently trying to crash-land just north of the town."[13]

One combat report suggests a longer than normal delay, and unlike most reports, this one was submitted by someone else.

"F/O Driver broke up and followed a 190 through cloud where he ran into approximately eight Me 109s. He closed on the Me 109s and observed strikes on two. One was pouring black smoke when he disappeared into cloud. F/O Driver claims two Me 109s as damaged. F/O Driver since the combat took place and before he had the opportunity of submitting a written report has been injured and confined to hospital. From the initial interrogation the following facts emerged and two Me 109s are provisionally claimed as damaged for F/O Driver awaiting his own report."[14]

Johnson's report made reference to a Spitfire crash-landing. This must have been the loss of W/O Bob Wallace. Wallace had flown operationally two days after arriving at the squadron 17 days before and flew several uneventful patrols. On his 6th flight he was in the dogfight of 15 June – and he survived, but with only two flights after that occasion, his luck ran out. W/O Robert George Wallace is buried at St. Gauberge-St. Coulombe Cemetery. His is the only Canadian grave in the cemetery.

When the battle was over, 421 claimed four victories with McElroy, Mayson, Johnson and F/L Roger Wilson credited with destroyed enemy aircraft. In German records III./JG 2 lost one, Unteroffizier Walter Sauder parachuted to safety and I./JG 1 lost two, Unteroffizier Paul Reissbeck and another unnamed, both killed. Because of the four burning crash sites reported by several pilots, it is assumed the Bf 109s were from III./JG 3 that did lose two aircraft and their pilots.

In summarizing the day's activities, here is how S/L Whalley summed it all up in the 127 Wing ORB:

"All three squadrons were engaged in operations during the day. F/O McRoberts of 421 Squadron engaged a FW 190 and claimed a damaged. Other pilots sighted enemy aircraft but no additional engagements took place on this particular operation. In a further operation carried out by 421 Squadron, 15 FW 190s and Me 109s were sighted and engaged. Four successful pilots were F/L Johnson – one FW 190; F/L Wilson – one FW 190; F/L McElroy – one FW 190; F/L Mayson – one FW 190; F/O Brandon – one FW 190 damaged; F/O Driver – two Me 109s damaged. Few enemy aircraft operated in this area during darkness, and no bombs were dropped though the activity on the beaches appeared to be about the same as usual. 403 Squadron claims two enemy aircraft destroyed and three damaged."[15]

The wing was ready for a good party that night – a good old Friday night bash. Just four days earlier, with great help from their W/Cs Brown and Buckham, they had the lads at Bognor Regis secure a whole keg of beer under the fuselage of a Spitfire to be delivered to 127 Wing. It arrived at B.2 amidst great fanfare resulting in a big party that first night and lesser ones the two evenings in between, so on Friday night they finished off the whole keg. No one worried about polishing off the beer because the squadron commanders could assure everyone that the big bosses, at this very moment, were arranging for a much larger shipment.

Bill McRae tells us more abut the beer supply.

"Beer was almost non-existent in the beachhead and whiskey was rationed. The beer problem was solved when someone got the idea of flying it across from England in an unused drop tank, then siphoning it into a barrel in France. This worked until someone used the tank for gasoline; we made one more trip with it after that but could not cope with the oily film that settled on top of the beer. Then the armourers managed to fasten the barrel itself on the bomb rack. This was the belly rack, we did not have wing racks. This arrangement worked well, until one day a reporter from the London tabloid, the Daily Mirror, saw it and used it as a front page story. Soon after, orders came down – no more beer flights from Britain. We would have killed that reporter had he ever shown his face again, but of course we ignored the order."[16]

Saturday 24 June

The big storm centred around 21 June had delayed the landing of three British divisions that Gen Montgomery considered absolutely necessary for the taking of Caen. They were 15th Scottish Infantry Division, the 43rd British Infantry Division and the 11th British Armoured Division. They were fresh troops, and they were essential to the task of breaking the stalemate that had settled along the front line. As soon as they were landed and deployed 25 June, Operation EPSOM began. Operation EPSOM was a frontal assault intended to punch a huge hole between stubborn Caen and the American salient at

Caumont to the south-west. When the hole was opened Caen could be encircled. The 127 ORB noted:

"Our squadrons carried out bombing of enemy targets during the day. Their objectives being bridges and enemy headquarters. In all cases the enemy flak was concentrated and extremely accurate but all our aircraft returned safely. The weather was very fine and the roads and airfield were beginning to get somewhat dusty. Dense clouds of dust hung over the area during the day. W/C Brown and S/L Whalley attended a conference at main headquarters of 83 Group during the afternoon. This conference was ordered by the Air Officer Administration and concerned the forthcoming push by the Army. It was disclosed that our commitments during the initial assault would be bombing and strafing ground targets, and the additional destruction of enemy aircraft as and when sighted. It was reported by intelligence that 600 to 700 enemy fighters and medium bombers had been moved up to within a 100-mile radius of our area by the enemy within the last 24 hours. All pilots hoped that this would mean some excitement and action.

"So beer has a smell. We managed to get some beer from England (36 gallons) and the rumour got quickly around. Many visitors decided to put in an appearance. These arrivals, in addition to our own personnel, quickly dispensed with the lot."[17]

Sunday 25 June

News reached the wing early in the morning that American troops had entered the outskirts of Cherbourg and expected to capture the city in the next day or two. Pastor S/L Crawford Scott held his usual Sunday church services at 0830 hours after all three squadrons had flown two dive-bombing missions, a patrol and a sweep of the Lisieux area. Everyone considered the fall of Cherbourg and the new British thrust which was starting that very morning, would bring about the long-awaited breakout and the news of the arrival of more enemy fighters was also greeted with great enthusiasm, for with the impressive successes the wing enjoyed on 15 June and 23 June, everyone was confident that honour and glory were just around the corner.

David Clark

"The three squadrons were active during the day carrying out patrols and armed recces over enemy territory. ... 421 Squadron claimed several enemy MT destroyed. 403 Squadron carried out two bombing shows with six Spitfires each but did not observe the results."[18]

Figure 41 – Churchs Service. *Pastor for 127 Wing, S/L Crawford Scott, conducts Sunday service, P/O Ronnie McCrae plays the portable organ and a group of ground crew and aircrew attend while in the background a 421 Squadron Spitfire waits to have its engine serviced.*

(Imperial War Museum CL236)

This day witnessed two events that caused a curious bitter-sweet experience to at first augment the euphoric tonic of the news, and then to dampen it in sorrow. The first event was the appearance of the missing administrative people who had left England and had their LCT torpedoed by a German E-Boat. The wing learned shortly after D-Day that some men from 3207 and 3209 Servicing Commandos went down with the ship and all the equipment was lost. The fate of the 127 Wing personnel aboard the LCT was not known for certain -- word had been received that some had been injured and that quite likely they had been sent back to England for medical treatment, but beyond that the wing knew nothing. As the days passed, and as the excitement that followed the invasion intensified, the missing persons were forgotten. What's more, with a million servicemen coming and going to and from France, to trace the whereabouts of small groups like that was impossible. However, this day at noon the missing group suddenly arrived. S/L Whalley wrote:

"The following officers, previously reported missing after being attacked by an E-Boat while en route to this country on D-Day-plus-one, arrived during the day: -- C.5466 S/L W J C MacArthur, Senior Medical Officer, C.7398 S/L R C Fisher, Senior Flying Control Officer, C.11542 F/L V R Perry, Medical Officer 421 Squadron, J.7517 F/L G E Tinkess, Flying Control, C.14671 F/O L L Aide, Flying Control. These officers look fit and well and appeared pleased to have returned. Naturally, we were just as pleased to see them."[19]

Both the medical staff and the Flying Control section staff had been doing double-duty with the absence of these senior officers. The medical staff and particularly the Flying Control personnel were intensely relieved to be rejoined with their missing compatriots. MacArthur and Fisher now completed the list of administrative officers needed to run the wing.

Just as the sweetness of the moment of reunion at midday added a reflective flavour to the ardour of the morning, so the evening brought a sombre note and shock. Everyone was reminded that they were in a war, and that war is dangerous. Whalley's words give only a minute indication of what the wing felt when tragedy struck at 2035 hours that evening.

"A Court of Inquiry was convened to investigate a flying accident involving J.5807 F/L C D Grant and J.11764 F/L R G Driver of 421 Squadron. Unfortunately, F/L Grant was killed and F/L Driver was taken to hospital seriously injured. The accident took place when the aircraft were taking off. F/L D J England of 416 Squadron was appointed president of the court and F/O C T Brown of 403 Squadron as a member of the court."[20]

Mention has been made of the very favourable weather that settled over Normandy after the big storm of 21 June. But with clear days and little rain, the airfields quickly became dusty again. Every time an aircraft taxied out along the dirt taxiways it kicked up clouds of dust – clouds sometimes rising 30 feet or more into the air. The dust was so bad and visibility at times so impaired, that the flying control people stationed members at the middle and ends of the runway to fire flares when the runway was cleared. Even those sitting on the wing of the Spitfire to direct with hand signals were unable to see. The official documents do not give details of what happened that Sunday, and unfortunately memories long after the fact are vague. But fifty years later from interviews with Bill Stronach and Bill Cook who were there, it seems that another squadron was taking off from the other end of the runway. Dust clouds billowed up over anything that moved. As each aircraft took off another swirling mass of dust was added to what went before. Charlie Grant and Gordie Driver thought everyone had taken off, and began taxiing out to take off when another aircraft roared down the runway. In trying to avoid the aircraft, Grant and Driver collided head-on. Cook's recollections were recounted in 1998:

> "Bitsy Grant was decapitated in the head-on crash while Driver was just wounded and out of the war. It was an English squadron coming the other way."

Stronach's recollections of those events were:

> "Gord Driver and Bitsy Grant were hit by a French squadron taking-off from the other end. The flares from the tower (said laughingly, for there was no tower) were all screwed up."

Both Grant and Driver were well liked by their peers. It was a sobering loss to take them both from the ranks of the wing in such a violent way. F/L Charles Donald Grant was buried at Arromanches, and his remains later transferred to Hottot-les-Bagues Cemetery. Driver spent months in the UK recuperating. It was long after the war was over before he was clear to fly again.

Monday 26 June

Monday's weather alternated between heavy downbursts that lasted for an hour or more and sunny interludes that made the damp earth steam. But the heavy rain did wonders for keeping down the dust.

Early in the morning, 12 aircraft of 403 Squadron were on an armed recce between Falaise and Lisieux when they spotted a tank and a half dozen trucks moving along a narrow road. They were at 4,000 feet altitude flying in an easterly direction. S/L Ed Wood ordered yellow section to go down and clean them out. Red and blue sections would provide top cover. Yellow section led by F/L Andy MacKenzie dove down, fired on the tank and started it smoking as it pulled off the road. They had just caused a bright fire in one of the trucks when from up above came the alert, "12 bandits -- angels six at 10 o'clock." Angels was the code word for a thousand feet of altitude.

Red section led by Wood and blue section led by F/L Hart Finley climbed to attack the Bf 109s of II./JG 2. Red section reached them first as F/O Bill Rhodes describes:

"We were flying about 4,000 feet in an easterly direction giving cover to yellow section which was attacking a tank. 15 Me 109s were seen approaching from north-east and slightly above. I climbed to get height and got into a gaggle of about seven Me 109s. I got on the tail of one and closing to 75 yards, allowing 30° deflection gave him a 2-second burst. About one quarter of his port wing fell away. He half-rolled and went down crashing into the ground. F/O Orr saw the aircraft crash. I climbed above the cloud layer and a number of 109s were milling around. I got onto the tail of a Me 109 which was making a steep turn. I closed to 50 yards and with 45° deflection gave him a 2-to-3-second burst. I saw cannon strikes on the port side of the cockpit near the wing root and pieces fell off. He disappeared into cloud."[21]

F/O George Nadon was flying wingman for Rhodes. His account follows:

"Two of the 109s met head-on with S/L Wood. One of these turned port and this brought him in front of me and in line astern. I was at about 200 yards and gave him a 2-second burst. I saw cannon strikes below the cockpit. He rolled over on his back and the pilot baled out and the aircraft went down in flames. S/L Wood saw the pilot bale out."[22]

In one pass, the pilots of 403 Squadron had destroyed two Bf 109s of II./JG 2. Both pilots, Unteroffizier Theodor Hartmann and Unteroffizier Gerhard Querengasser, were slightly wounded but parachuted to safety. Meanwhile yellow section climbed to join their comrades. F/O Doug Orr describes what happened next.

"Our section had gone down to attack a tank ... The other two sections were flying at about 4,000 feet providing cover. We were flying east at the time. Just after making the attack on the tank and while we were still on the deck, 15 Me 109s were observed flying in a north-easterly direction and at about 6,000 feet near Lisieux. We climbed up and under them and I managed to get on the tail of a Me 109. I closed to about 300 yards and allowing 25° deflection gave him a 2-to-3-second burst. He began to pour smoke and turned on his back. He disappeared into cloud. I followed but could not see him. I went up through cloud and I saw about seven Me 109s and a single Spitfire. The Spitfire was attacking one of the Me 109s. I saw part of the wing fall off the Me 109 and saw it half-roll and go down and crash. The Spitfire pilot was F/O Rhodes. I swung around and got behind two Me 109s. I closed to about 75 yards, and allowing 15° to 20° deflection fired a 2-second burst. Strikes were observed on port side of cockpit and pieces flew off. He rolled over on his back and went into the deck in flames near a small wood. F/O Rhodes and F/L Finley both confirm this."[23]

Rhodes, Nadon and Orr were awarded victories while Rhodes and Orr were also awarded damaged. This all occurred about 0640 hours. When 403 Squadron touched down at B.2 at 0725 hours the pelting rain was just starting, but the brief downpour let up enough for 416 Squadron to take off at 0805 hours on a patrol that ended when the rain pelted down again. With the pattern set, the day progressed with eleven patrols or sweeps carried out – often several at a time, but each time between bouts of torrential downpour. On three of these patrols enemy aircraft were seen at a distance, but each time they could not be caught. Charlie Grant's funeral was held in one of the downpours in a small army cemetery in Arromanches. Later in the afternoon there is a little note included in S/L Whalley's daily entry.

"During a conference presided over by W/C Brown in which W/C Buckham, and S/Ls Wood, Green, Conrad, Whalley and Fisher were in attendance, four or five FW 190s appeared from the clouds over the aerodrome and headed south as fast as they could go. These aircraft did not drop any bombs or carry out an attack. These were the first enemy aircraft we have seen over the aerodrome in several days. They were flying at about 6,000 to 7,000 feet when identified."[24]

That night the Canadian Legion put on a show for the whole wing. This was the second show they had staged and they followed up by presenting them twice a week from then on.

Tuesday 27 June

If Monday was bad, the weather on Tuesday was worse. A brief respite between 0800 and 1000 hours permitted each of the three squadrons to get airborne to do some dive-bombing in support of the army's Operation EPSOM, but as with the day before, as soon as they completed a mission the weather socked in and thus little ground support could be provided to the troops. On the dive-bombing mission flown by 421 Squadron around 0915 they destroyed six trucks and damaged two others, but the intense flak brought down F/O Jack Bamford. He crash-landed successfully but was immediately captured and spent the rest of the war as a POW. It was only after he had been repatriated at the end of the war that Bamford learned that his DFC had been granted and the notification came through the day after he was shot down.

Wednesday 28 June

It was very cloudy when the pilots woke up and although it became quite miserable at times in midday, the skies cleared in the afternoon. South-west of Caen, Operation EPSOM was in full gear. For three days the British armoured columns had been hammering their way yard-by-yard trying to cross the Odon River. The Odon flowed north-east into Caen while the much larger Orne flowed north-north-east into Caen. Into the triangular piece of land between these two rivers to a depth of 15 miles south-west of Caen struggled British and German armoured forces. This very morning the British 11th Armoured Division crossed the Odon River and drove two miles beyond.

Headquarters and 127 Wing planners worked with the army to plan maximum support. It would be a very full but exhilarating day even though the pilots had a very sketchy idea of how their missions fitted in with the big picture. The flying schedules posted at the three separated dispersal tents were mostly front line patrols, but with the intense battle going on just south-west of Caen one could expect anything.

At the 403 Squadron dispersal tent the list included every pilot on the roster. Six patrols were to be flown during the day – a total of 48 sorties with every pilot flying at least two sorties. Three patrols before noon were to be four-aircraft patrols; the remaining three were to be full squadron-strength patrols. All missions were spread out nicely over the afternoon and evening period. However as it turned out, 403 Squadron would fly two additional missions – a two-aircraft search mission for their downed pilot, and a two-aircraft escort mission protecting some VIPs.

At the 416 Squadron dispersal tent, the flying schedule also listed 48 sorties -- two armed recces and two front line patrols all at full squadron strength.

This day, 421 Squadron had a break with only two armed recces and a front line patrol to fly. The first was scheduled to take off just before three in the afternoon. If it had not been so cloudy the boys in 421 would have headed to the beaches. As it was, a few went into Bayeux in the morning.

The wing ORB started its summary for the day with the following words:

"From a point of view of operations and aircraft destroyed, it was another great day for our squadrons. In addition, a considerable amount of enemy wheel traffic was destroyed or seriously damaged.

All three squadrons took part in these operations and destroyed enemy aircraft and ground vehicles."[25]

This day was a traffic controller's nightmare. Short bursts of rain followed by sun helped keep some of the dust down in midday, but the amount of traffic on the airfield resulted in a faint permanent pall of dust hanging over the field and mud permanently underfoot. To give some idea of how busy it was at B.2 that day, here is the list of events that took place.

0505 four aircraft of 403 took off – returned 0640 – patrol, one victory Rhodes missing

0515 12 aircraft of 416 took off – returned 0620 – armed recce, two MT destroyed

0710 four aircraft of 403 took off – returned 0815 – patrol, Lanfranchi missing

0745 two aircraft of 403 took off – returned 0820 – search for Lanfranchi, aircraft seen

0940 four aircraft of 403 took off – returned 1030 – escorted Dakota from coast to US base

1005 four aircraft of 403 took off – returned 1115 – patrol, uneventful

1110 12 aircraft of 416 took off – returned 1235 – patrol, three victories

1210 12 aircraft of 403 took off – returned 1345 – patrol, uneventful

1445 12 aircraft of 421 took off – returned 1525 – armed recce, bombed bridge

1525 10 aircraft of 416 took off – returned 1640 – armed recce, two victories

1630 12 aircraft of 403 took off – returned 1750 -- armed recce, six MT fifty troops

1715 six aircraft of 421 took off – returned 1830 – patrol, two victories

2050 12 aircraft of 416 took off – returned 2210 – armed recce, fifteen MT

2110 12 aircraft of 403 took off – returned 2235 – patrol, uneventful

2220 12 aircraft of 421 took off – returned 2310 – armed recce, uneventful

S/L Whalley continues with the wing record in the ORB as follows:

Figure 42 -- MacKenzie, F/L Andy MacKenzie DFC was flight commander of 'A' Flight of 403 Squadron. This victory made him an ace. He went on to a record of 8 by war's end.

(McElroy collection)

"403 Squadron started off the day with F/L A R MacKenzie DFC, destroying one FW 190. Unfortunately, on this operation F/O W H Rhodes became a casualty. He was last seen following a FW 190. Later in the day other Spitfires of 403 Squadron found the aircraft near Gonneville T.2979. Apparently the pilot had crash-landed, but he was not himself seen. Two persons were standing on the wing of the missing Spitfire as our aircraft went over but immediately jumped off. It is hoped that F/O Rhodes managed to escape. At about the same time 416 Squadron attacked MT destroying two. The squadron sighted a number of FW 190s, but were unable to make contact. Four aircraft of 403 Squadron carried out a patrol of the forward lines on the next operation. F/O Lanfranchi called up to state that his engine had packed up and that he was baling out. His aircraft was later seen to be burning on the ground. No other particulars are available of this pilot."[26]

The two 403 pilots were listed as missing. Weeks later the Red Cross confirmed that Rhodes was uninjured but taken prisoner after he crash-landed behind enemy lines. F/O James Leon Lanfranchi was reported missing and was later reported killed in action. He is buried at the Canadian Cemetery at Bretteville-sur-Laize and his family donated a photo, correspondence, his personnel records and certificates to the Memorial Museum of the Battle of Normandy on the ring road outside Bayeux where they can be seen today.

Sometime around 0900 hours the whole of Normandy was covered with 10/10ths cloud with a low ceiling. Air operations were temporarily suspended, but by 1100 hours breaks in the cloud showered sunlight onto the battlefield in large splotches. The fighting on the ground was furious, and now swarms of aircraft were flung into the fray. To support the stubborn defensive efforts of the German army, the Luftwaffe sent III./JG 26 Bf 109s to dive-bomb the British troops while deploying I./JG 26 and II./JG 26 with their FW 190s to fly top cover. Approaching from the Bayeux area at 10,000 feet, 416 Squadron ran into this action. F/L Rainville reported;

"While flying east at 10,000 feet we saw six FW 190s flying west towards us at 12,000 feet. The enemy aircraft broke into two sections as we approached – one section breaking to our port, the other section to our starboard. I saw one of the enemy aircraft in starboard section come around and jettison his tank and apparently attempting to get on the tail of my number one who was attacking one of the FW 190s. I throttled back to allow the enemy aircraft to get ahead then closed to 400 to 300 yards and from 15° to 20° angle and gave him a one-second burst. Strikes were observed on front part of his fuselage. He broke away, made a complete orbit, flying in a gentle turn. I gave him another burst and I saw him jettison his hood and bale out."[27]

Both Rainville flying Red Two and his number one, F/L Danny Noonan, destroyed FW 190s. The victims were Unteroffizier Waldemar Speigel and Unteroffizier Werner Lissack – both of II./JG 26. At exactly the same time that Rainville, Noonan and the rest of red section and blue section attacked the FW 190s – 1125 hours – yellow section attacked the dive-bombers. F/O Gordon Farquarson reported:

"I was flying Yellow Three with 416 Squadron during a patrol in the Caen area, when we observed eight Me 109s. We were flying at 10,000 feet and in an easterly direction. The enemy aircraft were diving south and about 6,000 feet. We dove down on them. I followed one which started a climbing turn. I closed to 300 to 50 yards and gave him three 2-second bursts from dead astern to 15° angle off. The enemy aircraft took evasive action half-rolling diving through cloud and making right turns. I saw strikes on front part of fuselage and pieces fall off. He jettisoned his hood and baled out at about 4,000 feet and the aircraft went to the ground."[28]

The eight Bf 109s were those of III./JG 26 and between 1100 and 1200 hours they lost three aircraft. But it is known that minutes after the engagement, JG 26 ran into two squadrons of 144 Wing led by W/C Johnnie Johnson who claimed two Bf 109s while F/Os Robillard and Goodwin of 442 Squadron each claimed one Bf 109 as well. When it was all over, JG 26 had lost seven aircraft and two pilots killed. Five landed safely and though two were wounded, all of them returned to action. Neither 127 Wing nor 144 Wing lost an aircraft. S/L Whalley continues his description of the day's activities:

> "In the next operation 11 Spitfires from 421 Squadron carried out a bombing attack on a bridge in enemy territory and claim one hit and three near misses breaking the track on the bridge. The bridge itself remained intact. Other bridges were also attacked on this patrol with three near misses. All results being observed. During all of these attacks, heavy and intense light flak was encountered."[29]

The 421 Squadron ORB tells a slightly different story;

> "Dive-bombing at Bully T.996689 – 12 x 500 lb. 0.025 delayed-action bombs were dropped. Results not observed. Heavy accurate intense flak from area surrounding Caen. Weather: CAVU."[30]

The location Bully T.996689, given with the accuracy of an artillery target, is the location of a railway bridge that crosses the Orne River seven miles south of Caen. Early in the morning Typhoons had severely damaged the road bridge just two miles from Bully that was the major east-west artery south of Caen and it led to Evrecy in the heart of the action. Both the road bridge and the rail bridge were very important for sending men and supplies to reinforce the German defenders of the 9th SS Panzer Division. The 421 attack was intended to take out the rail bridge.

At 1525 hours ten Spitfires of 416 Squadron took off to patrol the front lines at 10,000 feet. Over Caen at 1630 hours they encountered a gaggle of about 30 Bf 109s plus FW 190s above and below the cloud. These were engaged and one Bf 109 was destroyed by F/L Pat Patterson.

The next action was an armed recce at 1630 hours when 12 Spitfires of 403 Squadron carried out an armed recce in the Caen/Argentan area. This is what they reported:

> "Area south Evrecy medium light flak, area Villers-Bocage meagre, heavy inaccurate flak. Convoy of 15 artillery tractors moving north

T.9439. Artillery moving approximately 100 feet apart. Attacked by section of two aircraft stopping convoy. Damage not determined. Squadron attacked 15 plus MT and Staff Car moving from side roads to main road running from Conde T.8532 to Thury-Harcourt, four rolled into ditch, three left smoking, other damage not determined. 50 infantry strafed moving north on road T.938482. Weather: 7/10ths at 4500 to 5000 feet, visibility 15 miles."[31]

At 1715 hours six aircraft from 421 Squadron took off on a front line patrol. They flew in fluid six formation – three pairs -- F/L John McElroy led with F/O Al Brandon on his wing; F/L Hank Zary flew number three with F/O Jim Flood on his wing and F/O Cookie Cook flying number five with F/O John Hamm on his wing. They covered the whole western area flying over to St. Lô and turning east toward Caen. Meanwhile 14 Bf 109s of III./JG 3 were escorting two other Bf 109s – aircraft of the reconnaissance gruppe I./NAG 13. The reconnaissance aircraft were trying to photograph the British positions from about 6,000 feet. For some curious reason the 14 escort aircraft were separated from the two reconnaissance aircraft by about half a mile, in a south-westerly direction. Into the space between, McElroy and his other five pilots burst through cloud and were upon them. McElroy, Brandon, Cook and Hamm broke left into the 14, while Zary and Flood broke right. The startled Germans barely had a chance to react. McElroy reported:

> "Diving down I broke cloud 100 yards behind him at 10° angle off. I gave him a 1-to-2-second burst and saw five or six strikes on port side of cockpit, engine and tail. The enemy aircraft pulled up gently for about 500 feet. I throttled back but passed him. The enemy aircraft dropped his nose and then began to go down in a vertical dive from about 4,000 feet. The enemy aircraft was apparently out of control and the pilot dead."[32]

Oberfähnrich Helmut Garzaroli of 8 Staffel was indeed dead at the controls. Brandon attacked another Bf 109 and emptied his ammunition into him but did not see smoke and lost him in cloud. He claimed only a damaged, but in fact another German pilot, Gefreiter Robert Emmerling of 8 Staffel III./ JG 3, was reported killed in action in this engagement. Meanwhile, Zary and his wingman Flood broke right into the two reconnaissance aircraft. The copy of Zary's Combat Report is poorly preserved, but Flood's says:

"My number one broke off to engage the two Me 109s to our right. He got on the tail of one and I observed many strikes finally seeing the enemy aircraft wreathed in flames go down."[33]

Flood went after the other aircraft but only claimed a damaged. However only one I./NAG 13 aircraft was lost – Leutnant Heinrich Weimer was reported FTR.

Returning now to S/L Whalley's description of the remaining events of the day, he rounds off the account with these words:

"During the day very important personages landed or visited the airfield. Admiral Sir Bertram Ramsay was expected to arrive but his flight was cancelled. AM Sir Arthur Tedder arrived by air and was met by AM Sir Arthur Coningham, AVM Broadhurst, AVM Brown and AC MacAvoy. A RN rear admiral, unidentified, and several brigadiers were also seen on the landing strip. The Sector Commander and Officer Commanding met these visitors. The majority of these officers left for England later in the day."[34]

The boys from 127 Wing were not the only ones to celebrate 28 June as a busy but extremely successful day. While the furious tank battles raged on the ground, the skies filled with hectic aerial fighting. The first history of the RCAF in World War II published one year after the war ended, had this to say about 28 June:

"Of the 34 enemy aircraft destroyed over Normandy that day, 26 fell to the Spitfire squadrons of MacBrien's sector, for the RCAF's biggest bag in one day." [35]

Saturday 29 June

The cloudy and damp weather continued on Saturday. Heavy showers at sun-up looked to be the order of the day, but about 0700 hours things cleared somewhat and aircraft took off. Though spotty, the weather was clear enough for operations until noon, then a downpour, an hour of clearing between 1300 hours and 1400 hours, more rain lasting several hours and a final clearing at 1900 hours. The wing managed to launch eight operations in the periods of clearing.

There was a serious loss to the wing in late morning when S/L Freddie Green DFC, commander of 416 Squadron, led his squadron at

1010 hours on an armed recce between Caen and Falaise. Passing just north of Caen on the return trip an hour later, Green's aircraft was badly damaged by flak and made barely flyable. Although he coaxed

it towards B.2, he crash-landed short of the airstrip in a field between B.3 and B.2 injuring his spine and cutting his forehead. He was immediately rushed to No. 52 Field Hospital where it was pronounced that he would not be able to fly for at least three or four months. That evening he was airlifted to England and F/L Johnny McElroy, DFC and bar, of 421 Squadron was promoted to acting S/L of 416 Squadron to replace Green. Green had been a staunch and reliable squadron commander for over two years. At one point, November 1942 to April 1943, he commanded 421 Squadron and after a rest in Canada, he came back to command 416 Squadron in October 1944.

Figure 43 -- Green. S/L Freddie Green had been commander of 416 Squadron since October 1943. A victim of flak, he was seriously injured when he crash-landed 29 July 1944.

(Canadian Forces Photo PL10347)

At 1300 hours S/L EePee Wood and 10 other 403 pilots took off on an armed recce from Caen south to Thury-Harcourt, east to Falaise and north to Mézidon. They flew in and out of cloud that nearly covered the sky and was stacked in layers from 5,000 feet up to 24,000 feet while light rain showers were scattered about. Between breaks in the cloud layer they managed to run into severe flak near Caen and to shoot up a truck and an open car near Thury-Harcourt. At one point they saw a gaggle of 15 or more Bf 109s, but the enemy disappeared into cloud soon after being spotted. East of Mézidon they ran into another small gaggle of three Bf 109s and two FW 190s, believed to be from I./JG 11 and II./JG 11. When the squadron encountered them, a FW 190 had picked out what he thought was a straggling Spitfire. He was attacking the aircraft of W/O Bob Shannon. F/L Doug Lindsay reported what happened.

"In the Lisieux area we were flying north due west of the town and at about 4,000 feet. To my port I saw a FW 190 flying north at approximately the same height, and on the tail of a Spitfire. The Spitfire rolled over on his back and went down. I broke around the FW 190. He broke left and dove down towards the deck. I followed him down getting on his tail. From dead line astern and at 300 yards range I opened fire giving him several 2-second bursts. Strikes were observed on the cockpit and wing roots and black smoke poured from the enemy aircraft. The 190 began to pull up and pieces fell away. He jettisoned his hood as I continued to fire and the pilot baled out but his parachute was not seen to open. The enemy aircraft rolled over on its back and went in exploding as it hit."[36]

Although the German pilot's parachute didn't open, Shannon's parachute did. He landed cleanly, buried his parachute and was hidden by the townspeople in a small farm house for two months until he was liberated by American troops on 21 August when he returned to his unit.

Sunday 30 June

Sunday's weather was again cloudy and damp. The wing flew 16 operations including one scramble and nine patrols, the remaining six were armed recces. Of theses 16 operations, four saw some action in which seven enemy aircraft were claimed with no losses. It started early when 421 Squadron flew an armed recce in the Caen/Lisieux area. At 0705 hours F/L Paul Johnson was leading the squadron. He related the following:

"We were flying approximately 15 miles north of Bernay at 8,000 feet and in a southerly direction when 15 Me 109s were seen flying south at the same height. They turned starboard and dove down through a hole in the cloud. I followed them down, lost them in cloud but picked them up again at cloud base which was about 1,000 feet. At this time we were south-west of Bernay. The remainder of the squadron had turned port. My number two and I engaged the enemy aircraft. I got on the tail of one and closing to 200 yards fired from dead astern. I gave him two short bursts and saw strikes on starboard aileron and wing and on fuselage. Black and white smoke poured from him. He went into a spin turning port and crashed into the ground exploding. The enemy aircraft was carrying jet tanks which he failed to jettison."[37]

In this same engagement F/L Roger Wilson, who was leading blue section claimed another Bf 109 destroyed. The two unfortunate pilots were Oberfähnrich Rolf Jutting, whose aircraft exploded upon impact with the ground, and Oberfähnrich Rolf Schobert who was listed as FTR. Both flew with II./JG 53.

On two separate occasions during the day 403 Squadron stumbled upon groups of enemy aircraft ducking in and out of cloud. They were aircraft from JG 1 and JG 3. F/O Hart Finley and F/O Doug Orr both submitted claims for single aircraft from these tussles. And while the next sizeable engagement involving 127 Wing went to 421 Squadron at 2030 hours north over Caen, the other Canadian Spitfire wings were reaping big rewards as well. At 1720 hours 144 Wing destroyed five Bf 109s of III./JG 27, and about the same time near Argentan 126 Wing destroyed three more Bf 109s from IV./JG 27. This particular jagdgeschwader -- JG 27 -- had a very bad day 30 June Between the three gruppen – I, III and IV of JG 27, they lost 11 Bf 109s and at least six pilots. The fate of three of the pilots is not known, only one was wounded while two were killed.

The aerial battle in which 421 Squadron found itself occurred near Lisieux – once again against Bf 109s of JG 27 -- eight aircraft against eight aircraft. I./JG 27 lost three Bf 109s. F/L Paul Johnson claimed two Bf 109s destroyed, bringing his total for the day to three and his career total to five, making him an ace. Johnson was 421 Squadron's second ace – Buck McNair having shot down eight while leading 421 Squadron in 1943 was its first ace. In addition to Johnson's pair, F/O Scotty McRoberts claimed one. It was the Canadian Spitfires alone that accounted for the staggering loss of aircraft of JG 27.

It had been a banner day, and it topped off a banner month. Since D-Day the Canadian Spitfire wings recorded 100 aircraft destroyed and another 37 probably destroyed or damaged[38]. The highest scoring squadron was 421 Squadron with 21 claimed destroyed. In addition, the Canadian Spitfire squadrons claimed six tanks, 13 armoured vehicles and 490 trucks destroyed.

That night the weather cleared around 2100 hours and aircrew and ground crew turned out to enjoy a calm evening and a delightful sunset, but the stillness was soon drowned with noise of an armada of bombers flying directly overhead at about 15,000 feet.

"All personnel watched aircraft of Bomber Command Lancasters carrying out a heavy and concentrated bombing attack to our south in the Beny Bocage area. Our pilots flew over the area after the bombers had left and reported that the entire village of Beny Bocage had been obliterated and the whole area, noted for its heavy flak and containing a number of German tanks and vehicles, looked like a large brown ploughed field."[39]

Chapter Nine – July

Saturday 1 July

Dominion Day – a day off from school or work had the boys been back home to celebrate it. First thing in the morning, while rain pelted down on the canvas roof, the teletype machine in the headquarters command truck chattered away printing three congratulatory signals – one each from Gen Eisenhower, AVM Broadhurst and G/C MacBrien.

The miserable weather that ended the month of June carried over into July, starting with a torrential downpour that let up from time to time but didn't end until noon. In driving rain or misty drizzle, both of which reduced visibility to the minimum, the wing sent off four 80-minute patrols spaced one-half-hour apart. They climbed above the low cloud layer to fly the length and breadth of the lodgement but none of the patrols was eventful.

It was the last flying day for F/L Hart Finley, 'B' Flight commander of 403 Squadron, and for his colleague F/L Pete Logan. Both had completed their tours sad to leave their comrades-in-arms. Two new pilots arrived from 83 Group headquarters to replace them and F/L Doug Lindsay took over command of 'B' Flight replacing Finley.

In the other two squadrons, this was the day that F/L Johnny McElroy of 421 Squadron officially became S/L McElroy of 416 Squadron, taking over the reins of command from Freddie Green who was now in capable hands in a hospital in England. F/L Hank Zary replaced McElroy as commander of 'B' Flight in 421 Squadron. Apart from these personnel changes and the congratulatory teletypes, it was a pretty dull day.

Sunday 2 July

Not so the next day. On Sunday, all three squadrons were coming and going all day and the airstrip was in a continuous buzz as ground crews prepared, patched, loaded and filled their beloved Spitfires. By two o'clock in the afternoon the weather had changed very little from early in the morning – three distinct layers of cloud at about 5,000, 7,000 and 12,000 feet. The layers broke up or filled in somewhat over time, ranging from 3/10ths to 6/10ths cover. Sun broke through occasionally, but for the most part it was just a bright cloudy day.

The wing had already flown five armed recces and two patrols with only a couple of destroyed trucks to show for it, when 12 aircraft of 403 Squadron fired up their Merlin engines and prepared to go on another patrol. S/L EePee Wood taxied his aircraft, with its prominent KH-A painted on each side, along one of the dirt strips accompanied by his wingman F/O Red Thomson. Behind him, moving in pairs were the other 10 Spitfires preparing for take-off on this squadron-strength patrol of the beachheads and the Cotentin Peninsula. On the wing of each Spitfire sat a ground crew member.

Two-by-two the Spitfires moved onto the wire mesh runway, wing-sitters jumped off, the aircraft gathered speed and took off. The adjutant noted the time at 1410 hours. The other pairs took off immediately after the leader, snapping up their undercarriage when they were a mere ten feet off the ground. As they climbed to form up over the sea, F/S Ron Forsyth's Spitfire began to run roughly and he turned back and landed. The remaining 11 aircraft climbed to 8,000 feet. F/L Doug Lindsay was flying his first day as the replacement commander of 'B' Flight.

They flew west cutting diagonally in over the coast beyond OMAHA beach, until just inland of the beaches past Carentan they wheeled right and flew north-west up the Cotentin Peninsula to Cherbourg before turning and retracing their steps. On the return route they flew inland along the bomb line until they were over Caen. From time to time light flak met them, but at Caen the flak was heavy, intense and very accurate, causing them to take evasive action until they were east of Caen and out of harm's way. At that moment – 1508 hours – they spotted about 20 Bf 109s 2,000 feet below them. As previously rehearsed, and without breaking radio silence, Wood went into a shallow dive to attack, leading red and yellow sections while Lindsay climbed with his blue section to provide some high cover. As he broke through the next higher layer of cloud Lindsay ran into another gaggle of about 15 Bf 109s. The lower formation consisted of I./JG 27 and IV./JG 27. The upper group were the aircraft of II./JG 53. All three of these Gruppen were based in fields around the town of Champfleury near Paris.

In the history of the action by these gruppen as described by Jean-Bernard Frappé, the records are confusing and we will return to this matter later, but let us start the description of the action with the combat reports of the pilots of 403 Squadron. Wood submitted the following report.

"As we came towards Caen, Bazaar (ground control) warned us of enemy aircraft in the vicinity. Blue section broke upwards through cloud. Red and yellow sections continued to fly at about 7,000 feet. Just north of Caen we saw 20-plus Me 109s. We broke into them and I got on the tail of one, and I fired at 600 yards, closing to 100 yards with 10° to 30° deflection. I gave him another long burst and saw strikes on the cockpit and along the fuselage. He broke to port. I had to disengage because other enemy aircraft were on my tail.

"I saw another enemy aircraft climbing from about 800 feet below. I fired at him and dead astern. I was so close I had to break for fear of hitting him. I fired, getting a number of strikes on his tail, wing roots and cockpit. The enemy aircraft continued on climbing slightly, suddenly turned and rolled on aileron turns. I saw flames shoot out of him as he was falling into a vertical dive. I kept watching him until he was about 3,000 feet from the deck and apparently out of control.

"I closed on a third Me 109. I got within 50 yards range and directly behind him. I saw strikes on cockpit and wing. I was forced to break off again because of other enemy aircraft."[1]

Wood claimed one aircraft destroyed and two damaged. We pick up the rest of the story from F/L Andy MacKenzie who led yellow section.

"Red and yellow sections engaged 20-plus Me 109s over Caen at approximately 8,000 feet. I closed to 400 yards on two 109s and they broke upward and to starboard. I closed on one to 300 yards and opened fire. It broke port and I then closed to 100 yards, after a long burst of 4-seconds the aircraft burst into flames, rolled on its back and I watched it crash in flames one-half-mile east of Caen.

"I saw another aircraft at about 6,000 feet climbing steeply towards the east. I closed to 150 yards firing about a 4-second burst. The port wheel fell down and I saw five cannon strikes on the cockpit. The aircraft then seemed to spiral down out of control but I was unable to watch the outcome as two enemy aircraft were attacking from four o'clock. I last saw the enemy aircraft at about 3,500 feet."[2]

F/O Bob Greene and F/L Mac Hill submitted a shared claim for the destruction of an enemy aircraft. Here is the way they reported -- first Greene's account, then Hill's.

"We were flying west toward Caen when we sighted 15-plus Me 109s ahead of us at about 6,000 feet. We chased them and fired a short burst at one of the 109s from line astern and 250 yard range. He slowed down and his port wheel dropped down. He started to go down and was weaving violently. His speed had increased greatly. I kept firing at him. My starboard cannon stopped and I ran out of ammunition. I called on F/L Hill to finish him off, which he did. The pilot finally baling out and the aircraft crashing into the ground."[3]

"We saw 15-plus Me 109s ahead of us and at the same height. We gave chase. The tailing section of three broke to starboard. I turned onto the last of the three and was about to open fire when another Spitfire almost collided with me and I had to break away. I looked back and saw this enemy aircraft being attacked by this Spitfire and saw strikes. I circled above them and the pilot of the Spitfire (F/O Greene) called up on the R/T and told me he was out of ammunition. I fired again from 300 yards with 10° deflection, a second burst and saw strikes on engine and wing root. White smoke poured from him and he started to go down. The pilot baled out at about 3,000 feet. The enemy aircraft went into the deck about 10 miles south-east of Caen."[5]

Lindsay took blue section up to attack the Bf 109s of II./JG 53 who were flying at 12,000 feet. For his pains he performed that rare feat of claiming three aircraft destroyed on one mission. His report was as follows:

"I was flying Blue One with 403 Squadron, on a front line patrol. We were flying west at about 6,000 feet near Caen, when Bazaar warned us of enemy aircraft in the vicinity. Our section broke upward through cloud to about 12,000 feet and sighted 15-plus Me 109s in front and approximately two miles away. We immediately tried to engage and closed slowly from line astern. The enemy aircraft were flying sections of five line astern. I attacked the port section and opened fire at 300 yards on the trailing enemy aircraft from line astern. I saw strikes around the cockpit and wing roots. Black smoke poured from him and he half-rolled then went diving straight down into the deck.

"I attacked the next one in line firing from 300 yards allowing 15° deflection and again got strikes on cockpit and wing roots. The coop-top was jettisoned and pilot baled out at about 2,000 feet, and the aircraft spun into the ground.

"The next enemy aircraft in line had dove down towards the deck by this time. I closed on him from 300 to 250 yards and with 10° to 15° angle off, fired seeing strikes on the cockpit. This pilot also baled out at about 2,000 feet." [6]

F/L Mac Gordon was with Lindsay when he performed this feat of nabbing three aircraft in a row. Gordon's report adds something to the drama of the battle up on top, but it also reveals something of the Intelligence Officer's role in corroborating all this. The intelligence officer was F/L Henry Martin.

"I was flying Blue Three with 403 Squadron on a front line patrol. We were flying west to our base at 6,000 to 7,000 feet and near Caen when control warned us of enemy aircraft in the area. Our section broke up through cloud to 12,000 feet and nearly about 20 Me 109s directly ahead of us and about two miles away. We gave chase toward south-west. They broke around in a circle. I got on the last one's tail and fired a fairly long burst with a full ring of deflection from about 200 to 75 yards. I saw strikes on cockpit and fuselage and wings. Black smoke poured from him and he rolled

261

Figure 44 -- Lindsay. F/L J D Lindsay was already credited with two destroyed, one shared and two damaged when he accomplished the feat of destroying three at one time -- making him an ace. By the end of the war he had six and one shared, and went on to claim two MIGs destroyed and three damaged in the Korean War.

(Canadian Forces Photo PL26643)

over into cloud. I got onto the tail of a second enemy aircraft and followed him around and down through cloud to about 6,000 feet. It was then that I saw an enemy chute come down through cloud.

"I opened fire on the second enemy aircraft from 150 yards from dead astern. I saw strikes and pieces fall away. The pilot baled out but his chute failed to open and the aircraft went down into deck."[7]

"Assessment of Me 109 damaged – F/L Gordon . F/L Gordon in his personal combat report is claiming one Me 109 damaged pending further assessment and a second Me 109 destroyed. At the time of the combat no other aircraft was in this area which was about 12 miles south-west of Caen. The 109 he claims as damaged was hit and with black smoke pouring from it, half-rolled into cloud at 9,000 feet. He then followed another Me 109 round and down through the cloud layer at 6,000 feet. It was then that he saw an enemy parachute come down through cloud.

"Blue section of 403 Squadron were the only section to engage enemy aircraft in this area, the other two sections having engaged another gaggle of enemy aircraft to the east of Caen. In blue section only F/L Lindsay and F/L Gordon fired at enemy aircraft. The pilots who baled out from aircraft engaged by F/L Lindsay were both seen to bale out at about 2,000 feet. F/L Lindsay orbiting around at about 1,000 feet in the area where the section had engaged the enemy aircraft saw five distinct fires on the ground which he states were in all possibility burning aircraft. In the engagement we suffered no casualties so those fires if they were burning aircraft would have been enemy aircraft. From the evidence it would appear that this Me

109 F/L Gordon is claiming as damaged might well be a destroyed; the parachute he saw at 6,000 feet coming from the Me 109 he damaged and which disappeared in cloud. It is requested that this claim of one Me 109 damaged be examined and re-assessed if it is deemed necessary."[8]

At the top of the combat report there is a hand-written annotation stating that the damaged was up-graded to a destroyed. So Gordon was officially awarded two Bf 109s destroyed. The final tally of claims by 403 Squadron was seven – three destroyed by Lindsay, two by Gordon, one by MacKenzie and one shared by Greene and Hill. All of the 403 Squadron aircraft returned safely to base, and there is no report of any substantial damage to any of the aircraft.

Now comes the mystery. As mentioned earlier, the expert on Luftwaffe activities during the Normandy Campaign is Jean-Bernard Frappé in his book '*La Luftwaffe – face au débarquement allié*'. In the book he confirms that three gruppen were near Caen at 1506 hours through 1516 hours this day. However, each of the gruppen claim having shot down P-47s – five P-47s in all and they claim they shot down a Spitfire as well. Even more difficult to explain is the declared losses. The Luftwaffe records suggest that it was three squadrons of US 9thAF P-47s that shot down nearly all their aircraft. In the whole day's activity no claims were made by the US 9thAF and only one claim of a Bf 109 made by LCol Ben Rimerman of 353rd Fighter Group of the 8thAF flying P-47s. Since 20 German fighters were shot down 2 July, it could have been any of these. I believe the facts are as follows -- I./JG 27 lost Unteroffizier Günter Weigmann KIA. IV./JG 27 lost Leutnant Walter Rabenstein FTR. And II./JG 53 who Lindsay and Gordon say lost five, actually recorded four lost – Feldwebel Alfred Ostemeyer parachuted safely but was slightly wounded, Leutnant Otto Russ FTR, Oberfähnrich Karl-Heinz Trettau FTR and Oberfähnrich Günter Worm FTR. In summary, whereas 403 claimed seven destroyed, there is a record of six German losses.

There was a great thrash in the officer's mess that night to celebrate 403 getting out of the doldrums in terms of successful action. It had been a busy day. S/L Whalley summed it all up in the notes that went into the 127 Wing ORB.

"Despite bad weather conditions, again typical of the weather we have had for the past ten days, aircraft of the three squadrons carried out eleven sorties. 421 Squadron carried out an armed recce to start the day off in the Villers-Bocage/Caen area. The aircraft attacked enemy MT seen moving north. The next two sorties were carried out by 416 and 403 Squadrons respectively but were uneventful. In the third sortie 416 Squadron carried out an armed recce in the Caen/Argentan area. With 11 aircraft in the squadron, they attacked MT near Argentan. Despite light and heavy flak being encountered, they left two vehicles smoking. 403 Squadron were detailed for the next flight and sent 12 aircraft up to dive-bomb Mézidon marshalling yards. One Spitfire was hit by flak but the pilot managed to return to base and land safely. The squadron dropped 12 500-pound MC .023 delay from 6000 to 3000 feet. Nine bombs were seen to land in the target area with good effect. Shortly afterwards, 12 aircraft of 421 Squadron carried out an armed recce in the Lisièux/Argentan area. MT were attacked and one was left smoking and two were damaged. During this operation two Me 109s were sighted but were lost when they dived through cloud. In the next patrol 416 Squadron returned to base without sighting any enemy targets. During the middle of the afternoon, 403 with 12 Spitfires, carried out a front line patrol with excellent results. The squadron engaged a number of enemy aircraft with the following results: -- three Me 109s destroyed by F/L J D Lindsay; one Me 109 destroyed by F/L A R MacKenzie DFC; one Me 109 destroyed by F/L M J Gordon; one Me 109 destroyed (shared) by F/L W J Hill and F/O R B Greene; three Me 109s damaged by S/L E P Wood; one Me 109 damaged by F/O F W Thomson; one Me 109 damaged by F/L M J Gordon; one Me 109 damaged by F/L A R MacKenzie DFC. 20-plus enemy aircraft were engaged during this operation. The next patrol by 421 Squadron with 11 aircraft was abortive but one of our aircraft was hit by flak but the pilot returned and landed safely. Two Me 109s were seen but the squadron was unable to engage. In the last two patrols of the day by aircraft of 416 and 403 Squadrons were uneventful. Owing to the very heavy rain falling in this area during the past week, the dust has been well and truly laid, and the topsoil has turned into mud making the roads very slippery and dangerous, but the airfield has remained serviceable despite these conditions. As I started to write this entry enemy ack-ack was heard in the distance and bursts were seen in the sky through the opening of my tent. With a pair of field glasses three Spitfires were seen to be carrying out a dive-bombing attack on a target (unknown) behind enemy lines. The flak was heavy and from the distance appeared to be rather accurate. On numerous occasions personnel of the wing are able to watch the ack-ack of the German gunners in addition to our own."[9]

Monday 3 July

Monday was a thoroughly miserable day. No flying was undertaken by 127 Wing until late afternoon, when four uneventful patrols were flown between 1500 hours and 2200 hours.

Tuesday 4 July

"Patrols were the order of the day – all of them in crummy weather and all of them uneventful except one. The pilots didn't realize it, but this was the start of the renewed effort to take Caen. The patrols were to ensure German fighters didn't get at the attacking Typhoons or at the troops themselves. At 1410 hours 12 aircraft led by S/L Wally Conrad left for a front lines patrol. The weather was 10/10ths cloud 2,000 to 10,000 feet and the flak around Caen was as heavy as ever. F/O Willie Warfield's aircraft was hit squarely and he had to crash-land it near Ranville north of Caen. F/O Warfield was only slightly injured – indeed he flew again the next day."[10]

Wednesday 5 July

Until this day, there had been a staging area at the end of the field where the wounded waited to be airlifted out of France by Dakotas of Transport Command. Several large tents and a couple of wood-covered lean-tos were off to the side and at least one Dakota was usually parked there. Wounded troops were brought from the field medical treatment centres or No. 52 Field Hospital and lodged in the tents awaiting airlift out to the UK. This activity had been going on ever since B.2 was first opened for operations about 10 June, but at first it was an ad hoc operation with just a trickle of casualties flown out. On 17 June the evacuation centre was officially set up at B.2, complete with more elaborate tents and other structures and few medical staff. Two hundred casualties were flown out that first day and in the next two weeks the daily figure went much higher. It operated at full capacity for nearly three weeks, but on 5 July, 127 Wing received a signal that the staging facilities for the evacuation of the wounded were being moved to B.8 Sommervieu -- the home of 39 Recce Wing. Because the number of casualties rapidly increased after the 4 July offensive when the Canadian and British offensive tried desperately to take Caen, the evacuation facility had to be moved closer to the action.

Figure 45 -- Medical airlift. *This photo shows the medical evacuation area at B.2 late in June. One C-47 is parked while another is starting to take-off, and raising a cloud of dust like that which claimed the life of F/L Charlie Grant.*
(Canadian Forces Photo PL 30086).

The intelligence officers, F/Ls Martin and Johnson gave the pilots a situation report. They described how the previous day the Canadian 3rd Division had launched a one-brigade assault on Carpiquet Airport. It was a success, but left the brigade holding a salient exposed on three sides to the Germans. This assault was the first phase of Operation CHARNWOOD – the effort to take Caen and break through the German lines. The second step was to be a massive carpet-bombing effort by RAF Bomber Command to annihilate the German artillery around Caen. This was to happen within two days. Finally the Canadian 3rd Division, British 59th Division and British 3rd Division would take the city. Typhoon squadrons would fly close support to the army and the firepower of artillery and the battlewagons HMS Rodney and HMS Belfast would precede the infantry attack.

12 aircraft each of 421 Squadron and 403 Squadron were on an armed recce in the Dreux/Chartres area when they came upon Bf 109s painted dark green with brown blots on them and black disks instead of swastikas. This is F/O Scotty McRoberts' combat report of the engagement that occurred at 1605 hours.

> "Near Bernay, 20-plus Me 109s were sighted below us travelling north-west. We bounced from out of the sun and I got on the tail of an Me 109 and fired several short bursts at about 5° deflection at a range of 150 yards. But observed no strikes. The Me broke port and I turned inside with about 15° to 20° angle off firing a long burst at 200 yards with strikes on tail, wings and engine. Clouds of smoke, white and black with flame started and finally obscured the whole enemy aircraft. I saw the hood jettisoned. The enemy aircraft began to dive down and was seen to disintegrate and disappeared into cloud at 5,000 feet.
>
> "I then broke to find the formation and while climbing I saw a lone 109 beneath cloud, I reefed round and dived on him as I opened fire from 300 yards angle of 15°. I saw strikes on wings and tail plane. Pieces were seen to fly off the left wing. I continued my attack closing to 150 yards, cutting the tail completely off. The pilot jettisoned the hood and baled out at approximately 500 feet."[10]

Figure 46 --The bosses. *This photograph was taken just around the beginning of July, after McElroy succeeded Freddie Green but before Buckham ended his tour. These were the bosses -- the commanding officers in 127 Wing. From left to right -- S/L EePee Wood commander of 403 Squadron, S/L Johnny McElroy commander of 416 Squadron, S/L Cam MacArthur chief medical officer, S/L Wally Conrad commander of 421 Squadron, W/C Buck McNair base commander of neighbouring B.3 (McNair was just visiting), S/L Bob Whalley chief administrative officer, W/C Brownsie Brown base commander of B.2, W/C Bob Buckham W/C (F) of 127 Wing, and G/C Tin Willy MacBrien officer commanding Number 17 Sector, 83 Group, 2ndTAF.*

(McElroy collection)

P/O D E Libbey reported:

"We bounced about 20 Me 109s which were at 15,000 feet, about 20 miles south-east of Caen. Yellow Three went down on two 109s. He got on the tail of one and the other broke into him; I went into this second enemy aircraft and gave him three bursts from about 20° off at about 150 yards. I saw strikes on tail unit and small pieces came off. He went over on his back and went down with white smoke pouring from him; I lost sight of him when he went into cloud at about 2,000 feet. F/L Paterson saw one go down on his back with smoke pouring from him at about the same time."[11]

We have been unable to precisely identify which Luftwaffe unit was involved in this battle, although it may have been IV./JG 27 for they lost four aircraft some time that afternoon.

Thursday 6 July

While 416 and 421 flew armed recces in the Caen to Falaises area attempting to cut off reinforcements coming to the support of the German troops at Caen, 403 Squadron flew 16 four-aircraft one-hour overlapping patrols over the beaches. This was to stop Ju 88s from laying mines in the sea lanes off the coast. They flew these patrols from 0515 hours until 2100 hours.

"During the morning and early afternoon there wasn't a cloud visible in this area. Despite the number of patrols, no enemy aircraft were sighted but 416 and 421 Squadrons damaged three and two MT respectively.

"A crew of three fitters under Sergeant DeLong and Corporal Stiles of Maintenance set up what is believed to be a new record for an engine change. Commencing at 0830 hours, this crew removed an engine from a Spitfire IXb and replaced it with a new engine, and including all the fittings on components, by 1930 hours on the same day. This is considered to be real teamwork and a good record – especially under field conditions."[12]

Friday 7 July

"The weather, which started off by being poor, improved considerably and resulted in seven operational flights being carried out by the squadrons. 416 Squadron attacked MT behind the enemy lines, leaving one smoking and damaging two. Shortly afterwards 403 Squadron attacked MT and damaged one, and followed up this operation by a further score leaving three MT smoking and damaging two. It was then 421 Squadron's turn to carry out an armed recce in which pilots left two MT smoking. The last patrol of the day by 416 Squadron was uneventful. Practically on all these patrols, heavy and accurate flak was encountered but fortunately all our aircraft returned safely. During the day Sir Archibald Sinclair, Secretary of State for Air, and Marshal of the RAF, Sir Charles Portal, landed on the strip in a Dakota aircraft. These very important personages were met by the Air Officer Commanding, 83 Group (AVM Harry Broadhurst), and the Officer Commanding the wing (W/C Mannifrank Brown). They proceeded to Group HQ located at Creully about two miles away almost immediately afterwards. Later in the day, they departed by air for the UK. During the few minutes they remained at this wing, they visited Intelligence and spoke to a number of pilots who were there."[13]

That night 800 Lancasters of RAF Bomber Command dropped 2,000 tons of bombs in 40 minutes across the north-western parts of the outskirts of Caen.

Saturday 8 July

416 Squadron flew 18 four-aircraft patrols over the beaches, while 403 and 421 Squadrons each flew three armed recces. They reported very heavy fighting around Caen. From first light this was the day when British and Canadian troops fought to capture the ground from their static positions of the last month through to the outskirts of Caen. The three-division attack met stubborn German resistance and the number of casualties on both sides was staggering.

> "421 Squadron attacked MT leaving two smoking and damaging two. A number of MT were later attacked by members of 403 Squadron and a number were left smoking. The pilots were unable to estimate the total number. These pilots reported very heavy fighting in the Caen sector and advised that a number of roads were streaming with French civilians apparently being evacuated."[14]

A big conference was held during the day. AM Tedder and AM Coningham flew in by Dakota aircraft and after a short chat at the edge of the strip they departed with AVM Broadhurst. Rumours were flying, and the rumours were saying there was to be a major reorganization of all the wings and sectors. Sectors were to be eliminated, some wings closed down and the remaining wings increased in size. It was believed there would be elimination of many jobs, and S/L Whalley expresses his own concerns about the loss of his job in the wing ORB.

"The result of the changes may and will probably mean that a number of the senior officers in the sector will soon be saying goodbye. Whether others will gain promotions is not known but until the axe falls, a certain amount of conjecture exists for those whose positions are now somewhat precarious. It is expected that officers in 144 Wing will generally be the losers and will be returning to the UK, others in 127 Wing and 126 Wing may be catching the same boat home. Whatever happens, those of us who have been with the wings since their formation have watched them grow into a smoothly operating machine. We have watched our squadrons make game with the enemy fit to face the enemy in an overseas theatre. The units were brought across the water a month ago and it is now realized that the many anxious days of worry behind us have reaped good results. For a number of us it will be tough to leave the sector as we have seen it grow from nothing into the most successful sector in the RAF. We would have liked to remain with our units to the end. Whoever gets our jobs, as and when we leave, will fall into what we consider to be an efficient and fine organization. Perhaps more could have been done to improve it but results have shown that the sector has not done too bad a job. In any event the next week will tell its tale and in the meantime those of us more directly concerned with the scheme of things will watch events very closely indeed."[15]

That night as Whalley anguished over losing his job, the bombers from Bomber Command came back and hit Caen again just before the British and Canadians moved into the city. Fierce fighting became hand-to-hand and house-to-house vicious fighting unlike anything seen before, except perhaps at Stalingrad.

Sunday 9 July

"Bad weather during the day permitted only four operational flights being carried out by the squadrons and these were all armed recces. 403 Squadron carried out the first in which they damaged four MT behind enemy lines. 421 Squadron then headed out and attacked an enemy column between Cabourg and Thury-Harcourt damaging three MT. In the afternoon 416 Squadron attacked MT and damaged two. On this operation 416 Squadron reported the first flying bombs they had seen. They were sighted near Trun at 3,000 feet travelling south-west at approximately 350 mph. 421 Squadron carried out the next operation, which was uneventful. All our aircraft returned safely.

"Rumour has it that big money says the war will be over in September. We all hope so but are not as optimistic as all that. All day long and on the previous night and day, the artillery pounded away at the Caen area and it was reported that an attack was progressing satisfactorily. In fact by mid afternoon the enemy had, except for small elements, left from that northern part of Caen area for the river Orne. Our troops were consolidating their positions on the riverbank and getting ready for the crossing. The previous night was most interesting for the vast majority of personnel in this wing. A large force of Lancasters attacked Caen from a low height, and all personnel, for the first time, saw the heavy bombers at work. After the attack, which left blankets of smoke soaring skywards, the Lancasters turned and proceeded northwards across the aerodrome. They were so low that squadron markings could be identified. It was an impressive sight and one which will be remembered by many for a very long time to come. No bombs were dropped on or near the aerodrome, although a very heavy barrage was directed at enemy aircraft which crossed over this area during the night. It was much heavier than usual and most personnel found that they could not sleep while the ack-ack was in action."[16]

Monday 10 July

The weather closed in around noon and stopped further flying, but before that time, 416 Squadron flew one armed recce and 421 Squadron flew 10 four-aircraft patrols while 403 had the day off. In the armed recce flown by 416, P/O Ronnie McCrae failed to return after being hit by intense flak at about 1000 hours, however he was back at the base for lunch.

"During the evening, the Wing Administrative Officer was faced with an unusual problem. Recently numbers of squadrons have landed here just before dark and because of bad weather conditions were unable to return to the UK. 29 American aircrew landed here this afternoon in C-47 aircraft and this was quite comfortably coped with; the pilots being accommodated in several marquees which we have erected for that purpose. However, the perplexing problem arose when Intelligence gravely informed the Senior Admin Officer that five American nurses were aboard and would also require accommodations over night. Arrangements were immediately made to send these nurses over to No. 52 Field Hospital, where it was understood that accommodation could be provided. At this time W/C Brown appeared and thought it would be a particularly poor show on our part to send them off elsewhere. He suggested that his caravan with the addition of an ambulance would solve the problem. It did. The girls were suitably entertained before turning in. It is understood that they spent a very comfortable night in their temporary quarters. The W/C continued to use his tent but it is not known whether he slept peacefully as his companions, in the same field, did. W/C Brown entertained them for breakfast in the morning in his personal dining room, and suitably saw them off when the aircraft departed for the UK."[17]

Tuesday 11 July

The weather was again poor, however the squadrons managed to get in five armed recces between downpours. F/O Glen Taylor of 421 in MK808 and F/L Ernie Treleaven of 416 in MK835 stopped some flak while on armed recces, but neither was seriously injured and both aircraft were easily repaired. F/L Mac Gordon of 416, who had been with the squadron longer than anyone else, reached the end of his tour and after a fond farewell from his colleagues, departed for England.

Wednesday 12 July

This day was 403 Squadron's turn to fly the four-aircraft beach patrols – 16 completely uneventful patrols. 421 Squadron flew two and 416 Squadron two other uneventful armed recces damaging a few vehicles, but then at 1740 hours both squadrons took off to escort 24 B-25 medium bombers on a mission to bomb airfields near Chartres. Over Caen, the Spitfire flown by F/L Blackie Campbell, MJ141, was shot down by flak. He managed to parachute to safety and to evade capture and found a friendly farm in which he hid until he was liberated 19 August by Canadian troops during the closing of the Falaise Gap. The bombing in the Chartres area was reasonably accurate and the bombers and their escorting Spitfires turned to fly north-west towards the coast and back to England. Just as the Spitfires of 421 Squadron left the bombers they spotted some enemy aircraft. F/O Scotty McRoberts relates what happened.

"We were escorting 24 Mitchells and just as the bombers were crossing the French coast near Trouville, 12-plus enemy aircraft were sighted flying south-west at about 15,000 feet. We were flying north at about 15,000 feet. We broke starboard into them. I got on the tail of an Me 109 but before I could fire, was in turn bounced by five enemy aircraft. I barrel-rolled and got on the tail of the second one. I closed to 350 to 300 yards and gave him a 2-second burst with about 15° to 20° deflection. I saw strikes on the cockpit and tail. By this time, tracer was coming over my port wing. My hood was shattered and my face was cut by glass. I broke hard starboard and was unable to see what happened to the enemy because of blood. I was using the Gyro gunsight."[18]

F/O Gordie Smith reported:

"We broke starboard into them. Three Me 109s climbed into the sun; my number two and I turned and got behind them. I followed two which made a gentle turn to port. From about 5° to 10° off and from 400 to 200 yards range, I opened fire giving him a 4-to-5-second burst. Strikes were observed on the port side of the fuselage and black smoke poured from him. He pulled hard to port and began to go down. I followed him for a distance but had to straighten out to prevent the second enemy aircraft getting on my tail. As I turned to get behind the second aircraft, I saw the first enemy aircraft still going down by this time pouring white and black smoke and in a rough spiral turn apparently out of control. At this time he would be about 5,000 feet.

"I got astern of the second enemy aircraft and about 50 yards range. I pulled right through giving him a 5-second burst. I got strikes on him along the fuselage. Large pieces flew off and the whole cockpit disintegrated. White smoke poured from him. He slid over and then went down straight with a very slight aileron roll out of control and went into the deck."[19]

F/O Jack Calvert was flying wing man to Smith. His account adds a bit more to the story.

"We broke starboard. Three enemy aircraft climbed into the sun. My number one and I followed. He attacked the two enemy aircraft on the port side and I went after the starboard one. He turned to port and I got behind at about 300 yards. I gave him a 2-second burst from 45° and saw strikes on the starboard wing, and bits flew off. He did a wing over and went straight down. I followed and he tried to turn but fell back and went down. I got dead astern and about 300 yards, gave him a 5-second burst, more strikes were observed on the engine, wings and fuselage and more pieces flew off and black smoke poured from him partially obscuring the enemy aircraft. The smoke was coming from both sides. He went on spiralling down out of control. I saw him going down until about 3,000 feet from the deck. I was alone and so broke off and climbed to pick up my number one."[20]

After assessing the combat reports, the intelligence officer, F/L Johnson, recommended one destroyed and one probably destroyed by Smith, one probably destroyed by each of McRoberts and Calvert. McRoberts was seriously injured in the encounter, and had to stuggle to get his damaged Spitfire MJ880 back to B.2. He was applauded for his efforts to do so, but although seriously hit the aircraft was repaired and back in service within two days. McRoberts was not as fortunate; he was granted sick leave four days later and after spending a week recuperating at B.2 was sent to the UK to be medically boarded. He had flown 183 operational hours, but wouldn't fly any more.

The record is not clear as to what German unit was encountered, but it was probably III./JG 3. Three Bf 109s of III./JG 3 were lost 12 July including Gefreiter Heinz Beyer who was FTR. The names of the other two are not known. The reason for the uncertainty is not location, claims and losses were reported as occurring in the Caen area, but it is the time that doesn't quite agree. The combat reports state 1815 hours, but the German losses are supposed to have occurred around 1700 hours. In terms of losses, this aerial battle resulted in three German losses and no Allied losses of aircraft but one pilot lost.

Thursday 13 July

With the rumour mill working overtime, it was a quiet day for the pilots. 403 and 421 each flew one armed recce, while 416 Squadron had the day off and spent it in Bayeux trying to find beer or wine.

Friday 14 July

Bastille Day was a day of contrasts. It was a day of sorrow for 403; a day of elation for 416; a so-so day like any other for 421; a day of great change for 443 Squadron.

Only two armed recces were flown by 403 Squadron and they lost a pilot on each mission. Shortly after noon 12 aircraft, while on an armed recce in the Falaise/Lisieux area, split up into sections and spread out. The four Spitfires of yellow section spotted a convoy consisting of about 30 armoured vehicles, flak-gun vehicles and trucks moving through the little village of St. Lambert about four miles south-west of Thury-Harcourt. The Spitfires destroyed the lead and trailing vehicles and were just beginning to attack the rest when a half-track flak gun hidden beside a house in the town fired point blank at the Spitfire of F/O Don Shapter as he flew low overhead. Shapter tried to climb his Spitfire MJ570 and circle for a place to set down, but crashed at the top of a nearby hill and was killed. The villagers extracted Shapter's remains from the twisted wreckage of his Spitfire, arranged a funeral and buried him in the yard surrounding the small parish church in St. Lambert. His grave became a symbol for the villagers and to this day they replace the flowers that nearly always adorn the grave. He is known as 'our Canadian' and one citizen, a man named André Louis-Auguste, built a flying three-quarter scale Spitfire replica, painted it in the colours of Shapter's Spitfire and flew it for many years after the war. As a ten-year-old boy he had seen Shapter shot down and was there with other villagers when they removed parts of the crashed Spitfire. Monsieur Louis-Auguste had incorporated parts of the Shapter aircraft inside his replica Spitfire as a living memory. The tragedy of Shapter's death is that his wife gave birth to a baby girl just a week before – a father who never saw his daughter and a girl who never saw her father.

At eight that evening 403 Squadron took off on the second armed recce of the day. Again German flak scored a direct hit, this time on MK881 flown by W/O William Powers. He had started with the squadron only days before, but this day he was shot down and killed in his exploded aircraft. He is buried in the St Charles de Percy War Cemetery.

After a day off in Bayeux, the pilots of 416 Squadron were assigned the job of flying 19 four-aircraft beach patrols. Normally the pilots hated this drudgery. It meant nearly every pilot had to fly at least once that day, and with only an hour-and-fifteen-minutes flight time, everyone had to hang around the dispersal tent most of the day. Little did they realize that on three of the patrols they would strike pay dirt. F/L Danny Noonan describes the first encounter at 1320 hours.

"I was flying east towards Villers at 2,500 feet through broken cloud as Blue One. With Blue Two (F/O Fraser) we saw three aircraft flying west through a flak barrage, slightly above to port. We broke port on to their tails and recognized two Me 109s and one FW 190. I engaged an Me 109 at about 600 yards, closing to 300 yards deflection 10°. There were cannon and machinegun strikes around the cockpit and fuselage, after giving four short bursts I saw a flash and broke to port onto the tail of the other Me 109. The pilot of first Me 109 was seen to bale out by F/O Fraser.

"I chased the second Me 109 through several layers of cloud, giving short bursts at 5° to 10° deflection and at 600 to 800 yards. The enemy aircraft took very little evasive action. After using all cannon ammunition, I saw the hood come off the enemy aircraft and it poured black smoke from the engine. I took several camera shots and then called on Blue Two to engage. Shortly after this, the pilot of the enemy aircraft baled out."[21]

F/O Bud Fraser had initially gone after the FW 190 and got in a couple of bursts before catching up again with his number one. As described by Noonan, Fraser polished off the second Bf 109. Noonan was granted one destroyed and one shared destroyed, while Fraser was granted a shared destroyed and one FW 190 damaged. It is suspected that the three lone aircraft were from JG 2. FW 190s were flown by I./JG 2 while II./JG 2 flew Bf 109s. If this assumption is correct then the FW 190 survived to fight another day while the two Bf 109s were lost when Unteroffizier Erich Schiek and Leutnant Paul Mungersdorf parachuted to safety.

In just over an hour – two patrols later – 416 Squadron struck again. Another four-Spitfire patrol flew for half an hour when coming back from the Pont L'Eveque area, spotted some enemy aircraft flying at 12,000 feet at 1430 hours. F/O Jackson Gould was flying Yellow Three. This is his combat report:

"Yellow One reported seven aircraft flying due west at 6,500 feet just on top of the cloud base. We recognized them as Me 109s. I half-rolled down on their number two and opened fire at 500 yards range with 30° deflection giving a 3-second burst. The enemy aircraft dived through cloud and no strikes were observed. I followed down through cloud and as no enemy aircraft were in view, I again climbed up through cloud and when forming up with yellow section I saw a single 109 coming through the cloud from port side. I broke port and attacked from dead astern, the enemy aircraft climbing steeply. I followed firing a 3-second burst at 300 yards range and dead astern and saw strikes on side of fuselage and cockpit. He turned starboard and dove straight down with glycol streaming, I closed to 100 yards firing dead astern and again saw strikes on cockpit, black smoke coming out, I followed down through cloud and saw the enemy aircraft go into the ground; cine film was used."[22]

Gould's wing man on this patrol was F/O 'Mush' Sharun flying Yellow Four. His combat report doesn't explain where he had been – perhaps asked by the patrol leader F/L Don Hayworth to go down and investigate something on the ground – but his report goes as follows:

"I was just joining yellow section on a patrol in the Pont L'Eveque area when I sighted a lone Me 109 north of Caen at nine o'clock, five thousand feet below me. I was then at 10,000 feet. This enemy aircraft was above 10/10ths cloud. I immediately dove down on him, manoeuvring to dead line astern. I opened fire at 200 yards. The Me 109 did not take evasive action. I fired a 4-second burst and saw strikes on his fuselage and his jet tank; this blew up. The enemy aircraft then went into a vertical dive through cloud – smoking. I followed and on breaking cloud at 2,500 feet saw the aircraft burning on the ground. F/O Gould saw the combat and the enemy aircraft go in a vertical dive through cloud smoking badly and confirms that when we followed down and broke cloud at 2,000 feet a burning aircraft was seen on the ground."[23]

The Canadian Spitfires had tangled with the Bf 109s of III./JG 1. This gruppe had apparently teamed up with I./JG 1 and I./JG 5, for all three of these gruppen were operating in the Caen/Bayeux area within minutes of each other. In the space of half an hour, German units claimed eight Allied aircraft destroyed – three Spitfires, four P-47s and one Typhoon. No Allied losses correspond to these figures, but three German aircraft were lost. It appears that over Caen, Gould and Sharun shot down Unteroffizier Rolf Stromer who was listed as FTR, and Unteroffizier Viktor Orend who parachuted and was captured.

Four more uneventful patrols were flown by 416 Squadron – four aircraft at a time, one patrol landing 10 minutes after the other took off. With very little change throughout the day, the cloud base hung 5,000 feet above the ground and varied from thin to thick. The procedure was unvarying; fly up and down the length of the lodgement; fly below the cloud to check out any ground action; fly above the cloud to find bogeys; fly for one hour and then get into the landing pattern in time to see your successors taking off. By the time the day was over, they had flown 19 patrols.

The next successful patrol was a dramatic one, for part of it occurred right over B.2 and hundreds turned out to witness the battle and cheer it on as though it were a Canadian hockey game. At 1900 hours F/L Dick Forbes-Roberts with F/L Bill Mason flying his wing, and F/L Pat Patterson with F/O Sandy Borland on his wing, took off on patrol number 15. Approaching Caen from the east, the four Spitfires were told enemy aircraft were in the area. They circled to check but found nothing and proceeded again in a westerly direction at 6,000 feet altitude. Suddenly at 1930 hours they found themselves closing with over 50 enemy aircraft descending slightly straight ahead towards them. Forbes-Roberts reported:

"We saw 50-plus enemy aircraft in two gaggles flying from 12 o'clock and slightly above. They fired at us from head-on and as we broke they scattered. I got on to the tail of a FW 190 and closed to about 100 yards, and with 15° to 20° deflection gave a 2-second burst. Strikes were seen on the cockpit and wing roots, and pieces flew off. Flames were seen coming from him. He pulled up and baled out, the enemy aircraft crashing on to B.2."[24]

With that first head-on exchange of gunfire, Mason's aircraft MK835 was badly hit. He immediately broke and dove down to get below the cloud deck, worked hard to control his Spitfire and managed a wheels-up crash-landing at B.2. When his aircraft slid to a stop in a clouds of dust and smoke, he was unhurt, but the aircraft was a write-off. F/L Pat Patterson continues the description of the battle.

"They fired at us from head-on. We broke and they scattered. I half-rolled on one and was pressing home the attack when another got on my tail. I broke around into this one and did two turns finally getting behind him. He half-rolled and went down. I followed and closing to 300 yards, gave a 4-second burst from astern. Strikes were observed on the tail and port wing root. Smoke poured from him and pieces flew off; he went down; the pilot baling out and the aircraft crashing into B.7 strip. F/O Borland saw the aircraft go in."[25]

Borland not only confirmed this kill, but had one of his own.

"When we broke I got on the tail of a FW 190 and chased him in and out of cloud. I fired a number of bursts at him from 600 to 200 yards, getting strikes on the fuselage and wings. I followed him south, and south-east of Bayeux saw the pilot bale out."[26]

This whole encounter, like the previous one is surrounded in mystery. 416 Squadron recorded the aerial battle as occurring at 1930 hours, and with three separate kills following immediately, the whole thing was probably over by 1935 hours. Around that time three German gruppen were in the Caen vicinity for they claimed eight Allied aircraft destroyed. The legendary Oberstleutnant Herbert Ihlefeld Gruppekommodore of JG 1 claimed a P-51 and a Spitfire at 1917 and 1919 hours respectively. These two victories brought his career total to 117. Hauptmann Grislawski led III./JG 1 and claimed a P-51, while other pilots of his gruppe claimed another P-51 and two Spitfires. This should not have been a trivial claim for it raised Grislawski's career total to 127. In addition a third gruppe, I./JG 5, claimed two more Spitfires. All this totalled eight Allied aircraft destroyed – according to the Germans. The first mystery is, there is no record of the Allies losing any aircraft at this time – with the exception of Mason's Spitfire. The three German gruppen lost four aircraft. They claim two of these were shot down by anti-aircraft fire.

Figure 47 -- Captured pilot. *On the back of this photograph Johnny McElroy wrote "Romanian Corporal of GAF, flying an Me 109G -- shot down by F/L Forbes-Roberts over the 'drome at B.2 on 14 July 1944. Squadron got 7 Huns that day."*

(McElroy collection)

The second mystery is that all four German aircraft shot down are recorded as Bf 109 G-5 or G-6s, but the 416 Squadron claims state that they shot down FW 190s. However, the photograph above contains Johnny McElroy's notes stating the aircraft was a 109. Therefore we conclude the captured pilot was either Fähnrich Franz Jungans or Unteroffizier Johannes Geilert. Let us leave the mystery, but to complete the story, here is the description of those who witnessed the dogfight from the ground.

> "The squadron hit the jackpot today and knocked seven Huns out of the skies. F/L Dick Forbes-Roberts was rather thoughtful, and

showed the ground crew just what went on during the dogfight. In fact he was so accommodating that the Hun landed just off the end of our strip. Nice shooting 'Dicko'. The rest of the boys to fatten their scores were: F/L Danny Noonan, F/Os Bud Fraser, Jackson Gould, Mush Sharun, Pat Patterson and F/S Eric Chambers our new pilot. This natcherly called for a big do in the Mess and the boys really done it up fine."[27]

That evening, 443 Squadron led by S/L Wally McLeod, his 24 pilots and administrative officers and 171 members of the 6443 Servicing Echelon moved from their base at B.3 Ste. Croix-sur-Mer to join 127 Wing at B.2. The wing that Johnnie Johnson led, 144 Wing, was disbanded, W/C Bob Buckham left for England – by boat – and W/C Johnnie Johnson took over operational control of 127 Wing. Despite the sombre mood of the officers of 403 Squadron who were mourning the loss of their two pilots, Shapter and Powers, McLeod and his squadron were truly welcomed and a great many new tents and new trucks were added to the Bazenville base.

Saturday 15 July

The weather was foul. A few aircraft could be heard in the skies over Caen at 0700 hours, but then things were socked in until afternoon. Several armed recces were planned but only three uneventful ones were implemented – the others washed out. Both 416 and 421 Squadrons didn't fly at all.

Sunday 16 July

It was 421 Squadron whose job it was to fly beach patrols all day long -- standard routine again, four aircraft off every hour on the half-hour, flying over the lodgement above and below the cloud, landing ten minutes after the replacement four took off. Cloud covered the sky 10/10ths with a base at 2,000 feet and a height between 6,000 and 10,000 feet. For one brief period in late afternoon it cleared completely and into this clearing at 1725 hours F/L John Paterson led the 11th patrol of the day. This day the patrol code name was Cradle and the ground control code name was Planet. After flying for nearly an hour Planet radioed Cradle that there was a bogey at angels eight, vector 040. Paterson noted the time at 1820 hours and dove to the attack:

"Sighted enemy aircraft at 8,000 feet on port side on reciprocal heading. Chased enemy aircraft and closed to about 200 yards at 6,000 feet just over Carpiquet Aerodrome – gave enemy aircraft a 2-second burst of machineguns and cannon after identifying him as an Me 109. Large pieces fell off and clouds of white smoke came back. Enemy aircraft rolled slowly to right and crashed in flames about a-mile-and-a-half south-west of the aerodrome. F/O Libbey, my number two, saw the pilot bale out at 5,000 feet and the crash was seen by F/O Libbey, F/O Smith and F/O Holness."[28]

It was a reinforcement unit that appears to have been the target of Paterson's attack. II./JG 52 was sent into Normandy with instructions to turn over its pilots and aircraft to JG 3. In this, their first appearance in Normandy, II./JG 52 lost three pilots and machines and two of them are believed to have been lost in the Caen area -- one early in the morning and the other around 1800 hours. If this assumption is correct then Paterson shot down either Leutnant Hermann Kelkel KIA or Feldwebel Heinz-Otto Birkenfeld FTR – most likely the former.

Two hours later, 403 Squadron was on an armed recce to the Argentan area when they ran into some good shooting as recorded in the 403 Squadron ORB:

"G C 16 – armed recce to Beny Bocage/Vire/Domfront/Thury-Harcourt – one Spitfire IXb Cat E – three Spitfires IXb Cat B – two Me 109s destroyed F/L MacKenzie, one Me 109 destroyed F/L Collier, two Me 109s destroyed and one probably destroyed F/O Boyle, one Me 109 probably destroyed and one Me 109 damaged F/O Garland. F/O W D O'Kelly missing. One MET flamer. Recce not effective Domfront to Thury-Harcourt area owing to combat with enemy aircraft.

"At 2010 hours when flying west at 6,000 feet eight miles east of Flers, sighted 50-plus Me 109s and one long-nosed FW 190 in two gaggles – one at 3,000 feet and the other just below our pilots on a converging course flying north-west. Combat ensued with above results. Wreckage of six aircraft in all seen, burning on ground (one might have been F/O O'Kelly who was last seen by F/L Brown immediately before diving to attack). Weather 5/10ths at 5,000 feet 10 miles visibility."[29]

The references to Spitfire IXb 'Cat E' and 'Cat B' relate to the method used by the RAF to categorize damage. Cat A was damage that could be repaired at the flight line, Cat B was damage that could be repaired at a Repair Depot – B.2 had 410 Repair and Service Unit resident on the base -- while Cat E was a write-off, so badly damaged as to be non-repairable. When viewed by the enemy, one Cat E and three Cat Bs might well be recorded as one destroyed and three damaged.

The German force consisted of about 25 Bf 109s of each of II./JG 3 and III./JG 3 plus one or two from III./JG 52, led by Oberleutnant Eberhard von Treuberg. Since D-Day II./JG 3 had lost 58 aircraft and III./JG 3 about 40. As mentioned, III./JG 52 was just in the process of being absorbed into JG 3 -- it must have been von Treuberg flying the long-nosed FW 190. Credit for the first German victory was claimed by von Treuberg or Unteroffizier Leube. These are likely the pilots who shot down O'Kelly in NH265. F/O Miall Bouchier O'Kelly joined 403 Squadron on the first of July. He survived only 16 days of combat. He is buried in Écouche Communal Cemetery south of Caen.

The pilots of 403 Squadron claimed five destroyed and two probably destroyed. In the engagement II./JG 3 recorded no losses, however, III./JG 3 recorded five losses including Oberleutnant Siegfried Sauer FTR, Unteroffizier Walter Hromada KIA, Unteroffizzier Harald Finkler safe but wounded, Unteroffizier Oswald Haibt KIA and Unteroffizier Walter Lederer FTR. But the truly remarkable thing is the loss of Leutnant Friedrich Wachowiak KIA of III./JG 52. Wachowiak was one of the replacements sent to bolster JG 3. He had the Iron Cross and 86 victories. The final count of the day was six German aircraft destroyed and only one pilot survived, one 127 Wing aircraft destroyed plus three easily repaired aircraft and one pilot killed.

Monday 17 July

This day's patrol duties started at noon, and the chore fell to the newly arrived 443 Squadron. In addition to the 12 patrols flown by 443, they flew four armed recces – all uneventful. 403 Squadron's only armed recce of the day recorded one interesting event, as told in the squadron ORB.

> "Only one show today, at about 1600 hours we got off on an armed recce and after dropping bombs on a railway and bridge at Sourdeval, a lone Jerry had enough nerve to attack us out of the sun. He more or less swooped out of the sun, and F/L Commerford, who was lagging a little bit got shot up and slightly wounded, and then Jerry immediately dived for the nearest cloud cover and made off."[30]

The German pilot who "had enough nerve to attack us" was none other than Major Klaus Meitusch Gruppekommandeur of III./JG 26. With JG 26 considered one of the top guns of the Luftwaffe, and Meitusch being number two to Pips Priller, this was no slouch! At 1640 hours he is reported to have attacked a Spitfire a little south and east of St Lô – exactly where 403 Squadron would have been at that time. Meitusch submitted a claim for a victory, the 72nd of his career. Later in the day at 2030 hours, the reverse happened to Major Meitusch. He was shot down and injured, but survived. Unlike Commerford, Meitusch went on to claim three more victories in the Normandy campaign.

F/L Lorne Commerford who was described as slightly injured, managed to get his aircraft back to B.2. Unfortunately Lorne Commerford was immediately hospitalized and sent back to the UK, grounded and he never flew again. At the time, his aircraft Spitfire ML420 was listed as being repairable at the base -- a Cat B -- but within a week it was written off and scrapped. Here was a case where the claim by Meitusch looked doubtful right after the event but within days it was known that both pilot and aircraft were lost.

Tuesday 18 July

The morning started with a tremendous display of bombing might. First the heavy bombers of the RAF Bomber Command and the US 8thAF, and later the medium bombers and fighter-bombers of 2ndTAF and US 9thAF attacked the area south-east of Caen -- in all, 4500 bombing sorties. Operation GOODWOOD was introduced by this bombing display. The Spitfire squadrons' job was to patrol and attack any Luftwaffe fighters that showed up and 127 Wing flew seven four-aircraft beach patrols and 17 squadron-strength patrols of the front lines. Although the US 9thAF had a couple of intense aerial battles with the Luftwaffe, 127 Wing found no enemy aircraft -- every patrol except one recorded as uneventful. That one exception was the first patrol of the day for 421 Squadron, when on an army support strafing run against German armoured vehicles, F/L Paul Johnson DFC and flight commander of 'A' pursued a German armed car so vigourously that he hit a tree knocking three feet off his starboard wing. His aircraft MK809 still flew, but it was nearly impossible to control and he could not gain altitude. Nevertheless, Johnson coaxed his Spitfire back toward home base, nearly made it but died when he crash-landed a half-mile from B.2. The airmen at the base saw him go in. He is buried at the Rivières Cemetery a half-a-mile down the road from where he crashed.

During that day, 127 Wing flew 195 sorties, the equivalent of every operational Spitfire the wing owned being flown four times. This day's effort was close to that of 27 July as the second greatest single day's effort for 127 Wing in Normandy.

Wednesday 19 July

Wednesday dawned overcast with solid rain that continued until afternoon. From 1400 hours to 2200 hours the wing flew 12 six-aircraft front line patrols and one squadron-strength armed recce. Four pilots were hit by flak. F/O Red Thomson of 403 Squadron was slightly injured but managed to land his Spitfire ML198 at the

American ALG A.12 Lignerolles south of Bayeux. F/O Stu Tosh of 403 Squadron crash-landed his Spitfire MK857 at Isigny but got a lift back to the base unhurt. F/L Cec Brown of 403 Squadron was hit by US friendly fire and landed NH232 at the American ALG A.3 Cardonville. F/L Alan Hunter of 443 Squadron had a hole shot through his port wing but returned to base.

Thursday and Friday, 20 and 21 July

The weather from the beginning of July had been mostly adverse but today was the start of another great storm just like the one that smashed the Mulberries exactly one month earlier. The skies cleared ever so slightly on the Thursday afternoon and then the storm roared in with heavy showers and winds that precluded any flying the rest of Thursday and all day Friday. However, in that brief respite midafternoon on Thursday, 443 Squadron had some success.

From the moment of joining 127 Wing 14 July, the other three squadrons had each had a moment of glory – 416 with eight claims on the 14th, 403 with five claims on the 16th, and 421 that led all Spitfire squadrons in June, followed up with three claims just before 443 Squadron arrived and one more on 16 July. S/L Wally McLeod, DFC and bar, was not happy with mediocrity. He was a veteran of the Malta campaign, had a career total of 19 victories, four of them claimed since D-Day. From the days in Malta McLeod had nursed the ambition to beat Buzz Beurling's record of victories and become the highest scoring Canadian pilot. As it turned out, he never beat Beurling's record but he became the highest-scoring RCAF pilot, since Beurling claimed nearly all his victories while flying with the RAF. But that story was still being played out.

McLeod met with his pilots seeking to know why they were not shooting down enemy aircraft. We don't know what they said in response, but we know that McLeod was not happy. At 1550 hours 12 aircraft of 443 Squadron flew on a sweep over Bernay. Visibility was poor with heavy cumulus clouds covering most of the sky down to a ceiling of 2,000 feet. Two of the aircraft had to return to base and the flight continued with a section of four led by McLeod, and a section of six led by F/L Larry Robillard.

> "Remaining four aircraft sighted a lone FW 190 on the deck in Bernay area and chased by S/L H W McLeod but before a burst could be fired, the Jerry pulled up sharply, climbed up to 1,000 feet and baled out, parachuting to safety and the aircraft crashed nearby. Claimed as a destroyed by S/L McLeod for his 20th victory. Remaining six aircraft led by F/L J S L Robillard attacked 30 FW 190s at 4,000 feet over Bernay; one Jerry destroyed by F/L Robillard and then his section nipped smartly away, the odds being too great."[31]

The FW 190 that panicked as McLeod moved in is believed to have been a stray pilot from III./JG 2 named Oberfeldwebel Rolf Schwingel. The pilot in the enemy aircraft claimed by Robillard was not seen to bale out. He is believed to have been Gefreiter Johannes Kamutski of 7 Staffel III./JG 51. The two victories brought McLeod's career total to 20 and Robillard's to seven, but it also restored the faith in themselves that this fine squadron had momentarily lost.

That night the officers of 127 Wing learned that with the miserable weather and with no aerial support, Operation GOODWOOD had ground to an inglorious halt after 400 British tanks had been lost and 6,000 casualties sustained.

Saturday and Sunday, 22 and 23 July

This weekend was memorable for the presence of a very important visitor -- Prime Minister Winston Churchill. Luckily, it was a weekend of boring patrols and a few armed recces none of which was exciting or productive. So everyone had a chance to enjoy the experience of a visit from the PM. In addition to describing the visit, the wing ORB provides an insight into life at B.2. in those July days in 1944.

> "22 July -- Bad weather continued, but six operational flights were carried out by the squadrons. These were all uneventful. During the afternoon a Dakota aircraft arrived from Transport Command with instructions to pick up a VIP who was returning to England by air. The VIP was Right Honourable Winston Churchill, Prime Minister

of Great Britain. However, the PM was enjoying his trip too much, and decided to delay his departure until the following day. The crew of the aircraft remained overnight. The pilot was G/C Morrison, Station Commander of Warmwell. During the night the enemy air force were active. One Ju 88 was shot down by ack-ack near the aerodrome. No bombs were dropped in our vicinity, but a number of leaflets were found in the surrounding fields, and these were picked up and retained as souvenirs by the airmen. The leaflets, it was ascertained, were absolute tripe and from the remarks of most persons it would appear that the mentality of the Hun is gradually being affected. It is hard to believe that any persons of even moderate intelligence would believe the propaganda that the Hun expounded. His communication was directed against the Communists and the necessity of a combination of German-British forces to counteract such a menace. According to the Germans our ideals were identical with his.

Figure 48 -- Churchill at B.2. The Prime Minister of Great Britain,, Sir Winston Churchill visited B.2 on 22/23 July. Here he is seen accompanied by G/C Bill MacBrien as Mr Churchil shakes the hand of W/C Johnnie Johnson -- the new W/C (F) of 127 Wing. Between Churchill and Johnson are W/C Paul Davoud (visiting B.2) and the PM's pilot G/C Morrison and to the right is S/L E P Wood of 403 Squadron.

(Imperial War Museum CL512)

"23 July – The Prime Minister of Great Britain, the Right Honourable Winston Churchill arrived here by air at 1530 hours. The whole wing were gathered en masse at the western end of the runway. The PM stepped out of the Air Officer Commanding's aircraft followed by the AOC, and was met by G/C MacBrien. The W/C ops and the squadron commanders were then introduced to the PM. Immediately afterwards the PM moved over towards the assembled wing. At a gesture from him the PM was immediately surrounded and he climbed onto a dais which had been placed in the centre of the large body of airmen. The PM spoke to those assembled for approximately ten minutes. His speech, and even more his presence, was the cause of great excitement for the wing. Few persons had previously seen the PM and it was a big day in their lives. The PM thanked the wing for the splendid work they had done and emphasized the continual need for cooperation between the various services. He mentioned the disruption in Germany and in his amicable style this created considerable laughter. He again emphasized our war aims which amounted solely to the defeat of our enemies and stressed that we had no territorial or other ambitions. With peace, we wanted to keep our empire, and run our empire without anybody else's interference. The G/C called for three cheers which were given very vociferously by the hundreds of airmen who were present. Immediately afterwards the PM climbed back into the AOC's aircraft and they took off to visit another wing. At 1830 hours the PM reappeared, with him this time was Gen Hastings Ismay, his military advisor, and other members of the PM's party. A Dakota aircraft of Transport Command was waiting to fly the PM back to the UK. The PM said good-bye to the AOC and G/C and climbed on board and the aircraft took off. The PM was escorted to the UK by aircraft of 421 Squadron. During the day operations were uneventful, though two aircraft of 403 Squadron were hit by flak 10 miles north of Argentan. Both aircraft returned to base and were categorized Cat B. In all the squadrons took part in 16 different shows during daylight."[32]

Monday 24 July

Back to work. Starting out cloudy, a bit foggy and with poor visibility, the weather was back to normal too. Squadrons flew five armed recces, a squadron-strength patrol of the front lines, a weather recce and a scramble – a normal day's work in a normal day's changeable Normandy weather. The only point of interest came at 2220 hours when 11 aircraft from 443 Squadron were scrambled after 83 Group Control detected some bogeys approaching the beachhead area. After getting them all in the air and finding no bogeys, it was some task to get them safely back on the ground through the heavy evening haze. One pilot mistakenly landed at B.4 airstrip thinking it was home.

Tuesday 25 July

Early in the morning, the drone of heavy bombers was again heard as B-17s of the US 8thAF flew overhead and Intelligence officers

Figure 49 -- Zary and Browne. This photo was taken in the fall of 1943 when F/O Danny Browne (at left) flew with 403 Squadron while F/O Hank Zary flew with 421. They were both Americans serving in the RCAF and by early 1945 Browne commanded 421 Squadron while Zary commanded 403.

(Canadian Forces Photo PL19872)

briefed the pilots of 127 Wing that Operation COBRA – the break-out attempt by the US First Army at St Lô was about to begin. 2ndTAF's job was to attack any columns that attempted to reinforce the Germans from the east. They flew 18 patrols over the eastern part of the lodgement while the US 9thAF patrolled the western portion. In addition 127 Wing launched nine armed recces into the whole area from Lisieux through Falaise and in the south-east to Flers.

403 and 416 Squadrons flew non-stop patrols. 443 Squadron flew the first armed recce at 0620 hours without success. Next it was 421 Squadron's turn. S/L Wally Conrad led 12 Spitfires off at 1030 hours on an armed recce due east to Pont l'Éveque and the Seine River area, the homeland of the enemy fighter airbases. A thin 10/10ths layer of cloud covered the sky at 15,000 feet and considerable ground haze rose to 7,000 feet. They flew past Pont l'Éveque to the Seine and at 1100 hours about 10 miles south-east of Rouen flying at 10,000 feet, they encountered a force of over 40 Bf 109s flying directly towards them at about 13,000 feet. F/L Hank Zary received credit for three victories in this engagement -- here is his combat report.

"I broke to the right as enemy aircraft opened fire. After an orbit to starboard I followed two enemy aircraft who pulled up climbing – one of them turning to port and diving. I fired at the latter 2-second (machinegun and cannon), saw strikes on starboard wing tip then enemy aircraft straightened out and dived gently. He then jettisoned his coop-top and baled out. The chute did not open.

"I climbed to join Spits above. I saw Pink Three (F/O Neil) fire at one Me 109 and saw strikes on fuselage and wing root. Enemy aircraft then half-rolled and went straight down – glycol and black smoke streaming from him. Two Me 109s came towards me, line astern, 50° to starboard and I fired a 4-second burst (machinegun and cannon) at second enemy aircraft and saw a huge explosion in cockpit. Enemy aircraft then disintegrated and fell down.

"I climbed again to circling Spits above at 7,000 to 8,000 feet. Four enemy aircraft then came down flying in an easterly direction, apparently homeward bound. I fired at last enemy aircraft who dived to the deck and I followed. I was out of ammunition, but remained above and behind him reporting enemy aircraft's position and lack of ammo to my S/L. I then dived on the enemy aircraft anyhow. The enemy aircraft turned sharply to starboard to evade, apparently hit a tree – then stalled into the ground. Smoke from this burning enemy aircraft was confirmed by Pink Three F/O Neil who replied to my request for confirmation."[33]

The dogfight lasted for quite a few minutes, for not only did Zary have several chances at different enemy aircraft, but so did F/O Bill Cook.

"During the ensuing dogfight I was turning to starboard when I saw an Me 109 turning to port, so I turned and fired a very short burst from 500 to 600 yards. The enemy aircraft turned to starboard and I fired a sighting burst then fired again under cowling as gyro was momentarily non-effective. I saw enemy aircraft going straight down at about 3,000 feet, white glycol smoke streaming from him.

"I then climbed to about 10,000 to 12,000 feet and saw an Me 109 turning slightly to starboard. I closed fast on him and opened fire from 150 yards, closing to 50 yards as he turned from starboard to port. Strikes appeared from the cockpit right up along the engine and black and white smoke poured out. I had to pull up to avoid hitting him. I then saw him go straight down smoking and flaming. He then baled out while at approximately 3,000 feet and the enemy aircraft crashed into woods. Brown Four (F/O Holness) confirms hitting the ground."[34]

The 40 Bf 109s were from III./JG 1 led by Gruppekommandeur Hauptmann Erich Woitke, and I./JG 5 led by the superstar Gruppekommandeur Hauptmann Theodor Weissenberger. III./JG 1 had been so badly mangled in June that it was withdrawn to Germany to regroup. It had only returned 5 July with Woitke at its helm. One of Woitke's staffel leaders, Hauptmann Erich Maetzke, claimed the first victory over the Spitfires, but that was followed by Weissenberger claiming two, and two other German pilots claiming one apiece – total of five claims. The two for Weissenberger raised his career total claims to 200 – 25 of them claimed in Normandy. The Allied claims were three for Zary, one for Cook (the first attack described in his report was considered a damaged) and one for P/O Ed Levere -- a total of five claims.

And what were the facts? One Spitfire pilot, F/O George Allan Cashion of 421 Squadron in MJ987, was shot down and killed. He is buried at Charlevoix Cemetery. There is no evidence that any of the other Spitfires were even damaged. As to the Germans, their records show five Bf 109s were lost from III./JG 1. Hauptmann Erich Maetzke was shot down and safely parachuted, but he was seriously wounded and hospitalized, Feldwebel Eugen Grunenwald was killed, Unteroffizier Heinrich Esser was safe but wounded, and two other pilots were missing with no details known. Final score – Germany lost five, Allies one.

But before any celebrating could take place there were to be more losses. On an armed recce about 1830 hours, flying over Villers-Bocage F/O Tom Munro of 443 Squadron experienced engine trouble in MJ514 and was forced to bale out. He was captured as soon as he landed. Then about 2100 hours while on an armed recce, F/O Fredrick William Ward, only three weeks with 421 Squadron, was hit by flak while strafing trucks and did not get out of MK796 when it was seen to crash. He is buried at Bretteville-sur-Laize Cemetery. This had been a day of victories for 127 Wing, but it had been a day when they lost three good men.

Wednesday 26 July

The day started early for 416 Squadron as they were on low eastern patrol from dawn until noon with four-aircraft patrols taking off every hour starting at 0535 hours. In the meantime, 403 took off at 0625 hours on an armed recce to Pont l'Éveque on the first of three sweeps for the day. The next to get going was 443 when they left at 0822 to bomb a bridge north of Bernay on the first of three armed recces for them this day. 421 Squadron got to sleep in because their first of three armed recces took off only at 0920 hours bound for Argentan. After flying patrols, 416 Squadron flew two armed recces in the rest of the day. The targets for all these armed recces were a smattering of all the staging points behind enemy lines – Pont l'Éveque, Lisieux, Argentan, Falaise, Fécamp, Domfront, Condes and Dreux. 127 Wing score was two tanks seriously damaged, four vehicles left burning furiously and seven vehicles left smoking – all picked up at different times throughout the day. 421 paid for their sleep-in by being on readiness from 1600 hours until late at night.

The only excitement from all these missions occurred when 443 Squadron, on an armed recce to Dreux, encountered a mixed gaggle of more than 40 FW 190s of III./JG 2 and I./JG 26, and Bf 109s of II./JG 2 and I./JG 6. This large crowd was trying to corner and destroy the Mustangs of 122 Squadron. They had shot down P/O Galloway of 122 Squadron when the Spitfires of 443 joined in. Roused with anger, the pilots of 122 Squadron led by their commander S/L Stillwell, flung themselves in and claimed six victories, while F/L George Stephens of 443 Squadron shot down a FW 190 with the expenditure of only nine rounds from each cannon at 200 yards range. The end result of the exchange was one Bf 109 and two FW 190s destroyed compared to the single loss of the 122 Squadron Spitfire. Unteroffizier Reinhold Uter parachuted from his Bf 109 and landed safely, but the two FW 190 pilots, Unteroffizier Karl Loose and Unteroffizier Christian Bauer, were listed as KIA and FTR respectively. P/O Galloway of 122 Squadron was captured when he landed.

The squadron records tell us that in the morning, B.2 had 49 guest aircraft land for servicing and re-arming – all Spitfires. The base had 72 resident Spitfires from the four squadrons in 127 Wing and the ground crews were used to refuelling and re-arming about 140 of their own aircraft each day, but an additional 35% workload was not something to look forward to, however, they handled the matter with ease and prided themselves on what they accomplished.

That night there was a movie in the officer's mess, and immediately afterward it was announced that in addition to his DFC and bar, S/L Wally McLeod had been awarded the Distinguished Service Order (DSO) for having destroyed 20 enemy aircraft. That was cause for a great party.

Thursday 27 July

In a pretty nice day for flying, 127 Wing spent most effort on patrols. 443 Squadron flew eight-aircraft front line patrols that took off every two hours and lasted about an-hour-and-a-half. The first patrol took off at 0730 hours and the last landed at 2255 hours. 421

Squadron flew eight-aircraft front line patrols that overlapped the 443 patrols, but they started at 0630 hours and continued only until 1100 hours. They were then on readiness until late in the day when they were sent on two armed recces – an uneventful sweep of Argentan and Domfront and a dive-bombing mission to hit a lock near Le Havre. Visibility was becoming a problem for this last mission so results were uncertain. 403 Squadron had one early morning armed recce on which they left one tank smoking and three vehicles a little worse for wear near Falaise, and then they flew eight-aircraft front line patrols picking up where 421 left off. At 1700 hours when the cloud cover that had been about 5/10ths all day had increased to cover 10/10ths of the sky, they flew four-aircraft low eastern patrols until dark. Not one of these many missions was eventful except for the few vehicles claimed.

It was 416 Squadron that had the excitement of the day. At 0620 hours, 12 Spitfires from 416 took off in a clear sky with scattered cloud. This day their call-sign was Bulldog. They formed up and headed south for the area between Argentan and Alençon. They flew in fluid six formation, with two sections called green and yellow. This is S/L Johnny McElroy's combat report.

> "I was leading Bulldog squadron on an armed recce – approached Alençon from east at 5,500 feet. I saw two FW 190s below us, the first had wheels and flaps down, coming in to land on landing strip running north and south between road and railroad approximately three miles north-east of Alençon. I attacked 90° as enemy aircraft was coming over edge of field. I opened fire as enemy aircraft touched down – firing a 3-second burst (machine gun and cannon) saw my fire lick up dirt around enemy aircraft which rolled on. F/O Sharun (Yellow Two) saw the enemy aircraft break in half and ground loop to the right ending up alongside hedge and trees at end of field, aircraft was smoking on ground."[35]

They had stumbled upon the latest airfield used by II./JG 1 – Semallé. The background is interesting. II./JG 1 came to Normandy from its base at Montdidier 10 June and took up residence at Le Mans. That base was bombed the very next day with five FW 190s completely destroyed and seven severely damaged. They moved two miles outside of Alençon to a little airstrip that offered more protection of trees, in the village of Essay. When this base was discovered and bombed by 35 B-24s 17 June, II./JG 1 moved two miles away to Semallé, a place where two airstrips were surrounded on three sides by trees. At this new base they found enough trees to hide all their aircraft as soon as they were on the ground. On one occasion in late June when II./JG 1 just happened to have aircraft lined up on the runway, Semallé was bombed again and this time 15 were destroyed. John McElroy and 416 Squadron could now attest that the Semallé airstrip was being used again. But before we leave this topic, compare this history of repeated bombing of German fighter bases to the fact that German bombing of the exposed Allied fighter bases occurred only three times. What better measure of air supremacy could there be?

Several aircraft of II./JG 1 had been on a flight, probably a weather reconnaissance mission and were just returning to base when Johnny McElroy caught their leader Leutnant Ulrich Brenner as he was landing. Brenner was quite seriously injured in the crash but survived. Three other FW 190s were flying in the circuit about to land. F/L Danny Noonan takes up the story.

> "I was flying Green One at 5,500 feet when Yellow Five – F/L England – reported three aircraft on the deck at nine o'clock three miles north-east of Alençon. The enemy aircraft turned towards the runway, I dived down and got behind one of them, which I recognized as FW 190s. I slowed down to avoid overshooting and enemy aircraft broke starboard, then port, and before I could fire he flicked to port and hit the ground, exploding at once and burned. This was seen by F/L England and several other members of the squadron."[36]

It was Unteroffizier Fritz Milde who crashed and was killed. One of the other two aircraft that were in the landing circuit was attacked by F/L Don Hayworth and F/S Eric Chambers, although the FW 190 escaped leaving a long trail of smoke. Hayworth and Chambers were awarded a shared probably destroyed. The final claim was two destroyed and one shared probably destroyed; actual losses were two Germans, no Canadians.

As usual, the officers had other things to talk about. This day saw S/L Wally Conrad reach the end of his third tour -- his first tour was in North Africa where he served with long-time friend George Keefer in 274 Squadron. Conrad was on his second tour in the fall of 1943 when he was involved in an aerial collision over northern France. He baled out, had his parachute stream and not fully deploy, but was saved by landing in a huge haystack from which he survived and evaded capture. With the help of the French Underground he travelled the long route through France, crossed the Pyrenees and Spain to Gibraltar from where he was flown back to England. When he returned he was granted leave in Canada then posted to command 421 Squadron. He had a career total of six-and-a-half destroyed, three probables and eleven-and-a-half damaged, and he had a reputation as a fair and understanding leader. Conrad had led 421 Squadron since January and was highly respected by his men -- he was going to be missed.

Conrad was to be replaced as squadron commander of 421 by Bill Prest who had been the leader of 'A' Flight in 443 Squadron. F/L Gordon Troke would replace Bill Prest so it was time to congratulate all three. And, of course, it was time to congratulate Johnny McElroy on the destruction of his 10th enemy aircraft. But the best reason to celebrate was stated simply in the 416 Squadron ORB:

> "In the evening about 20 Canadian nurses visited the mess and it certainly livened things up a bit."[37]

Friday 28 July

It rained in the morning but was beautiful after that. Once again it was a day for patrols, for all squadrons except 421 who had the middle of the day off. Late in the evening, led by the newly appointed S/L Bill Prest, they bombed a road north-east of Mortain. In addition to the patrols, each of the other three squadrons flew an uneventful armed recce all in the Falaise/Flers/Domfront area. However the patrols afforded some excitement.

It was the sixth front line patrol that 416 Squadron had flown that day. Led by F/L Don Hayworth, they were flying in fluid six formation at 4,000 feet and had completed four of the six circuits when between the clouds they spotted two Bf 109s above and ahead of them. The time was 1850 hours.

"I was flying Yellow Three on a patrol west of Caen at angels four. Two Me 109s were reported above at 11 o'clock. I gave chase, one of the Me 109 broke right into cloud, I followed and came out of cloud immediately behind the enemy aircraft at 200 yards, and I fired a long burst 5-seconds machine gun and cannon. The enemy aircraft began to smoke and pulled up into cloud, reappeared almost immediately. I fired another burst (2-seconds machine gun and cannon) closing to 100 yards, I lost enemy aircraft in cloud again and found him again and gave him a third burst. I lost the enemy aircraft for the third time in cloud. Yellow Six (P/O McCrae) coming up from behind saw the enemy aircraft enveloped in flames plunging straight down and disappear in cloud."[38]

This was F/L Dyke England's combat report, for which he was awarded one destroyed. Another member of the patrol, F/O Mush Sharun tackled the other Bf 109. Here is his report.

"I was flying Yellow Five on a patrol just west of Caen, at 4,000 feet. I sighted two Me 109s at 11 o'clock at 2,000 feet above and about one-half-mile to the side. I immediately gave chase. The enemy aircraft split up, one turned left, the other right. I followed the one turning left. Opening fire from dead astern at 800 yards, the first burst of about 3-seconds (machine guns and cannon) no strikes observed. I closed in to about 400 yards, fired another 3-second burst (machine guns and cannon) getting strikes on the wing roots on both sides of the cockpit – large pieces flew off the enemy aircraft. The enemy aircraft then went out of control and dove vertically into the ground near the forest just south of Bretteville. The pilot of the enemy aircraft baled out about 1,000 feet and landed near vicinity of the crash. Confirmed by F/L Hayworth and P/O McCrae."[39]

The enemy unit is not known for sure, but a new jagdgeschwader gruppe – II./JG 52 – appeared in Normandy skies a week earlier, and loss lists indicate that they lost two Bf 109s on this date. If this is the correct gruppe then the Bf 109 that went down in flames was Feldwebel Richard Osing KIA, and the pilot who baled out was the leader of the new gruppe, Oberleutnant Eberhard von Treuberg. He landed safely.

Six aircraft of 416 Squadron took off on the next patrol but F/L Johnny Rainville had to turn back when the engine of MJ874 began to act up; the remaining five led by S/L Johnny McElroy, continued on.

They were near Caen when the air controller at 83 Ground Control vectored them to proceed east to Lisieux and at 1945 hours they engaged the enemy. Here's the way F/L Neil Russell described it.

> "I was Green Two on front line patrol and we were vectored to west of Lisieux. We climbed above cloud 7,000 feet and saw approximately 50 Liberators at 11 o'clock at 15,000 feet. 20-plus FW 190s were seen to half-roll and attack the Liberators, then break down into our formation. I followed Green One into a steep climbing turn to port but was a bit behind. At that moment a FW 190 started to come down at nine o'clock to me. As he came down I got in a 2-second burst from 45° (machine guns and cannon) at 300 to 400 yards. He then turned right and down and I got onto his tail very easily. I fired three or four 2-second bursts hitting him on the fuselage and right wing. Large pieces came off his fuselage, there appeared to be an explosion and a great deal of flame and smoke. He went down and I got another burst (2-second machine guns and cannon) and part of his right wing came off. He then went straight down spinning and burning. I saw him below cloud still spinning straight down and burning. He appeared to be about 2,000 feet at that time. The squadron was then ordered to reform so I did not see him hit the ground. S/L McElroy (Green One) saw a Spitfire on the tail of a FW 190 at the time of my attack and reports that it was on fire and pieces falling off. After my first burst the enemy aircraft took no evasive action whatsoever."[40]

The evidence suggests that the pilot that Russell shot down was Unteroffizier Herbert Addicks of III./JG 54 who is listed as FTR.

Saturday 29 July

It was a beautiful warm day, and the wing was released at 1300 hours after flying 14 uneventful patrols and three uneventful armed recces. Many – pilots, ground crew, chefs and every trade went to the beach and enjoyed a day lounging in the sun, invigorated by the cold waters of the Channel.

Sunday 30 July

During the night a front went through and in the morning it was cool and cloudy, as most airmen at the base turned out to watch 700 heavy bombers fly overhead on their way to bomb the Caumont area. After the breakfast hour, the weather improved and it turned out to be a beautiful day with much summer cloud. Eight armed recces were flown and one scramble -- only the scramble proved eventful.

At 1500 hours, 12 Spitfires of 443 Squadron were scrambled to intercept more than 30 enemy aircraft reported south of the beachhead. 10 minutes after take-off, two aircraft turned back, F/O Wes Gilbert because of mechanical failure, and F/O John Irwin to escort him. The remaining 10 aircraft led by S/L Wally McLeod carried on. The sky was covered 9/10ths with cloud varying from 4,000 feet to 9,000 feet, but it was summer cloud, separated into floating icebergs of billowy white. It was the kind of sky that was good for surprising a foe, just as it was the kind of sky that was good for getting away from one. McLeod tells what happened.

"I was leading Potter squadron in the Mortagne area, observed 30-plus Me 109s on the deck proceeding east. I led red section down to attack, blue section having become separated from me previously. I fired at a Me 109 and missed, chased another east for some time. Fired short burst, starting him smoking badly. Closed to 100 yards, fired and the pilot baled out at 500 feet. The enemy aircraft crashed and exploded."[41]

The dogfight started between Mortagne and Alençon and the chase that followed spread as far east as Dreux, for it was over Dreux that McLeod got his 21st kill. F/O Bill Bentley also claimed a victory. He tells of his victory.

"I was flying Red Four at 2,500 feet in a south-easterly direction approximately 20 miles south-east of Dreux when Red Leader (S/L McLeod) reported 30-plus on deck at three o'clock. Our section turned starboard and dived to attack, then I climbed to attack an Me 109 which was climbing to port. I fired a short ineffective burst from long range then closed in to an astern at 100 yards. I fired another short burst (2-seconds) observing strikes on port side of cockpit and wing root. Large pieces flew off and there was an explosion at the wing root. The enemy aircraft spun off a turn and I then had to break off. S/L McLeod (Potter Leader) confirms that the enemy aircraft crashed into the ground and exploded."[42]

In the battle, F/O Lorne Foster was hit in the buttock when a shell exploded under him. He managed to get home safely, but was sent directly to No. 52 Field Hospital – and he wasn't able to sit down for a very long time. His aircraft MJ741 was much better off, for it was immediately repaired and made available in two days.

Although there is some doubt, it appears that the Bf 109s were those of I./JG 27 – that beleaguered jagdgeschwader that 127 Wing seems to have hounded again and again. That day they lost three Bf 109s in combat – Obergefreiter Arnim Porath FTR, Gefreiter Ernst Koss FTR and Oberleutnant Diethelme Laufhutte safe. Final score appears to have been Germans zero, Canadians three.

Monday 31 July

The month ended with an uneventful set of four patrols and four armed recces – the total score for which was two flaming vehicles, two smoking vehicles and a road bridge with a hole in it. Late in the day W/C Rolf Berg of 132 Wing led 22 Spitfires of 331 and 332 Norwegian Squadrons into B.2 where the pilots were fed, entertained in the mess and bedded down for the night.

Operations in July

In July, 127 Wing flew 2699 sorties, and had 443 Squadron been with them a full month, the total would have been nearly 3000. The pilots claimed 13 destroyed, seven probably destroyed, and 17 damaged. They lost six pilots killed in action, two shot down but evaded capture, one shot down and captured and three safe but seriously wounded. 11 Spitfires were destroyed and 13 more were seriously damaged but ultimately repaired.

Chapter Ten – August

The last few days of July were filled with beautiful summer weather punctuated from time to time with a typical Norman rain spell or two, but as if nature wanted to mark the changing of the month, August came in with sticky hot days complete with thick early morning fog and uncomfortably high humidity. After all the rain and cloud, a hot Norman summer was about to begin.

Tuesday 1 August

The squadrons carried out 10 flights this day, but only 403 and 416 Squadrons claimed any credits. In the late afternoon, 403 Squadron while on an armed recce between Flers and Mortain, sighted a large convoy of military trucks. They attacked and set four vehicles on fire and left four others smoking in the ditch. They also ran a staff car off the road and destroyed a motorcycle. Later in the evening, 416 Squadron on another armed recce, attacked scattered vehicles driving in ones and twos on the roads near Falaise. Three were left smoking and five were damaged. All other patrols and sorties were uneventful.

Wednesday 2 August

The 127 Wing ORB describes this day well.

"The weather was duff during the first part of the morning and the first operation was not carried out until after lunch. However, the Air Officer Commander-in-Chief, RCAF Overseas, AM Breadner arrived by air from the UK at 1140 hours. He was met by Air Officer Commanding, 83 Group, AVM Broadhurst, the Air Officer Administration, A/C Montgomery, G/C MacBrien Officer Commanding the (127) Wing, and a number of staff officers. With the AOC-in-C's party were the following – G/C Truscott, G/C Graham and G/C Morrow. The AOC-in-C carried out an inspection on part of the camp, visited Intelligence and met all the pilots. From there he visited the airmen's mess, and after a short inspection of 410 Repair and Service Unit, departed by air for another Canadian wing. In the late afternoon the AOC-in-C returned and the party left France to return to the UK at 1945 hours. Operations during the day were mostly uneventful. No enemy aircraft were sighted. 416, 421 and 443 Squadrons carried out an escort of Mitchells and Bostons. 421 Squadron on this operation attacked MT leaving one in flames and another damaged."[1]

Figure 50 -- Breadner at B.2. From left to right are unknown (at back), G/C Bill MacBrien, AM Breadner, most senior RCAF officer overseas, S/L EePee Wood of 403, S/L J F Johnny McElroy of 416, S/L Bill Prest new squadron commander of 421, S/L Wally McLeod of 443, F/L Andy MacKenzie and F/L Doug Lindsay.
(Canadian Forces Photo PL31094)

Thursday 3 August

The morning fog gave way to complete overcast on Thursday, but it was still very warm. The order of the day called for patrols over the front lines with each squadron flying one armed recce and 421 flying two. 403 and 416 Squadrons shared the four-aircraft front line patrol chore, flying 16 missions between them. Three of the armed recces were dive-bombing missions, on one of them, 403 Squadron got lucky.

They took off at 1855 led by S/L EePee Wood and headed south at 5,000 feet. The sky was half-filled with summer cumulus clouds with their base just above the heads of the 403 Spitfires as they flew, the tops of the clouds climbed to about 9,000 feet. The 12 aircraft were flying towards the target, a bridge near l'Aigle, when through haze they spotted a gaggle of more than 20 Bf 109s far below them. Half the aircraft of 403 Squadron carried 500-pound bombs, these were immediately jettisoned west of l'Aigle. F/L Doug Lindsay described what happened at 1930 hours.

> "While flying Black Five on an armed recce over l'Aigle at approximately 5,000 feet in a westerly direction, I spotted 20-plus Me 109s flying due east over l'Aigle 4,000 feet below. I broke around and gave chase closing very slowly. I opened fire (4-to-5-second burst of cannon and machine guns) at about 400 yards, getting several strikes on wing and fuselage. I claim this Me 109 damaged.
>
> "I then noticed another aircraft straggling on my right and broke around on to him; opening fire several short bursts (cannon and machine guns of 1-to-2-seconds each) from 400 yards closing to 50 yards. I saw strikes on the wing roots and tail. The enemy aircraft poured white smoke and pieces fell off. The tail fell off and I saw the enemy aircraft crash into a field in area north-west of Dreux." [2]

The records of III./JG 1 show that Unteroffizier Brechtold claimed the destruction of a Spitfire at l'Aigle at 1937 hours, however 403 Squadron does not record any aircraft damaged or destroyed. The German records also show the Bf 109s of III./JG 1 claimed two P-51s and that they lost an unnamed pilot. Because of the stated time and place it is assumed III./JG 1 was the adversary and the unnamed pilot was the one shot down by Lindsay.

This mission was Lindsay's last flight of his current tour. On 2 July he shot down three enemy aircraft in one session with the same aircraft he flew today – ML411 – KH-Z. He was immediately awarded the DFC. Now he had completed his tour and finished it in glory, credited with a total of six victories and one shared victory. He was not finished here, for after a leave in Canada he would return to 403 Squadron and complete the war with the squadron picking up a couple of damaged adversaries. In the Korean War in the 1950s he was credited with shooting down two Mig 15s with his F-86 Sabre jet fighter.

This day saw the end of another pilot's tour of duty. F/L Danny Noonan of 416 Squadron temporarily hung up his spurs this day as well. He was credited with four enemy aircraft destroyed and three shared victories. Noonan received his DFC two months later in October. The squadron ORB adds a note:

"F/L Danny Noonan, of Kingston Ontario, finished his tour and left today for England and a well-deserved rest. Danny very kindly left ten pounds for the ground crew, and went higher still in the estimation of the men who worked for him."[3]

Friday 4 August

Every day the squadrons had to fly patrols and 416 Squadron flew four-aircraft front line patrols in the morning while 421 flew four-aircraft low eastern patrols from noon until dark. Before flying the patrols, 421 Squadron teamed up with 403 Squadron and the 24 Spitfires were joined by two other squadrons from another wing to escort 48 Mitchells and 24 Bostons dropping bombs in the Vire and Flers area. Much activity was noted on the ground because the British break-out was in full-swing and a little further south, the Germans too were seen hustling about in the early signs of Hitler's planned counter-offensive.

416 Squadron flew an armed recce sweep along the road between Argentan and Falaise, while 443 Squadron dive-bombed a railway line east of Argentan.

"An item of very good news and of considerable interest to everybody was received during the day. Aircrew leave was to commence immediately and pilots were to be flown by transport aircraft to and from the UK. Commencing approximately the first of September ground crew, at the discretion of unit commanders, were also to be granted leave in the UK proceeding to and from by ship. In both instances leave was to give everybody seven clear days in the UK. Headquarters immediately started to work on a roster which would be fair to all ranks."[4]

Saturday 5 August

The morning haze was heavier than usual and lasted longer -- only in the evening did the sun break through with authority. Four aircraft were scrambled at 0845 hours but it took great efforts to get them back down in one piece. After that there was no flying until 1700 hours when 443 Squadron started the first of five four-aircraft high eastern patrols, and both 403 and 416 took off on armed recces to Falaise and Dreux respectively.

It was on the 403 Squadron armed recce that two pilots were lost. While strafing north of Lisieux, F/O John Benson Earle flying MJ784 was shot down by flak and killed. He is buried at Bretteville-sur-Laize Cemetery. A quarter of an hour later north-east of Caen, W/O Jack Wilcox's Spitfire MK810 was hit and though slightly wounded, he flew it back to Allied territory and crash-landed the aircraft at a forward base. He stayed there overnight and made his way back to the squadron the following day.

Sunday 6 August

Heavy ground fog and heavy dust which hung over the airfield reduced visibility and ruled out flying for much of this warm and humid day. In the early afternoon some of the haze burned off and

403 flew front line patrols while the other three squadrons got in one good -- though uneventful -- armed recce each.

At 1700 hours 421 Squadron took off with six aircraft carrying 500-pound bombs and six aircraft flying escort. The target was a chateau just west of Falaise thought to be an enemy command post and although the bombing was carried out, the results could not be observed because visibility was so poor. Shortly after the bombing, W/O Douglas Guest's aircraft MK421 developed engine trouble and he had to crash-land behind enemy lines close to Falaise where he was immediately captured by German troops.

Monday 7 August

Heavy ground mist in the morning prohibited flying again. For days the German army had mustered its armour for the attack on Mortain and the ground fog each day was better than smoke to disguise this activity. The German army launched its offensive this Monday morning, drove through Mortain and ten miles beyond. 2ndTAF Typhoons blunted and then stopped this attack in a dramatic show of the power of an aerial rocket attack. Although the pilots weren't aware of their role in trying to counter this offensive, 127 Wing squadrons flew eight armed recces, half of them dive-bombing bridges, roads and a marshalling yard at Flers, the other half as sweeps in the same region.

> "Most of the boys are starting to sport various degrees of tan, due to the excellent weather we have been having the past few days."[5]

Tuesday 8 August

For the first time in August, the day started and continued as a beautifully sunny summer day with a light blue sky. Everyone was busy -- 403 flew three armed recces, 416 flew five front line patrols and then two armed recces, 421 flew 12 front line and low eastern patrols, 443 flew one armed recce and then 10 front line patrols.

Figure 51 -- 443 Spitfires. *Spitfires of 443 Squadron are parked at the dispersal area after returning from a long-range mission.*

(Imperial War Museum CL87)

The front line patrol flown by four aircraft of 443 Squadron and led by F/L Gordon Troke was different. Flying at 11,000 feet in light haze that made it difficult to see, Troke spotted a lonely Bf 109 flying two thousand feet below them. The four Spitfires broke and fell in behind the enemy aircraft, but before a shot could be fired, the Bf 109 pilot rolled his aircraft over on its back, jettisoned the canopy and baled out. Troke and the other three pilots submitted a claim for a destroyed Bf 109, credit for which was divided by the four pilots. The tape over their gun ports was untouched when they landed.

The endless patrols and usually uneventful missions were beginning to tell upon the pilots and ground crew. A boredom was seeping into the words in the wing records and the records of each of the four squadrons. We noted the reference to getting tans the day before, and the same author, F/O Robert Howe adjutant of 416 Squadron, wrote this day:

> "Another scorcher today. All the pilots who were not flying went to the beach nearby and had a swim. It was a compulsory parade and most of the boys enjoyed it. Some of the gang had a great thrash in

the mess during the evening to celebrate the birthday of one of the boys."[6]

Wednesday 9 to Friday 11 August

The level of effort continued as it had been, tempered only by an occasional weather disturbance. In these three days they flew 77, 128 and 43 sorties respectively – just a bit lower average than the 88 average sorties per day so far in August. But the difference was lack of quality, the sorties offered very little excitement.

On Wednesday, 416 flew off to bomb barges in the Seine. They spotted 20 and sank two, and reported near misses on four others. The Seine is shallow enough that a sunk barge just settled to the bottom but had its superstructure still standing well above the waterline and one had to look very closely to make sure it wasn't just low in the water. This mission provided a moment of excitement when two Spitfires strafed a 30-foot motor launch heading south, sank it and left eight crew members floundering around in the muddy waters of the Seine.

All off-duty airmen, pilots and ground crew alike were getting to the beach as often as possible and all comparing the deeper and deeper tans they were sporting. Several new pilots arrived to replace losses and bring complement up to full strength. News of promotions and decorations were received -- 421 Squadron was pleased for Hank Zary who was awarded the DFC, and they were just as pleased to learn that Wally Conrad, their ex-squadron commander, was awarded a bar to his DFC.

It was at the end of this three-day period that the full impact of the Falaise Gap was made known to all the personnel at B.2. The intelligence officers drew maps on the blackboard showing changes in the Allied position and as with D-Day, the importance of closing the gap seemed to herald for many the vision of the war being over by Christmas. The population of B.2 consisted of 104 pilots, 59 ground officers and men attached to the four squadrons, and 41 ground officers and 889 ground personnel associated with the wing headquarters and they all learned about the Falaise Gap at the same time.

No personnel were lost or wounded; no aircraft were lost or damaged; no enemy aircraft were claimed, but in the three days 64 bombs were dropped – for seven hits and 10 near misses, 19 trucks left in flames and 24 left smoking, plus the two barges and one motor launch mentioned earlier.

Saturday 12 August

This was a day of patrols. 403 Squadron was spared, but 416 flew five two-aircraft low eastern patrols, 421 flew three four-aircraft front line patrols and 10 two-aircraft low eastern patrols, and 443 flew nine four-aircraft front line patrols. In addition to the early patrols, 416 got in two armed recces, while 443 flew one. 443 Squadron's armed recce was a 12-aircraft mission with half carrying 500-pound bombs, sent to bomb locks and a dam on the Seine north-east of Evreux. While returning from this mission the aircraft flown by F/O John Bentley ML303, developed a glycol leak, the engine overheated, and he had to shut down. The record does not state whether this was caused by flak or was just a mechanical failure. The 443 ORB tells us;

> "F/O W J Bentley is missing after an armed recce this morning. He attempted to bail out north-west of Bernay after a glycol leak had made it impossible to fly his aircraft any further. Unfortunately he was caught on the coupe top cover and went in with the aircraft."[7]

F/O William John Bentley of Willowdale Ontario, is buried at St. Valery-en-Caux Cemetery.

There was another 443 Squadron aircraft lost to flak this day, but fate was much kinder to F/O Wes Gilbert. He crash-landed his aircraft at B.19 Lingèvres, six miles south of Bayeux. He was unhurt, and though his aircraft MK800 stayed at B.19 for repair, Gilbert returned to the base and flew the following day.

However, while operations cost the life of one pilot and nearly cost the life of another, there was always the lighter side -- occasionally chronicled in the squadron record.

Figure 52 -- Servicing in the field*. Ground crew at B.2 physically lift this 403 Squadron Spitfire up in order to have its landing gear fully extended after a crash-landing.*

(Imperial War Museum CL186)

"Commanding Officer McElroy returned from leave today and is not suffering from anything that a few days rest won't cure. Bill Palmer left today to visit his wife in Scotland, and also the new addition to the Palmer household. Bill can't understand how babies get bald so early in life."[8]

Sunday 13 August

Briefings concerning the way the battle was proceeding were well attended and everyone awaited anxiously to hear the most recent developments. Though the activities the wing was undertaking did not vary greatly, the ennui that seeped into the daily reports a week earlier was now gone and a new vigour imparted a little more urgency and interest to what the wing was doing and what was going to happen.

"10 armed recces were carried out by our squadrons during the day. Operations during the morning were hampered by poor visibility.

443 Squadron was airborne at 0836 hours on an armed recce in the Argentan and L'Aigle area – uneventful. At 1110 hours, 403 Squadron was up on an armed recce in the Falaise and Argentan area. Score in MT, five flamers, 12 smokers and two damaged. Six aircraft of 443 Squadron were airborne at 1126 hours on an armed recce in the Falaise and Argentan area -- one flamer, three smokers and two damaged was the score. 416 Squadron was off at 1140 hours on a dive-bombing show on barges in the Seine -- two hits and four near misses were obtained on a lock near St. Cyr and four near misses on a lock near Bonniers. 403 Squadron was airborne at 1330 hours on a show in the Condes and Flers area. Score was two flamers, two smokers and one damaged. A large number of civilians were seen moving east from the Falaise area. 421 Squadron carried out an uneventful recce in the Argentan and Bernay area at 1330 hours. 416 Squadron got five flamers, two smokers and four damaged on an armed recce in the Trun and L'Aigle area. At 1600 hours, three enemy ambulances stopped and personnel waved white flags. 403 Squadron was up at 1700 hours in its third armed recce of the day -- three smokers and one damaged were the score in MT. At 1800 hours 421 Squadron was up on an armed recce in the Bernay region. Very little movement was seen. Score two smokers and one damaged. 416 Squadron carried out the last armed recce of the day being airborne at 2046 hours. The area covered was Falaise to Dreux but no movement was seen. 302 Squadron landed at B.2 after providing target support to Bostons attacking tactical targets. The squadron claimed five flamers in MT. 107 sorties were flown during the day."[9]

Monday 14 and Tuesday 15 August

Everyone could sense the impending springing of the trap. Typhoon squadrons were flying all-out, attacking German armour and the signs were there that soon huge congregations of trucks would be appearing, but as if to rest the Spitfire pilots before the arduous task of slaughter in a killing ground, furlough in the United Kingdom and rotating releases of squadrons characterized these two days. Three uneventful armed recces were flown while 443 Squadron was on readiness on Monday, and six more armed recces while 403 and 416 flew patrols on Tuesday. In the two days they flew 138 sorties – a quarter of the level they would be asked to achieve in another three days.

Wednesday 16 August

While the fighting around Falaise was at its most ferocious, the Spitfire pilots seemed to be holding their breath. The intensity of activity was starting to build up but wasn't close to being there yet. Seven armed recces netted three tanks damaged, 11 vehicles left in flames, 27 left smoking and 29 damaged.

The wing ORB describes a diversion when the most important mission of the day became a trip by three senior officers to Rennes in Brittany.

"On hearing that the food question in Rennes was most satisfactory, the S/L Administration, Messing Officer and French Interpreter departed after an early breakfast to that fair city. After a most enjoyable drive, most of which was taken up turning in and out of American convoys, Rennes was reached. Our mission was not a disappointment. The Fordson truck was quickly loaded, and for very reasonable prices, with pears, tomatoes, cucumbers, and believe it or not, eggs. The egg establishment was very sorry as they informed us that they only had 27 dozen left, but we could take these if we wished. Before the proprietor had a chance to change his mind, the SLA quickly sealed the box, paid, and left the place.

"A tour around the business section was also made, and extremely little damage could be seen with the exception of bridges which had been blown out over the river which runs through the centre of the city. This caused considerable damage to surrounding buildings. No other damage was seen. The bridges had been demolished by the retreating Hun. Rennes was found to be officially out-of-bounds to American troops, and there were very few of our Allies to be seen. Two A/Cs and two W/Cs were the only air force personnel whom we saw in the place. They, like ourselves, were on a school-boys holiday and were taking full advantage of the commodities which Rennes was offering to sell. This wing's party brought back a considerable stock of cosmetics with the intention of re-selling it to officers on our strength, whom it was felt would like to take back such things as souvenirs and presents on their return to the United Kingdom."[10]

Thursday 17 August

Thursday was hot, humid and foul. Heavy cloud, some rain, some haze – just a terrible flying day until noon. The first mission to get off was an armed recce by 443 Squadron at 1117 hours, aimed at sweeping the Bernay/Lisieux/Falaise/Argentan area. They didn't see any concentrations of trucks, but saw many scattered groups of vehicles and armour, out of which they claimed four flamers and three smokers. S/L Wally McLeod's aircraft MK636 developed a glycol leak and he nursed the over-heating Spitfire engine to Falaise but no further. He performed a successful dead-stick landing in a field somewhere near the bomb line while an Auster artillery spotting aircraft watched him go down. The army spotter landed nearby in the field, picked McLeod up and obligingly flew him back to B.2 and dropped him off before the flying control officers of the wing knew that S/L McLeod's aircraft was down. A warm message of appreciation went out to the spotter squadron together with Wally McLeod's thanks.

The second armed recce to go was 403 Squadron, off at 1400 hours to Lisieux and Bernay. Over Lisieux the flak was intense and F/O Gordon Weber's aircraft NH232 was badly hit and he was seen to bale out. Although he was listed as missing, Weber managed to evade capture and returned to the squadron ten days later on 27 August. One other Spitfire was hit – that flown by Sgt Jim Forsythe -- but he brought his plane back to base and aircraft MJ955 was promptly repaired.

416 and 421 Squadrons took off at 1510 and 1530 hours respectively, and surprisingly they didn't see much. They managed to report nine flamers and seven smokers between them achieved at scattered locations. All aircraft had been back for half an hour when the next two armed recces took off at 1750 hours. 403 and 443 Squadrons swept the roads around Trun where they spotted over 400 vehicles – mostly trucks but a few tanks, and quite a few flak

vehicles. The description was "intense, accurate, light flak." Together, the two squadrons claimed 29 flamers and 40 smokers, but three aircraft were hit by flak. F/O Art Horrell of 443 Squadron received a direct hit that blew a hole through the wing of his NH208, however with skill and some luck he managed to nurse his Spitfire back to home base. Not so lucky were F/O Harry Boyle of 403 Squadron who was hit and seen to crash, and F/O Mike Garland of 403 Squadron -- both were listed as missing. Someone thought they saw Garland bale out of ML183. It was true and he baled out, landed safely, evaded capture, and returned to the squadron in early September after 127 Wing had moved from B.2. F/O Harold Vern Boyle, on his second

Figure 53 -- 421 Spitfire. *After being re-fuelled and rearmed, a 421 Spitfire is ready to take off again and attack.*

(Imperial War Museum CL782)

tour, did not get out of his aircraft MK299 -- he was killed in the crash and is buried at Castillon-en-Auge Cemetery.

It had been a very rough day – three pilots reported missing, four aircraft lost and two more damaged. There was just one bit of good news, F/L Cuppy Cuthbertson, much-liked member of 416 Squadron got his first victory.

> "At 1902 (hours) I took off with orange section 416 Squadron on an armed recce. Huns were spotted in Lisieux area shortly afterwards. I saw aircraft milling about at nine o'clock in Lisieux area at 8,000 feet. We climbed into the dogfight and I saw a FW 190 turning with a Typhoon. I got on the Focke Wulf's tail firing from 200 to 300 yards (3-second burst of machine guns and cannon). I didn't see any strikes and he pulled straight up into cloud. I followed him through firing from 100 yards almost line astern (2-to-3-second burst). He half-rolled back into cloud as I continued firing from 10° off. He straightened out between the layers of cloud and as I continued firing he began to smoke and went straight through the bottom layer of cloud and I saw him go in and explode in flames on the ground south-east of Lisieux."[11]

416 Squadron stumbled upon a real scrum. Typhoons of 266 Squadron and 184 Squadron had each been bounced by the FW 190s and Bf 109s of I./JG 2 and II./JG 2. They had already shot down two Typhoons – F/S Love of 266 Squadron was killed, while P/O Downing of 184 Squadron baled out and was captured. The Typhoon was a real workhorse, but when clean it could fight as well as most other fighters, however it was rarely clean for it could carry an awesome array of bombs or rockets. The embattled Typhoons climbed to get some position and spread out between Lisieux and Vimoutiers. While 416 Squadron came to the rescue at Lisieux and beat off the FW 190 attack there, another Canadian squadron – 401 – was attacking JG 2 aircraft a few miles away at Vimoutiers. Between the attacks of the Spitfires and ground fire from Allied troops, JG 2 lost four aircraft – all four pilots killed or missing -- Gefreiter Fritz Woelm FTR, Unteroffizier Gehrard Körmig KIA, Oberfähnrich Karl-Heinz Hecker FTR and Unteroffizier Johannes Austel KIA.

Three more armed recces were flown that day. They reported seeing many vehicles burning and very few moving but they shot up whatever they could. By the end of the day the wing could claim 196 smokers and flamers, one tank destroyed and one FW 190 destroyed. It looked as though the cost had been three pilots killed and a lot of aircraft lost. Luckily, two of the three lost pilots returned within weeks, only Boyle didn't make it back.

Before we leave Thursday 17 August we have one more glimpse of what became of all the eggs and perfumes bought by the officers who drove into Rennes the day before.

"PMC opened shop as a concerted rush took place by numerous officers to purchase the loot which we had brought back from Rennes. His tent reeked of perfume and powders. 50 pounds of cosmetics that he had purchased quickly disappeared. Our loot had been so good in Rennes on the 16th that the G/C agreed to send the Messing Officer back for a further lot of produce including cosmetics. The Messing Officer did extremely well, arriving in Rennes sufficiently early to corner the market for eggs. He returned with enough eggs to serve breakfast for the next week. In addition, more cucumbers, tomatoes and pears were bought. Another large supply of cosmetics was cornered and these were turned over to the PMC for re-sale. The change in diet is most agreeable and the additional vitamins, which the pilots are getting, should please the medical staff. I know it pleases our innards.

"It might be mentioned here that there is a tremendous contrast in the attitude of the French population in the Rennes district towards us as compared to the Normandy beachhead area. Perhaps it is because the beachhead had suffered considerable bombing and much demolition. One can travel for many miles through the Brest Peninsula without seeing signs of a war whatsoever. A number of towns and villages in the beachhead area have been completely destroyed. There are probably similar cases in the Brest Peninsula but these were not seen around Rennes. The country in this spot resembles parts of the lovely English countryside. French civilians, from the year-old to the aged, have acquired the Churchill salute. They stand in clusters or in ones and twos along the highways, and as the troops pass they wave and cheer them on. In Normandy the people seem to have lost the ability to smile. In that part of the Brest Peninsula which we saw, they were all smiles, extremely cooperative and most friendly. It would have to be seen to be believed, but along the road many children were seen with eggs in their hands for sale. Men with bottles of wine and cider and glasses requested you to come and drink with them. The Allied air forces, especially the British air forces, stand very high in the estimation of the Brest Peninsula's population. It was found that they could not do enough for us. A number of officers on days off have gone down in a disbelieving mind but have returned with the same story."[12]

Friday 18 August

"It was the busiest day in the history of the wing. Approximately 290 operational hours were flown by our aircraft. About 30,000 rounds of 20mm ammunition were expended on the Hun. Nearly 500 enemy vehicles were destroyed or damaged by our squadrons. These enemy vehicles are split up as follows: 160 flamers, 174 smokers and 152 damaged. In addition, three tanks were destroyed and 14 damaged. One engine of a train found in the Bernay area was destroyed. Out of 264 sorties carried out, 192 were armed recces. At 1800 hours all patrols and readiness was cancelled and a concerted effort from the entire wing was requested to attack transport in the Vimoutiers area. From then onwards until dusk every available aircraft including the G/C's Spitfire V, was put in the air. They took off in twos and flew until they ran out of ammunition. They returned to base, were refuelled and re-armed, and were off again. When operations finished, 486 vehicles of one kind or another had been destroyed or damaged, making an average of two-and-a-half vehicles per sortie flown. A number of our aircraft were hit by flak and several crash-landed away from base, but only one pilot, F/O Leyland of 421 Squadron, was missing. A few enemy aircraft were sighted but our pilots were unable to make contact. 421 Squadron carried out one successful air sea rescue patrol. Two Spitfires of the squadron located the survivor and dropped a dinghy to him, which landed within 20 yards. The pilot swam to the dinghy and was seen to climb in. It has been subsequently ascertained that the pilot belonged to 126 Wing and the wing has extended its congratulations to the 421 Squadron on their effort.

"During the day another sale of cosmetics was directed by the PMC. The goods were bought up as quickly as before. Mylady, possibly in England, but probably more often in Canada, will receive souvenirs of our officers' tour of France."[13]

F/O Jack Leyland of 421 Squadron started with the squadron 9 August. In the nine days he had been with the squadron he flew eight times without incident, but on this day, flak in the Mézidon area set his aircraft MJ820 on fire and although he set it down within Allied lines, he sustained scalp wounds and burns. He was flown out of

France, hospitalized in the UK and the following week declared non-effective – the air force term for unable to fly any more.

Saturday 19 August

The wing thought it would continue what had started the day before, but orders came down that 403 Squadron was to be placed on defensive readiness which meant they had the day off, and only three squadrons were geared up for more frenzy in the killing ground. However, just as they got into the swing of things a heavy electrical storm moved in to cut the day short and they ended up flying only 12 armed recces for a total of 144 sorties. Notwithstanding the reduced activity they claimed 60 flamers, 78 smokers and six tanks destroyed

Figure 54 -- Church at B.2. *F/L Danny Noonan, P/O Bill Palmer, F/O Mush Sharun, F/L Don Hayworth, and F/O Art McFadden sing hymns with S/L Crawford Scott while P/O Ronnie McCrae plays the portable organ perched on Gerry cans.*
(Canadian Forces Photo PL30422)

– just a pittance compared to the day before -- but they were thankful that there were no casualties.

Sunday 20 August

The weather front that moved in bringing Saturday's thunder storm brought with it a very changeable following day punctuated with heavy downpours and ended the day with continuous rainfall.

The slaughter in the gap was mostly over. Thousands of Germans surrendered – sometimes in large groups waving a white flag to aircraft, asking them to accept their surrender. In the preceding six days the squadrons of 127 Wing recorded the following totals of flamers – 9, 11, 37, 160, 60, and 17 -- a total of 294 flamers. In addition, they reported 321 smokers and 333 damaged. The 2ndTAF had 15 wings of fighters and fighter-bombers and they all had a go at the massed German vehicles squeezed into the sector delineated by the villages of Trun, Chambois and Vimoutiers -- the stench from the carnage was still strong at several thousand feet altitude.

Monday 21 August

During the night the downpour turned into a raging storm. In a peculiar turn of events the 21st day of each month -- June, July and August -- occasioned a severe storm in Normandy. There was no flying at all due to the immense weather disturbance that covered north-western France and southern UK with high winds and heavy rain.

Tuesday 22 August

After a clearing of the storm came another day of patrols. 403 Squadron flew four two-aircraft low eastern patrols and then two armed recces. 416 Squadron flew an armed recce then eight two-aircraft low eastern patrols. 421 Squadron flew six four-aircraft front line patrols and then an armed recce. 443 Squadron flew an armed recce and then seven four-aircraft front line patrols. Total vehicles left flaming numbered 18 and 10 others were left smoking. W/O Shannon of 403 Squadron, reported missing 29 June, returned this day after being liberated by American troops.

Wednesday 23 August

The pilots of the wing had been exhilarated with the turkey-shoot of enemy vehicles on the 18th and 19th before the storm, but now they were disappointed that the volume of activity had fallen off and the site of the action shifted to the Seine river, for that suggested the Luftwaffe had vanished and that aerial battles were a thing of the past. This proved to be quite untrue.

The first armed recces of the day were launched by 403 and 416 Squadrons respectively at 1000 and 1100 hours. They were uneventful, so when 421 and 443 Squadrons took off at 1230 hours, the 24 pilots thought this would be more of the same. Two 443 pilots and three 421 pilots returned due to mechanical failure and the gaggle of Spitfires now numbered 19. Led by W/C Johnnie Johnson, they circled Paris from the south at 7,000 feet and while coming around to the north sighted a large number of FW 190s below them, and another large number of Bf 109s flying cover above them. F/O George Ockenden of 443 Squadron noted:

"While flying as Potter Red Five leading a section of two, in the Senlis area on a fighter sweep, aircraft were reported by controller as we turned north. From south Paris area they were sighted shortly afterwards at approximately 5,000 to 6,000 feet by F/L Robillard flying in blue section and identified as FW 190s. W/C Johnson, leading our flight, led the attack by diving down to engage. Myself and number two (F/O Horrell) had to break to starboard across the W/C as four Me 109s attacked head on. We attacked two FW 190s chasing them in about a 50° dive closing from 300 to 200 yards. The one I fired at with cannon and machine guns (short bursts) streamed white vapour apparently from the belly tank but we were forced to disengage.

"The two enemy aircraft continued to dive and the one Red Six fired at hit the deck while mine continued along the deck. I then climbed to attack two Me 109s turning over my head and got on to the tail of the second which left its leader. I closed firing short bursts (1-to-2-seconds) of machine guns and cannon from 500 yards closing to about 150 yards, the enemy aircraft turning and weaving all the time. I observed strikes on port wing and fuselage in at least two bursts then he streamed smoke and began diving, pieces falling off; as I overshot him the pilot baled out about 300 feet below me and the aircraft went straight in.

"After encounters with several other enemy aircraft I broke away climbing to 10,000 feet. Seeing a single Me 109 attempting to climb away I attacked opening fire at 500 yards with one cannon only (one cannon was jammed) and machine guns and closing to 250 to 300 yards observing light strikes around the cockpit. The enemy aircraft went into a spin, the pilot baling out about 5,000 feet and the aircraft flat spinning into the trees. I then climbed up and reformed on a single Spitfire that was in the sky."[14]

W/C Johnson led the diving attack on the FW 190s below them and shot down two of them. This brought his personal record from 35 to 37 putting him far ahead of all others as the highest scoring Allied fighter pilot in the European Theatre. From the combat report above, Ockenden claimed two destroyed and one damaged. There was another claim for two destroyed by F/L Eric Smith of 421 Squadron;

"I was flying Pink Five with Cradle squadron at 5,000 to 6,000 feet in Senlis area flying due north when aircraft were reported by controller north of our formation. These soon proved to be enemy aircraft, 15 of which were sighted at 4,000 to 5,000 feet by my section. I followed Pink One (S/L Prest) down to them singling out one Me 109 from the gaggle firing 2-to-3-second burst (machine guns and cannon) from 20° closing to 10° at range of 350 closing to 250 yards. I saw strikes all along the fuselage and the enemy aircraft exploded and burst into flame, which enveloped whole of aircraft. I then broke away to look around and then resumed attack firing at another Me 109 from same angle 2-to-3-second bursts from 400 to 300 yards range. There were strikes all over the enemy aircraft and about four feet of his starboard wing left, the unit flying vertically upward and white smoke poured from engine. I then broke off attack, did an orbit and when I next saw enemy aircraft he was in inverted dive which he stayed until he hit the ground. I did not see him bale out."[15]

There is one other combat report that has to be quoted here. It was submitted for F/O Jack Neil by F/L Benton Gilmour. Neil was listed as missing after this engagement and so was unable to submit his own claim.

"I was in Cradle pink section flying Pink Four at 8,000 feet flying north in Senlis area. Controller reported aircraft in our path and were identified as enemy aircraft shortly afterwards. A small group of enemy aircraft came in to attack our section from above and behind and I saw Pink Three (F/O Neil) turn on the tail of one of them (a FW 190) and the enemy aircraft did a normal turn to port and I saw strikes on fuselage – then his coupe top came off and the enemy aircraft went down tail over nose for three thousand feet. Brown Three (F/L Gilmour) confirms that the pilot baled out. Immediately someone called out over RT for pink section to break – I lost the section and suddenly found myself on the tail of a FW 190. Before I could fire I was attacked from behind and above by another FW 190. This enemy aircraft overshot and I got on his tail, he drew away so I followed reducing range in a dive until at 600 yards range I fired a 1-to-2-second burst (cannon and machine guns) observing strikes. I followed him as he reached the deck, then fired another burst of machine guns and cannon 2-to-3-seconds and either the aileron or the wing tip came off. He slowed down and I fired another 4-second burst (machine guns and cannon) from 200 yards. I saw strikes all over the enemy aircraft the coupe top came off and the enemy aircraft hit the ground and burst into flames. Though I was unable to jettison my jet tank, I had no difficulty in keeping up with the enemy aircraft. Cine gun used – gyro sight fitted. I claim one FW 190 as destroyed for F/O Neil who has been listed as missing."[16]

Comparing all accounts, the intelligence officer concluded about 80 German aircraft had been involved. Three German units were flying in the Paris area at that time (1335 hours) and we conclude that I./JG 2, I./JG 11 and II./JG 26 all claimed shooting down Spitfires and reported losses – 10 of them. However all three of those units flew FW 190s. Whose Bf 109s were they? Although we do not have a fix as to time, III./JG 27 lost three Bf 109s in the Paris area. Given these assumptions, we can tally the overall dogfight as follows. 443 Squadron claimed six aircraft destroyed – two FW 190s by Johnson, two FW 190s by Ockenden, one FW 190 by F/L Larry Robillard, one by F/O Alan Horrell. 421 Squadron also claimed six aircraft destroyed – two by F/L Eric Smith, one by F/O Robert Holness, one by Gilmour, one by Hoare, and one by Neil. The Canadians lost F/O Glen Taylor of 421 Squadron in MJ880, killed in action, F/O Jack Neil of 421 in MK115, prisoner of war and F/O Robert Dunn of 443 Squadron in MK468, prisoner of war. F/O Glen Whitcomb Taylor is buried in the only Commonwealth grave in Forfry Cemetery.

The Germans lost 13 pilots. I./JG 2 lost four -- Unteroffizier Kurt Dreissig safe, Fahnrich Hans Gunther KIA, Hauptmann Siegfried Bogs KIA and an unknown. I./JG 11 lost five – Unteroffizier Karl Brunner safe, Leutnant Kurt Ebener POW, Leutnant Kurt Hubinek POW, Oberfähnrich Alfred Wittig FTR and an unknown. II./JG 26 lost one – Obergefreiter Heinz Nieter safe. And III./JG 27 lost three – Gefreiter Josef Steigenberger KIA, Oberleutnant Dietrich Sponnagel safe, and Feldwebel Heinrich Eickhof KIA. Five of these 13 German pilots were killed or missing.

Thursday 24 August

Six armed recces were flown, one early in the morning and the others late in the day. The distance between B.2 and the front lines had now been increased to such an extent that aircraft found no available ground targets until they had just about reached the limit of their range. They were obviously far, far behind the front lines and the rumour mill became rife with talk of relocating closer to the front -- everyone hoped that meant Paris.

Friday 25 August

Word was received that the wing would move to B.26 Illiers l'Éveque – the captured airbase just recently vacated by the Bf 109s of III./JG 3. The move was scheduled for Monday and Tuesday. The squadrons flew 142 sorties in the form of 30 patrols and four armed recces, so uneventful that the total count was two flamers and two smokers.

Saturday 26 August

S/L Whalley, Administrative Officer, S/L Hamilton, Technical Officer, F/L Cameron, Signals Officer and F/L McNab, Intelligence Officer left at 0600 hours and drove the 130 miles from B.2 to the site of the new base at B.26. It took four hours. When they arrived the airfield construction unit was already at work and very soon after, three Spitfires flown by W/C Johnson, S/L Prest and F/L England set down on the heavily-cratered field. After sorting out where everything should be located, the Spitfires took off and the scouting party started the return drive home at 1710 hours, arriving home just as darkness descended. Upon their return, they learned that the move was now brought forward by one day. They also learned that there had been a couple of small dogfights.

Figure 55 -- 416 Spitfire. *Looking very much alone, this single 416 Squadron Spitfire sits on the field of B.2 airstrip waiting for its pilot.*

(Canadian Forces Photo PL 30299)

At 0830 hours 421 Squadron took off on an armed recce for Gournay just east of Rouen. 416 Squadron took off 25 minutes later on an armed recce bound for Gisors, also east of Rouen and only ten miles from 421's target. F/O Willie Warfield of 421 Squadron reported:

> "I was flying Brown One giving top cover to pink section with five other aircraft as pink section was strafing in the Gournay area. While at 10,000 feet we sighted 20-plus FW 190s at 12,000 feet and immediately climbed into them. I made two separate attacks but they were apparently very good pilots and managed to spiral down away before I could open fire. The third aircraft I attacked dove straight down and I followed closely gaining on him considerably and when he did recover it put me right on top of him so I was able to force him into the ground rather than close my throttle and position myself behind him. The FW 190 hit the ground at a very shallow angle and ploughed through two fields after which he hit a wood and exploded, setting the immediate area on fire. I did not fire my guns or use my camera but my number two (F/L Cunningham) remained within three or four wingspans distance throughout."[17]

Piecing the story together, it seems that 602 Squadron of 125 Wing was returning from an armed recce near Rouen when it ran into the FW 190s of II./JG 6. 602 Squadron records indicate they lost one Spitfire to flak and another to friendly fire attacked by a US P-47 and ran out of fuel and crashed trying to get away. Both pilots F/S Menzies and W/O Ellison were safe. The 602 Spitfire pilots claimed shooting down two JG 6 FW 190s. They were bounced by I./JG 26 and II./JG 26, but the rest of 602 got away. All three of the German units had just days before moved from their airfields south of Paris to new airfields north and east of Rouen. Leading I./JG 26 was their Gruppekommandeur Major Boris, while leading II./JG 26 was their Gruppekommandeur Hauptmann Lang. The JG 26 units claimed shooting down seven Spitfires. To get to these totals the Germans must have claimed the 602 aircraft shot down by their pilots.

No sooner was the first encounter over – at about 0900 hours – when 421 Squadron showed up and tangled with part of the combined force, while ten minutes later 416 Squadron came along and battled with the rest of the huge German formation about five miles away.

Willie Warfield was right, these were very experienced super-aces with whom he was fighting. While Warfield picked up a victory, two 421 Squadron pilots were shot down -- F/O D E Libbey in MK661 parachuted to safety but was taken captive by German troops, but F/O James McVeigh Flood's aircraft ML308 was shot down and Flood was killed. He is buried at Dieppe Cemetery.

Major Boris claimed a Spitfire, his 39th; Hauptmann Lang claimed two Spitfires bringing his Normandy total to 27 and his career total to 172 -- making him the top-scoring Luftwaffe pilot in Normandy. His fellow II./JG 26 pilot Leutnant Vogt claimed his career 35th. Meanwhile 416 Squadron tangled with what appears to be another part of this large force and both F/L Dave Harling and F/O Mush Sharon claimed victories.

> "I was flying Bulldog Yellow One in the Gournay area at 6,000 feet when smoke trails were seen above at approximately 15,000 feet. We started to climb and at 9,000 feet I attacked a straggling FW 190 from a formation of approximately six enemy aircraft. I fired a 2-second burst (cannon and machine guns) from 600 yards to 400 yards with 10° deflection. The enemy aircraft broke to starboard and half-rolled right down. I followed firing short bursts all the way until he hit the ground in a wood east of Gournay and exploded."[18]

Time for this attack was listed by Harling as 0910 hours – ten minutes after Warfield's attack – and the location was the same. So far so good, but then comes Sharun's combat report.

> "I was flying Bulldog Yellow Five – at 4,000 feet in area of Breteuil when I sighted eight-plus aircraft which I later identified as Me 109s. These were at 12,000 to 15,000 feet travelling north. I immediately, with my number two (F/O Cameron), turned and climbed after them. We overtook them at 12,000 to 13,000 feet in the Forges area. I closed in on the port outside man and opened fire 3-to-4-second burst (cannon and machine guns) at approximately 400 yards obtaining strikes immediately on all over the fuselage and main plane. The enemy aircraft started smoking badly and rolled on its back and went straight down hitting the deck in the Forges area."[19]

The difficulty with Sharun's report is that German records show only three Bf 109s lost that day, and all of them in the Rouen area between 1450 hours and 1507 hours – a time that fits nicely with the claims of two Allied squadrons who were operating over Rouen at that time. So it is not easy to summarize this battle except to say between 602, 421 and 416 Squadrons, four aircraft were lost, two pilots safe, one KIA and one POW. They claimed five German aircraft destroyed. The German JG 6 and JG 26 figures record five losses three safe and two KIA.

Sunday 27 August

The first echelon of the move to B.26 started leaving at 0600 hours in groups of 20 trucks and leaving every hour, the last part of 'A' Echelon arrived at B.26 about 1800 hours. The weather was none too good, but only four uneventful armed recces were flown out of B.2 this day – for three of the squadrons it was the last operational flights to take off from B.2. Only 403 would fly one more day from the base.

Monday 28 August

While 403 Squadron flew three four-aircraft front line patrols along the Seine starting at 0710 hours, the remaining 60 Spitfires began taking off in pairs on the 20 minute ferry flight to the new airstrip at B.26. As they arrived they were serviced so quickly by the 'A' Echelon crew that two armed recces were sent off from the new base at 1100 hours. Before the day was over, seven armed recces were flown from B.26, eight more front line patrols were flown, and the Dakotas and remaining trucks arrived carrying the rest of the wing. By the end of the day, nothing remained at B.2 but dust, sommerfeldt tracking and an assorted collection of mechanical refuse that was quickly whisked away by the local farmers.

One of the armed recces had some excitement associated with it. F/L Doug Orr of 403 Squadron submitted this combat report.

"I was flying leading Kapok squadron on an armed recce in the Beauvais-Montdidier-Amiens area flying at 5,000 feet when an aircraft was reported by White Four (F/O Scott) landing on the aerodrome below us south-east of Amiens. I told Kapok squadron to remain above the airport as I expected intense flak. I turned 90° and came in dead astern as a FW 190 was touching down. I opened fire from 800 yards with machine guns and cannon and continued firing 2-to-3-second bursts until I had closed to approximately 50 yards. I observed strikes all over fuselage with a concentration of large flashes on starboard wing. This aircraft swung about 40° to runway and hit the ground starboard wing first. I stayed on the deck across the drome and as I pulled up to 3,000 feet and circled the drome I observed a large volume of smoke coming from the FW 190 on the ground."[20]

Soon after this action, the squadron flew on to strafe some ground targets, and while strafing, W/O Milton Eldon Soules of 403 Squadron in his Spitfire MJ572 was hit by flak and Soules died when his aircraft crashed to the ground. He is remembered on panel 254 at Runnymede Memorial. He was the last member of 127 Wing to die in the Normandy Campaign.

Summing Up

It was all over but the partying. The German military commander in Paris surrendered two days earlier. The few tattered remnants of the German Seventh Army that got across the Seine were incorporated into the Fifteenth Army, and together were scurrying across France as fast as possible to take up new defensive positions in Belgium and Holland. All Luftwaffe units had been evacuated to German soil. Allied ground forces were following as best they could, trying to keep in contact with the fleeing Germans, but the supply lines suddenly became impossibly long. Four days after moving to the new base, 127 Wing was ordered to completely suspend all further operations. Logistic considerations demanded that all of their 200 trucks be commandeered to carry supplies to the front. This was not applied to the whole air force but to many units like 127 Wing. There seemed no more tangible evidence that the Normandy Air War was over.

As with July, six pilots lost their lives in August. Three pilots were shot down and evaded capture while three others were shot down and captured. Two pilots were severely injured. Fourteen

Spitfires were lost and five others seriously damaged but returned to service.

Figure 56 -- Monument. *To the south-west of where the airstrip was located, in front of the wall surrounding the Bazenville parish church, there is a monument -- a replica of a Spitfire wing commemorating 403, 416 and 421 Squadrons and 83GCC that operated there.*

(author's photo)

From D-Day to the end of August, 127 Wing flew 8,984 sorties – an average of 106 sorties per day. They claimed 89 destroyed enemy aircraft, they claimed nearly 400 flamers, as many smokers and a long list of locomotives, goods cars, barges and midget submarines destroyed. The action cost the lives of 22 pilots but no ground crew. Seven pilots were shot down and made prisoners of war; seven were shot down and evaded capture to return to duty. 46 Spitfires were lost. How do these kinds of statistics compare to the experience of other equivalent units?

Starting with claims of enemy aircraft destroyed, the nine Canadian Spitfire squadrons made 239 claims for destroyed aircraft in Normandy.[21] Apparently 401 Squadron claimed 43 while the lowest three squadrons each claimed 19.[22] From the records upon which this book was based 421 Squadron claimed 37, 443 Squadron at 23, 403 Squadron 21, 416 Squadron 20. That places the squadrons of 127 Wing at second, fourth, fifth and sixth – right in the middle of the pack.

But looking at the cost in lives, the wing lost one (Chadburn), 403 lost seven, 416 lost one, 421 lost 12, and 443 lost three before joining 127 Wing and one after, for a total of four. That's an average of 6.3 killed in action per squadron. Total number of Canadian Spitfire pilots killed in Normandy was 58 – an average of 6.4 for each of the nine squadrons, and removing 127 results increases the average for the others to 6.6. So 127 Wing was slightly better.

In terms of aircraft lost, the nine Canadian Spitfire squadrons lost 118 Spitfires, about 13.1 per squadron. The squadrons of 127 Wing lost 46 Spitfires (plus the additional 3 for 443) for an average of 12.2 - - they were a bit better regarding the Queen's property, however these figures were higher than the average. Total number of Spitfires lost in Normandy by 30 squadrons was 326 -- 10.9 per squadron, and 353 P-47s were lost by the 33 US 9thAF squadrons who flew them, about 10.7 per squadron.

Now the really interesting comparison is to be made against their adversaries – the once triumphant Luftwaffe. Using the same relationships, we find quite different numbers. Compared to the 46 Spitfires lost by 127 Wing, II./JG 3 lost 116, IV./JG 27 lost 98. III./JG 3 lost 93. Indeed from the 21 jagdgeschwaders that served in Normandy the average number of aircraft lost was 62.7. Since the JG was usually three squadrons, this is twice the loss rate of the Allied squadrons. Add to that the fact that few if any of the German units were even at half-battle strength throughout the campaign suggests the loss rate was much higher.

It would be interesting to try to compare the number of lives lost as well, but because of the very high proportion of German airmen listed as FTR – failed to return, or missing, -- the numbers would be misleading.

127 Wing Honour Roll in Normandy

W/C Lloyd Vernon **Chadburn**, DSO, DFC, C de G, killed 13 June 1944, age 25, Rainville Cemetery, Normandy, Section V, Row R, Grave2. (Oshawa, Ontario)

403 Squadron

P/O Harry Vern **Boyle**, killed 17 August 1944, age uncertain, Castillon-en-Auge Churchyard, Calvados, France, only military grave (hometown unknown)
F/O John Walter Benson **Earle**, killed 5 August 1944, age 28, Bretteville-sur-Laize Canadian War Cemetery, Calvados, France Section XIX.Row F Grave 9. (Westmount, Quebec) P/O James Leon **Lanfranchi**, killed 28 June 1944, age 26, Bretteville-sur-Laize Canadian War Cemetery, Calvados, France Section XXVIII Row H Grave 2. (Montreal, Quebec)
F/O Miall Bourchier **O'Kelly**, killed 16 July 1944, age uncertain, Ecouche Communal Cemetery, Orne, France, only military grave (hometown unknown)
WO William Charles **Powers**, killed 14 July 1944, age 23, St. Charles de Percy War Cemetery, Calvados, France Section VIII Row B Grave 10. (hometown unknown)
F/O Donald John **Shapter**, killed 14 July 1944, age 24, St. Lambert Churchyard, Calvados, France, only military grave (Toronto, Ontario)
WO Milton Eldon **Soules**, killed 28 August 1944, age 22, Runnymede Memorial, Surrey, United Kingdom Panel 254. (Orilia, Ontario)

416 Squadron

P/O Joseph Cyril Robert **Maranda**, killed 8 June 1944, age uncertain, Runnymede Memorial, Surrey, United Kingdom Panel 251. (hometown unknown)

421 Squadron

F/O George Allan **Cashion**, killed 25 July 1944, aged 23, Cemetery 942 -- Charlevoix, Normandy -- the only Canadian grave. (Montreal, Quebec)

F/L Frank Joel **Clark**, killed 13 June 1944, age 23, Bretteville-sur-Laize Cemetery, Normandy, Section XXIV, Row C, Grave 5. (Montreal, Quebec)

F/O Lorne Franklin **Curry**, killed 15 June 1944, age 27, Bretteville-sur-Laize Cemetery, Normandy, Section XXIV, Row B, Grave 3. (Windsor, Ontario)

F/L William John **Drope**, killed 7 June 1944, age 21, Bayeux Cemetery, Normandy, Section IV, Row F, Grave 11. (Regina, Saskatchewan)

F/O James McVeigh **Flood**, killed 26 August 1944, age 22, Dieppe Cemetery, Normandy, Section IV, Row M, Grave 56. (Hurst, Ontario)

F/L Charles Donald **Grant**, killed 25 June 1944, age 24, Hottot-les-Bagues Cemetery, Normandy, Section I, Row A, Grave 11. (Consecon, Ontario)

F/O Robert Jackson **Grigg**, killed 7 June 1944, age 23, Runnymede Memorial, Surrey, panel 246. (Sault St. Marie, Ontario)

F/L Paul Gilbert **Johnson**, killed 18 July 1944, age 24, Revières Cemetery, Normandy, Section XVIU, Row H, Grave 8. (Bethel, Connecticut)

F/O Robert Wilson **Murray**, killed 13 June 1944, age 24, Brookwood Military Cemetery, Sussex, Section 52, Row E, Grave 9. (hometown unknown)

F/O Glen Whitcomb **Taylor**, killed 23 August 1944, age uncertain, Forfry Cemetery, the only Commonwealth grave in the cemetery. (hometown unknown)

WO Robert George **Wallace**, killed 23 June 1944, age 21, Ste. Gauberge-Ste. Colombe cemetery, the only Canadian grave. (Tilbury, Ontario)

F/O Frederick William **Ward**, killed 25 July 1944, age uncertain, Bretteville-sur-Laize Cemetery, Section XXIV, Row C, Grave 6. (hometown unknown)

443 Squadron

F/O William John **Bentley**, killed 12 August 1944, age 24, St. Valery-en-Caux Franco-British Cemetery, Seine-Maritime, France Row B Grave 10. (Willowdale, Ontario)

What Became of 127 Wing?

The wing went on to fight in the later stages of the war through north-western Europe and into Germany itself until they were disbanded in the summer of 1945. All four squadrons stuck together in 127 Wing. They lost pilots as the war came to its conclusion, but those lost were not part of the Normandy effort and so not mentioned in this narrative. However, two of those who survived Normandy and are mentioned here, did not survive the war. Wally McLeod commander of 443 Squadron, who registered his 21st victory in Normandy in July, failed to return after a battle over Nijmegen in September. Willie Warfield of 421 Squadron, who had destroyed three enemy aircraft, crashed and died in December coming back from an armed recce in foul weather. The others split three-to-one between those who went back to civvie street and those who stayed in the air force, but they all found useful lives and never forgot the days they spent in the Normandy Air War.

David Clark

Appendix "A" – Abbreviations

17 – B-17 Flying Fortress heavy bomber
20 – A-20 Havoc medium bomber
24 – B-24 Liberator heavy bomber
25 – B-25 Mitchell medium bomber
26 – B-26 Marauder medium bomber
38 – P-38 Lightning twin engine fighter
47 – P-47 Thunderbolt fighter
51 – P-51 Mustang fighter
87 – Ju 87 Stuka dive-bomber
88 – Ju 88 medium bomber
88 mm – 88 millimetre German guns
190 – Focke Wulf 190
2Lt – Second Lieutenant
AA – shot down by anti-aircraft fire
ACM -- Air Chief Marshal
ACG -- Airfield Construction Group
ADGB – Air Defence of Great Britain
ALG – Advanced Landing Ground
angels – code for altitude, as in 'angels 6' meant 6,000 feet
A R – armed recce, general search and destroy mission
bar – as in "DFC and bar" – to receive the award a second time
Bf 109 -- see Me 109
Bf 110 -- see Me 110
brown job – airman's slang for a foot soldier
BS – bomber squadron (USAAF)
CatA – aircraft repair category, can be repaired by unit
CatB – aircraft repair category, beyond unit capability
CatE – aircraft repair category, a write-off
CatEm – aircraft lost over enemy territory, unrecoverable
CAVU -- ceiling and visibility unlimited
Cpt -- Captain
CL – collision, either in the air or on the ground
CO – commanding officer
Col – Colonel
DFC – Distinguished Flying Cross – RAF medal for officers
DFM – Distinguished Flying Medal – RAF medal for NCOs and non-NCOs
DSO – Distinguished Service Order – RAF medal for senior officers
Do – Dornier
Do 17 – a German medium bomber used in Spain and in the Battle of Britain
e/a – enemy aircraft
EAB -- Engineering Aviation Battalion
EOT – end of tour, when a fighter pilot had flown 150 operational hours
erk – slang for ground crew
err – damage due to pilot error
EVD – shot down but evaded capture
FF -- shot down by friendly fire
FG – fighter group (USAAF)
Fhr -- Fähnrich
flak – anti-aircraft fire
F/L – Flight Lieutenant
F/O – Flying Officer
FS – fighter squadron (USAAF)
F/S – Flight Sergeant

FTR – failed to return from mission
FW – Focke Wulf 190
Fw – Feldwebel (German Sergeant)
G/C – Group Captain
GCC – ground control centre
Gefr – Gefreiter (German Lance Corporal)
Gen -- General
GF – abbreviation for 'shot down by German Fighter'
GSU – general servicing unit, the administrative unit that directed replacements
Haupt – Hauptmann (German Flight Lieutenant)
He – Heinkel
He 111 -- a German medium bomber used in Spain and Battle of Britain
HE – high explosive
JG – Jagdgeschwader (Luftwaffe wing or group)
Ju – Junkers German aircraft builder
Ju 88 -- German medium bomber used in Spain, Battle of Britain and Normandy
KIA – killed in action
LCol – Lieutenant Colonel
LCI – Landing Craft Infantry, usually the standard Higgins boat
LCT – Landing Craft Tank
LST – Landing Ship Tank, a ship that beaches and unloads
Lt – Lieutenant or Leutnant (Luftwaffe)
MACR – missing air crew record (US source of loss data)
Maj – Major
Me 109 – Messerschmitt Bf 109
Me 110 – Messerschmitt Bf 110 twin engine fighter
MF – mechanical failure as cause of loss
MT – motor transport, term used for military trucks
Mos or Mossie – de Havilland Mosquito twin engine bomber or night fighter
n/e – 'non-effective' term used to retire pilots because of health or injury
NCO – Non-commissioned Officer
No-ball Target -- V-1 pilotless bomb site
Obfhr – Oberfähnrich (German Warrant Officer)
Obfw – Oberfelswebel – (German Flight Sergeant)
Oblt – Oberleutnant (German Flying Officer)
Obstlt – Oberstleutnant (German Wing Commander)
Ogfr – Obergefrieter (German Airman 2)
ORB – Operations Record Book or squadron history
PM -- Prime Minister
P/O – Pilot Officer
POW – prisoner of war
prang – slang for a crash
Ramrod – effort to bring up enemy fighters to attack a small number of bombers
Ranger – daylight incursion to disrupt enemy's use of airfields
R/T – radio transmitter
Safe – lived through military engagement
SCU -- Service Commando Unit
Sgt -- Sergeant
S/L – Squadron Leader
Sp – Supermarine Spitfire fighter
sprog – slang for a rookie fledgling pilot
Spit -- Supermarine Spitfire fighter
sprog – a rookie pilot
Temp – Hawker Tempest fighter
Typh – Hawker Typhoon fighter-bomber
Uffz – Unteroffizier (German LAC or Corporal)
u/s – unserviceable

VC – Victoria Cross – highest military honour in Commonwealth
W/C – Wing Commander
WND -- wounded or injured
W/O – Warrant Officer

Appendix "B" – Comparative Ranks

Comparative aircrew ranks and the shortened forms of these ranks used in this book.

Luftwaffe		RAF, RCAF, RAAF, RNZAF		USAAF	
OFFICERS					
Oberst	Obst	Group Captain	G/C	Colonel	Col
Oberstleutnant	Obstlt	Wing Commander	W/C	Lieutenant Colonel	LCol
Major	Maj	Squadron Leader	S/L	Major	Maj
Hauptmann	Hptm	Flight Lieutenant	F/L	Captain	Cpt
Oberleutnant	Oblt	Flying Officer	F/O	First Lieutenant	Lt
Leutnant	Lt	Pilot Officer	P/O	Second Lieutenant	2Lt
NCOs					
Oberfähnrich	Ofhr				
Fähnrich	Fhr	Warrant Officer	WO	Warrant Officer	WO
Oberfeldwebel	Ofw	Flight Sergeant	F/S	Master Sergeant	M/S
Feldwebel	Fw	Sergeant	Sgt	Sergeant	Sgt
Unteroffizier	Uffz	Leading Airman	LAC	Corporal	Corp
Obergefreiter	Ogfr	Airman 2	AC2	Lance Corporal	LCp
Gefreiter	Gefr				

Appendix "C" -- Order of Battle -- June 1944

SECOND TACTICAL AIR FORCE at 6 June 1944.
AM Arthur Coningham – Officer Commanding
No.83 (Composite) Group (source Cruc of War p.269)
AVM Harry Broadhurst – Officer Commanding

No. 15 Sector

122 Wing
 19 Squadron, Mustang III -- QV
 65 Squadron, Mustang III -- YT
 122 Squadron, Mustang III -- MT

125 Wing
 132 Squadron, Spitfire IX -- FF
 602 Squadron, Spitfire IX -- LO
 453 (Australian) Squadron, Spitfire IX -- FU

No. 17 (RCAF) Sector (G/C W MacBrien)

126 (RCAF) Wing (W/C George Keefer) (W/C Dal Russel 14Jul)
 401 (Canadian) Squadron, Spitfire IX -- YO
 411(Canadian) Squadron, Spitfire IX -- DB
 412 (Canadian) Squadron, Spitfire IX -- VZ

127 (RCAF) Wing (W/CLloyd Chadburn) (W/C Bob Buckham 14Jun) (W/C Johnnie
 Johnson 14Jul)
 403 (Canadian) Squadron, Spitfire IX -- KH
 416 (Canadian) Squadron, Spitfire IX -- DN
 421 (Canadian) Squadron, Spitfire IX -- AU

144 (RCAF) Wing (W/C Johnnie Johnson) (disbanded 14 July)
 441 (Canadian) Squadron, Spitfire IX -- 9G
 442 (Canadian) Squadron, Spitfire IX -- Y2
 443 (Canadian) Squadron, Spitfire IX -- 2I

No. 22 Sector (G/C Paul Davoud)

121 Wing (W/C Bob Davidson)
 174 Squadron, Typhoon 1b -- XP
 175 Squadron, Typhoon 1b -- HH
 245 Squadron, Typhoon 1b -- MR

124 Wing (W/C Basil Carroll)
 181 Squadron, Typhoon 1b -- EL
 182 Squadron, Typhoon 1b -- XM
 247 Squadron, Typhoon 1b -- ZY

143 (RCAF) Wing (W/C M T Judd)
 438 (Canadian) Squadron, Typhoon 1b -- F3
 439 (Canadian) Squadron, Typhoon 1b -- 5V
 440 (Canadian) Squadron, Typhoon 1b -- I8

39 Recce Wing (W/C Bunt Waddell)

400 (Canadian) Squadron, Mosquito XVII -- SP
168 Squadron, Spitfire XIV
414 (Canadian) Squadron, Spitfire XIV -- RU
430 (Canadian) Squadron, Spitfire XIV -- G9

Spotting Wing

652 Squadron, Auster
653 Squadron, Auster
658 Squadron, Auster
659 Squadron, Auster
662 Squadron, Auster   ET

David Clark

83 Group Reserve Squadrons in ADGB
64 Squadron, Spitfire V -- SH
130 234 Squadron, Spitfire V -- AZ
303 (Polish) Squadron, Spitfire V -- RF
345 (French) Squadron, Spitfire Vb -- 2Y
350 (Belgian) Squadron, Spitfire Vb -- MN
402 (Canadian) Squadron, Spitfire V -- AE
501 Squadron, Spitfire V -- SD
611 Squadron, Spitfire V -- FY
... plus 3 squadrons of Mustang IIIs

~~~~~~

No. 84 Group
AVM L. O. Brown Officer Commanding

No. 18 Sector

131 (Polish) Wing
302 (Polish) Squadron Spitfire IX -- WX
308 (Polish) Squadron, Spitfire IX -- ZF
317 (Polish) Squadron, Spitfire IX -- JH
132 (Norwegian) Wing (W/C Rolf Berg)
127 Squadron, Spitfire IX -- 9N
66 Squadron, Spitfire IX -- LZ
331 (Norwegian) Squadron, Spitfire IX -- FN
332 (Norwegian) Squadron, Spitfire IX -- AH
134 (Czech) Wing (W/C Tomas Vybiril)
310 (Czech) Squadron, Spitfire Vc -- NN
312 (Czech) Squadron, Spitfire Vc -- DU
313 (Czech) Squadron, Spitfire Vc -- RY

No. 19 Sector

135 Wing
222 Squadron, Spitfire IX -- ZD
349 (Belgian) Squadron) Spitfire IX -- GE
485 (New Zealand) Squadron) Spitfire IX -- OU
145 (French) Wing
329 (French) Squadron, Spitfire IX -- 5A
340 (French) Squadron, Spitfire IX -- GW
341 (French) Squadron)Spitfire IX -- NL
133 (Polish) Wing
129 Squadron, Mustang III -- DV
306 (Polish) Squadron, Mustang III -- UZ
315 (Polish) Squadron, Mustang III -- PK

No. 20 Sector
123 Wing (W/C Desmond Scott)
198 Squadron, Typhoon 1b -- TP
184 Squadron, Typhoon 1b -- BR
609 Squadron, Typhoon 1b -- PR
136 Wing (W/C Ed Reyno)
164 Squadron, Typhoon 1b -- FJ
183 Squadron, Typhoon 1b -- HF
263 Squadron, Typhoon 1b -- HE
146 Wing (W/C John Baldwin)
193 Squadron, Typhoon 1b -- DP
197 Squadron, Typhoon 1b -- OV
257 Squadron, Typhoon 1b -- FM

266 Squadron, Typhoon 1b -- ZH

35 Recce Wing

2 Squadron , Mustang I -- OI
4 Squadron, Spitfire IX -- TV
268 Squadron, Mustang I

84 Group Reserve Squadrons in ADGB

149 Wing
33 Squadron, Spitfire IX -- 5R
74 Squadron, Spitfire IX -- 4D
233 Wing
80 Squadron, Spitfire IX -- W2
229 Squadron, Spitfire IX -- 9R
274 Squadron, Spitfire IX/Tempest V -- JJ

No. 85 Group (night fighter and miscellaneous)

AVM C Hamilton Officer Commanding
141 Wing
264 Squadron, Mosquito XIII -- PS
410(Canadian) Squadron, Mosquito VI -- RA
322 (Dutch) Squadron, Spitfire XIV -- 3W
142 Wing
124 Squadron, Spitfire IX -- ON
147 Wing
488 (New Zealand) Squadron, Mosquito VI -- ME
604 Squadron, Mosquito XIII -- NG
148 Wing
29 Squadron, Mosquito VI -- RO
91 Squadron, Spitfire XIV -- DL
409 (Canadian) Squadron, Mosquito XIII -- KP
150 Wing
3 Squadron, Tempest V -- JF
56 Squadron, Spitfire IX -- US
486 (New Zealand) Squadron, Tempest V -- SA

Reserves from ADGB

406 (Canadian) Squadron, Mosquito XII -- HU
418 (Canadian) Squadron Intruder, Mosquito VI -- TH

No. 2 Group (from Bomber Command) (AVM B E Embry)

137 Wing
88 Squadron, Mitchell II -- RH
226 Squadron, Mitchell II -- MQ
342 (Lorraine) Squadron, Boston IIIa -- OA
138 Wing
107 Squadron, Mosquito VI -- OM
305 (Polish) Squadron, Mosquito VI -- SM
613 Squadron, Mosquito VI -- SY
139 Wing
98 Squadron, Mitchell II -- OE
180 Squadron, Mitchell II -- EV
320 (Dutch) Squadron, Mitchell II -- NO
140 Wing
21 Squadron, Mosquito VI -- UP
464 (Australia) Squadron, Mosquito VI -- SB
487 (New Zealand) Squadron, Mosquito VI

343

Headquarters Group

> 34 Wing
>> 16 Squadron, Spitfire IX PR -- EG
>> 69 Squadron, Wellington XIII -- W1
>> 140 Squadron, Mosquito -- ZW
> 3 Naval Wing
>> 808 Squadron, Seafire III
>> 885 Squadron, Seafire III
>> 886 Squadron, Seafire III
>> 897 Squadron, Seafire III
> Aerial Spotters Wing
>> 26 Squadron, Spitfire V -- XC
>> 63 Squadron, Spitfire V -- NE

COASTAL COMMAND

19 Group

> 30 squadrons defending south-west approach to Neptune
> 21 squadrons defending the north-east approach to Neptune

NINTH TACTICAL AIR FORCE.(General Lewis H Brereton)

IX FIGHTER COMMAND (Brig Gen RR Etheral)

IX Tactical Air Command (Maj Gen Elwood Quesada)
70th Fighter Wing
> 48th Fighter Group, P-47 (Col Geo Wertenbaker)
>> 492nd Squadron, -- F4
>> 493rd Squadron, -- I7
>> 494th Squadron, -- 6M
> 367th Fighter Group, P-38 (Col Charles Young)
>> 392nd Squadron, -- H5
>> 393rd Squadron, -- 8L
>> 394th Squadron, -- 4N
> 371st Fighter Group, P-47 (Col Bingham Kleine)
>> 404th Squadron, -- 9Q
>> 405th Squadron, -- 8N
>> 406th Squadron, -- 4W
> 474th Fighter Group, P-38 (Col Clinton Wasem)
>> 428th Squadron, -- 7Y
>> 429th Squadron, -- F5
>> 430th Squadron, -- K6

71st Fighter Wing
> 366th Fighter Group, P-47 (LCol Norm Holt)
>> 389th Squadron, -- A6
>> 390th Squadron, -- B2
>> 391st Squadron, -- A8

368th Fighter Group, P-47 (Col Gil Meyers)
    395th Squadron, -- A7
    396th Squadron, -- C2
    397th Squadron, -- D3
370th Fighter Group, P-38 (Col Seth McKee)
    401st Squadron, -- 7F
    402nd Squadron, -- E6
    485th Squadron, -- 9D

84th Fighter Wing
    50th Fighter Group, P-47 (Col William Greenfield)
        10th Squadron, -- T5
        81st Squadron, -- 2N
        313th Squadron, -- W3
    365th Fighter Group, P-47 (Col Reg Stacker)
        386th Squadron, -- D5
        387th Squadron, -- B4
        388th Squadron, -- C4
    404th Fighter Group, P-47 (Col Carrol McColpin)
        506th Squadron, -- 4K
        507th Squadron, -- Y8
        508th Squadron, -- 7J
    405th Fighter Group, P-47 (Col Robert Delashew)
        509th Squadron, -- G6
        510th Squadron, -- 2Z
        511th Squadron, -- K4

Recon Group
    67th Tac Group, (Col George Peck)
        107th Tac Recon Squadron, P-51
        109th Tac Recon Squadron, P-51
        30th Photo Recon Squadron, P-38 F-5
        33rd Photo Recon Squadron, P-38 F-5 -- SW

XIX Tactical Air Command (Maj Gen Otto Weyland)

100th Fighter Wing
    354th Fighter Group, P-51 (Col George Bickell)
        353rd Squadron, -- FT
        355th Squadron, -- GQ
        356th Squadron, -- AJ
    358th Fighter Group P-47 (Col Cecil Wells)
        365th Squadron, -- CH
        366th Squadron, -- IA
        367th Squadron, -- CP
    362nd Fighter Group, P-47 (Col Morton Magaffin)
        377th Squadron, -- E4
        378th Squadron, -- G8
        379th Squadron, -- B8
    363rd Fighter Group, P-51 (Col Jim Tipton)
        380th Squadron, -- A9
        381st Squadron, -- B3
        382nd Squadron, -- C3

303rd Fighter Wing
    36th Fighter Group, P-47 (Col Van Slayden)
        22nd Squadron, -- 3T

        23rd Squadron, -- 7U — rendered as:

23rd Squadron, -- 7U
53rd Squadron, -- 6V
373rd Fighter Group, P-47 (Col William Schwartz)
    410th Squadron, -- R3
    411th Squadron, -- U9
    412th Squadron, -- V5
406th Fighter Group, P-47 (Col Anthony Grossetta)
    512th Squadron, -- L3
    514th Squadron, -- O7
    513th Squadron, -- 4P
Recon Group
    10th Photo Group, (Col William Reid)
       34th Photo Recon Squadron, P-38 F-5
       31st Photo Recon Squadron, P-38 F-5
       12th Tac Recon Squadron, P-51
       15th Tac Recon Squadron, P-51

IX Bomber Command

97th Bomber Wing
    409th Bomber Group, A-20 (Col Preston Pender)
       640th Squadron, A-20 -- WS
       641st Squadron, A-20 -- 7F
       642nd Squadron, A-20 -- E2
       643rd Squadron, A-20 -- 5L
    410th Bomber Group, A-20 (Col Ralph Rhudy)
       644th Squadron, A-20 -- 5D
       645th Squadron, A-20 -- 7X
       646th Squadron, A-20 -- 8U
       647th Squadron, A-20 -- 6Q
    416th Bomber Group, A-20 (Col Harold Mace)
       668th Squadron, A-20 -- 5H
       669th Squadron, A-20 -- 2A
       670th Squadron, A-20 -- F6
       671st Squadron, A-20 -- 5C

98th Bomber Wing
    323rd Bomber Group, B-26 (Col Wilson Wood)
       454th Squadron, B-26 -- RJ
       455th Squadron, B-26 -- YU
       456th Squadron, B-26 -- WT
       457th Squadron, B-26 -- VT
    387th Bomber Group, B-26 (Col Tom Seymour)
       556th Squadron, B-26 -- FW
       557th Squadron, B-26 -- KS
       558th Squadron, B-26 -- KX
       559th Squadron, B-26 -- TQ
    394th Bomber Group, B-26 (Col Tom Hall)
       584th Squadron, B-26 -- K5
       585th Squadron, B-26 -- 4T
       586th Squadron, B-26 -- H9
       587th Squadron, B-26 -- 5W
    397th Bomber Group, B-26 (Col Richard Joiner)
       596th Squadron, B-26 -- U2
       597th Squadron, B-26 -- 9F
       598th Squadron, B-26 -- X2
       599th Squadron, B-26 -- GB

1st Pathfinder Squadron, B-26 -- 1H

99th Bomber Wing
    322nd Bomber Group, B-26 (Col Glenn Nye)
        449th Squadron, B-26 -- PN
        450th Squadron, B-26 -- ER
        451st Squadron, B-26 -- 5S
        452nd Squadron, B-26 -- DR
    344th Bomber Group, B-26 (Col Reginald Vance)
        494th Squadron, B-26 -- K9
        495th Squadron, B-26 -- V5
        496th Squadron, B-26 -- N3
        497th Squadron, B-26 -- 7I
    386th Bomber Group, B-26 (Col Joe Kelly)
        552nd Squadron, B-26 -- RG
        553rd Squadron, B-26 -- AN
        554th Squadron, B-26 -- RV
        555th Squadron, B-26 -- YA
    391st Bomber Group, B-26 (Col Gerald Williams)
        572nd Squadron, B-26 -- P2
        573rd Squadron, B-26 -- T6
        574th Squadron, B-26 -- 4L
        575th Squadron, B-26 -- O8

IX Troop Carrier Command (Brig Gen P L Williams)

50th Troop Carrier Wing
    439th Troop Carrier Group, C-47 (Col Charles Young)
        91st Squadron, C-47 -- L4
        92nd Squadron, C-47 -- J8
        93rd Squadron, C-47 -- 3B
        94th Squadron, C-47 -- D8
    440th Troop Carrier Group, C-47 (Col Frank Krebs)
        95th Squadron, C-47 -- 9X
        96th Squadron, C-47 -- 6Z
        97th Squadron, C-47 -- WB
        98th Squadron, C-47 -- 8Y
    441st Troop Carrier Group, C-47 (Col Theodore Kershaw)
        99th Squadron, C-47 -- 3J
        100th Squadron, C-47 -- 8C
        301st Squadron, C-47 -- Z4
        302nd Squadron, C-47 -- 2L
    442nd Troop Carrier Group, C-47 (Col Charles Smith)
        303rd Squadron, C-47 -- J7
        304th Squadron, C-47 -- V4
        305th Squadron, C-47 -- 4J
        306th Squadron, C-47 -- 7H

52nd Troop Carrier Wing
    61st Troop Carrier Group, C-47 (Col Willis Mitchell)
        14th Squadron, C-47
        15th Squadron, C-47 -- Y9
        33rd Squadron, C-47
        59th Squadron, C-47 -- X3
    313th Troop Carrier Group, C-47 (Col James Roberts)
        29th Squadron, C-47
        47th Squadron, C-47 -- N3

48th Squadron, C-47 -- Z7
49th Squadron, C-47 -- 5X
314th Troop Carrier Group, C-47 (Col Clayton Styles)
    32nd Squadron, C-47 -- 2B
    50th Squadron, C-47 -- Q9
    61st Squadron, C-47 -- S2
    62nd Squadron, C-47 -- E3
315th Troop Carrier Group, C-47 (Col Hamish McLelland)
    34th Squadron, C-47 -- NM
    43rd Squadron, C-47 -- UA
    309th Squadron, C-47
    310th Squadron, C-47
316th Troop Carrier Group, C-47 (Col Harvey Berger)
    36th Squadron, C-47 -- 2E
    37th Squadron, C-47 -- W7
    44th Squadron, C-47 -- 4C
    45th Squadron, C-47 -- T3
349th Troop Carrier Group, C-47
    23rd Squadron, C-47 -- Q8
    312th Squadron, C-47 -- 9J
    313th Squadron, C-47 -- 3E
    314th Squadron, C-47

53rd Troop Carrier Wing
    434th Troop Carrier Group, C-47 (Col William Whiteacre)
        71st Squadron, C-47 -- CJ
        72nd Squadron, C-47 -- CU
        73rd Squadron, C-47 -- CN
        74th Squadron, C-47 -- ID
    435th Troop Carrier Group, C-47 (Col Frank McNees)
        75th Squadron, C-47 -- 5H
        76th Squadron, C-47 -- CW
        77th Squadron, C-47 -- 1B
        78th Squadron, C-47 -- CM
    436th Troop Carrier Group, C-47 (Col Adriel Williams)
        79th Squadron, C-47 -- S6
        80th Squadron, C-47 -- TD
        81st Squadron, C-47
        82nd Squadron, C-47 -- 3D
    437th Troop Carrier Group, C-47 (Col Cedric Hudgens)
        83rd Squadron, C-47 -- I2
        84th Squadron, C-47 -- Z8
        85th Squadron, C-47 -- 9D
        86th Squadron, C-47 -- 5K
    438th Troop Carrier Group, C-47 (Col John Donahue)
        87th Squadron, C-47 -- 3X
        88th Squadron, C-47 -- M2
        89th Squadron, C-47 -- 4U
        90th Squadron, C-47 -- Q7

US EIGHTH AIR FORCE

FIGHTER GROUPS

65th Fighter Wing
    4th Fighter Group – P-51 (Col Donald Blakeslee) (Debden)
        332nd Squadron (Maj James Goodson) -- VF

334th Squadron (Maj Howard Hively) -- QP
335th Squadron (Maj Robert Ackerly) -- WD
56th Fighter Group – P-47 (Col Hubert Zemke) (Boxted)
61st Squadron -- HV
62nd Squadron -- LN
63rd Squadron -- UN
355th Fighter Group – P-51 (Col William Cummings) (Steeple Morden)
354th Squadron -- WR
357th Squadron -- OS
358th Squadron -- YF
361st Fighter Group – P-51 (Col Thomas Christian) (Bottisham)
374th Squadron -- B7
375th Squadron -- E2
376th Squadron E9
479th Fighter Group – P-38 (LCol Kyle Riddle) (Wattisham)
434th Squadron -- L2
435th Squadron -- J2
436th Squadron -- 9B

66th Fighter Wing
55th Fighter Group – P-51 (Col George Crowell) (Wormingford)
38th Squadron (Maj Clayton Peterson) -- CG
338th Squadron -- CL
343rd Squadron -- CY
78th Fighter Group – P-47 (Col Frederic Gray) (Duxford)
82nd Squadron -- MX
83rd Squadron -- HL
84th Squadron -- WZ

339th Fighter Group – P-51 (Col John Henry) (Fowlmere)
503rd Squadron -- D7
504th Squadron -- 5Q
505th Squadron -- 6N
353rd Fighter Group – P-47 (Col Glen Duncan) (Raydon)
350th Squadron -- LH
351st Squadron -- YJ
352nd Squadron -- SY
357th Fighter Group – P-51 (Col Donald Graham) (Leiston)
362nd Squadron -- G4
363rd Squadron -- B6
364th Squadron -- C5

67th Fighter Wing
20th Fighter Group – P-38 (LCol Harold Rau) (Kingscliffe)
55th Squadron (Maj Morris McClary) -- KI
77th Squadron (Maj Merle Gilbertson) -- LC
79th Squadron (Maj Delynn Anderson) -- MC
352nd Fighter Group – P-51 (Col Joe Mason) (Bodney)
328th Squadron -- PE
486th Squadron -- PZ
487th Squadron -- HO
356th Fighter Group – P-47 (LCol Phillip Tukey) (Martlesham Heath)
359th Squadron -- OC
360th Squadron -- PI
361st Squadron -- QI
359th Fighter Group – P-51(Col Avelin Tacon) (East Wretham)
360th Squadron -- CS

368th Squadron -- CV
369th Squadron -- IV
364th Fighter Group – P-51 (Col Roy Osborn) (Hovington
383rd Squadron -- N2
384th Squadron -- 5Y
385th Squadron -- 5E

Appendix "D" -- Loss Data

	LUFTWAFFE				2nd TAF				US 9thAF				US 8th AF		ALLIES	
	Me	FW	tot	cum	Sp	Ty	tot	cum	47	38	tot	cum	tot	cum	tot	cum
Jun 6	1	17	22	22	9	8	23	23	8	2	23	23	20	20	64	66
7	36	22	71	93	18	17	44	67	23	3	29	52	16	36	89	155
8	14	14	30	123	6	2	11	78	3	0	4	56	13	49	28	183
9	9	8	18	141	3	1	5	83	0	1	6	62	0	49	11	194
10	25	3	32	173	12	3	25	108	16	2	21	83	14	63	60	254
11	6	2	10	183	9	1	12	120	3	0	5	88	10	73	27	281
12	26	24	50	233	11	8	19	139	6	1	9	97	15	88	43	324
13	6	6	19	252	4	2	6	145	5	0	9	106	3	91	18	342
14	14	5	24	276	3	5	14	159	10	1	14	120	3	94	31	373
15	14	12	31	307	5	6	13	172	6	0	9	129	1	95	23	396
16	3	2	10	317	6	3	12	184	3	1	4	133	0	95	16	412
17	10	18	33	350	6	3	14	198	10	5	23	156	6	101	43	455
18	3	1	15	365	6	2	13	211	6	1	8	164	0	101	21	476
19	0	1	2	367	5	0	7	218	0	1	2	166	8	109	17	493
20	16	12	29	396	2	1	5	223	0	4	5	171	2	111	12	505
21	9	1	10	406	2	0	9	232	3	2	7	178	0	111	16	521
22	22	7	29	435	7	2	17	249	16	14	31	209	2	113	50	571
23	6	15	23	458	7	4	24	273	2	0	3	212	5	118	32	603
24	12	19	35	493	1	4	12	285	8	0	10	222	2	120	24	627
25	30	6	38	531	3	1	5	290	2	8	13	235	0	120	18	645
26	7	5	13	544	0	0	0	290	0	0	3	238	0	120	3	648
27	21	7	28	572	4	2	9	299	4	0	4	242	5	125	18	666
28	17	10	29	601	6	1	8	307	0	0	0	242	0	125	8	674
29	14	7	22	623	2	1	8	315	2	1	6	248	0	125	14	688
30	20	2	23	646	5	0	7	322	4	3	7	255	0	125	14	702
Jul 1	9	1	11	657	2	0	2	324	0	0	0	255	4	129	6	708
2	13	7	21	678	3	0	4	328	1	0	1	256	0	129	5	713
3	0	0	2	680	2	2	5	333	0	1	1	257	0	129	6	719
4	21	16	38	718	8	0	9	342	2	1	8	265	6	135	23	742
5	22	14	39	757	2	1	4	346	3	1	6	271	9	144	19	761
6	14	13	27	784	2	7	9	355	3	4	9	280	2	146	20	781
7	12	4	16	800	3	2	5	360	3	1	5	285	0	146	10	791
8	1	2	4	804	1	1	3	363	5	0	15	300	1	147	19	810
9	3	0	4	808	2	1	5	368	0	0	1	301	2	149	8	818
10	2	2	5	813	3	0	4	372	2	0	2	303	0	149	6	824
11	8	2	12	825	3	2	6	378	4	2	7	310	1	150	14	838
12	7	7	16	841	5	1	8	386	5	1	7	317	0	150	15	853
13	3	4	8	849	1	3	4	390	2	0	2	319	0	150	6	859
14	15	4	21	870	5	0	5	395	5	3	8	327	0	150	13	872
15	0	3	4	874	2	2	5	400	0	0	0	327	0	150	5	877
16	10	7	17	891	1	4	5	405	1	0	2	329	0	150	7	889

	LUFTWAFFE				2ndTAF				US 9thAF				US 8thAF		ALLIES	
	Me	FW	tot	cum	Sp	Ty	tot	cum	47	38	tot	cum	tot	cum	tot	cum
17	11	9	20	911	5	1	6	411	3	0	7	336	0	150	13	897
18	14	7	21	932	4	10	15	426	10	5	18	354	0	150	33	930
19	6	3	10	942	3	4	8	434	2	2	6	360	0	150	14	944
20	2	10	12	954	1	1	2	436	4	1	5	365	0	150	7	951
21	0	0	0	954	0	0	0	436	0	0	0	365	0	150	0	951
22	4	1	5	959	3	0	6	442	0	1	1	366	0	150	7	958
23	3	2	5	964	1	0	2	444	3	4	8	374	0	150	10	968
24	16	5	21	985	4	0	4	448	1	1	3	377	0	150	7	975
25	16	9	26	1011	8	6	20	468	2	0	3	380	2	152	25	1000
26	12	7	20	1031	2	6	12	480	10	3	14	394	0	152	26	1026
27	9	12	22	1053	4	4	11	491	8	2	11	405	2	154	24	1050
28	4	8	14	1067	1	1	3	494	8	0	11	416	0	154	14	1064
29	2	2	8	1075	0	2	6	500	5	1	6	422	0	154	12	1076
30	8	4	13	1088	3	3	9	509	10	0	11	433	0	154	20	1096
31	3	4	9	1097	3	3	6	515	4	3	8	441	0	154	14	1110
Aug 1	8	3	11	1108	3	1	6	521	2	1	3	444	4	158	13	1123
2	5	3	11	1119	3	1	4	525	3	0	3	447	0	158	7	1130
3	7	2	13	1132	1	2	7	532	1	0	2	449	1	159	10	1140
4	7	0	12	1144	1	2	7	539	8	2	12	461	0	159	19	1159
5	1	6	11	1155	1	1	4	543	0	1	1	462	0	159	5	1164
6	8	5	17	1172	3	1	8	551	2	0	5	467	0	159	13	1177
7	7	9	24	1196	4	5	13	564	8	1	16	483	5	164	34	1211
8	4	4	14	1210	2	3	6	570	7	1	13	496	6	170	25	1236
9	7	3	11	1221	2	4	6	576	6	1	13	509	0	170	19	1255
10	11	6	19	1240	0	4	6	582	8	2	11	520	7	177	24	1279
11	4	1	9	1249	4	1	11	593	2	1	4	524	0	177	15	1294
12	1	2	5	1254	4	6	12	605	2	0	2	526	8	185	22	1316
13	9	8	17	1271	3	4	8	613	9	4	19	545	9	194	36	1352
14	5	10	15	1286	8	4	12	625	6	7	13	558	3	197	28	1380
15	6	5	13	1299	7	4	13	638	4	2	6	564	0	197	19	1399
16	12	1	16	1315	2	1	16	654	2	0	5	569	0	197	21	1420
17	2	7	10	1325	4	9	13	667	2	4	6	575	4	201	23	1443
18	20	14	34	1359	9	17	30	697	4	3	8	583	17	218	55	1498
19	11	5	19	1378	4	11	17	714	5	1	6	589	0	218	23	1521
20	6	7	14	1392	2	1	5	719	4	1	5	594	0	218	10	1531
21	4	2	7	1399	0	0	1	720	0	0	0	594	0	218	1	1532
22	13	10	23	1422	1	1	2	722	1	2	4	598	0	218	6	1538
23	14	12	26	1448	5	0	5	727	4	3	7	605	0	218	12	1550
24	1	2	3	1451	1	1	4	731	1	0	1	606	0	218	5	1555
25	9	40	49	1500	4	5	11	742	2	18	27	633	0	218	38	1593
26	3	7	10	1510	15	3	18	760	3	0	4	637	0	218	22	1615
27	1	6	7	1517	2	2	4	764	9	1	11	648	0	218	15	1630
28	4	1	5	1522	4	0	5	769	2	1	4	652	0	218	9	1639

Appendix "E" -- Number of Sorties and Claims by 127 Wing

date		403	416	421	443	TOTAL	
June	6	45	45	48		138	
	7	47	45	48		140	
	8	36	46	32		114	
	9	11	11	12		34	
	10	47	47	47		141	
	11	34	10	33		77	
	12	36	24	24		84	
	13	0	31	43		74	
	14	25	11	14		50	
	15	24	24	24		72	claims 10 - 0 - 1
	16	24	20	20		64	
	17	4	17	14		35	claims 0 - 0 - 1
	18	16	9	5		30	
	19	0	0	0		0	
	20	2	0	0		2	
	21	0	0	8		8	
	22	23	6	22		51	
	23	34	18	26		78	claims 6 - 0 - 7
	24	12	15	12		39	
	25	29	20	28		77	
	26	33	27	33		93	claims 3 - 0 - 3
	27	11	30	12		53	
	28	50	36	30		116	claims 7 - 0 - 3
	29	34	32	23		89	claims 1 - 0 - 0
	30	41	27	56		124	claims 6 - 0 - 1
July	1	30	4	34		68	
	2	34	42	46		122	claims 6 - 1 - 5
	3	24	11	7		42	
	4	30	17	47		94	
	5	24	32	26		82	claims 3 - 0 - 3
	6	34	10	21		65	
	7	22	35	25		82	
	8	36	72	36		144	
	9	11	10	23		44	
	10	0	7	42		49	
	11	12	12	17		41	
	12	72	23	36		131	claims 1 - 3 - 0
	13	12	0	12		24	claims 0 - 0 - 1

date		403	416	421	443	TOTAL	
	14	24	71	30		125	claims 8 - 0 - 2
	15	30	0	0	12	42	
	16	12	10	10	63	95	claims 6 - 2 - 1
	17	12	22	24	40	98	
	18	43	51	48	53	195	
	19	26	29	2	12	69	
	20	0	12	12	12	36	claims 2 - 0 - 0
	21	0	0	0	0	0	
	22	18	0	6	0	24	
	23	6	0	2	40	48	
	24	34	7	12	23	76	
	25	40	68	36	36	180	claims 5 - 1 - 3
	26	36	48	32	36	152	claims 1 - 0 - 0
	27	56	34	49	58	197	claims 2 - 1 - 0
	28	18	58	12	31	119	claims 3 - 0 - 1
	29	24	32	12	21	89	
	30	23	17	35	28	103	claims 2 - 0 - 1
	31	12	23	16	12	63	
Aug	1	12	12	12	28	64	
	2	32	22	14	12	80	
	3	40	48	24	12	124	claims 1 - 0 - 1
	4	12	28	40	24	104	
	5	12	12	16	20	60	
	6	20	12	12	12	56	
	7	22	23	12	36	93	
	8	33	31	32	52	148	Claims 1 - 0 - 0
	9	24	24	16	13	77	
	10	15	47	36	30	128	
	11	2	17	12	12	43	
	12	30	34	36	48	148	
	13	36	36	21	14	107	
	14	12	12	12	10	46	
	15	14	24	18	36	92	
	16	12	20	24	12	68	
	17	35	23	24	36	118	claims 1 - 0 - 0
	18	63	74	62	65	264	
	19	0	48	48	48	144	
	20	20	12	24	12	68	
	21	0	0	0	0	0	
	22	31	28	32	40	131	
	23	35	32	32	40	139	claims 12 - 0 - 3
	24	12	24	12	36	84	
	25	42	24	46	30	142	
	26	24	24	23	0	71	claims 1 - 0 - 0
	27	12	12	12	12	48	

date		403	416	421	443	TOTAL	
	28	24	48	48	24	144	claims 1 - 0 - 0
Aug	29	24	0	0	0	24	
	30	0	0	0	4	4	
							claims 89 - 8 - 37
Jun 6-15		305	294	325	0	924	
Jun 16-30		313	257	289	0	859	
Jul 1-15		395	346	402	12	1155	
Jul 16-31		763	827	729	908	3227	
Aug 1 -15		316	382	313	359	1370	
Aug 16-31		334	369	387	359	1449	
June		618	551	614	0	1783	
July		1158	1173	1131	920	4382	
Aug		650	751	700	718	2819	
TOTALS		2426	2475	2445	1638	8984	

Appendix "F" -- 127 Wing Claims and Losses

| Time | Place | Sq | Name | Serial | ----CLAIM---- | | | ----LOSS--- | | |
					Des	PD	Dam	Type	Cat	Fate
7 June 1944										
1300	UTAH beach	421	F/L W J Drope	MJ554				MF	CatEm	KIA
2000	St Catherine Pt.	421	F/O R J Grigg	NH183				MF	CatEm	KIA
8 June 1944										
1300	UTAH beach	416	W/O J C Maranda	MJ929				MF	CatEm	KIA
9 June 1944										
2100	OMAHA beach	403	F/L E C Williams	MJ827				FF	CatEm	POW
2100	OMAHA beach	403	F/O E D Kelly	MJ952				FF	CatB	safe
10 June 1944										
1630	beachhead	421	F/L P G Johnson	MJ954				AA	CatB	safe
1550	Tangmere	421	P/O J H Tetroe	MK120				Err	CatE	safe
11 June 1944										
1530	ELS Poupeville	403	F/L A R MacKenzie	n/a				AA	CatB	safe
13 June 1944										
0750	Isle of Wight	421	F/O R W Murray	MJ235				MF	CatEm	KIA
1300	Caen	Wg	W/C L V Chadburn	MJ824				CL	CatE	KIA
1300	Caen	421	F/L F J Clark	NH415				CL	CatE	KIA
1330	B.2 Bazenville	416	F/S W L Saunders	ML292				MF	CatB	safe
14 June 1944										
2300	beachhead	403	WO S Roth	MK859				MF	CatA	safe
15 June 1944										
1950	Caen/Cabourg	421	F/O J Bamford	MK809	3			109		
1950	Caen/Cabourg	421	F/L J N Paterson	MJ820	2			109		
1950	Caen/Cabourg	421	F/O W Warfield	MK199	2			109		
1950	Caen/Cabourg	421	F/L J K McElroy	MK472	1			GF	CatE	safe
1950	Caen/Cabourg	421	F/L W N Stronach	NH344	1			109		
1950	Caen/Cabourg	421	F/O W F Cook	MK994	1			109		
1950	Caen/Cabourg	421	F/L C D Grant	MJ870			1	109		
1950	Caen/Cabourg	421	F/L B Gilmour	MK687				GF	CatE	safe
1950	Caen/Cabourg	421	F/O L R Curry	MK941				GF	CatEm	KIA
1950	Caen/Cabourg	403	F/O R L Reeves	MK974				AA	CatE	EVD
17 June 1944										
1600	beachhead	421	F/O J Flood	PL275				AA	CatB	safe
1930	Caen	403	W/O A B Clenard	MK570				GF	CatEm	EVD
1930	St. Lo	403	F/O W H Rhodes	MK194			1	190	CatB	safe
2100	B.2 Bazenville	416	F/O G H Farquarson	MJ787				AA	CatB	safe
23 June 1944										
1215	Caen	421	F/O H C McRoberts	n/a			1	190		
1630	Caen/Bayeux	403	F/L M J Gordon	MK730	1		1	190		
1630	Caen/Bayeux	403	F/L P Logan	MK881	1		1	190		
1630	Caen/Bayeux	403	F/O B K Oliver	MH928			1	190		

Time	Place	Sq	Name	Serial	CLAIM Des	PD	Dam	LOSS Type	Cat	Fate
2130	Caen/Falaise	421	F/L P G Johnson	MK809	1			190		
2130	Caen/Falaise	421	F/L R C Wilson	MJ920	1			190		
2130	Caen/Falaise	421	F/L J F McElroy	MK468	1			190		
2130	Caen/Falaise	421	F/O G L Mayson	MJ880	1			190		
2130	Caen/Falaise	421	F/O A C Brandon	MK962			1	190		
2130	Caen/Falaise	421	F/O R G Driver	MJ275			2	109		
2130	Caen/Falaise	421	F/S R G Wallace	n/a				GF	CatEm	KIA
25 June 1944										
2035	B.2 Bazenville	421	F/L C D Grant	MJ870				CL	CatE	KIA
2035	B.2 Bazenville	421	F/O R G Driver	PL275				CL	CatE	WND
26 June 1944										
0700	Falaise/Lisieux	403	F/O J D Orr	ML411	1		1	109		
0700	Falaise/Lisieux	403	F/O W H Rhodes	ML248	1		1	109		
0700	Falaise/Lisieux	403	F/O G R Nadon	MJ988	1			109		
1115	Cabourg	403	F/L J D Lindsay	ML420			1	190		
1900	Cherbourg	421	F/O H C McRoberts	MJ793				AA	CatB	safe
27 June 1944										
0945	Falaise	421	F/O J Bamford	MK969				AA	CatEm	POW
28 June 1944										
0600	front lines	403	F/O W H Rhodes	ML248				AA	CatEm	POW
0600	front lines	403	F/L A R MacKenzie	MJ187	1			190		
0720	front lines	403	F/L J Lanfranchi	MJ988				MF	CatEm	KIA
1130	Caen	416	F/L D E Noonan	MJ770	1			190		
1130	Caen	416	F/L J D Rainville	MJ874	1			190		
1130	Caen	416	F/O G H Farquarson	MJ787	1			109		
1500	Caen	421	F/O H C McRoberts	MJ855				AA	CatB	WND
1610	front lines	416	F/L G R Patterson	MK837	1			190		
1610	front lines	416	F/L D R Cuthbertson	MJ611			1	190		
1800	front lines	421	F/L J F McElroy	MK468	1			109		
1800	front lines	421	F/L H P Zary	NH412	1			109		
1800	front lines	421	F/O A C Brandon	MK962			1	109		
1800	front lines	421	F/O J N Flood	MK891			1	109		
29 June 1944										
1100	Caen	416	S/L F E Green	MK790				AA	CatEm	WND
1330	Lisieux	403	F/L J D Lindsay	MJ988	1			190		
1330	Lisieux	403	W/O2 R C Shannon	MH928				GF	CatEm	EVD
30 June 1944										
0650	Caen/Falaise	421	F/L P G Johnson	MK809	1		1	109		
0650	Caen/Falaise	421	F/L R C Wilson	MK891	1			109		
1300	Falaise/Lisieux	403	F/L H R Finley	ML415	1			109		
2010	beach patrol	421	F/L P G Johnson	MK809	2			109		
2010	beach patrol	421	F/O H C McRoberts	MK365	1			109		

Time	Place	Sq	Name	Serial	CLAIM Des	PD	Dam	Type	LOSS Cat	Fate
1 July 1944										
0935	B.2 Bazenville	421	P/O O E Levere	n/a				err	CatB	safe
2 July 1944										
1508	Caen	403	F/L A R MacKenzie	MJ348	1		1	109		
1508	Caen	403	F/L J D Lindsay	ML411	3			109		
1508	Caen	403	F/L M J Gordon	MK730	1		1	109		
1508	Caen	403	F/L W J Hill	MJ570	0.5			109		
1508	Caen	403	F/O R B Greene	MK859	0.5			109		
1508	Caen	403	S/L E P Wood	ML180		1	2	109		
1508	Caen	403	F/O F W Thomson	MK881			1	109		
1515	Caen/Bayeux	421	F/L G E Stephenson	ML140				AA	CatB	safe
4 July 1944										
1445	Caen	421	F/O W Warfield	MK407				AA	CatB	safe
5 July 1944										
1110	Vire	403	F/L J D Lindsay	ML411			1	190		
1110	Vire	403	F/O J D Orr	MJ348			1	190		
1600	Bernay	421	F/O H C McRoberts	MJ569	2			109		
1600	Bernay	421	F/O C E Libby	MJ855	1			109		
1600	Bernay	421	S/L W A Conrad	ML308			1	109		
8 July 1944										
1140	Bernay	421	F/O W Warfield	NH412				AA	CatB	safe
10 July 1944										
1010	Falaise	416	P/O J E MaCrae	MK117				AA	CatE	safe
1010	Falaise	416	F/L N G Russell	MJ611				AA	CatB	safe
11 July 1944										
1015	Caen	416	F/L E H Treleaven	MK835				AA	CatB	safe
1220	Vire	421	F/O G W Taylor	MK808				AA	CatB	safe
12 July 1944										
1840	Cabourg	416	F/L J L Campbell	MJ141				AA	CatEm	EVD
1830	Chartres	421	F/O G M Smith	MJ295	1	1		109		
1830	Chartres	421	F/O H C McRoberts	MJ880		1		109	CatB	safe
1830	Chartres	421	F/O J Calvert	NH299		1		109		
13 July 1944										
1845	Alencon	443	F/L W A Prest	ML417			1	109		
14 July 1944										
1320	Villers-Bocage	416	F/L D E Noonan	MJ770	1			109		
1320	Villers-Bocage	416	F/L D E Noonan	MJ770	0.5			109		
1320	Villers-Bocage	416	F/O A J Fraser	NH411	0.5		1	109		
1430	Lisieux	416	F/O J B Gould	MK559	2			109		
1430	Lisieux	416	F/O M R Sharun	MJ953	1			109		
1430	Lisieux	416	F/S R E Chambers	NH408			1	109		
1520	Thury-Harcourt	403	F/O D J Shapter	MJ570				AA	CatEm	KIA
1920	over B.2	416	F/L R D Forbes-Roberts	MJ828	1			190		

Time	Place	Sq	Name	Serial	CLAIM			LOSS		
					Des	PD	Dam	Type	Cat	Fate
1920	over B.2	416	F/L G R Patterson	MK837	1			190		
1920	over B.2	416	F/O A G Borland	MJ575	1			190		
1920	over B.2	416	F/L W F Mason	MK835				190	CatE	safe
2045	Thury-Harcourt	403	WO W C Powers	MK881				AA	CatEm	KIA
16 July 1944										
1750	Cabourg	421	F/L J N Paterson	MJ820	1			109		
2010	Vire/Domfront	403	F/L A R MacKenzie	NH232	2			109		
2010	Vire/Domfront	403	F/L J E Collier	MK628	1			109		
2010	Vire/Domfront	403	F/O H V Boyle	MK780	2	1		109		
2010	Vire/Domfront	403	F/O M I Garland	ML183		1	1	109		
2010	Vire/Domfront	403	F/O M B O'Kelly	NH265				GF	CatEm	KIA
17 July 1944										
1300	low eastern	443	P/O F R Kearns	NH298				MF	CatB	safe
1620	St Lo	403	F/L L P Commerford	ML420				GF	CatE	WND
18 July 1944										
'0530	Caen	416	F/O J R Gould	MK559				FF	CatB	safe
'0530	Caen	416	F/O G Cameron	MJ953				FF	CatB	safe
0900	eastern patrol	421	F/L P G Johnson	MK809				CL	CatE	KIA
19 July 1944										
1530	St Lo	403	F/L C T Brown	NH232				AA	CatB	safe
1530	St Lo	403	F/O S A Tosh	MK857				AA	CatE	safe
1530	St Lo	403	F/O F W Thomson	ML198				AA	CatB	safe
20 July 1944										
1500	Bernay	443	S/L H W McLeod	MK636	1			190		
1500	Bernay	443	F/L J L Robillard	MK315	1			190		
25 July 1944										
0700	East'n patrol	403	F/O C J Thomlinson	ML318				AA	CatB	Safe
1100	Rouen	421	F/L H P Zary	MK920	3			109		
1100	Rouen	421	F/O W F Cook	MJ891	1		1	109		
1100	Rouen	421	F/O E H Levere	ML140	1			109		
1100	Rouen	421	F/O J W Neil	MK407		1		109		
1100	Rouen	421	F/L L R Thorne	MK796			1	109		
1100	Rouen	421	F/O G M Smith	MK661			1	109		
1100	Rouen	421	F/O G A Cashion	MJ987				GF	CatEm	KIA
1830	Villers-Bocage	443	F/O T G Munro	MJ514				AA	CatEm	POW
2000	Argentan/Dom	421	F/O F W Ward	MK796				AA	CatEm	KIA
26 July 1944										
1915	Dreux	443	F/O G R Stephen	ML153	1			190		
27 July 1944										
0710	Alencon	416	S/L J F McElroy	ML250	1			190		
0710	Alencon	416	F/L D E Noonan	MK837	1			190		
0710	Alencon	416	F/L D W Hayworth	MK559		0.5		190		
0710	Alencon	416	F/S R E Chambers	NH408		0.5		190		

Time	Place	Sq	Name	Serial	CLAIM			LOSS		
					Des	PD	Dam	Type	Cat	Fate
28 July 1944										
1830	Caen	416	F/O M R Sharun	MK559	1			109		
1830	Caen	416	F/L D J England	MJ872	1			109		
1830	Caen	416	F/O A J Fraser	MJ611			1	109		
1940	Caen	416	F/L N G Russell	NH611	1			190		
30 July 1944										
1530	Alencon	443	S/L H W McLeod	MK636	1			109		
1530	Alencon	443	F/O W J Bentley	NH244	1			109		
1530	Alencon	443	P/O R A Hodgins	ML153			1	109		
1530	Alencon	443	F/O L B Foster	MJ741				GF	CatB	WND
1 August 1944										
3 August 1944										
1930	L'Aigle	403	F/L J D Lindsay	ML411	1		1	109		
5 August 1944										
1815	Mezidon	403	F/O J W Earl	MJ784				AA	CatEm	KIA
1815	Benouville	403	WO J A Wilcocks	MK810				AA	CatE	WND
6 August 1944										
1515	B.2 Bazenville	416	F/L J D England	MJ872				CL	CatB	safe
1730	Falaise	421	W/O D W Guest	MK421				MF	CatEm	POW
1900	Creil/Gournay	443	F/O R B Henderson	NH347				MF	CatB	safe
8 August 1944										
1415	Argentan	443	F/L G W Troke	ML184	0.25			190		
1415	Argentan	443	F/O W J Sherman	MJ171	0.25			190		
1415	Argentan	443	F/O A J Horrell	NH208	0.25			190		
1415	Argentan	443	F/O D J Wegg	NH244	0.25			190		
12 August 1944										
1200	Dreux/Bernay	443	F/O W J Bentley	ML303				MF	CatEm	KIA
17 August 1944										
1215	Falaise	443	S/L H W McLeod	MK636				MF	CatB	safe
1430	Bernay	403	P/O G R Weber	NH232				AA	CatEm	EVD
1815	Trun	403	F/O H V Boyle	MK299				AA	CatEm	KIA
1815	Trun	403	P/O W L Garland	ML183				GF	CatEm	EVD
1845	Trun	443	F/O A J Horrell	NH208				AA	CatB	safe
1930	Lisieux	416	F/L D R Cuthbertson	NH411	1			190		
18 August 1944										
1530	Trun	403	W/O2 K Harvey	MJ752				AA	CatB	safe
2040	Mezidon	421	F/O J Leyland	MJ820				AA	CatEm	safe
23 August 1944										
1330	Senlis	421	F/L E S Smith	MK365	2			190		
1330	Senlis	421	F/O R E Holness	MJ891	1			190		
1330	Senlis	421	F/L T H Hoare	MK573	1			190		
1330	Senlis	421	F/L B T Gilmour	MK575	1			190		
1330	Senlis	421	F/O J W Neil	MK115	1			190	CatEm	POW

Time	Place	Sq	Name	Serial	CLAIM Des	PD	Dam	LOSS Type	Cat	Fate
1330	Senlis	421	F/L Stronach	MJ714			1	190		
1330	Senlis	421	F/O G W Taylor	MJ880				GF	CatEm	KIA
1330	Senlis	Wg	W/C J E Johnson	MK392	2			190		
1330	Senlis	443	F/L J S L Robillard	MK315	1			109		
1330	Senlis	443	F/O G F Ockenden	MJ799	2		1	109		
1330	Senlis	443	F/O A J Horrell	MJ779	1			109		
1330	Senlis	443	F/O E H Fairfield	ML424			1	109		
1330	Senlis	443	F/O R W Dunn	MK468				GF	CatEm	POW
26 August 1944										
0930	Lyons	421	F/O W Warfield	MJ714	1			190		
0930	Lyons	421	F/O J M Flood	ML308				GF	CatEm	KIA
0930	Lyons	421	F/O O E Libbey	MK661				GF	CatEm	EVD
28 August 1944										
1430	Beauvais	403	F/L J D Orr	ML262	1			190		
1430	Beauvais	403	W/O M E Soules	MJ572				GF	CatEm	KIA

Appendix "G" – 127 Wing Aircrew

Note: SC = Squadron Commander, AFC = A Flight Commander, BFC = B Flight Commander

403 PILOTS
(pilots on roster from the last day of the preceding month)
June 1944

S/L R A Buckham	SC		to W/C(F) 14 Jun
	SC	S/L E P 'Ed' Wood	From 402 16 June
P/O H V 'Harry' Boyle			
F/L C T 'Cec' Brown			
		F/S Steve Butte	started 10 June
P/O N V Chevers			
WO A B Clenard			GF 17 June EVD
		F/L L P Commerford	started 30 June
F/O W A Doyle			
F/L H R 'Hart' Finley	BFC		
		F/S Ron Forsyth	started 10 June
F/L M J 'Mac' Gordon			
F/O R B Greene			
		F/S K Harvey	started 2 June
F/L W J Hill			
F/L J Hodgson			AA 2 June KIA
F/L W G Hume			
P/O E D Kelly			FF 9 June WND
		F/O R J 'Bob' Lawlor	started 13 June n/e 29 June
P/O J Lanfranchi			MF 28 June KIA
F/L J D 'Doug' Lindsay			
F/L P 'Pete' Logan			
F/L A R 'Andy' MacKenzie	AFC		
		F/O G R Nadon	Started ? June
		F/O K Oliver	started 20 June
F/O J D 'Doug' Orr			
F/O J Preston			EOT 12 June
F/O R 'Dick" Reeves			AA 15 June EVD
F/O W H Rhodes			AA 28 June POW
W/O S 'Sid' Roth			MF 14 June safe
P/O K F Scott			
		W/O2 R C Shannon	FTR 29 June EVD
F/O D J 'Don' Shapter			
F/O R 'Red' Thomson			
		P/O C J Tomlinson	Started 30 June
F/O Whitaker			
W/O J A L Wilcocks			
F/L E C Williams			FF 9 June POW

416 PILOTS

June 1944

S/L F E Fred Green	SC		AA 29 Jun WND
	SC	S/L J F McElroy	from 421 start 30 Jun
		P/O D 'Dave' Blackstock	start ? n/e 22 Jun
		P/O C 'Charlie' Bryce	start 28 Jun
F/O A C 'Sandy' Borland			
F/L J L 'Black' Campbell			
F/L D R 'Cuthy' Cuthbertson			
F/L D J 'Dyke' England			
F/O G H Farquarson			
F/L R D 'Dick' Forbes-Roberts			
F/O A J 'Bud' Fraser			
W/O L N Guillot			GF 1 Jun KIA
F/O J R 'Jackson' Gould			
F/L D W 'Dave' Harling			
F/L D W 'Don' Hayworth			
W/O J C Maranda			MF 8 June KIA
F/L W F 'Bill' Mason			
F/L J B McColl			
P/O J E 'Ronnie' McCrea			
F/O A R McFadden			
F/L D E 'Danny' Noonan	BFC		BFC 30 June
P/O W H 'Bill' Palmer			
F/L G R 'Pat' Patterson			
F/L D M Prentice	AFC		EOT 30 June
F/L J B 'Johnny' Rainville			
		F/S W 'Bill' Saunders	started 2 June
F/O W J 'Bill' Simpson			
F/O M R 'Mush' Sharun			
F/O R R St. Georges			
F/O A J 'Taffy' Tafuro			

421 PILOTS

June 1944

S/L W A 'Wally' Conrad	SC		
F/O J N 'Jack' Bamford			AA 27 June POW
F/O A C 'Brandy' Brandon			
		F/O G A Cashion	started 26 June
F/O J 'Jack' Calvert			
F/L F J 'Frank' Clark			CL 13 June KIA
F/O W F 'Cookie' Cook			
F/O L F 'Lorne' Curry			GF 15 June KIA
F/O R G 'Gord' Driver			CL 25 June WND
F/L W 'Johnny' Drope			MF 7 June KIA
		F/O J M Flood	started 14 June
F/L B T 'Benton' Gilmour			GF 15 June safe

F/L E L 'Ed' Gimbel	BFC		to USAAF 4 June
F/L C D 'Bitsy' Grant			CL 25 June KIA
F/O R J 'Bob' Grigg			MF 7 June KIA
		F/O J Hamm	started 9 June
F/L P 'Paul' Johnson	AFC		AA 10 June safe
F/O H Leblond			
		P/O E H Levere	started 26 June
		F/O O E Libbey	started 27 June
		F/O G L Mayson	started 9 June n/e 27 June
F/L J F 'Johnny' McElroy	BFC		to S/L 416 29 June
F/O H C 'Scotty' McRoberts			AA 28 June WND
F/O R W 'Bob' Murray			MF 13 June KIA
F/L J N 'John' Paterson			
		F/O R W Perkins	started 27 June
F/S W 'Bill' Saunders			to 416 2 June
		F/L E S Smith	started 15 June
F/O G M 'Gordie' Smith			
		F/L G E Stephenson	started 26 June
F/O W N 'Bill' Stronach			
P/O J H 'John' Tetroe			n/e 16 June
F/L L R 'Len' Thorne			
		F/O J Ulmer	started 27 June
		F/S R G Wallace	started 6 June GF 23 June KIA
F/O W 'Willie' Warfield			
F/L R C 'Roger' Wilson			
F/L H P 'Hank' Zary	BFC		BFC 29 June

403 PILOTS

July 1944

S/L E P 'Ed' Wood	SC		
P/O H V 'Harry' Boyle			
F/L C T 'Cec' Brown			FF 19 Jul WND
F/S S 'Steve' Butte			
		Sgt Campbell	start 1 July
P/O N V Chevers			
		F/L J E Collier	start ?
F/L L P Commerford			GF 17 Jul WND
F/O W A Doyle			
F/L H R 'Hart' Finley	BFC		EOT 1 July
F/S R 'Ron' Forsyth			
		F/O Garland	start ?
F/L M J 'Mac' Gordon			EOT 11 July
F/O R B Greene			
F/S K Harvey			
F/L W J Hill			
F/L W G Hume			

P/O E D Kelly			
F/L J D 'Doug' Lindsay	BFC		BFC 1 JUly
F/L P 'Pete' Logan			EOT 1 July
F/L A R 'Andy' MacKenzie	AFC		EOT 31 Jul
F/O G R Nadon			
		F/O D 'Doug' O'Kelly	start 1 July GF 16 July KIA
F/O K Oliver			
F/O J D 'Doug' Orr			
		W/O W C Powers	started ? July AA 14 July KIA
F/O R 'Dick Reeves			
W/O S 'Sid' Roth			
P/O K F Scott			
F/O D J 'Don' Shapter			AA 14 July KIA
F/O R 'Red' Thomson			FF 19 July safe
P/O C J Tomlinson			AA 25 Jul safe
		F/O S A 'Stu' Tosh	start ? FF 19 Jul safe
F/O Whitaker			
W/O J A L Wilcocks			

416 PILOTS

July 1944

S/L J F 'Johnny' McElroy	SC		
P/O D 'Dave' Blackstock			
F/O A C 'Sandy' Borland			
P/O C 'Charlie' Bryce			n/e 3 July
		F/O G 'Gord' Cameron	start 3 July FF 18 July safe
F/L J L 'Black' Campbell			AA 12 July EVD
		F/S E 'Eric' Chambers	start 8 July
F/L D R 'Cuppy' Cuthbertson			
F/L D J 'Dyke' England			
F/O G H Farquarson	AFC		AFC 1 July
F/L R D 'Dick' Forbes-Roberts			
F/O A J 'Bud' Fraser			
F/O J R 'Jackson' Gould			FF 18 July safe
F/L D W 'Dave' Harling			
F/L D W 'Don' Hayworth			
F/L W F Mason			AA 14 Jul safe
F/L J B McColl			
P/O J E 'Ronnie' McCrea			AA 10 Jul safe
F/O A R McFadden			
F/L D E 'Danny' Noonan	BFC		
P/O W H 'Bill' Palmer			
F/L G R 'Pat' Patterson			
F/L J B 'Johnny' Rainville			
		F/L Neil Russell	start 4 July, AA 10 July safe
F/S W 'Bill' Saunders			
F/O W J 'Bill' Simpson			

F/O M R 'Mush' Sharun			
F/O R R St. Georges			
F/O A J 'Taffy' Tafuro			
		F/L E H Treleaven	start 8 July, AA 11 July safe

421 Squadron

July 1944

S/L W A 'Wally' Conrad	SC		EOT 27 Jul
	SC	S/L W A 'Bill' Prest	From 443 SC 28 July
F/O A C 'Brandy' Brandon			7 Jul n/e sick
F/O G A Cashion			GF 25 Jul KIA
F/O J 'Jack' Calvert			
F/O W F 'Cookie' Cook			
F/O L F Curry			
		F/O W A Evans	start 28 July
F/O J M Flood			
F/L B T 'Benton' Gilmour			
		WO D W Guest	start 28 July
F/O J Hamm			
		F/O R E Holness	start 9 July
F/L Paul G Johnson	AFC		CL 18 July KIA
F/O H Leblond			
P/O E H Levere			
F/O O E Libby			
		F/O E H Mann	start 27 Jul
F/O H C 'Scotty' McRoberts			21 July n/e
		F/O J W Neil	started 6 July
F/L John N Paterson			
F/O R W Perkins			to 441 6 July
F/L E S Smith			
F/O Gordie M Smith			
F/L G E Stephenson			AA 2 July safe
F/O Bill N Stronach			
		F/O G W Taylor	start 11 July
F/L Len R Thorne			EOT 26 July
F/O J Ulmer			
		F/O F W Ward	started 22 Jul AA 25 Jul KIA
F/O Willie Warfield			AA 8 Jul safe
F/L Roger C Wilson	AFC		AFC 19 July
F/L Hank P Zary	BFC		

443 PILOTS

July 1944			
S/L H W 'Wally' MacLeod	SC		
F/L P G Blades			

F/O W J Bentley			
F/O E H Fairfield			
P/O P E Ferguson			
F/O L B Foster			AA 30 Jul WND
F/L H B Fuller			To ? 2 Jul
F/O W A Gilbert			
F/L H T Hallihan		started 9 Jul	To 442 10 Jul
F/O R A Hodgins			
F/O A J Horrell			AA 25 Jul safe CatAC
F/O L E Hunt		started 28 Jul	
F/L A Hunter			AA 19 Jul safe CatAC
F/O J R Irwin			
P/O F R Kearns			MF 17 Jul safe
F/O T G Munro			AA 25 July POW
F/O G N Ockenden			
F/O P E Piche			
F/L W A 'Bill' Prest	BFC		to 421 27 Jul
F/L L 'Larry' Robillard	AFC	from 442 9 Jul	
F/O C E Scarlett			
F/O G R Stephen			
F/L E B Stovel			
P/O A M Thomas		started 28 Jul	
F/L G W Troke	BFC		BFC 27 July
F/O W I Williams			N/e 31 July
F/L F A Wilson	AFC		EOT 9 Jul
P/O D J Wegg		started 20 Jul	

403 Squadron

August 1944

S/L E P Wood	SC		
P/O H V 'Harry' Boyle			GF 17 Aug KIA
		F/O W F Bridgman	to 416 Sq 10 Aug
F/L C T Brown			
F/S Steve Butte			
Sgt Campbell			
P/O N V Chevers			
F/L J E Collier	AFC		AFC 1 Aug
F/L L P Commerford			
F/O W A Doyle			
P/O Earle			GF 5 Aug KIA
F/S Ron Forsyth			
F/O M Garland			GF 17 Aug EVD
F/O R B Greene			
F/S K Harvey			AA 18 Aug safe
F/L W J Hill			
F/L W G Hume			
P/O E D Kelly			
F/L J D 'Doug' Lindsay			EOT 3 Aug
F/O G R Nadon			
F/O K Oliver			
F/O J D 'Doug' Orr	BFC		BFC 6 Aug

F/O R 'Dick' Reeves			
W/O 'Sid' Roth			
P/O K F Scott			
		WO M 'Milt' Soules	start ? GF 28 Aug KIA
F/O 'Red' Thomson			
P/O C J Tomlinson			
F/O S A Tosh			
F/O Whitaker			
		F/O R B Gordon Weber	AA 17 Aug EVD
WO J A L Wilcocks			AA 5 Aug WND safe

416 PILOTS

August 1944

S/L J F 'Johnny' McElroy	SC		
P/O D 'Dave' Blackstock			returned from n/e 7 Aug
F/O A C 'Sandy' Borland			
		F/O Bridgman	From 403 10 Aug
F/O G 'Gord' Cameron			
F/S Eric Chambers			
F/L D R 'Cuthy' Cuthbertson			
F/L D J 'Dyke' England			
F/O G H Farquarson	AFC		EOT 24 Aug
F/L R D 'Dick' Forbes-Roberts			EOT 5 Aug
F/O A J 'Bud' Fraser			
F/O J R 'Jackson' Gould			AA 18 Aug safe CatAC
F/L D W Dave Harling			
F/L D W Don Hayworth			EOT 5 Aug
F/L W F Mason			
		F/L 'Leo' Mault	started 9 Aug
F/L J B McColl			
P/O J E 'Ronnie' McCrea			
F/O A R McFadden			EOT 24 Aug
F/L D E 'Danny' Noonan	BFC		EOT 3 Aug
P/O W H 'Bill' Palmer			
F/L G R 'Pat' Patterson	BFC		BFC 3 Aug
F/L J B 'Johnny' Rainville			
		P/O W 'Bill' Roddie	started 9 Aug
	AFC	F/L A 'Art' Sager	From 402 AFC 24 Aug
F/S W 'Bill' Saunders			
F/O W J 'Bill' Simpson			
F/O M R 'Mush' Sharun			
		F/L L 'Larry' Spurr	started 23 Aug
F/O R R St. Georges			
F/O A J 'Taffy' Tafuro			
F/L E H Treleaven			

421 PILOTS

August 1944

S/L W A 'Bill' Prest	SC		
F/O J 'Jack' Calvert			
F/O William F Cook			
F/O L F Curry			
F/O W A Evans			
F/O J M Flood			GF 26 Aug KIA
F/L Benton T Gilmour			
WO D W Guest			MF 6 Aug POW
F/O J Hamm			
		F/L T H Hoare	started 9 Aug
F/O R E Holness			
F/O H Leblond			
P/O E H Levere			
		F/O Langmuir	started 29 Aug
		F/O J Leyland	started 9 Aug AA 18 Aug WND n/e
F/O O E Libbey			GF 26 Aug EVD
		P/O Marsden	started 24 Aug
		P/O McDonald	started 29 Aug
		Sgt McIntosh	started 25 Aug
		F/O McKellar	
		F/L J D Mitchener	started 13 Aug
F/O J W Neil			GF 23 Aug POW
F/L J N 'John' Paterson			n/e sick 16 Aug
		W/O M Price	started 29 Aug
F/L E S Smith			
F/O Gordie M Smith			
F/L G E Stephenson			
F/O W N 'Bill' Stronach	BFC		BFC 12 Aug
F/O G W Taylor			GF 23 Aug KIA
F/O J Ulmer			n/e 24 Aug
		F/O E M Veenis	started 1 Aug
F/O W 'Willie' Warfield			
F/L Roger C Wilson	AFC		
F/L H P 'Hank' Zary	BFC		EOT 12 Aug

443 PILOTS

August 1944

S/L H W 'Wally' MacLeod	SC		AA 22 Aug safe
F/L P G Blades			
F/O W J Bentley			AA 12 Aug KIA
F/O Borrell			
F/O R W Dunn		started 6 Aug	GF 23 Aug POW
F/O E H Fairfield			
P/O P E Ferguson			
F/O L B Foster			

F/O W A Gilbert			AA 12 Aug safe CatAC
F/O R A Hodgins			
F/O A J Horrell			AA 17 Aug safe
F/O L E Hunt			
F/L A Hunter			
F/O J R Irwin			
P/O F R Kearns			
Ff/O G Ockenden			
F/O P E Piche			
F/L L 'Larry' Robillard	AFC		
F/O C E Scarlett			N/e 31 Aug
F/O G R Stephens			EOT 30 Aug
F/O W J Sherman		started 6 Aug	
F/L E B Stovel			
P/O A M Thomas			
F/L Troke	BFC		
P/O Wegg			

BIBLIOGRAPHY

127 Wing Operations Record Book, National Archives of Canada, Microfilm C – 12,425

403 Squadron History, 403 Squadron, Oromucto, NB, 2001, ISBN 0-9688969-0-1

403 Squadron Operations Record Book. National Archives of Canada, Microfilm C – 12,268

416 Squadron History, The Hangar Bookshelf, Belleville ON, 1984, ISBN 0-920492-00-4

416 Squadron Operations Record Book. National Archives of Canada, Microfilm C – 12,287

421 Squadron History, Canada's Wings, Stittsville ON, 1982, ISBN 0-920002-16-1

421 Squadron Operations Record Book. National Archives of Canada, Microfilm C – 12,295

443 Squadron Operations Record Book. National Archives of Canada, Microfilm C – 12,320

Andrews, Paul, Adams, William, The Mighty Eighth Combat Chronology, Eighth Air Force Memorial Foundation, 1997 (no ISBN number)

Astor, Gerald, The Mighty Eighth, Dell, NYC, 1997, ISBN 0-440-22648-1

Benamou, Jean-Pierre, Murphy, Geoffrey, Normandie 1944 -- La 2nd Tactical Air Force, Magazine Hors-Série, N° 11, Éditiond Heimdal, Bayeux, 1989

Blackburn, George, The Guns of Normandy, Maclellan & Stewart, Toronto ISBN 0-7710-1053-8

Bracken, Robert, Spitfire -- the Canadians, Boston Mills, Erin, Ontario, 1995 ISBN 1-55046-148-6

Bracken, Robert, Spitfire II -- the Canadians, Boston Mills, Erin, Ontario, 1995 ISBN 1-55046-267-9

Caldwell, Donald., JG26 – Top Guns of the Luftwaffe, Ivy Books, New York, 1991 ISBN 0-8041-1050-6

Cooper, M., The German Air Force – 1933 –1945 An Anatomy of Failure, Jane's, London, 1981, ISBN 07106-0071-2

Copp, Terry, A Canadian's Guide to the Battlefields of Normandy, Wilfred Laurier University, Waterloo, 1994 ISBN 0-9697955-0-5

D'Este, Carlo, Decision in Normandy, Collins, London, 1983, ISBN 0-00-217056-6

Forbes, Robert, Gone is the Angel , Brown Book Company, Toronto 1997, ISBN 0-9681875-0-1

Franks, Norman, Fighter Command Losses of WWII Vol 3, Midland, 2000, ISBN 1-85780-093-1

Frappé, Jean-Bernard, La Luftwaffe face de débarquement allié, Heimdal, Bayeux, 1999, ISBN 2-84048-126-X

Godefroy, H. Lucky Thirteen , Stoddart, Toronto, 1987, ISBN 0-7737-5102-5

Greenhous, Harris, Johnston and Rawling, The Crucible of War 1939 – 1945, U of Toronto Press, 1994 ISBN 0-8020-0574-8

Halliday, Hugh, Typhoons and Tempests CANAV Books, Toronto, 1992 ISBN 0-921022-06-9

Johnson, J E, Wing Leader, Ballantine Books, New York, 1967 (no ISBN number)

Keegan, John, The Second World War,, Penguin Books, New York, 1990 ISBN 0-1401-1342-X

Kellett J., Davies J., A History of the RAF Servicing Commandos

McAndrew, W, Graves, D, Whitby, M, Normandy 1944 – The Canadian Summer, Art Global, Montreal, 1994, ISBN 2-920718-56-8

Milberry, L, Halliday, H, Royal Canadian Air Force 1939 to 1945, CANAV Books, Toronto, 1990, ISBN 0-921022-04-2

Milberry, L, Canada's Air Force at war and peace, Vol 1, CANAV Books, Toronto, 2000, ISBN 0-921022-11-5

Milberry, L, Canada's Air Force at war and peace, Vol 2, CANAV Books, Toronto, 2000, ISBN 0-921022-12-3

Morgan, Eric, Shacklady, Edward, Spitfire -- the History Key Publishing, Stamford, England, 1987, ISBN 0-946219-10-9

Olmstead, W., Blue Skies – The Autobiography of a Canadian Fighter Pilot, Stoddart, Toronto, 1987

Olynyk, Frank, USAAF (European Theatre) Credits for the Destruction of Enemy Aircraft in Air-to-Air Combat in WWII, 1987 (no ISBN number)

Public Records Office documents – AIR 24/1496 – Second Tactical Air Force ORB

Public Records Office documents – AIR 26/179 through 212 – ORBs for 121 Wing through 148 Wing

Public Records Office documents – AIR 50/138 – 403 Squadron Combat Reports

Public Records Office documents – AIR 50/145 – 416 Squadron Combat Reports

Public Records Office documents – AIR 50/147 – 421 Squadron Combat Reports

Public Records Office documents – AIR 50/154 – 443 Squadron Combat Reports

Ramsay, W G, D-Day Then and Now, Volumes I and II, Church House, London, 1995 ISBN 0-900913-84-3

Rust, Kenneth, Ninth Tactical Air Force, Aero Publication, 1970, (no ISBN number)

Roy, R H, 1944 - The Canadians in Normandy, - Canadian War Museum Historical Publication No.19, Macmillan of Canada, 1984 ISBN 0-7715-9796-7

Scutts, Jerry, P-47 Thunderbolt Aces of the Ninth and Fifteenth Air Forces, Osprey, 1999, ISBN 1-85532-906-9

Shores, Chris, Williams, Clive, Aces High, Grubb Street London, 1994 ISBN 1-898697-00-0

tacey, Col. C P, Canada's Battle in Normandy, King's Printer, Ottawa, 1946 (no ISBN number)

Stacey, Col. C P, Volume III -- The Victory Campaign , Queen's Printer, Ottawa, 1966 (no ISBN number)

Terraine, John, The Right of the Line, Hodder and Stoughton, London, 1985, ISBN 0-340-26644-9

Whitaker, D and S, Victory at Falaise, the soldier's story, HarperCollins Canada, Toronto, 2000 ISBN 0-00-638498-6

Wilmot, C., The Struggle for Europe, Collins, London, 1957 (no ISBN number)

INDEX

About the Author

Dave Clark was only thirteen when his older brother was killed in a Spitfire in the skies over Normandy – seven days after D-Day. Years later, when he retired, he realized how little he knew about the circumstances of the tragic death and set about gathering research material from books, fellow amateur historians and original microfilms. He went to the UK and France, built a web site, participated actively in Internet bulletin boards devoted to World War II aviation and corresponded with veteran pilots. Four years later he had enough material to chronicle every major aerial encounter of fighters over Normandy. Combining this database with a day-by-day account of one RCAF wing of Spitfires provided enough material for a book.

Footnotes

Footnotes to Chapter One

[1] Quoted in 'D-Day Then and Now' by Winston G. Ramsay page 6.

[2] The Transportation Plan was opposed because of the great number of French civilians who were killed or wounded in the course of accomplishing the mission.

[3] This list was compiled from '50th Division Operational Order No.1' as reproduced in Winston Ramsay's book 'D-Day Then and Now' page 442.

[4] These figures are quoted in Reginald H. Roy's book '1944 – The Canadians in Normandy', Canadian War Museum Publication, Macmillan 1984 — page 39.

[6] Hitler's Directive Number 51, 27 November 1943, as quoted in 'D-Day Then and Now', page 40.

Footnotes for Chapter Two

[1] In his definitive history of the campaign in north-west Europe, Chester Wilmott cites two reasons for the difficulties the Americans encountered at OMAHA (1) Bradley's insistence upon direct frontal assault, and (2) his reluctance to use any of the specialized equipment offered by the British for clearing beaches. See Wilmott, page 265.

[2] Most regimental records of the assaulting forces emphasize that heavy bombing and naval bombardment prior to the landings failed to knock out any of the defences. The bombing was generally too far inland to be effective, but unknown to the assaulting troops who faced field artillery and machine guns at the beaches, 25 out of the 27 large coastal batteries were knocked out by bombing and especially naval gunfire.

[3] Air Chief Marshal Sir Trafford Leigh-Mallory, London Gazette, 31 December 1946 as quoted in Winston Ramsey's 'D-Day Then and Now', page 146.

[4] 'Crucible of War' Greenhous, Harris, Johnston, Rawling, Department of National Defence, page 280.

[5] Public Record Office document AIR 25/699 – 'Bigot' plan Appendix K

[6] from PRO document AIR 24/1496 Operations Record Book for 2ndTAF, page 17.

[7] 'D-Day – June 6 1944', Stephen Ambrose, page 239.

[8] 'Ninth Tactical Air Force in WWII', Kenneth Rust, page 84.

[9] PRO document AIR 24/1496 Operations Record Book for 2ndTAF, p. 17

[10] These figures — like all other Allied loss figures quoted in this book — are derived from PRO document AIR 24/1496 Operations Record Book for 2ndTAF, 'RAF Fighter Command Losses' Volume 3, Norman Franks, 'Ninth Tactical Air Force in WWII', Kenneth Rust, 'The Mighty Eighth Combat Chronology', Paul Andrews and William Adams.

[11] These figures — like all other Luftwaffe loss figures quoted in this book — are derived from 'La Luftwaffe — en face du débarquement', Jean Bertrand Frappé.

Footnotes to Chapter Three

[1] Chester Wilmott points out that the German Navy told the German High Command that the Allies were capable of invading with 20 divisions. When it was ascertained that the Allied attack consisted of only six assaulting divisions, the Germans were convinced Calais was the real target.

[2] The reference 'T.9439' is a location reference for the maps used by the Allies in Normandy. See Figure 4.

[3] Quoted in Carlo D'Este, Decision in Normandy, p.268.

[4] One Ju 88 was actually downed when it became entangled by a barrage balloon cable.

[5] Hauptmann Weissenberger would go on to claim 25 victories in the Normandy Campaign for a career total of 208. That made him the second highest scoring Luftwaffe Pilot in Normandy (after Hauptmann Lang of II./JG 26 who claimed 28 in Normandy).

[6] Many Americans joined up before the US entered the war, and flew with RAF Fighter Command. They were concentrated in two FSs called the 'Eagle Squadrons'. In 1943 as new FSs were being formed in the UK many of these pilots transferred to the newly-formed US 8thAF.

[7] The code word for altitude was 'angels' hence 'angels eight' meant 8,000 feet of altitude. This is why the title of the book is 'Angels Eight' — the safe level to fly above light and medium flak.

[8] PRO document AIR 24/1496 Operations Record Book for 2ndTAF, page 27

[9] ibid, page 26

[10] ibid, page 30

[11] ibid, page 31

[12] Cherbourg began to receive cargo 16 July 1944, and then became the major port for Allied logistic supply until Antwerp was opened in the middle of November 1944.

[13] By the end of June the British Army was severely stretched to find replacements, and the Canadian Army was similarly short of supply because of the political difficulties with conscription. It was the Americans who then poured in replacement troops in increasing numbers.

Footnotes to Chapter Four

[1] Unlike ground troops, the British and Canadian Air Forces were brimming with trained, experienced replacements.

[2] Several groups have claimed this very important victory, but the most persuasive comes from the 602 Squadron records that describe strafing a German staff car, killing the driver and the car turning over on its side landing in a ditch. Weeks later, intelligence reports described this same sequence of events in reporting Rommel's injury.

[3] In spite of the persistent appearance of German Junkers Ju 88 bombers over the Mulberries, beaches and Cherbourg, there was no report of serious damage being done by these attacks. Allied logistics personnel were far more worried about just keeping up with the pace of material unloading than about the bombers.

[4] "Ninth Tactical Air Force in WWII", Kenneth Rust,, page 96

[5] ibid, page 97

Footnotes to Chapter Five

[1] PRO document AIR 24/1496 Operations Record Book for 2ndTAF – 3 August 1944

[2] Public Records Office document AIR 26/185 – 125 Wing ORB – 3 August 1944

[3] Hitler had ordered von Kluge to assemble nine panzer divisions to mount the attack on Avranches. Von Kluge knew he could not wait long enough to assemble these forces and so attacked with only the 4 divisions.

[4] Panzer Lehr lost 160 officers, 5400 men and 120 tanks in June. By the beginning of August, after a month of losses and few reinforcements, it was at less than a third its original strength of 18,000 men and 200 Tiger tanks. By 7 August, it had fewer than 50 guns and tanks to contribute to the Mortain counter-attack.

[5] PRO document AIR 24/1496 Operations Record Book for 2ndTAF – 7 August 1944

[6] But the German losses in armour were greater than the Allies imagined. In the 3 months May to July, German factories produced 2313 tanks while 1730 were destroyed — per Wilmott page 386

[7] PRO document AIR 24/1496 Operations Record Book for 2ndTAF – 13 August 1944

[8] ibid – 18 August 1944

[9] These two claims brought Hauptmann Emil Lang's career record to 172 and his claims in Normandy to 27. Before the day was over he would claim one more for a total of 28 claims in Normandy — the highest scoring ace in Normandy.

[10] 'Ninth Tactical Air Force in WWII', Kenneth Rust,, page 110

[11] PRO document AIR 24/1496 Operations Record Book for 2ndTAF – 31 August 1944

[12] Casualty figures are always suspect to some degree, and historians have quoted many figures for Normandy casualties. These are the figures quoted by Carlo D'Este, page 431.

[13] These figures are quoted in the official history of the RAF, 'Right of the Line' by John Terraine, page 663.

Footnotes for Chapter Six

[1] Note the spelling of 'Johnnie'. Most spell this nickname as 'Johnny' but even before he became a W/C, James Edgar Johnson insisted everyone spell his nickname 'Johnnie'.
[2] Canada's was the largest contribution to the training of aircrew for the RAF, but other centres of aircrew training were located in the United States, Australia, New Zealand and Rhodesia.
[3] Olmstead W., 'Blue Skies – The autobiography of a Canadian Spitfire Pilot', p. 23
[4] ibid
[5] Godefroy H., 'Lucky Thirteen' p. 84
[6] Olmstead, p. 38
[7] Godefroy, p. 156
[8] As an example, when 421 Squadron was first formed 9 April 1942, the official establishment was 17 aircraft, 23 pilots (11 airmen and 12 officers) and 108 ground crew. However as pilots became plentiful in 1943, the total increased to about 30.

Footnotes for Chapter Seven

[1] Public Records Office AIR 26/187 – 127 Wing ORB 6 June 1944
[2] National Archives of Canada reel C-12294 – 6 June 1944
[3] Public Records Office AIR 26/187 — 7 June 1944
[4] National Archives of Canada reel C-12268 – 403 Squadron 9 June 1944
[5] e-mail from Bill Mason 14 January 2001
[6] ibid
[7] Public Records Office AIR 26/187 – 127 Wing ORB 14 June 1944
[8] Public Records Office AIR24/1497 – Servicing Commandos ORB 6 and 7 June 1944
[9] Public Records Office AIR 26/187 – 127 Wing ORB 14 June 1944
[10] As related to the author by William Mason, November 2000
[11] according to Lloyd Chadburn's biographer Robert W. Forbes, Gone is the Angel, Brown Book Company, Toronto, 1997, p.267.
[12] as related in "Lucky Thirteen", Hugh Godefroy, Stoddart, Toronto, 1987 p. 266
[13] Public Records Office AIR 50/147 no. 72
[14] Public Records Office AIR 50/147 no. 113
[15] Public Records Office AIR 50/147 no. 94
[16] Public Records Office AIR 50/147 no. 23
[17] Public Records Office AIR 50/147 no. 116
[18] Public Records Office AIR 50/147 no. 4 and 5
[19] Public Records Office AIR 26/187 — 16 June 1944 – 127 Wing ORB
[20] National Archives of Canada reel C-12268 – 16 June 1944 – 403 Squadron ORB
[21] National Archives of Canada reel C-12287 – 16 June 1944 – 416 Squadron ORB
[22] National Archives of Canada reel C-12294 – 16 June 1944 – 421 Squadron ORB

Footnotes for Chapter Eight

[1] based upon Public Record Office document AIR 24/1534
[2] private note to the author from Bill McRae, December 2001
[3] ibid
[4] ibid
[5] ibid
[6] Public Record Office document AIR 37/876
[7] The 9th Air Force in WWII", Kenneth C.Rust, Aero Publishing, 1970, p.86
[8] Public Record Office document AIR 50/138 – 73 and 74
[9] Public Record Office document AIR 50/138 – 56 and 57
[10] Public Record Office document AIR 50/147 — 3
[11] Public Record Office document AIR 50/147 — 74
[12] Public Record Office document AIR 50/147 — 82
[13] Public Record Office document AIR 50/147 — 57
[14] Public Record Office document AIR 50/147 — 30
[15] Public Record Office document AIR 26/187 – 127 Wing ORB – 23 June 1944
[16] e-mail from Bill McRae December 2001
[17] Public Record Office document AIR 26/187 – 127 Wing ORB – 24 June 1944
[18] Public Record Office document AIR 26/187 – 127 Wing ORB – 25 June 1944
[19] ibid
[20] ibid
[21] Public Record Office document AIR 50/138 — 139
[22] Public Record Office document AIR 50/138 — 90
[23] Public Record Office document AIR 50/138 — 99
[24] Public Record Office document AIR 26/187 – 127 Wing ORB – 26 June 1944
[25] Public Record Office document AIR 26/187 – 127 Wing ORB – 28 June 1944
[26] ibid
[27] Public Record Office document AIR 50/145 — 78
[28] Public Record Office document AIR 50/145 — 29
[29] Public Record Office document AIR 26/187 – 127 Wing ORB – 28 June 1944
[30] National Archives reel C-12294 and 5 – 421 Squadron ORB – 28 June 1944
[31] National Archives reel C-12268 – 403 Squadron ORB – 28 June 1944
[32] Public Record Office document AIR 50/147 — 75
[33] Public Record Office document AIR 50/138 — 34
[34] Public Record Office document AIR 26/187 – 127 Wing ORB – 28 June 1944
[35] "The RCAF Overseas", Oxford University Press, Toronto, 1945, p. 238
[36] Public Record Office document AIR 50/138 — 137
[37] Public Record Office document AIR 50/147 — 58
[38] These figures are quoted from "The RCAF Overseas", Oxford University Press, Toronto, 1945, p. 242
[39] Public Record Office document AIR 26/187 – 127 Wing ORB – 30 June 1944

Footnotes for Chapter Nine

[1] Public Records Office document AIR 50/138 — 172
[2] Public Records Office document AIR 50/138 — 76
[3] Public Records Office document AIR 50/138 — 60
[5] Public Records Office document AIR 50/138 — 65
[6] Public Records Office document AIR 50/138 – 130 and 131
[7] Public Records Office document AIR 50/138 — 58
[8] Public Records Office document AIR 50/138 — 59
[9] Public Records Office document AIR 26/187 — 127 Wing ORB – 2 July 1944
[10] ibid
[10] Public Records Office document AIR 50/147 — 80
[11] Public Records Office document AIR 50/147 — 65
[12] Public Records Office document AIR 26/187 — 127 Wing ORB – 6 July 1944
[13] ibid
[14] ibid
[15] ibid
[16] ibid
[17] ibid
[18] Public Records Office document AIR 50/147 — 81
[19] Public Records Office document AIR 50/147 – 107 and 108
[20] Public Records Office document AIR 50/147 — 19
[21] Public Records Office document AIR 50/145 – 59 and 60
[22] Public Records Office document AIR 50/145 — 34
[23] Public Records Office document AIR 50/145 — 89
[24] Public Records Office document AIR 50/145 — 30
[25] Public Records Office document AIR 50/145 — 64
[26] Public Records Office document AIR 50/145 — 5
[27] National Archives of Canada reel C-12287 – 416 Squadron ORB – 16 July 1944
[28] Public Records Office document AIR 50/147 —?
[29] National Archives of Canada reel C-12268 – 403 Squadron ORB – 16 July 1944
[30] ibid – 17 July 1944
[31] National Archives of Canada reel C-12320 – 443 Squadron ORB – 20 July 1944
[32] Public Records Office document AIR 26/187 — 127 Wing ORB – 22 and 23 July 1944
[33] Public Records Office document AIR 50/147 – 122 and 123
[34] Public Records Office document AIR 50/147 — 117
[35] Public Records Office document AIR 50/145 — 47
[36] Public Records Office document AIR 50/145 — 61
[37] National Archives of Canada reel C-12320 – 443 Squadron ORB – 27 July 1944
[38] Public Records Office document AIR 50/145 — 28
[39] Public Records Office document AIR 50/145 — 90
[40] Public Records Office document AIR 50/145 — 131
[41] Public Records Office document AIR 50/154 — 65
[42] Public Records Office document AIR 50/154 — 2

Footnotes for Chapter Ten

[1] Public Records Office document AIR 26/187 — 127 Wing ORB – 2 August 1944
[2] Public Records Office document AIR 50/138 — 127
[3] National Archives reel C-12287 – 416 Squadron ORB – 3 August 1944
[4] Public Records Office document AIR 26/187 — 127 Wing ORB – 4 August 1944
[5] National Archives reel C-12287 – 416 Squadron ORB – 7 August 1944
[6] ibid – 8 August
[7] National Archives reel C-12320 – 443 Squadron ORB – 12 August 1944
[8] National Archives reel C-12287 – 416 Squadron ORB – 12 August 19
[9] Public Records Office document AIR 26/187 — 127 Wing ORB – 13 August 1944
[10] ibid – 16 August 1944
[11] Public Records Office document AIR 50/145 — 25
[12] Public Records Office document AIR 26/187 — 127 Wing ORB – 17 August 1944
[13] ibid – 18 August 1944
[14] Public Records Office document AIR 50/154 — 47
[15] Public Records Office document AIR 50/147 — 105
[16] Public Records Office document AIR 50/147 — 49
[17] ibid — 25
[18] Public Records Office document AIR 50/145 — 38
[19] ibid — 92
[20] Public Records Office document AIR 50/138 — 103
[21] these figures come from 'The Crucible of War' official history of the RCAF, page 321
[22] ibid